About the Author

Nur Masalha is Reader in Religion and Politics, and Director of the Centre for Religion and History and the Holy Land Research Project, St Mary's University College, UK. He is the editor of *Holy Land Studies: A Multidisciplinary Journal*. His books include *Imperial Israel and the Palestinians* (2000) and *The Politics of Denial* (2003).

Contents

Acknowledgements

This book has been inspired by the ideas of six extraordinary individuals who sadly are no longer with us: Edward W. Said, Michael Prior, Samih Farsoun, Israel Shahak, Hisham Sharabi and Michael Adams. I have been extremely fortunate to count these formidable intellectuals among my best friends. For many years they have encouraged me and helped me with ideas, discussions, criticism and moral support. Many institutions have also contributed to making this work possible, foremost of which is my own School of Theology, Philosophy and History, St Mary's College. I have been director of the School's Holy Land Research Project since it was co-founded with Michael Prior in February 2001. Since then the Project has benefited from the spirited encouragement of the head of the School, Dr Michael Hayes. The support of the Arts and Humanities Research Council (UK), the Jerusalem Fund (Washington DC) and the Palestine Studies Trust (Exeter) is gratefully acknowledged. Other institutions which helped me with source material for the book are the SOAS library in London, the Israel State Archives (Jerusalem), the Central Zionist Archives (Jerusalem), and the Hebrew University of Jerusalem libraries. I would also like to thank the many friends and colleagues who have helped me with ideas and logistics, including Ilan Pappé, Naseer

Aruri, Bashir Abu-Manneh, Isabelle Humphries, Stephen Sizer, Isma'el Abu-Sa'ad, Duncan Macpherson, As'ad Ghanem, Donald Wagner, Carol Lourdas, Tim Niblock, Oren Ben-Dor, Jeff Halper, Paul Kelemen, Lisa Taraki, Rosemary Sayigh, Yasir Suleiman and Peter Miano. At Zed I am particularly grateful for the useful comments and practical help of two commissioning editors, Anna Hardman and Ellen McKinlay. Finally, I owe an enormous debt to my wife, Dr Stephanie Cronin, for her brilliant ideas and practical suggestions, without which this work would not have been completed. Any credit for this book should be shared with the people I mention above, but the deficiencies and shortcomings are mine alone.

Introduction

(Conclude)

There are over 4 million Palestinian refugees in the Middle East and nearly 70 per cent of all Palestinians are refugees. The mini-holocaust (Palestinian *Nakba*, or catastrophe in Arabic) and the exiling of hundreds of thousands of indigenous people which took place with the creation of the State of Israel in 1948 – established in the name of the Bible[1] – is one of the great war crimes of the twentieth century. The State of Israel was built on old biblical symbols and legends and modern Zionist myths, and the Zionist claim to Palestine was based on the notion that God had given the land to the Jews. But does the Bible justify political Zionism, the military conquest and destruction of historic Palestine by the Israelis in 1948, and the current Israeli building of the separation/apartheid wall in occupied Palestine? This is the key question raised by this book.

Political Zionism emerged from the conditions of late-nineteenth-century Eastern and Central Europe as a radical break from 2,000 years of rabbinical Judaism and Jewish tradition. The founding fathers of Zionism were almost all atheists or religiously indifferent. Although, in the interests of gaining international support, political Zionism appealed to the biblical narrative to legitimise the Zionist enterprise, it was basically a secular, settler colonialist movement, with non-religious and frequently anti-religious dispositions. Historically the term *Eretz Yisrael* (the 'Land of Israel') was a religious term embedded in the Jewish tradition. The 'Land of Israel' was revered by generations of Jews as a place of holy pilgrimage and ecclesiastical territory, but never as a future secular state. For two millennia Jewish tradition and religion strictly ordered Jews to await the coming of the Messiah and the 'end of time' before returning to the land. This is also illustrated by the fact that several currents of traditional and orthodox Judaism are still deeply anti-Zionist. More crucially, Palestine (or the Holy Land) was never a major centre for Judaism during the last 2,000 years. Although the Holy Land was central in the religious imagination of Jews, this was not translated into political, social, economical, demographic, cultural and intellectual realities.

Of course it is important politically for the Zionists to predicate a constant and enduring Jewish presence in Palestine, and in the city of Jerusalem in particular. But the claim that political Zionism expressed 2,000 years of yearning for Jewish political and religious self-determination is a modern myth – invented in Europe in the mid to late nineteenth century. Nation-building through the invention of tradition was a typical European practice: using collective memory selectively by manipulating bits of the religious past, suppressing some and elevating and mobilising others in an entirely functional way and for political purposes; thus mobilised collective memory is not necessarily authentic but rather useful politically. The reinvention of the Jewish religious tradition and the synthesising of a new secular Jewish national tradition were latecomers among the national movements of Eastern and Central Europe and were born out of the historical and ideological conditions of those European countries. Like other nationalist movements, political Zionism looked for 'historical roots' and sought to reinterpret distant pasts in the light of newly invented nationalist ideologies. Central to the debate in this book about 'the Hebrew Bible and Zionism' is the idea of the concoction of a new national Jewish tradition by political Zionism – an invented European colonial discourse which included the secularisation, nationalisation and racialisation of the Hebrew Bible and its deployment in support of the settlement and colonisation of modern Palestine.

In modern times the biblical paradigm of 'chosen people–promised land' has been deployed in favour of secular European political Zionism.

This book explores the invention and mobilisation of the ethnocentric paradigm of 'promised land–chosen people' and its links to modern Zionist myths, especially the nationalised and mythologised concept that the Hebrew Bible provides for the Jews a sacrosanct 'title-deed' to the land of Palestine and beyond signed by God, for the alleged moral legitimacy of the establishment of the State of Israel, and for its policies towards the indigenous inhabitants of Palestine. The work also discusses the biblical and mythical justification for Zionism and subjects Zionism's own narratives, presuppositions, myths and symbols to a thorough critique. It also explores a wide range of themes related to the biblical paradigm and its deployment in favour of political Zionism, as well as other permanent themes of political Zionism. These themes include the mythical 'gift of land' to Abraham and its 'conquest' by Joshua, the myth of a ubiquitous and perennial longing on the part of the Jewish diaspora to 'return', the myth of 'a land without a people', the deep-seated inclination among Zionists to see Palestine as a country without its Arab inhabitants, the erasure of Palestinian villages and deletion of the reality of historic Palestine, the invention of a new Hebraic consciousness and the historicisation of the Bible as a collective national enterprise, biblical naming and the Hebraicisation of Palestine's landscape and geographical sites since 1948 and archaeology in the service of settler colonialism.

The role of biblical archaeology (discussed in Chapters 1, 2 and 7), with its biblical paradigm of 'elect people–promised land', in privileging the narrative associated with Zionist settlers and Israelis over those of the indigenous (predominantly Muslim) inhabitants of Palestine is a major theme of this work. From its beginning in the nineteenth century the Western discipline of biblical archaeology, with its complete disregard for the historical, demographic and political realities of Palestine, was at the heart of the colonial tradition. It was established to validate Western roots in the Holy Land and authenticate the historicity of the Hebrew Bible. Virtually all biblical archaeologists were Western Christians or Jews with a strong commitment to the historicity of the Bible, and interpreted their finds in light of the scriptures. No wonder, therefore, that archaeological findings confirmed the Bible when researchers used the Old Testament to identify, date and interpret the significance of the towns, buildings, pottery and other artefacts they unearthed. The same biblical archaeology became central to the founding myths of Zionism and to its creation of a new Hebraic consciousness. Driven by an invented tradition and the need to establish the veracity of the Old Testament, biblical archaeology was passionately Zionist. Moreover, while the attitudes of British archaeologists towards the Third World began to change in the post-Second World War period, Israelis, by contrast, chose to consolidate the colonial tradition of the West (Benvenisti 2002: 304). After the establishment of the State of Israel in 1948 biblical archaeology became an obsession, firmly institutionalised as a cornerstone of Israel's civic religion, testifying to exclusive Jewish claims to the land of Palestine (Rose 2004: 7–25). The discipline of biblical archaeology has since been employed by Israeli academic institutions and the state to de-emphasise the Arab and Muslim connection to the land, to foster Jewish nationalism and state-building, and to legitimise the dispossession of the indigenous inhabitants of Palestine.

The subject of 'the Bible and Zionism' is often dealt with in the West in abstract, with little attention to Zionism's disastrous consequences for the indigenous inhabitants of Palestine. Palestinian demography and the land issue were always at the heart of the struggle between the Zionist settlers and the indigenous Palestinians. The deployment of the militarist traditions of the Hebrew Bible in the Zionist struggle with the indigenous population of Palestine is another major theme of this work. In the struggle with the Palestinians for land and territory, David Ben-Gurion and other founding fathers of the Israeli state studied, revived and celebrated the heroic battles of the ancient zealots, and the (rather mythologised) fortified biblical positions such as Massada and Bitar. However, despite its biblical mythologies and distinct nationalist rhetoric ('exile and return'), political Zionism followed the general trajectory of the great colonialist projects in Africa, Asia and the Americas, seeking to displace or subdue the indigenous population of the land (Ruether 1998: 113).

From the beginning of the modern Zionist settlement in Palestine, European Jewish settlers had to confront the reality that their project immediately clashed with the ethnic, religious and demographic realities of Palestine and precipitated conflict with the indigenous inhabitants. In particular, Palestinian demography and the land issue were at the heart of the struggle between the Zionist settlers and indigenous Palestinians. Even in 1947, the indigenous Palestinians were the overwhelming majority in the country and owned much of the land. In 1948 the predominantly East European settler community in Palestine, or the Jewish Yishuv, was about a third of the total population and owned, after fifty years of colonisation and land purchases, only 6 per cent of the land. In the 1930s and 1940s, the general endorsement of 'transfer' (in different forms: voluntary, agreed and compulsory) by the Zionist leadership was designed to achieve two crucial objectives: (1) to clear the land for European Jewish settlers and would-be immigrants, and (2) to establish an ethnocratic, mono-religious and fairly homogenous Jewish state. During the same period key leaders of Labour Zionism, such as Ben-Gurion, then chairman of the Jewish Agency, strongly believed that Zionism would not succeed in setting up a homogenous Jewish state and fulfilling its imperative of absorbing the expected influx of Jewish immigrants from Europe if the indigenous inhabitants were allowed to remain.

The idea of 'transferring' the Palestinians – a euphemism denoting the organised removal of the Arab population of Palestine to neighbouring or distant countries – was held widely in Israel after 1948. In fact, the concept – delicately described by its proponents as population exchange, Arab return to Arabia, emigration, resettlement and rehabilitation of the Palestinians in Arab countries, and so on – is deeply rooted in Zionism. As demonstrated in my book *Expulsion of the Palestinians: The Concept of 'Transfer' in Zionist Political Thought 1882–1948* (1992), the transfer notion was embedded in the Zionist perception that the Land of Israel or Palestine is a Jewish birthright and belongs exclusively to the Jewish people as a whole, and, consequently, Palestinians are 'strangers' who should either accept Jewish sovereignty over the land or depart. The book also showed that the concept had occupied a central position in the strategic thinking of the Zionist movement and the Yishuv as a solution to the Zionist land and 'Arab demographic' problems.

The justifications used in defence of the 'transfer plans' in the 1930s and 1940s formed the cornerstone of the subsequent argumentation for transfer, particularly in the proposals and plans put forward after 1947 and in the wake of the 1967 conquest of the West Bank and Gaza. After 1967, proponents of ethnic cleansing continued to assert, often publicly, that there was nothing 'immoral' about these proposals; that the earlier twentieth-century 'transfer' of Greeks and Turks, Indians and

Pakistanis, Germans and other Europeans provided a 'precedent' for similar measures vis-à-vis the Palestinian Arabs; that the uprooting and transfer of the Palestinians to Arab countries would constitute a mere relocation from one district to another; that the Palestinians would have no difficulties in accepting Jordan, Syria or Iraq as their homeland; that the Palestinian Arabs had little emotional attachment and few real ties to the particular soil in Palestine and would be just as content outside the 'Land of Israel'; that the Palestinian Arabs were marginal to the Arab nation and their problems might be facilitated by a 'benevolent' and 'humanitarian' policy of 'helping people to leave'. Such assertions were crucial to legitimise Zionism's denial of the Palestinians' right to self-determination in Palestine before 1948 or even in part of Palestine (the West Bank and Gaza) after 1967. Proponents of ethnic cleansing asserted that the Palestinians were not a distinct people but merely 'Arabs', an Arab population, or 'Arab community' that happened to reside in the land of Israel. Closely linked to this idea of the non-existence of the Palestinians as a nation and their non-attachment to the particular soil of Palestine was the idea of their belonging to an Arab nation with vast territories and many countries. After all, if the Palestinians did not constitute a distinct separate nation and were not an integral part of the country and were without historical ties to it, then they could be transferred to other Arab countries without undue prejudice. Similarly, if the Palestinians were merely a marginal local part of a larger population of Arabs, then they were not a major party to the conflicts with Israel; therefore Israeli efforts to deal over their heads were justified. It is thus that Israeli pronouncements were full of references to the vast Arab territories and to the notion that the Palestinians were bound to other centres in Syria, Iraq and the Arabian Peninsula, the homeland of the Arab people.

This book is unique in four respects. First, most works on Palestine-Israel tend to focus on current affairs, giving inadequate attention to the historical context. Also works which address religious questions do not reflect a depth of scholarship or familiarity with modern history and politics. Second, a distinctive feature of this work is its extensive use of the Zionist and Israeli archives. The work integrates a critical discussion of 'the Bible and Zionism' against the background of modern history of Palestine and issues related to interfaith discourse. Third, what distinguishes this book is the strength of the multidisciplinary and multilinguistic approach it adopts. The work addresses a range of aspects of the complex discourse (history, theology, biblical studies, archaeology, politics, human rights), whereas conventionally books display a much narrower focus. Fourth, the works avails itself of the most up-to-date scholarship on the subject, and is written with a critical edge, speaking to both an academic and a more public audience.

Structurally the book consists of three distinct parts and nine chapters which deal with the historical evolution of Christian and Jewish Zionisms and their biblical and theological justification as well as various critiques of biblical Zionism. Part I, comprising Chapters 1 and 2, traces the journeys of secular Jewish and messianic Christian Zionisms, mainly from the nineteenth century onwards. It discusses the historical roots and development of both Jewish and Christian Zionisms and critiques their mythical justifications and biblical discourse. Chapter 1, in particular, examines the rise of political Zionism from the 1880s to 1967 and its devastating consequences for the indigenous inhabitants of Palestine, resulting in the destruction of much of Palestine and the 1948 Palestinian catastrophe. This part explores the sharp political and ethical issues arising from the use and abuse of the Bible by Christian Zionists, as much as by Jewish Zionists, to justify the occupation and settlement of Palestine, with its inevitable consequences of the forced expulsion and subjugation of the indigenous Palestinian people.

Chapter 1 explores the use and misuse of the figurative biblical language to justify secular political Zionism and the founding myths of Israel. It examines Zionist myths such as 'a land without a people' and the claims that until the arrival of European Jewish settlers Palestine was virtually barren, desolate and empty, waiting to be made fertile and populated by Israel; that the land is the rightful property of Jews (a divinely 'chosen people'); and that it was their superiority defined by their superior military power. This (mythical) continuum between the ancient and the modern implied that this was a difficult land, resisting agriculture, and could only be made to yield up its produce by the extraordinary effort of modern Jewish immigrants, socialist Zionist pioneers and Israel's genius. The claims that only under Jewish cultivation did Palestine become a productive country; that only Israel can make the land (and desert) bloom; that most Palestinians arrived in the area only within the past century, have long been part of the Zionist justification for Jewish immigration to Palestine, the founding of the State of Israel, its territorial expansion and the dispossession of the Palestinians.

Chapter 2 focuses on the politics of Christian Zionism, with special reference to evangelical dispensationalism and the question of Jerusalem. It explores the historical roots of Christian (Protestant) Zionism and prophetic politics since the sixteenth century onwards and traces how the Zionist agenda has been variously interpreted by liberal Protestants and evangelicals, both before and after 1948 and 1967. This chapter also explores the rise of crusading Christian fundamentalism since 1967, with its 'Armageddon' theology and its obsession with the Muslim holy shrines in Jerusalem.

Part II, comprising Chapters 3, 4 and 5, focuses on the national colonial theology of neo-Zionism and traces the journey from a secular to a sacred Jewish Zionism. Since its establishment in 1948 the Israeli state, which had been built mainly by atheist Jewish Zionists, has undergone a slow but constant process of clericalisation, with leading Labour Zionists and founding fathers of the state (notably Ben-Gurion) seeking a link with religious Judaism – thus cementing the alliance between the sword and the Torah, between the secular establishment of Zionism and the Zionist religious parties. This continuing process of clericalisation of the Israeli state has been accelerated since 1967, and has had serious implications for interfaith relations and the relationship between religion and the state in Israel–Palestine. Furthermore, since the occupation of East Jerusalem and the West Bank by Israel in 1967, Jewish fundamentalism has developed into a major force, with a considerable influence on the attitudes and votes of many Israelis. The new messianic fervour centres on the building of the Temple on the site of the Muslim shrines in Jerusalem. Chapters 3, 4 and 5 explore the theology of two strands of Jewish fundamentalism in Israel: the Zionist nationalist 'messianic' camp, and the ultra-orthodox rabbis and non-Zionist religious parties. It explores the doctrinal differences between these two concerning the 'messianic doctrine', their attitudes towards Palestinian Christians, and their impact on Israeli foreign and domestic policies.

Several chapters in this book (Chapters 2–6) also address the rise of a variety of fundamentalisms (Jewish, Christian and Muslim) since 1967 and the implications for community, ethnic and interfaith relations in Israel and Palestine. Chapter 4, in particular, examines the social and political conditions under which Jewish fundamentalist attitudes have evolved and explores attitudes towards the 'sacred geography' of Jerusalem and rights of occupancy, within the wider context of multi-faith relations. Since the early 1970s Gush Emunim rabbis and political leaders have routinely compared Palestinians to the ancient Canaanites or Amalekites, whose extermination or expulsion by the ancient Israelites was, according to the Bible, predestined by divine design. Some leaders of the messianic movement prefer to use Joshua's 'destruction and subjugation of the Canaanites' as a model for the application of Israeli policy towards the contemporary 'Palestinian problem'. Chapter 5 examines the way in which religious nationalist and fundamentalist currents in Israel have nationalised and racialised the medieval theology of Moses Maimonides, the most illustrious example of the golden age of Arabo-Islamic-Judaic symbiosis, to justify Israeli racist and ethnic cleansing policies towards the indigenous Palestinians; in 1982 an Israeli chief rabbi used Maimonides to justify the Israeli invasion of Lebanon. The chapter examines the 'reinvention' of both Maimonides and the classical heritage of Arabo-Judaism by Jewish fundamentalists, who metamorphose Maimonides from a rationalist and universalist philosopher into an anti-Arab religious zealot and a xenophobic Zionist messianic. The chapter shows how Maimonides' classic Arabic philosophical magnum opus, *Dalalat al-Hairin* (the *Guide of the Perplexed*), a great monument of Jewish–Arab symbiosis in the Middle Ages, has been reinvented and mythologised as a Jewish nationalist philosophical tract in modern-day Israel.

Part III (Chapters 6, 7, 8 and 9) focuses on a wide range of critiques of 'the Bible and Zionism' and discusses the challenge of political Islam in Palestine, of the new archaeology of the Holy Land, post-colonialism and secular democracy. Chapter 6 examines the transformation of Palestinian nationalism from the secular to the sacred and the impact of Jewish religious nationalism on the rise Palestinian religious nationalism and the Palestinian organisation Hamas. Chapter 7 focuses on the challenges of the new archaeology of Israel–Palestine and of the new biblical scholarship for both the biblical academy and nationalist historiography. It demonstrates how recent findings of Israeli archaeologists and biblical scholars undermine the hegemonic Zionist claim (discussed in Chapter 1) that 'the Bible is our Mandate'. The chapter argues that on the basis of recent archaeological and scientific evidence, the historicity of the Old Testament is completely demolished.

The sharp moral, ethical and political issues arising from the use of the Bible by Christians, as much as by Jews, to justify the occupation and settlement of Palestine, are highlighted in the last two chapters of the book. Chapters 8 and 9 provide two post-colonialist critiques of the 'Bible and Zionism' – critiques based on the seminal works of Michael Prior (biblical scholar and liberation theologian) and Edward Said, both of whom articulated the aspirations of many indigenous and oppressed peoples, and of the disenfranchised and marginalised. Chapter 8 pays particular attention to the works of Prior and the challenge of Palestinian liberation theology. The chapter highlights the contribution of Prior in providing a moral critique of the Bible and Zionist colonialism in Palestine. Despite the acknowledged role of the Bible in the Zionist narrative – 'the Jews' sacrosanct title-deed to Palestine' – no biblical scholar, apart from Prior, has addressed the issues critically. Prior is in favour of a radical liberation theology which confronts the biblical paradigm of 'promised land–chosen people'. Prior argues that the biblical claim to the divine promise of land is integrally linked to the claim of divine approval for the extermination of the indigenous people and dismisses biblical passages deemed 'ethnocentric, xenophobic and militaristic' (1999a: 161-2; 1999c: 181). He also exposes the failure of biblical scholarship to address, full square, the moral questions inherent in the biblical texts.

Chapter 9, in some sense, concludes the book by focusing on Edward Said's post-colonial discourse and by offering the prospect of a new political vision derived from a join Palestinian–Israeli struggle for equality and democracy. The chapter explores Said's thinking on the question of Palestine over three decades and revisits Zionist responsibility for the ongoing Palestinian catastrophe. The chapter pays particular attention to Said's critique of Redemptionist Zionism, both secular and religious, which has long traded on biblical myths, on the 'uniqueness' and 'exceptionalism' of the Jewish people, and on orientalist discourses and colonialist practices.

Said demonstrated the historical importance of biblical stories like that of Exodus for settler-colonial societies in Palestine and elsewhere. In his 'resistance' reading of the Bible, Said shows how modern Zionist readings and re-imagining of the Old Testament stories have become a thinly veiled apology for the colonial policies of the Israeli state. Said's secular humanist approach, his advocacy of strict separation between religion and the state, and his secular democratic vision for Palestine-Israel is central to the conclusions drawn by this work. Said's search for an alternative to the deeply flawed Oslo process led him back to the one-state solution, based on equality and justice and a joint Palestinian-Israeli struggle. Said's rethinking of the Palestine question was an indictment of narrow brands of ethnic–religious–tribal (Jewish and Arab) nationalisms. For him, Zionist 'ethnocracy' and settler colonialism have brought about the death of the two-state solution, and this meant that the architects of the Oslo accords had inadvertently set the stage for a single non-sectarian state in historic Palestine. Rather than a political programme for a future settlement, Said championed an anti-apartheid struggle that can only derive from a long-term Palestinian-Jewish struggle for equality, expressed within a single, secular democratic framework.

PART I

The Bible, Zionism and the
Invention of Tradition

I

'The Bible is Our Mandate': Zionism, the Hebrew Bible and the Palestinian Catastrophe, 1881-1967

The Jews' Sacrosanct Title Deed to Colonise Palestine?

It is frequently argued that Zionism is in essence an unchanging idea that expresses 2,000 years of yearning for Jewish political and religious self-determination to be exercised over the 'promised land'. Because political Zionism has culminated in the creation of the State of Israel, it is also often argued that its historical realisation has confirmed its unchanging essence, and no less important, the (brutal) means used for its realisation (Said 1980: 56-7). The conviction held by Westerners and Zionists (both secular and religious) that God and the Bible have given the 'Jews' Palestine (the 'promised land') in perpetuity is one of the underpinnings of modern political Zionism and Israeli settler colonialism in Palestine.

The term 'Zionism' was first coined in the late nineteenth century, and this reflected the fact that European political Zionism was a product of modern European nationalist and colonialist movements of the period (Prior 1997a: 107-19). While the Bible was not the only 'justification', it certainly was the most powerful one, without which political Zionism was only another conquering European ideology. Read at face value, in a literalist fashion, and without recourse to doctrines of universal human rights and international law, the Old Testament indeed appears to propose that the taking possession of ancient Palestine and the forcible expulsion of the indigenous population (the Canaanites) was the fulfilment of a divine mandate. A scrutiny of the language used in the Old Testament in relation to the emergence of political Zionism from the late nineteenth century onwards shows the way in which a secular European conquering ideology and movement mobilised the figurative language of the Jewish religion into a sacrosanct 'title deed' to the land of Palestine signed by God (Wetherell 2005: 69–70). Very little is said about the actual genealogy and provenance of Zionism, especially its European settler-colonial context of the late nineteenth century from which Zionism drew its force; and almost nothing is said about what the creation of the State of Israel entailed for the indigenous inhabitants of the land (Said 1980: 57). Despite its distinct features and its nationalist ideology ('return' to the land of the Bible) political Zionism followed the general trajectory of colonialist projects in Africa, Asia and Latin America: European colonising of another people's land while seeking to remove or subjugate the indigenous inhabitants of the land (Ruether 1998: 113).

The Bible has been utilised by modern secular Zionism as 'history' rather than theology or a source of belief (Shindler 2002a: 101). Paradoxically, however, the secular Zionist claim to Palestine is based on the biblical paradigm and the notion that God had given the land to the Jews. In modern times this ethnocentric paradigm of 'chosen people–promised land' has been deployed in favour of secular political Zionism and settler colonialism in Palestine (Prior 1999c: 138). In 1937 David Ben-Gurion (1886–1973), a Russian Jew, later to become the first prime minister and chief architect of the State of Israel, told the British Royal Commission visiting Mandatory Palestine that the 'Bible is our Mandate' (Ben-Gurion 1970: 107; also Rose 2004: 7). Ben-Gurion, who is revered in Israel as the 'Father of the Nation', was a non-believer and deeply secular Zionist. From its earliest days in the late nineteenth century secular Jewish Zionism embraced the Protestant Zionist biblicist doctrine[1] of exclusive land ownership. This fundamentalist doctrine was premised on the notion that the Hebrew Bible provides for the Jews' sacrosanct 'title deed' to colonise Palestine, and gives moral legitimacy to the establishment of the State of Israel and its current policies towards the indigenous Palestinians. The nationalised and racialised European doctrine, which viewed the Jews in racial terms, was not only central to Zionist politics in the late nineteenth century but was ever pervasive within mainstream Christian theology and biblical scholarship (Prior 1999c: 170-1). The link between Zionist myth-making, Zionist settler colonialism, territorial expansion into the occupied West Bank and the use of the Hebrew Bible is reflected in the claim of Ben-Gurion that the Bible was the Chosen People's sacrosanct title deed to Palestine, 'with a genealogy of 3,500 years' (Ben-Gurion 1954: 100). A leading advocate of the historicisation of the Bible, Ben-Gurion wrote:

> The message of the Chosen People makes sense in secular, nationalist and historical terms.... The Jews can be considered a self-chosen people.... Though I reject theology, the single most important book in my life is the Bible. (Ben-Gurion 1970: 120-25)

The biblical paradigm is based on the Hebrew Bible and its narrative of the earliest history of the Israelites. This history is identified with the three patriarchs, Abraham, Isaac and Jacob, who, according to biblical genealogy, are to be dated between 2200 and 1990 BC (Lemche 1995: 29). According to the book of Genesis, the history of the Israelites began with 'Abram', a Babylonian from Ur in what is now southern Iraq, who set out with his wife, father and nephew northwest to Haran in southern Turkey, where the voice of Jehovah (Yahweh) told him to go south into Canaan (Gen. 11:31; 12:1, 5). But the Hebrew Bible also traces all the nations of the region, including the Arabs, to Abraham and his family. The Moabites and Ammonites derive from his nephew Lot; the Jews and southern Arabs from Abraham's sons, Isaac and Ishmael, respectively. There follow Isaac's sons Esau – father of the Edomites and other desert tribes – and Jacob; then Jacob's twelve sons, each of whom ruled one of the twelve tribes of Israel. Isaac and Jacob lived in Canaan until Jacob was forced by famine to flee to Egypt with his sons, where one of them, Joseph, was sold to slavery in Egypt and rose to a position of prominence under the Pharaohs.

A second series of biblical events revolves around the enslavement of the descendants of Jacob in Egypt, and the miraculous escape of the Israelites led by Moses, who continued to Mount Sinai, where a law was laid down including the Ten Commandments and where a covenant was concluded establishing Jehovah as the God of his 'chosen people'. However, because of the Israelites' disobedience the Sinai march towards 'the promised land' turned into forty years of wanderings in the desert. Finally, after the death of Moses, the Israelites entered Canaan from the east, crossing the River Jordan, and swiftly conquered and sacked Jericho – the world's oldest known inhabited city[2]–and killed the inhabitants, after the city's walls came tumbling down miraculously. Then they went on to conquer the rest of 'the promised land' and slaughter all of the original inhabitants. These events, memorialised in major Jewish festivals, occupy four of the first five books of the Bible traditionally attributed to Moses. The wanderings of the patriarchs, the Exodus from Egypt, the desert march and Joshua's conquest of the 'promised land' have all provided the foundation of the notion of 'religious liberation' within traditional Judaism. But the same Exodus and conquest paradigm has also become central to the foundational myths of modern secular political Zionism.

The Invention of Tradition:
Synthesising and Masculinising a Nation

Nation-building with the invention of tradition was a typical European practice of using collective memory selectively by manipulating certain bits of the national and religious past, suppressing others and elevating and mobilising others in an entirely functional way and for political purposes; thus mobilised, memory is not necessarily authentic but rather useful politically (Said 1999b: 6–7). Competing modes of modern nation-building and nationalist myth-making have received extensive critical reappraisal in the works of Benedict Anderson (1991: 6, 11-12), Eric Hobsbawn (1990, 1996), Anthony Smith (1971, 1984, 1986) and Ernest Gellner (1983). Hobsbawm's most comprehensive analysis of nation-building and myth-making in Europe is found in *Nations and Nationalism since 1780*. Published in 1990 under the subtitle 'Programme, Myth, Reality', his work is about the 'invention of tradition', the creation of national culture, and the construction national of identities from a mixture of folk history and historical myths (Hobsbawm 1990). In *The Invention of Tradition* (1996) Hobsbawm and Terence Ranger explore the way social and political authorities in the Europe of the mid-nineteenth century set about creating supposedly age-old traditions by providing invented memories of the past as a way of creating a new sense of identity for the ruler and the ruled (1996: 1-14, 263-83).

'Land redemption' (*geolat adama*), 'land conquest' (*kibbush adama*), emigration and Jewish statehood in Palestine, settler colonisation and demographic transformation of the land, the obsessive search for rootedness, the historicisation of the Bible as a collective national enterprise and the creation of a new Hebraic consciousness, the Judaisation of Palestine and the Hebraicisation of its landscape and geographical sites – all have been permanent themes of 'modern, dynamic and productive' Zionism. The reinvention of both the Jewish past and modern Jewish nationhood in Zionist historiography and the creation of a new Hebraic consciousness have received some scholarly attention (Myers 1995; Ram 1995: 91-124; Piterberg 2001: 31-46; Raz-Krakotzkin 1993: 23-56, 1994: 113-32). Political Zionism, which originated in the conditions of late-nineteenth-century eastern and central Europe, was a radical break from 2,000 years of Jewish tradition and rabbinical Judaism. Jewish nationalism was in fact a latecomer among the national movements of Eastern and Central Europe and it was born out of the historical and ideological conditions of those countries in Europe; like other nationalist movements there, it looked for 'historical roots' and sought to reinterpret distant pasts in the light of newly invented nationalist ideologies. According to American Jewish historian and theoretician of nationalism Hans Kohn, Zionist nationalism 'had nothing to do with Jewish traditions; it was in many ways opposed to them'.[3] Furthermore, according to the adopted German *volkisch* theory, people of common descent should form one common state. But such ideas of tribal nationalism ran counter to those held by liberal nationalism in Western Europe, whereby equal citizenship regardless of religion or ethnicity – not 'common descent' – that determined the national character of the state.[4]

Secular Jewish nationalism is a classical case of the invention of tradition in late-nineteenth-century Europe and a synthesising of a nation project. Political Zionism mobilised a re-imagined biblical narrative – a post-exilic tradition invented during the Persian empire by urban intellectuals many centuries after the events they describe (see Chapter 7) – which was reworked in the late nineteenth century for the political purposes of a modern European movement intent on colonising the land of Palestine. As an invented (European) tradition, Zionism was bound to be a synthesising project. Zionism's rejection of a perceived 'feminised' diaspora and its obsession with synthesising a nation are reflected by the fact that its symbols were an amalgam, chosen not only from the Jewish religion and the militant parts of the Old Testament but also from diverse modern traditions and sources, symbols subsequently appropriated as 'Jewish nationalist', Zionist or 'Israeli': Hannah Arendt showed that 'Herzl thought in terms of nationalism inspired from German sources' (quoted by Kohn 1958, in Khalidi 2005: 813); the music of Israel's national anthem, haTikva, came from the Czech national musician Smetana; much of the music used in nationalist Israeli songs originated in Russian folk songs; even the term for an Israeli-born Jew free of all the 'maladies and abnormalities of exile' is in fact the Arabic word for *sabar*, Hebraicised as (masculine and tough) *tzabar* or *sabra* (Bresheet 1989: 131), the prickly pear grown in and around the hundreds of Palestinian villages destroyed by Israel in 1948 (see below). Even the 'national anthem of the Six Day War', Na'omi Shemer's song 'Jerusalem of Gold', was a plagiarised copy of a Basque lullaby (see below).

The invention of a Jewish nationalist tradition and construction of a new collective consciousness in the nineteenth century – a tradition recast with a 'historical depth' and ancient roots – was in line with other East and Central European national projects of the age. According to Israeli sociologist Baruch Kimmerling, this project should be credited to two outstanding Jewish historians: German biblical critic Heinrich Graetz (1817-1891) and Russian Simon Dubnow (1860-1941), both of whom used Jewish (especially religious) and non-Jewish sources and texts to reconstruct a collective consciousness of Judaism as an 'ancient nationality' existing from time immemorial. Dubnow thought that the Jews had been transformed into a European nation and that it was upon them to demand the status of a national minority within the European or American nation-states. Other writers – such as Lithuanian novelist Abraham Mapu, in his novel *Love of Zion* (1845), within the French Romantic tradition – sought to create a sense of Jewish collectivity within the framework of the biblical Jewish kingdom in ancient Palestine (Kimmerling 1999: 339-63).

From the Bible and the Jewish religion Zionism took some central ingredients but gave them different meanings and contexts. These were, Kimmeling writes,

(1) The definition of the boundaries of the collectivity as including all the Jews in the world. (2) The target territory, from the a priori perspective that emigration from Europe and establishing a society on another continent and amidst other peoples is an acceptable and legitimate practice in the context of the colonial world order. (3) Large, if selective, selections from the religious symbols of Judaism, including the Holy tongue, Hebrew, and the attempt to secularize it and to transform it to a modern language. (4) The Bible and especially the Books of Joshua, Isaiah and Amos. The Book of Joshua provided the muscular and militaristic dimension of conquest of the land and annihilation of the Canaanites and other ancient people that populated the 'Promised Land,' while the Books of Isaiah and Amos were considered as preaching for social justice and equality (a kind of proto-socialism). (Kimmerling 1999: 339)

Although it was possible to construct a Jewish theory of social justice and liberation with strong dependence on the Old Testament prophets, in reality, however, political Zionism developed a theory of ethnic and racial superiority on the basis of the land and conquest traditions of the Hebrew Bible, especially on the Book of Joshua and those dealing with Israelite origins that demanded the subjugation and destruction of other peoples. It is hardly surprising, therefore, that the book of Joshua is required reading in Israeli schools. Although, as we shall see in Chapter 7, the Israelite 'conquest' was not the 'Blitzkrieg' it is made out to be in the Book of Joshua, this book holds an important place in the Israeli school curriculum and Israeli academic programmes partly because the founding fathers of Zionism viewed Joshua's narrative of conquests as a precedent for the establishment of Israel as a nation (Burge 2003: 82). Professor Benjamin Beit-Hallahmi of Haifa University wrote in 1992:

Most Israelis today, as a result of Israeli education, regard the Bible as a source of reliable historical information of a secular, political kind. The Zionist version of Jewish history accepts most Biblical legends about the beginnings of Jewish history, minus divine intervention. Abraham, Isaac and Jacob are treated as historical figures. The descent into Egypt and the Exodus are phases in the secular history of a developing people, as is the conquest of Canaan by Joshua. The Biblical order of events is accepted, but the interpretation is nationalist and secular.

The historicization of the Bible is a national enterprise in Israel, carried out by hundreds of scholars at all universities. The starting point is Biblical chronology; then evidence (limited) and speculation (plentiful) are arranged accordingly. The Israeli Defence Ministry has even published a complete chronology of Biblical events, giving exacts dates for the creation of the world...

Claiming this ancient mythology as history is an essential part of Zionist secular nationalism, in its attempt to present a coherent account of the genesis of the Jewish people in ancient West Asia. It provides a focus of identification to counter the rabbinical, Diaspora traditions. Teaching the Bible as history to Israeli children creates the notion of continuity. It is Abraham ('the first Zionist', migrating to Palestine), Joshua and the conquest of Palestine (wiping out the Canaanites, just like today), King David's conquest of Jerusalem (just like 1967). (1992: 119)

In a similar vein Meron Benvenisti, former deputy mayor of Jerusalem, explained that in the state school curriculum and in the army the subject of 'knowledge' of the land of the Bible (*yedi'at haaretz*) is obsessional. Furthermore, knowledge of the land is both masculinised and sexualised. On the obsessive search for rootedness by Zionist institutions and the treatment of the Bible as (mythologised) 'history' by a predominantly secular Israeli society, Benvenisti had this to say:

The Bible became a guidebook, taught by reference to the landscape, less for its humanistic and social message – and not for its divine authorship. There is nothing more romantic and at the same time more 'establishment' than to be connected in some fashion with this cult. Its priests are the *madrichim* – guides and youth leaders. An extensive institutional network sustained *yedi'at haaretz* [knowledge of the biblical country]: research institutes, field schools, the Society for the Preservation of Nature in Israel (SPNI), the Jewish National Fund, youth movements, paramilitary units, the army. (Benvenisti 1986: 20)

Those who conceived the expression *yedi'at haaretz*, Benvenisti wrote, were undoubtedly aware of the biblical meaning of *yedi'a*, an act of sexual possession: 'And Adam knew Eve, his wife' (1986: 19).

The land and conquest traditions of the Hebrew Bible, in particular, were singled out by the founding fathers of Zionism as the origins of the birth of the nation. The same masculinised traditions provided Zionism with a tribal form of ethnic and racial nationalism. In his important work *The Founding Myths of Israel* (1998) the Israeli historian Zeev Sternhell argues that what was presented to the world as an Israeli social democracy was in fact a 'nationalist socialist' ideology designed to create a new community of blood and common descent, to redeem the 'biblical land'

by conquest and to submit the Jewish individual to an ethnic collectivity driven by messianic fervour. Focusing on the 'nationalist socialist'
ideology of Labour Zionism, which dominated the Jewish community
in Palestine and then the State of Israel from the 1930s into the 1970s,
Sternhell illustrates ideological parallels between it and early-twentieth-
century tribal and *volkisch* 'organic nationalism' of Eastern and Central
Europe, which condemned liberalism – along with individual and civic
rights – and universalism on moral intellectual and political grounds
(Sternhell 1998: 10-11, 16, 27). Instead Labour Zionists gave precedence to
the realisation of their nationalist project: the establishment in Palestine
of a sovereign Jewish state. In this project socialism was deployed merely
as a useful mobilising myth. Sternhell agues that Zionism as a whole was
a tribal form of nationalism of 'blood and soil' emphasising religion and
ethnicity, promoting the cult and myths of ancient history, the revival of
seemingly a dead language, the advocacy of the supremacy of the Hebrew
language over Yiddish in Zionist colonies in Palestine,[5] a desperate drive
for cultural renewal and a bitter struggle for political independence and
territorial expansionism.

   The analogies between Eastern and Central European populist nationalisms and Labour Zionism go further; Zionist nationalist socialists
repudiated liberal individualism and were suspicious of bourgeois liberal
democracy. In this illiberal legacy of Labour Zionism, Sternhell finds the
seeds of current Israeli problems – the lack of a constitution, an inadequate
concept of universal human rights, the failure to separate religion and
state, and so on. Deflating the socialist pretensions of Labour Zionism,
Sternhell implies that socialist Zionists and the right-wing revisionist
movement of Betar, founded by a Russian Jew, Vladimir (Zeev) Jabotinsky
(1880-1940), through Menahem Begin (1913-1992) and Yitzhak Shamir
to Binyamin Netanyahu, were all integral nationalists. He argues that
Labour Zionism ran its course with the founding of the state and there
were no social perspectives or ideological directions, beyond a nationalism
based on 'historical rights to the whole land of Israel'. This settler-colonial
legacy of Labour Zionism, with its obsession with land settlement, ethnic
and demographic separation (*hafrada*), continued after the founding
of the Israeli state in 1948. With no social perspectives or ideological
directions beyond a racialist *volkisch* nationalism and mystical attitudes

towards the land, based on abstract 'historical rights to the whole land of Israel', the mould set in the pre-state period did not change. After 1967, unable to come to terms with Palestinian nationalism, Labour Zionism had inevitably pursued its settler colonialism in the occupied territories and tried to test the Zionist method of 'creating facts on the ground' (Sternhell 1998).

Furthermore, Zionist nation-building, ever-expanding settlements, territorial ambitions and the effective use of the conquest legends of the Hebrew Bible went hand in hand. Zionists claim that events described in the Old Testament establish the right of twentieth-century Jews to found an ethnic Jewish state in Palestine. Contrary to the archaeological and historical evidence, the view that the Bible provides Jews with a title deed to the 'whole land of Israel' and morally legitimises the creation of the State of Israel and its 'ethnic cleansing' policies towards the native Palestinians is still pervasive in Jewish Zionist circles.

The 'Iron Wall' Doctrine, the Book of Joshua and Militarist Zionism

Different Zionist leaders and intellectuals took different ingredients from the various books of the Hebrew Bible. The Book of Joshua provided Ben-Gurion, Jabotinsky and muscular Zionism with the militaristic tradition of the Bible: of military conquest of the land and subjugation of the Canaanites and other ancient people that populated the 'promised land'. Both Ben-Gurion and Jabotinsky – both were directly responsible for many of the founding myths of Zionism – were, in particular, highly suspicious of liberal democracy. Both embraced a form of militarist Jewish 'nationalism' and both repeatedly invoked Joshua to justify Zionist attitudes towards the indigenous inhabitants of Palestine (Masalha 1992: 24–5, 28–9). Ben-Gurion in addition (unlike Jabotinsky) embraced 'state socialism' – which from the 1930s into the 1950s dominated first the Yishuv (the pre-1948 Jewish settlement in Palestine) and then the State of Israel. The doctrine of the 'Iron Wall' (see below) was to form a central plank in the attitudes of the Yishuv settlers towards the Palestinian Arabs. Furthermore from 1929 onwards Ben-Gurion began using – albeit with a modified meaning – the 'Iron Wall' approach Jabotinsky had coined in articles in the early

1920s. Thus in 1929 Ben-Gurion wrote of the need for an 'Iron Wall of [Zionist] workers' settlements surrounding every Hebrew city and town, land and human bridge that would link isolated points' and that would be capable of enforcing the doctrine of exclusive Hebrew labour (*'avoda 'ivrit*) and Hebrew land (*adama 'ivrit*) (Masalha 1992: 24–5).

Although Ben-Gurion's 'state socialism' was denounced by Jabotinsky – who believed that the Bible was a superior text to *Capital* since it was based on capitalism and private enterprise (Shindler 2002a: 99) – Labour Zionism was in fact an amalgam form of integral tribal and *volkisch* nationalism. This invented tradition considered the Jews as a race and a biological group, and borrowed heavily from illiberal nationalisms in Central and Eastern Europe (Sternhell 1998). Ben-Gurion's obsessive advocacy of the ethnic cleansing of Palestine in the 1930s and 1940s (see below) was related to this nationalist rejection of both liberal forms of universalism and Marxism, along with individual rights and class struggle. Instead, it gave precedence to the realisation of an ethnocratic settler project: the establishment in Palestine of a mono-religious, ethnic settler state. In this project, state socialism was deployed both as a useful mobilising myth and as an essential tool for collective (Jewish) control of the land. Although largely secular, Labour Zionism instrumentally emphasised Jewish religion and Jewish ethnicity, promoted the cult and mythologies of ancient history and biblical battles, revived a seemingly dead language, built up a powerful army, surrounded its ethnically exclusive Yishuv with an 'Iron Wall' (Shlaim 2000; Masalha 2000) and waged a bitter struggle for political independence and territorial expansion throughout the land. Muscular 'nationalist socialist' Zionism repudiated liberal individualism and was suspicious of bourgeois liberal democracy (Sternhell 1998).

For Ben-Gurion and other founding fathers of Zionism the invention of a tradition and the synthesising of a nation meant that the Hebrew Bible was not a religious document or the repository of a theological claim to Palestine; it was reinvented as a nationalised and racialised sacred text central to the modern foundational myths of secular Zionism. As a primordialist movement of secular nationalism, asserting the antiquity of Jewish nationalism (Smith 1986), inspired by Eurocentric ethnic, *volkisch* and racial ideologies, Ben-Gurion viewed the Bible in an entirely functional way: the biblical narrative functioned as a mobilising myth and as a 'historical account' of Jews' 'title to the land' – a claim (as we shall see in Chapter 7) not necessarily borne out by recent archaeological findings. For Ben-Gurion it was not important whether the biblical narrative was an objective and true record of actual historical events. It is not entirely clear whether Ben-Gurion assumed that the ancient events Israel was re-enacting had actually occurred. But as he explains: 'It is not important whether the [biblical] story is a true record of an event or not. What is of importance is that this is what the Jews believed as far back as the period of the First Temple' (Pearlman 1965: 227; also Rose 2004: 9).

Ben-Gurion represented a radical secular Zionist revolution against Jewish traditionalism. His ambivalence towards both Jewish traditionalism and the religious city of Jerusalem in particular was expressed by the fact that in 1906 when, at age 20, he emigrated to Palestine, he did not bother to visit the city until three years later (Wasserstein 2002: 5). His Jewish nationalism was a form of secular (East European) nationalism and he sought to redefine the Hebrew Bible and traditional Judaism along similar lines. For him the Hebrew Bible was central to Jewish myth-making and Israel's civic religion. Ben-Gurion tried to give political Zionism – and all Zionist politics and policies – a 'historical character' linked to the Hebrew Bible. As a deeply secular man, he used the Bible instrumentally as a nationalist tool to further Zionist objectives.

Like Ben-Gurion, many secular Labour Zionists displayed from the outset a deeply ambivalent attitude towards Jerusalem. Although the movement's name is derived from the word 'Zion', which was originally the name of a fortress in Jerusalem, Zionism reinvented the religious yearnings of generations of Jews for Jerusalem – which were expressed in the prayers and customs mourning Jerusalem's destruction – and trans-lated them into political action. Furthermore, Zionism had ambitions to create a new Jewish society that would be different from Jewish life in the Diaspora and did not see multi-religious and pluralistic Jerusalem as the appropriate place for the founding of such a new society. Not only was it full of aliens (native Arabs) but it was also inhabited by the 'old Jewish Yishuv', whose members were part of the anti-Zionist ultra-orthodox com-munity. It is no wonder, therefore, that the Zionists preferred to build the new (and exclusively) Jewish city of Tel Aviv on the Mediterranean coast, just outside the Palestinian city of Jaffa. Tel Aviv was founded in 1910 in a region which, according to the Bible, was ruled by the Philistines (not the Israelites) from the twelfth century BC onwards. It was named after a Babylonian city mentioned in Ezekiel (3:15) and chosen by Zionist leader Nahum Sokolow as the title of his Hebrew translation of Theodor Herzl's Zionist novel *Altneuland* (*Old New Land*, 1902). The ethnic-religious exclusiveness of the European Jewish Yishuv was illustrated by the fact that during the Mandatory period its Zionist leaders preferred to live in the ethnically exclusive Tel Aviv rather than in multi-religious Jerusalem. Those Zionist immigrants who chose to live in Jerusalem settled outside the historic city and built new Jewish neighbourhoods and the first Jewish university – the Hebrew University. Tel Aviv remained home to the Histadrut and all the Hebrew daily papers, and, while Zionist leaders of the Yishuv continued to swear by the name of Jerusalem, they did not live there and most of the Jewish immigrants to Palestine, about 80 per cent, settled along the Mediterranean coast, a region that (according to Professor Avishai Margalit of the Hebrew University) had never been the historic homeland of the Jewish people.[6]

However, like other founding fathers of the State of Israel, who were secular or atheist Jews, Ben-Gurion made extensive use of 'elect people-promised land' ideas and kept stressing the 'uniqueness' of the Jewish people. He liked to invoke the biblical Prophet Isaiah who enjoined the Jews to be 'a light unto the nations'. He was also quick to put the ethnocentric concepts of 'promised land–chosen people' to use for their political value, both as a means of attracting believing Jews to the Zionist cause and as a way of justifying the Zionist enterprise in Western eyes and the eyes of world Jewry.[7] The relatively moderate Israeli leader Moshe Sherret, who had served as foreign minister and (and for a short period) prime minister in the 1950s, had this to say about Ben-Gurion's ethnocentric Zionism and messianic tendency: '[Ben-Gurion's] constant stress on the uniqueness of the Jewish people is another aspect of his egocentrism – cultural egocentrism. The third aspect of a messianic mission vis-à-vis Israel and Jewry' (quoted in Shindler 2002a: 64).

Ben-Gurion also, and crucially, argued that he was fighting all Zionist battles with the help of the Hebrew Bible.[8] Already in his first published work, in Yiddish, entitled: *Eretz Yisrael: Past and Present* (1918), which he co-authored with Yitzhak Ben-Tzvi – later to become the second president of Israel – he argued that the Jewish 'return' to Palestine is actually a 'repeat' of Joshua's conquest of ancient Palestine.[9] The 1948 Palestine war drew Ben-Gurion ever nearer to the biblical narrative, as seen from his frequent references to biblical figures and biblical battles of conquest. Apparently the Book of Joshua was the biblical book to which Ben-Gurion was most drawn. On more than one occasion Ben-Gurion pointed to an 'unbroken line of continuity from the days of *Yehoshua bin Nun* [Joshua son of Nun] to the IDF' (Israel Defence Force) in and after 1948.[10] When he spoke of sweeping Jewish offensives in the 1948 war, he apparently did so in language evocative of the Book of Joshua. The Israeli army, he declared, had 'struck the kings of Lod and Ramleh, the kings of Belt Naballa and Deir Tarif, the kings of Kola and Migdal Zedek'.[11]

Twentieth-century Zionist nationalism and settler colonialism imagined itself closely linked with the original Hebrew covenant.[12] In *God's Peoples: Covenant and Land in South Africa, Israel, and Ulster*, Akenson (1992) shows how the Hebrew Bible has formed the fundamental pattern of mind of the three societies of apartheid South Africa, Zionist Israel, and Protestant Northern Ireland, and how the dominant peoples of these countries have based their cultural identity on a belief in a covenant with an all-powerful militant God. By going back to muscular parts of the Hebrew scriptures that defined the 'promised land–chosen people' and told the people to conquer it, the religious purpose of the Bible was declared to be the same as the purpose of the secular Israeli state (Akenson 1992).

Shortly after Israel's 1967 conquests, the country's leading novelist Amos Oz, in an article in the Hebrew daily *Davar*, wrote:

> Some of our first arrivals thought that, by right, the Arabs should return to the desert and give the land back to its owners, and, if not, that they (the Zionists) should 'arise and inherit', like those who conquered Canaan in storm: 'A melody of blood and fire ... Climb the mountain, crush the *plain*. All you see – inherit ... and conquer the land by the strength of your arm...' (Tchernichovsky, 'I Have a Tune').[13]

Shaul Tchernichovsky (1875-1943), a Russian Jew and one of the most influential Hebrew poets, was greatly influenced by the muscular culture of ancient Greece. In his Hebrew poems he contributed to the development of militant muscular Zionism by calling upon the Jewish youth to remember the heroic battles of the biblical zealots. He celebrated 'blood and soil' and the virility and primitive heroism of the Israelite tribes, emerging (according to the Bible) from the desert under Joshua's leadership, over-running and conquering Canaan. Not surprisingly, Tchernichovsky also had a major influence on Jabotinsky's 'Iron Wall' doctrine of military might which would protect Greater Israel.[14] Jabotinsky, the leader of the Revisionist Betar movement, the forerunner of the present-day Likud, developed his concept of militant Zionism in his historical novel *Samson* (1930) – named after the legendary biblical figure who is said to have lived during the period when the Israelites were oppressed by the power of the Philistines. In the novel the final message masculine Samson sends to the Israelites consists of two words: 'Iron' and 'King', the two themes the Israelites were told to strive for so that they would become the lords of Canaan (cited in Bresheet 1989: 123).

Earlier in the 1920s Jabotinsky developed his 'Iron Wall' theme to explain that Zionist settlement in Palestine can only be carried out against the wishes of the country's Arab majority. In an article entitled 'The Iron Wall: We and the Arabs' (1923), Jabotinsky cited both the conquest methods of the Spaniard colonists in Mexico and Peru and Joshua to justify Zionist policies towards the indigenous Palestinians and the transforma-tion of Palestine into the 'Land of Israel':

> Every reader has some idea of the early history of other countries which have been settled. I suggest that he recall all known instances. If he should attempt to seek but one instance of a country settled with the consent of those born there he will not succeed. The inhabitants (no matter whether they are civilized or savages) have always put up a stubborn fight. Further-more, how the settler acted had no effect whatsoever. The Spaniards who conquered Mexico and Peru, or our own ancestors in the days of Joshua ben Nun behaved, one might say, like plunderers ... Zionist colonization, even the most restricted, must either be terminated or carried out in defiance of the will of the native population. This colonization can, therefore, continue and develop only under the protection of a force independent of the local population – an iron wall which the native population cannot break through. This is, in toto, our policy towards the Arabs. To formulate it any other way would only be hypocrisy.[15]

After Jabotinsky's death in the United States in 1940, a Revisionist group around Abraham Stern broke with Betar Revisionism and cre-ated the Stern Gang, or Lehi (Fighters for the Freedom of Israel), whose political programme called for the setting up of a Jewish state from the Nile to the Euphrates and for the 'transfer' (the Hebrew euphemism for ethnic cleansing) of the Palestinians to other countries in the Middle East (Masalha 2000: 44; Shindler 2002a: 100). Stern, who constantly spoke of rebuilding the Third Temple, sought to synthesise a mixure of biblical militarism and messianic religiosity with an admiration for contemporary Italian Fascism and with an anti-British military struggle in Palestine, adopted 'Yair' as a *nom de guerre* after Elaazar Ben-Yair, who (according to one biblical tradition) had committed suicide at Massada rather than fall into the hands of the Romans or accept Roman hegemony (Shindler 2002a: 22-4, 2002b: 100).

In the struggle with the indigenous inhabitants of Palestine for land and territory, Ben-Gurion (Labour Zionism), Jabotinsky (Betar Zionism) and Stern (Stern Gang) studied, revived and celebrated the heroic (but rather mythological) battles of the ancient zealots, and biblical names such as Betar and Massada, those legendary small fortified positions which held out in desperate struggles against the Romans (Kohn 1958, in Khalidi 2005: 819); Jabotinsky's 'Iron Wall' doctrine, in particular, with its revival of militarist biblical traditions from Joshua to Samson, and its celebation of modern militarism, has formed a central plank in Zionist attitudes towards the indigenous inhabitants of Palestine, through the early Mandatory period to the 1948 Palestinian catastrophe to the 'Separation (Apartheid) Wall' in the occupied West Bank.

Interestingly, however, the initial mobilisation of biblical myths in favour of Zionism – and in particular the notion that the Hebrew Bible provides the Jews with a 'title deed to the land' – did not originate with Jewish Zionism; historically it was deeply rooted in the post-Reformation Protestant doctrine that Jewish restoration to Palestine would lead to the fulfilment of biblical prophecies and the second coming of Christ. As we shall see in Chapter 2, from the sixteenth century onwards Christian and biblical Zionism and the establishment of European settler colonies in Asia, Africa and the Americas were joined. However, Christian and Jewish 'Zionisms', originating in different ideological contexts, were also drawn to different ingredients in the Old Testament to justify Zionism, the military conquest of Palestine and the imposition of the Zionist political agenda as expressed in the State of Israel.

The rise of biblical Christian Zionism in the mid- to late nineteenth century prepared the ground for the emergence of European Jewish Zionism in the late nineteenth century. Clearly political Zionism, which was founded by Theodor Herzl in the 1890s, was influenced by its contemporary, Christian Zionism (Merkley 1998: 15-21). Ironically, however, Herzl's Zionism was a basically secular movement, with non-religious and frequently anti-religious dispositions. Although the Bible was always in the background as a support, the Jewish state would not be a theocracy. In the late nineteenth century the Zionist programme was generally opposed by both wings of Judaism, Orthodox and Reform, as being anti-religious (by the Orthodox) and contrary to the universality of Judaism (by Reform Jewry). Indeed the founding fathers of Jewish Zionism were almost all atheists or religiously indifferent. Moses Hess (1812-1875), a leading precursor of Zionism, was typical: a secular German Jew and a socialist, he contributed to Marx's *Communist Manifesto* (written in 1848) and was even credited with the term 'religion as the opium of the masses'. Following the rise of nationalism in Italy, Hess became a Zionist. His booklet *Rome and Jerusalem: The Last National Question*, published in 1862, called for a Jewish national movement similar to the Italian Risorgimento. Hess died in Paris, although at his request he was buried in the Jewish cemetery in Cologne. However, in 1961 his remains were transferred to Israel where they were buried in the Kinneret cemetery alongside other secular founding fathers of Labour Zionism such as Nahum Syrkin, Ber Borochov and Berl Katznelson.

Although many early Jewish Zionists were secular, socialists and atheists, they were quick to put the 'promised land–chosen people' ideology to use for its political value, both as a means of attracting believing Jews to their cause and as a way of justifying their colonial project in European Christian eyes. In the interests of gaining international support, the biblical narrative was an appealing way of legitimising the Zionist movement. This alliance between secular Jewish nationalists and Christian Zionists was mutually beneficial. Herzl himself was introduced to William Henry Hechler (1845-1931),[16] the chaplain of the British embassy in Vienna, half German and a close associate of Lord Shaftesbury, and a supporter of the restoration of the Jews to Palestine and rebuilding the Temple. He had been tutor to Prince Ludwig, the heir to the Grand Duke Frederick of

Baden, and was happy to introduce Herzl to his former master and other diplomatic figures on the European scene (Vital 1988: 75; Merkley 1998: 16-17).[17]

Where Are the Biblical Boundaries of the 'Land of Israel'?

The biblical boundaries of the so-called Land of Israel are entirely fictional. Although the term *Eretz Yisrael* (the Hebrew for the 'Land of Israel') is used occasionally in the Hebrew Bible (1 Samuel 13:19), it has carried only religious and spiritual connotations in Diaspora Judaism. In fact the term was used widely only in the nineteenth century with the rise of secular Zionism in Europe, and with the secularisation and nationalisation of this term by different Zionist groups (Shindler 2002b: 93). Moreover there is no historical or even religious map of the scope and boundaries of the 'Land of Israel', and no Jewish religious definition of the borders. As a result different European Zionist camps drew on completely different sources to support their different scope and boundaries of the 'biblical land of Israel' (Shindler 2002b: 92-3). Furthermore, modern secular European Zionist definitions of the term *Eretz Yisrael* were largely based on economic and settler colonial factors such as good agriculture, access to water from the Litani and Jordan rivers, and efficient transportation facilities rather than any imagined biblical boundaries of the 'promised land' (Shindler 2002b: 96-7).

However, the entire spectrum of Zionist opinion believed, and still believes, that *Eretz Yisrael* extends to the east of the River Jordan; in Zionist terminology, *Eretz Yisrael* is basically separated by the Jordan river into two major parts: 'the western land of Israel' (*Eretz Yisrael Hama'aravit*), which includes Israel proper and the 1967 occupied territories, and 'the eastern land of Israel' (*Eretz Yisrael Hamizrahit*), situated mainly in the modern state of Jordan. However, while certain sections of the Zionist movement (particularly right-wing Revisionists) insisted that the modern Jewish state should be established in 'the whole of *Eretz Yisrael*', the majority accepted the British-dictated reality and focused on the area of the Palestine Mandate. Yet, while the majority believed that the State of Israel could realistically be established only in part of *Eretz Yisrael*, it remained committed to the ultimate vision of 'the whole Land of Israel'.

Furthermore, the concept of exclusive Jewish 'rights' in the 'land of the Bible' was never confined only to the territorial maximalists of Zionist Revisionism or Israel's extreme right. Ben-Gurion's chief aide during the Mandatory period and Israel's first foreign minister, the Ukraine-born Moshe Shertok had this to say in 1914:

> We have forgotten that we have not come to an empty land to inherit it, but we have come to conquer a country from a people inhabiting it, that governs it by the virtue of its language and savage culture.... Recently, there has been appearing in our newspapers the clarification about 'the mutual misunderstanding' between us and the Arabs, about 'common interests' [and] about 'the possibility of unity and peace between two fraternal peoples.' ... [But] we must not allow ourselves to be deluded by such illusive hopes ... for if we cease to look upon our land, the Land of Israel, as ours alone and we allow a partner into our estate – all content and meaning will be lost to our enterprise. (cited in Morris 2000: 91)

Five years later, at the Paris Peace Conference, which opened in January 1919 to dispose of the territories captured from the defeated powers, Germany, Austria-Hungary and the Ottoman Empire, Chaim Weizmann, then leading the Zionist Commission that was to put forward Zionist political and territorial claims, called for the imposition of a British Mandate over an enlarged Palestine extending north to the Litani river in what is now Lebanon and east to the Hijaz railway line, which is well east of the Jordan river. It was at that conference, too, that Weizmann called for a Palestine 'as Jewish as England is English' (Litvinoff 1983: 256–7).

During the British Mandate (1922–48) the Zionists insisted on Palestine being referred to officially as the (biblical) 'Land of Israel', but the most that the mandatory authorities were willing to concede was the use of the Hebrew for *Eretz Yisrael* after the name Palestine on all official documents, currency, stamps, and so on (Rolef 1993: 101). Throughout the Mandatory period, the pragmatic and gradualist Zionist state-builders, led by David Ben-Gurion and his Mapai party (*Mifleget Po'alei Eretz Yisrael*, or the Land of Israel Workers' Party) dominated the Yishuv's politics, with right-wing territorial maximalists of Zionist Revisionism (who sought Jewish sovereignty over all of Mandatory Palestine and Transjordan and whose traditional slogan, still officially valid, was, 'Both banks of the Jordan – this is ours and that one is also') winning only a minority of

Jewish votes. In 1937, Ben-Gurion, an eminent realist and an archetypal pragmatic expansionist, was willing to accept the British Royal (Peel) Commission partition proposal and the establishment of a Jewish state in part of the country, although throughout he remained strongly committed to a vision of Jewish sovereignty over all of Palestine as the ultimate goal of Zionism (Morris 1987: 5). Ben-Gurion's objective was a Jewish state expanding into the whole of Palestine.

The Mythical Continuum

The idea that political Zionism expressed two thousand years of yearning for Jewish political and religious self-determination is an invented tradition – invented in Europe in the mid- to late nineteenth century. The 'land of the Bible', or Palestine, was never a major centre for Judaism during the last two thousand years. Although the Holy Land was central in the religious imagination of Jews, this was not translated into political, social, economical, demographic, cultural and intellectual realities. The first Zionist migration to Palestine (redemptive 'ascent' or *'aliyah* to the Land of Israel, in Zionist terminology), was in 1881–82, with most of the immigrants coming from Eastern Europe. In all, nearly 35,000 Jewish immigrants came from Eastern Europe to Palestine during the First Aliyah; almost half of them left the country within several years of their arrival, but some 15,000 established new rural settlements, and the rest moved to the towns. In comparison, during the 1880s hundred of thousands of Jews emigrated from Eastern Europe to the Americas. Prior to the First Aliyah, however, the number of Jews living in the whole of Palestine was approximately 24,000 – most of them non-Zionist orthodox Jews living in Jerusalem – which amounted to less than 5 per cent of the total population (Chapman 2002: 37).

Nevertheless, Zionist Jewish nationalists continued to talk about the 'unbroken chain of Jewish presence' in Palestine, from the earliest times to the rise of Zionism in the late nineteenth century. Of course it is important politically for Zionist Israelis to predicate a constant and enduring Jewish presence in Palestine, and the city of Jerusalem in particular, for two thousand years (Wasserstein 2002: 2). Moreover, in modern times the 'land of the Bible' and other phrases related to both biblical and modern terminology have been invested with far-reaching historical, geopolitical and ideological connotations in both Israeli rhetoric and Western scholarship (Whitelam 1996: 40). The reconstruction of the past by Zionist authors has often reflected their own political and religious ideologies. Both Zionist authors and biblical scholars in the West have based the 'historical claims' of modern Zionism to *Eretz Yisrael* on the biblical (mythical) narrative of the twelve tribes that conquered and lived on the land during the Israelites' pre-monarchical era; other Zionist claims have been based on the biblical 'Davidic or Solomon kingdoms' – whose historicity are highly questionable; see Chapter 7 – and the subsequent southern and northern kingdoms of Judea and Israel, the early second Temple period, the Hasmonean era, or the Kingdom of Herod.[18]

During the Mandatory period Ben-Gurion was fixated by the Book of Joshua and its conquest narrative. As we shall see in Chapter 7, the archaeological evidence shows the conquest narrative of Joshua to be completely mythical. By 1948 Ben-Gurion was arguing for an 'unbroken line of continuity' from the (mythical) days of Joshua to the recently formed Israeli army. This mythical continuum between the days of Joshua and modern Israel was meant to convey the idea that the land can only yield up its produce by the extraordinary effort of the 'returning' Jewish settlers and Zionist pioneers and Israel's genius. The colonialist claims that only under Jewish cultivation did Palestine become a productive country, that only Israel can make the land (and desert) bloom, that most Palestinians arrived in the area only within the past century, have long been part of the Zionist justification for Jewish immigration to Palestine, the founding of the State of Israel, its territorial expansion and the dispossession of the Palestinians (Whitelam 1996: 40-45).

Attitudes to the Indigenous Population of Palestine

From the beginning of the modern Zionist settlement in Palestine, European Jewish settlers had to confront the reality that their project immediately clashed with the ethnic, religious and demographic realities of Palestine and precipitated conflict with the indigenous inhabitants. In particular Palestinian demography and the land issue were at the heart of the struggle between the Zionist settlers and indigenous Palestinians.

Even in 1947 the indigenous Palestinians were the overwhelming majority in the country and owned much of the land. The Jewish community or Yishuv (mainly East European settlers) was about a third of the total population and owned, after fifty years of land purchases, only 6 per cent of the land.

Two of the founding fathers of Zionism, Yitzhak Ben-Tzvi and Ben-Gurion, initially raised the idea of assimilation of the Palestinian peasants and turning them into Jews. This suggestion was based on the (not far-fetched) notion that the Palestinian peasants might be the descendants of the ancient Israelites who had lived during the period of the second Temple, beginning around the fifth century BC, and who (according to Ben-Tzvi and Ben-Gurion) had survived the Romans' 'destruction' of the country and had remained in Palestine. Those Jewish inhabitants had accepted Islam many generations later.[19] In the 1920s Ben-Gurion and Ben-Tzvi argued that if the rural Palestinian Arabs were originally Jewish, this should facilitate the job of their Hebraicisation and eventually turning them into Jews (Wiemer 1983: 36). However, in the 1930s, with the intensification of the Palestinian resistance to Zionism, the general endorsement of 'transfer' by Ben-Gurion and other leaders of the Jewish Agency (in different forms: voluntary, agreed and compulsory) was designed to achieve two crucial objectives: (1) to clear the land for Jewish settlers and would-be immigrants, and (2) to establish an ethnocratic, mono-religious and fairly homogenous Jewish state. During the same period key leaders of Labour Zionism, such as Ben-Gurion, then chairman of the Jewish Agency, strongly believed that Zionism would not succeed in setting up a homogenous Jewish state and fulfilling its imperative of absorbing the expected influx of Jewish immigrants from Europe if the indigenous inhabitants were allowed to remain. In 1952, even after the 1948 Nakba and expulsion of three-quarters of a million Palestinians, Ben-Tzvi was still arguing in internal debates of the Mapai ruling party that if 'disloyal [Israeli] Arabs should be discovered, then this will enable us to treat them differently, to expel them' (cited in Wiemer 1983: 36).

The establishment of Jewish political sovereignty over Greater Israel constitutes the vital focus of action for Israel's territorial maximalists. The Likud and other right-wing parties reject Israeli withdrawal from any territories of the so-called western *Eretz Yisrael* – west of the Jordan river, or the West Bank. Moreover, since the Sinai peninsula was not considered by Likud Zionism as part of 'biblical Israel' the Israeli withdrawal in the early 1980s (endorsed by Prime Minister Menahem Begin) was not resisted as strongly as might be a possible future withdrawal from the West Bank. Although at present the Likud Party's support for settlement and territorial expansionism is largely confined to the post-1967 occupied territories (the West Bank, Gaza and the Golan Heights), this support is in large measure the result of adherence to Jabotinsky's Greater Israel: concern for the territorial integrity of an imagined biblical Israel. When in 1949 the Labour government acquiesced in the annexation of the West Bank to the Transjordan state of King 'Abdullah, Begin denounced the Israeli government for betraying Zionism and (imagined) biblical territories of a Jewish state to be set up on both sides of the River Jordan:

> Who gave the government the right to hand over the cave of Machpela, Rachel's tomb's ... Gilead and Bashan to a foreigner, an enemy, an oppressor? – sites which had been historically hallowed for 120 generations. (quoted in Shindler 2002a: 45)

For Begin and Revisionist Zionism the West Bank ('Judea and Samaria') are situated at the heart of 'biblical Israel', in Zionist terminology in the 'western Land of Israel'. In a speech in the Knesset on 3 May 1950 Begin, then leader of the Revisionist Herut party (later the Likud), denounced the annexation of the West Bank by the Jordanian kingdom, a state, he said, that existed in 'our homeland'. In a biblical analogy Begin labelled '[King] 'Abdullah "the Ammonite slave", describing him by his Arabic name: 'Allah slave [who] will rule 80 per cent of our homeland' (Shindler 2002b: 46). The Israeli academic Yonathan Shapiro recently commented on the deployment of biblical myths in Revisionist Zionism and the Likud:

> [such] myths are based on an interpretation of historical events and concrete events that is not necessarily consonant with reality. To argue that the boundaries of Mandate Palestine (with or without the Jordan) were the borders of the historic Land of Israel was devoid of factual historical basis. But Herut, like Betar and like the Revisionist Party, which also embraced this principle, never bothered to examine the subject ... although this camp contained scholars and researchers who knew it lacked historical foundation. Correlation between myth and reality was unnecessary. (quoted in Shind/ 2002b: 47)

Other, more radical, supporters of post-1967 neo-Zionism, such as the highly influential settlement movement of Gush Emunim, also use the same biblical myths and legends and dream of territorial expansionism far beyond 'Judea and Samaria'. As the late Ehud Sprinzak, of the Hebrew University, a prominent expert on Gush Emunim and Israel's radical right, observes:

> When Gush [Emunim] ideologues speak about the complete [whole] Land of Israel they have in mind not only the post-1967 territory, but the land promised in the Covenant (Genesis 15) as well. This includes the occupied territories – especially Judea and Samaria, the very heart of the historic Israeli nation, and vast territories that belong now to Jordan, Syria and Iraq. (Sprinzak 1991: 113)

The June War of 1967 marked a decisive turn in the history of Zionism, the State of Israel and the Palestinians, particularly those living in the occupied West Bank and the Gaza Strip. The overwhelming Israeli victory, the seizure of the remainder of historic Palestine with its sizeable Arab population, the resultant outburst, and later upsurge, of messianic Zionism and growing Israeli confidence all contributed to the prompt and inevitable revival of the project of territorial expansionism. As has already been shown, in the wake of the 1967 conquests the perception and myths of Greater biblical Israel was found not only in the maximalist revisionist camp of Herut (later the Likud), but increasingly gained ground in all mainstream Zionist parties.

'Jerusalem of Gold' and the Myth of an Empty and Deserted Land

The State of Israel was built on old biblical symbols and legends and modern Zionist myths.
¹ to Zionist foundational myths is the theme that the land, until
an Jewish settlers, was virtually barren, desolate and
tile and populated by Israel; it was the rightful
,' (Whitelam 1996: 40–45). A few weeks after
leading novelist, Amos Oz, wrote an article in
w daily *Davar* in which he drew attention to the
mong Zionist Israelis to see Palestine as a country

without its indigenous inhabitants. He also pointed to the revival of a 'transfer' (ethnic cleansing) discourse in Israel: 'One often hears talk about pushing the Palestinian masses back to rich Kuwait or fertile Iraq.'[20]

Oz also drew attention to Naʿomi Shemer's song 'Jerusalem of Gold', which encapsulated this deep-seated inclination among Israeli Jews to see Palestine as a country without its Arab inhabitants. The song 'Jerusalem of Gold', which came to be defined as a kind of 'national anthem of the Six Day War',[21] was commissioned by the municipality of Jewish Jerusalem, was written for a music festival held on the eve of the war,[22] and became a national hit after the Israeli seizure of East Jerusalem, the West Bank and the Gaza Strip, and throughout the years the song has enjoyed the unofficial status of a second national anthem.[23] After the Israeli army conquered the Old City of Jerusalem, its senior commanders rushed to the 'Western Wall' – according to Jewish tradition, a remnant of the ancient Jewish Temple – and the whole country was swept by the intoxication of victory, mixed with a semi-religious redemptionist mysticism.[24] 'Jerusalem of Gold' is the most popular song ever produced in Israel and in 1967 it swept the country overnight, genuinely expressing Israeli territorial aspirations following the new conquests. Shemer herself received the Israel Prize for her unique contribution to the Israeli song, although she later confessed, on her deathbed, that the 'Jerusalem of Gold' melody was a copy of a Basque lullaby she heard some years earlier from a Spanish singer.[25] The song contains the following passages about Arab Jerusalem:

Jerusalem of Gold
How did the water cisterns dry out, the market-place is empty,
And no-one visits the Holy Mount in the Old City [site of the Dome of the
    Rock and al-Aqsa Mosque].
And through the cave within the rock winds are whining,
And no-one descends down to the Dead Sea en route for Jericho ...
Jerusalem of Gold ...
We have returned to the water cisterns, to the market-place and the square.
A shofar[26] sounds on the Holy Mount in the Old City.
And in the caves within the rock a thousand suns do glow,
We shall again descend to the Dead Sea en route for
Jericho.[27]

In the post-1967 period Israeli politicians constantly spoke of 'Judea and Samaria' as 'rightful' parts of the Jewish state – claims made on the basis of the Old Testament and without a reference to the rights of the land's indigenous inhabitants. The same biblical rhetoric was also linked to the myth of 'a land without a people' (Masalha 1997) and is not just an infamous fragment of early Zionist propaganda: it is ubiquitous in much of the Israeli historiography of nation-building. A few weeks after the 1967 war, Oz drew attention to the deep-seated inclination among Israelis to see Palestine as a country without its indigenous inhabitants:

> When I was a child, some of my teachers taught me that after our Temple was destroyed and we were banished from our country, strangers came into what was our heritage and defiled it. The desert-born Arabs laid the land waste and let the terraces on the hillsides go to ruin. Their flocks destroyed the beautiful forests. When our first pioneers came to the land to rebuild it and to redeem it from desolation, they found an abandoned wasteland. True, a few backward, uncouth nomads wandered in it.[28]

The mega-narrative of Zionism contains several intertwined foundational myths which underlie contemporary Israeli culture. These include the 'negation of exile' (*shlilat ha-galut*), the 'return to history' (*ha-shiva la-historia*), the 'return to the Land of Israel' (*ha-shiva le-Eretz Yisrael*) and the myth of 'empty territory' (Piterberg 2001: 31–46).[29] The 'negation of exile' allows Zionism to establish a line of unbroken continuity between ancient Palestine and a present that renews it in the resettlement of Palestine (Piterberg 2001: 31). These slogans run through state education in Israel and find strong expression in children's literature. One such work for children contains the following excerpt:

> Joseph and some of his men thus crossed the land [Palestine] on foot, until they reached Galilee. They climbed mountains, beautiful but empty mountains, where nobody lived ... Joseph said, 'We want to establish this Kibbutz and conquer this emptiness. We shall call this place Tel Hai [Living Hill] ... The land is empty; its children have deserted it [reference is, of course, to Jews]. They are dispersed and no longer tend it. No one protects or tends the land now.' (Gurvitz and Navon 1953: 128, 132, 134, in El-Asmar 1986: 83)

In a similar vein, Israel's leading satirist, Dan Ben-Amotz, observed in 1982 that 'the Arabs do not exist in our textbooks [for children]. This is apparently in accordance with the Jewish–Zionist–socialist principles we have received. "A-people-without-a-land-returns-to-a-land-without-people"' (Ben-Amotz 1982: 155).

In his *Davar* article, Oz offers a liberal Zionist explanation of the connection between the 'land without a people' formula, the popularity of Shemer's song 'Jerusalem of Gold', and the emergence of the transfer 'talk' after the war:

> It seems that the enchantment of 'renewing the days of old' is what gave Zionism its deep-seated inclination to see a country without inhabitants before it ... How fitting would it have been for the Return to Zion to have taken the land from the Roman legions or the nations of Canaan and Philistia. And to come to a completely empty country would have been even better. From there, it is only a short step to the kind of self-induced blindness that consists in disregarding the existence of the country's Arab population, or in discounting it and its importance on the dubious grounds that it 'has created no valuable cultural assets here', as if that would permit us to take no notice of its very existence. (In time, Na'omi Shemer would express this state of mind in her song 'Jerusalem of Gold': ... the marketplace is empty/ And no-one goes down to the Dead Sea/ By way of Jericho.' Meaning, of course, that the marketplace is empty of Jews and that no Jew goes down to the Dead Sea by way of Jericho. A remarkable revelation of a remarkably characteristic way of thinking.) (Oz 1988)

This characteristic thinking echoes strongly the deep-seated theme of 'land without a people' and naturally leads to the revival of the ethnic cleansing project, a fact illustrated by the attitude of Na'omi Shemer, the poet laureate of Greater Israel's supporters, toward the indigenous inhabitants of Palestine.

Na'omi Shemer's views on ethnic cleansing were supported by one of the famous 'heroes' of the Israeli army, Meir Har-Tzion,[30] 'who was considered the ultimate Israeli warrior, a kind of Jewish Rambo' (Kimmerling 2003: 51-2). Har-Tzion had served in 'Unit 101', which, under the command of Ariel Sharon, carried out 'retaliatory' operations against Arab targets in the 1950s. The unit was responsible for the attack on the Arab village of Qibya, to the south-west of Hebron in 1953 in which sixty-three villagers were slaughtered, and also carried out the expulsion of the al-'Azazmeh tribe from the Negev to Sinai. In January 1979 Har-Tzion said: 'I do not say that we should put them [the Arabs] on trucks and kill them. ... We must create a situation in which for them it would not be worth living here, but [to leave] to Jordan or Saudi Arabia or any other Arab state'.[31] Har-Tzion promptly was applauded by Shemer in an article in the Histadrut (Labour-controlled) daily *Davar*:

Arab emigration from Israel, if it is done with mutual respect and positive will
... is likely to be the right solution ... it is possible that it will be recognized as
a most human possibility after much suffering and only after hard and bitter
civil war – but talking about it is permitted and must be now; ... why is the
exodus of one million French from Algeria a progressive and human solution
and the exodus of one million Arabs from Israel [is not]?[32]

Shemer and Har-Tzion are not marginal figures in Israel. Shemer is Israel's
most famous and popular songwriter. Har-Tzion, who was brought up and
educated in Kibbutz 'Ein Harod, was a national hero; he was described
by general Moshe Dayan (1915–1981) as 'the brightest soldier in Jewish
history since [Simon] Bar-Kohkva' (quoted in Schiff and Haber 1976: 178)[33]
– the messianic leader of the last Jewish rebellion against the Romans in
132 and 135.[34]

Such statements echoed classical mainstream Zionist argumentation in
justification of Arab removal. The argument that support for the 'transfer'
concept does not come only from a fringe group is also illustrated by the
fact that some of the nation's leading authors, novelists and poets, such
as Natan Alterman, Haim Hazaz, Yigal Mossenson and Moshe Shamir (all
of whom supported Israel's retention of all the territories seized in 1967),
publicly supported the idea of transfer in the post-1967 era (Nisan 1986:
119, 200; Shiloah 1989: 8; Shamir 1991: 95-9). These leading literary
figures also were closely associated with mainstream Labour or left-wing
Zionism in the pre-1948 period and the first two decades of the State of
Israel.

Haim Hazaz (1898–1973) was another example of a leading author who
supported the 'transfer' concept in the post-1967 era. As a prolific Hebrew
novelist, his works have won him numerous awards, including the Bialik
Prize and the Israel Prize, the top prize awarded by the State of Israel.
Hazaz, in an article published in *Davar* on 10 November 1967, echoed the
Labour Zionist biblical rhetoric of the pre-1948 period:

There is the question of Judea and Ephraim [the West Bank], with a large
Arab population which must be evacuated to neighbouring Arab states. This
is not an exile like the exile of the Jews among the Gentiles. ... They will be
coming to their brothers to large and wide and little populated countries.
One culture, one language and religion. This is 'transfer' such as that which
took place between Turkey and Greece, between India and Pakistan ... putting
the world aright in one place through exchanging [the Arab population] to

its designated place. We will assume responsibility f[
planning, organising and financing. (quoted in Ben-

Avraham Yoffe, who also was a member of the Knesse[
1974 to 1977, believed that the extension of Israeli sovereignty ov[
and Samaria and Gaza would cause 'part [of the Arab inhabitants]
emigrate from here and the other part to remain as loyal citizens of the
State of Israel' (Masalha 2000: 39).

Mainstream Zionism rejected the views of a liberal minority – to which
Amos Oz belongs – which argued that Palestine is also the homeland of the
Palestinian people. Therefore one needs to go beyond Oz's explanation to
understand the background against which 'transfer' thoughts and debates
promptly resurfaced after 1967. This background consists of the standard
mainstream Zionist 'solution for the Palestinian problem', which was predicated on the claim for monopolised Jewish ownership and Zionist domination of the 'land of the Bible'. This being the case, Zionism was bound to
base its conception of Jerusalem upon a mythologised entity, 'Jerusalem of
Gold', and to involve abstract historical and ideological rights in the newly
acquired territories, as well as resting its claim on territorial expansion and
domination and the actual 'redemption of land' through settlement. One
implication of the claim for monopolised ownership of a country shared by
another people is the 'transfer' solution. Against this background transfer
proposals and plans inevitably were put forward by mainstream labour
leaders – including ministers – immediately after the 1967 victory.

These images and formulas of 'underpopulated and untended land'
gave those who propounded them a simple and self-explanatory Zionism.
These myths not only justified Zionist settlement but also helped to suppress conscience-pricking among Israeli Jews for the dispossession of the
Palestinians before, during and after 1948: if the 'land had been deserted',
then no Zionist wrongdoing had taken place.

Even in the 1990s, Israeli leaders such as Binyamin Netanyahu (Likud
prime minister 1996-99) were still propagating the myth of an underpopulated, desolate and inhospitable land to justify the Zionist colonisation of Palestine and obliviousness to the fate of its native inhabitants
(Netanyahu 1993: 39-40). Moreover, this (mythical) continuum between
the ancient and the modern means this is a difficult land, one that resists
agriculture and that can only be 'redeemed' and made to yield up its

be called Palestine, a country without a people, and, or
exists the Jewish people, and it has no country. What ᴗ
than to fit the gem into the ring, to unite this people with ᴗ
owners of the country [the Ottoman Turks?] must, therefore, ᴗ
and convinced that this marriage is advantageous, not only for the ᴗ
people and for the country, but also for themselves. (Weizmann, 28 Maᴗ
1914, in Litvinoff 1983: 115-16)

A few years after the Zionist movement obtained the Balfour Declaration, Zangwill wrote:

If Lord Shaftesbury was literally inexact in describing Palestine as a country
without a people, he was essentially correct, for there is no Arab people living
in intimate fusion with the country, utilising its resources and stamping it
with a characteristic impress; there is at best an Arab encampment. (Zangwill
1920: 104)

This and other pronouncements by Weizmann and other leading Zionists
embodying European supremacy planted in the Zionist mind the racist
notion of an empty territory – empty not necessarily in the actual absence
of its inhabitants, but rather in the sense of civilizational barrenness
– justifying Zionist colonisation at the expense of the native population
and their eventual removal.

Disposable People: Zionism Seen by Its Victims

Neither Zangwill nor Weizmann intended these demographic assessments
in a literal fashion. They did not mean that there were no people in
Palestine, but rather that there were no people worth considering within
the framework of the notions of European white supremacy that then held
sway. In this connection, a comment by Weizmann to Arthur Ruppin,
head of the colonisation department of the Jewish Agency, is particularly
revealing. When asked by Ruppin about the Palestinian Arabs and how
he (Weizmann) obtained the Balfour Declaration in 1917, Weizmann
replied: 'The British told us that there are some hundred thousand negroes
[*kushim* in Hebrew] and for those there is no value' (Heller 1984: 140).
Such pronouncements by Weizmann, Zangwill and other leading Zionists
planted in the Zionist mind the racist notion of an empty territory – empty
not necessarily in the sense of an actual absence of inhabitants, but rather

in the sense of a 'civilisational barrenness' justifying Zionist colonisation at the expense of the native population and its eventual removal.

In earlier works (Masalha 1992, 1997, 2000), which are largely based on Hebrew and Israeli archival sources, I have dealt with the evolution of the theme of 'population transfer' – a euphemism denoting the organised removal of the Arab population of Palestine to neighbouring or distant countries. I have shown that this concept – delicately described by its proponents as 'population exchange', 'Arab return to Arabia', 'emigration', 'resettlement' and 'rehabilitation' of the Palestinians in Arab countries, and so on – was deeply rooted in mainstream Zionist thinking and in the Yishuv as a solution to Zionist land and political problems. Although the desire among Zionist leaders to 'solve' the 'Arab question' through transfer remained constant until 1948, the envisaged modalities of transfer changed over the years according to circumstances. From the mid-1930s onwards a series of specific plans, generally involving Transjordan, Syria and Iraq, were produced by the Yishuv's transfer committees and senior officials.

The justifications used in defence of the transfer plans in the 1930s and 1940s formed the cornerstone of the subsequent argumentation for transfer, particularly in the proposals put forward after 1948 and in the wake of the 1967 conquest of the West Bank and Gaza. After 1967, Zionist territorial maximalists and proponents of transfer continued to assert, often publicly, that there was nothing immoral about the idea. They asserted that the Palestinians were not a distinct people but merely 'Arabs', an 'Arab population', or an 'Arab community' that happened to reside in the Land of Israel.

Closely linked to this idea of the non-existence of the Palestinians as a nation and their non-attachment to the particular soil of Palestine was the idea of their belonging to an Arab nation with vast territories and many countries. As Ben-Gurion put it in 1929, 'Jerusalem is not the same thing to the Arabs as it is to the Jews. The Arab people inhabit many great lands' (Teveth 1985: 39). And if the Palestinians did not constitute a distinct, separate nation, had little attachment to Jerusalem, were not an integral part of the country and were without historical ties to it, then they could be transferred to other Arab countries without undue prejudice. Similarly, if the Palestinians were merely a marginal, local segment of a larger population of Arabs, then they were not a major party to the conflicts with Israel; therefore Israeli efforts to deal over their heads were justified.

Despite their propaganda slogans of an underpopulated land, of Palestine's 'civilisational barrenness' and of their making 'the desert bloom', all of which were issued partly for external consumption, the Zionists from the outset were well aware that not only were there people on the land, but that they were there in large numbers. Zangwill, who had visited Palestine in 1897 and come face to face with the demographic reality of the country, himself acknowledged in a 1905 speech to a Zionist group in Manchester that 'Palestine proper had already its inhabitants. The pashalik [province] of Jerusalem is already twice as thickly populated as the United States, having fifty-two souls to the square mile, and not 25 per cent of them Jews' (Zangwill 1937: 210). Abundant references to the Palestinian population in early Zionist texts show clearly that from the beginning of the Zionist settlement in Palestine, the Palestinian Arabs were far from being an unseen or hidden presence.

Thus, Yitzhak Epstein, an early settler leader who arrived in Palestine from Russia in 1886, warned not only of the moral implications of the Zionist colonisation but also of the political dangers inherent in the enterprise. In 1907, at a time when Zionist land purchases in the Galilee were stirring opposition among Palestinian peasants forced off land sold by absentee landlords, Epstein wrote an article entitled 'The Hidden Question' in which he strongly criticised the methods by which Zionists had purchased Arab land. In his view, those methods entailing dispossession of Arab farmers were bound to cause political confrontation in the future. Reflected in the Zionist establishment's angry response to Epstein's article are two principal features of mainstream Zionist thought: the belief that Jewish acquisition of land took precedence over moral considerations, and the advocacy of a physically separate, exclusionist and literally 'pure' Jewish Yishuv. 'If we want Hebrew redemption 100 per cent, then we must have a 100 per cent Hebrew settlement, a 100 per cent Hebrew farm, and a 100 per cent Hebrew port', declared Ben-Gurion at a meeting of the Va'ad Leumi, the Yishuv's National Council, on 5 May 1936 (Ben-Gurion 1971-72: 163).

The idea of 'transfer'/ethnic cleansing is old as modern political Zionism and has accompanied its evolution and praxis during the past century (Masalha 1992, 1997).[37] Ben-Gurion, in particular, was an enthusiastic and committed advocate of the transfer 'solution'. The importance he attached not merely to transfer but forced transfer is seen in his diary entry for 12 July 1937:

> The compulsory transfer of Arabs from the valleys of the proposed Jewish state could give us something which we never had [an Arab-free Galilee], even when we stood on our own feet during the days of the First and Second Temple. (Ben-Gurion 1972: 297–9)

Ben-Gurion was convinced that few, if any, Palestinians would 'voluntarily' transfer themselves to Transjordan. He also believed that if the Zionists were determined in their effort to put pressure on the British Mandatory authorities to carry out 'compulsory transfer', the plan could be implemented:

> We have to stick to this conclusion in the same way we grabbed the Balfour Declaration, more than that, in the same way we grabbed Zionism itself. We have to insist upon this conclusion [and push it] with our full determination, power and conviction. ... We must uproot from our hearts the assumption that the thing is not possible. It can be done.

Ben-Gurion went as far as to write in his memoirs: *'We must prepare ourselves to carry out* the transfer' (Ben-Gurion 1972, vol. 4: 297–9; emphasis in the original). A letter to his son Amos, dated 5 October 1937, shows the extent to which transfer had become associated in his mind with expulsion. Ben-Gurion wrote:

> We must expel Arabs and take their places ... and, if we have to use force – not to dispossess the Arabs of the Negev and Transjordan, but to guarantee our own right to settle in those places – then we have force at our disposal. (Teveth 1985: 189)

At the Twentieth Zionist Congress, held 3–21 August 1937, Ben-Gurion emphasised that transfer of Arab villagers had been practised by the Yishuv all along:

> Was the transfer of the Arabs ethical, necessary and practicable? ... Transfer of Arabs had repeatedly taken place before in consequence of Jews settling in different districts.[38]

A year later, at the Jewish Agency Executive's transfer discussions of June 1938, Ben-Gurion put forward a 'line of actions' entitled 'The Zionist Mission of the Jewish State':

The Hebrew State will discuss with the neighbouring Arab states the matter of voluntarily transferring Arab tenant farmers, workers and *fellahin* from the Jewish state to neighbouring states. For that purpose the Jewish state, or a special company ... will purchase lands in neighbouring states for the resettlement of all those workers and *fellahin*.[39]

Ben-Gurion elaborated on the idea in his 'Lines for Zionist Policy' on 15 October 1941:

We have to examine, first, if this transfer is practical, and secondly, if it is necessary. It is impossible to imagine general evacuation without compulsion, and brutal compulsion. ... The possibility of a large-scale transfer of a population by force was demonstrated, when the Greeks and the Turks were transferred [after the First World War]. In the present war [the Second World War] the idea of transferring a population is gaining more sympathy as a practical and the most secure means of solving the dangerous and painful problem of national minorities.[40]

Ben-Gurion went on to suggest a Zionist-inspired campaign in Britain and the United States that would aim at influencing Arab countries, especially Syria and Iraq, to collaborate with the Jewish Yishuv in implementing the transfer of Palestinians in return for economic gains.

There is a great deal of evidence showing that in the pre-1948 period, 'transfer'/ethnic cleansing was embraced by the highest levels of Zionist leadership, representing almost the entire political spectrum. Nearly all the founding fathers of the Israeli state advocated transfer in one form or another, including Theodor Herzl, Leon Motzkin, Nahman Syrkin, Menahem Ussishkin, Chaim Weizmann, David Ben-Gurion, Yitzhak Tabenkin, Avraham Granovsky, Israel Zangwill, Yitzhak Ben-Tzvi, Pinhas Rutenberg, Aaron Aaronson, Vladimir Jabotinsky and Berl Katznelson.

Menahem Ussishkin, a Russian Jew and one of the leading figures of the Yishuv, long the chairman of the Jewish Agency Fund and a member of the Jewish Agency Executive, publicly called for the transfer of the Palestinians to other parts of the Middle East. In an address to journalists in Jerusalem on 28 April 1930, he stated:

We must continuously raise the demand that our [Biblical] land be returned to our possession. ... If there are other inhabitants there, they must be transferred to some other place. We must take over the land. We have a greater and nobler ideal than preserving several hundred thousands of Arab *fellahin*.[41]

Eleven years earlier, in an address to the representatives of the Western powers at the Versailles Peace conference in February 1991, the deeply secular Ushishkin had this to say:

> In the name of the largest Jewish community, the Jews of Russia, I stand here before you ... in order to put forward the historic demand of the Jewish people: for our return to our own borders; for the restoration to the Jews of the land that was promised to them four thousand years ago by the Power Above. ... That country was forcibly taken from the Jewish people 1800 years ago by the Romans. ... And now I ... come ... to you who serve both politically and culturally as the heirs to the Romans and make my demand to your. Restore that historic robbery to us. (quoted in Shindler 2002b: 97)

In August 1937, Berl Katznelson, who was one of the most popular and influential leaders of the Mapai Party (later the ruling Labour Party), had this to say in a debate at the World Convention of Ihud Poʻalei Tzion (the highest forum of the dominant Zionist world labour movement) about ethnic cleansing:

> The matter of population transfer has provoked a debate among us: Is it permitted or forbidden? My conscience is absolutely clear in this respect. A remote neighbour is better than a close enemy. They [the Palestinians] will not lose from it. In the final analysis, this is a political and settlement reform for the benefit of both parties. I have long been of the opinion that this is the best of all solutions ... I have always believed and still believe that they were destined to be transferred to Syria or Iraq.[42]

A year later, at the Jewish Agency Executive's discussions of June 1938, Katznelson declared himself in favour of maximum territory and the 'principle of compulsory transfer':

> What is a compulsory transfer? ... Compulsory transfer does not mean individual transfer. It means that once we resolved to transfer there should be a political body able to force this or that Arab who would not want to move out. Regarding the transfer of Arab individuals we are always doing this. But the question will be the transfer of much greater quantity of Arabs through an agreement with the Arab states: this is called a compulsory transfer. ... We have here a war about principles, and in the same way that we must wage a war for maximum territory, there must also be here a war [for the transfer 'principle']. ... We must insist on the principle that it must be a large agreed transfer. (Protocol of the Jewish Agency Executive meeting, 12 June 1938)[43]

In the early 1940s Katznelson found time to be engaged in polemics with the left-wing Hashomer Hatza'ir about the merits of transfer. He said to them: don't stigmatise the concept of transfer and rule it beforehand.

> Has [kibbutz] Merhaviya not been built on transfer? Were it not for many of these transfers neither Merhaviya or [kibbutz] Mishmar Ha'emek or other socialist Kibbutzim would have been set up. (Gorny 1987: 304; also Katznelson 1949: 241, 244; Shapira 1984: 335)

Supporters of 'voluntary' transfer included Arthur Ruppin, a co-founder of Brit Shalom, a movement advocating bi-nationalism and equal rights for Arabs and Jews; moderate leaders of Mapai such as Moshe Shertok and Eli'ezer Kaplan, Israel's first finance minister; and leaders of the Histadrut (Jewish Labour Federation) such as Golda Meyerson (later Meir) and David Remez (Masalha 1992).

Perhaps the most consistent, extreme and obsessive advocate of 'compulsory transfer' was Yosef Weitz, a Polish Jew who arrived in Palestine in 1908 and later became director of the settlement department of the Jewish National Fund (JNF) and head of the Israeli government's official Transfer Committee of 1948. Weitz was at the centre of Zionist land-purchasing activities for decades. His intimate knowledge of and involvement in land purchase made him sharply aware of its limitations. As late as 1947, after half a century of tireless efforts, the collective holdings of the JNF – which constituted about half of the Yishuv total – amounted to a mere 3.5 per cent of the land area of Palestine. A summary of Weitz's political beliefs is provided by his diary entry for 20 December 1940:

> Amongst ourselves it must be clear that there is no room for both peoples in this country. ... After the Arabs are transferred, the country will be wide open for us; with the Arabs staying the country will remain narrow and restricted. ... There is no room for compromise on this point ... land purchasing ... will not bring about the state. ... The only way is to transfer the Arabs from here to neighbouring countries, all of them, except perhaps Bethlehem, Nazareth, and Old Jerusalem. Not a single village or a single tribe must be left. And the transfer must be done through their absorption in Iraq and Syria and even in Transjordan. For that goal, money will be found – even a lot of money. And only then will the country be able to absorb millions of Jews ... there is no other solution. (Weitz 1940: 1090-91)

A countryside tour in the summer of 1941 took Weitz to a region in central Palestine. He recorded in his Diary seeing large [Arab] villages crowded in population and surrounded by cultivated land growing olives, grapes, figs, sesame, and maize fields. ... Would we be able to maintain scattered [Jewish] settlements among these existing [Arab] villages that will always be larger than ours? And is there any possibility of buying their [land]? ... and once again I hear that voice inside me called: *evacuate this country*. (Weitz 1941: 1204; emphasis in the original)

Earlier in March 1941 Weitz wrote in his Diary after touring Jewish settlements in the Esdraelon Valley (Marj Ibn 'Amer): 'The complete evacuation of the country from its [Arab] inhabitants and handing it to the Jewish people is the answer (Weitz 1941: 1127). In April 1948 Weitz recorded in his Diary:

I made a summary of a list of the Arab villages which in my opinion must be cleared out in order to complete Jewish regions. I also made a summary of the places that have land disputes and must be settled by military means. (Weitz 1948: 2358)

In 1930, against the background of the 1929 disturbances in Palestine, Weizmann, then president of both the World Zionist Organisation and the Jewish Agency Executive, actively began promoting ideas of Arab transfer in private discussions with British officials and ministers. He presented the colonial secretary, Lord Passfield, with an official, albeit secret, proposal for the transfer of Palestinian peasants to Transjordan, whereby a loan of 1 million Palestinian pounds would be raised from Jewish financial sources for the resettlement operation. Lord Passfield rejected the proposal. However, the justification Weizmann used in its defence formed the basis of subsequent Zionist transfer arguments. Weizmann asserted that there was nothing immoral about the concept of transfer; that the transfer of Greek and Turkish populations in the early 1920s provided a precedent for a similar measure regarding the Palestinians; and that the uprooting and transportation of Palestinians to Transjordan, Iraq, Syria or any other part of the vast Arab world would merely constitute a relocation from one Arab district to another. Above all, for Weizmann and other Jewish Agency leaders, transfer was a systematic procedure, requiring preparation, money and a great deal of organisation, which needed to be planned by strategic thinkers and technical experts.

'The Transfer Committees', 1937–48

While the desire among the Zionist leadership to be rid of the 'Arab demographic problem' remained constant until 1948, the extent of the preoccupation with, and the envisaged modalities of, transfer changed over the years according to circumstances. Thus, the wishful and rather naive belief in Zionism's early years that the Palestinians could be 'spirited across the border', in Herzl's words, or that they would simply 'fold their tents and slip away', to use Zangwill's formulation, soon gave way to more realistic assessments. Between 1937 and 1948 extensive secret discussions of transfer were held in the Zionist movement's highest bodies, including the Zionist Agency Executive, the Twentieth Zionist Congress, the World Convention of Ihud Po'alei Tzion (the top forum of the dominant Zionist world labour movement), and various official and semi-official transfer committees.

Many leading figures justified Arab removal politically and morally as the natural and logical continuation of Zionist colonisation in Palestine. There was a general endorsement of the ethical legitimacy of transfer; the differences centred on the question of compulsory transfer and whether such a course would be practicable (in the late 1930s/early 1940s) without the support of the colonial power, Britain.

From the mid-1930s onwards the transfer solution became central to the assessments of the Jewish Agency (then effectively the government of the Yishuv). The Jewish Agency produced a series of specific plans, generally involving Transjordan, Syria or Iraq. Some of these plans were drafted by three 'Transfer Committees'. The first two committees, set up by the Yishuv leadership, operated between 1937 and 1944; the third was officially appointed by the Israeli Cabinet in August 1948.

As of the late 1930s, some of these transfer plans included proposals for agrarian legislation, citizenship restriction and various taxes designed to encourage Palestinians to transfer 'voluntarily'. However, in the 1930s and early 1940s, Zionist transfer proposals and plans remained largely confined to private and secret talks with British (and occasionally American) senior officials. The Zionist leadership generally refrained from airing the highly sensitive proposals in public. (On one occasion, Weizmann, in a secret meeting with the Soviet ambassador to London, Ivan Meiski, in February

1941, proposed transferring a million Palestinians to Iraq in order to settle Polish Jews in their place.) More importantly, however, during the Mandate period, for reasons of political expediency, the Zionists calculated that such proposals could not be effected without Britain's active support and even actual British implementation. Moreover, the Zionist leadership was tireless in trying to shape the proposals of the Royal (Peel) Commission of 1937, which proposed a partition of Palestine between Jews and Arabs. It has generally escaped the attention of historians that the most significant transfer proposal submitted to the commission – the one destined to shape the outcome of its findings – was put forward by the Jewish Agency in a secret memorandum containing a specific paragraph on Arab transfer to Transjordan.

Jewish David against an Arab Goliath?
The Palestinian Nakba and Politicide

The 1948 Palestine war is known to Palestinians as the *Nakba*, the 'disaster' or 'catastrophe',[44] and to Israelis as the 'War of Independence' (*Melhemet Ha'atzmaut*) or 'War of Liberation' (*Melhemet Hashehrur*). In the middle of the war, in May, the Zionist leadership issued the 'Declaration of Independence', which stated:

> the Land of Israel was the birthplace of the Jewish people. Here their spiritual, religious and national identity was formed. Here they ... created a culture of national and universal significance. Here they wrote and gave the Bible to the world.

While the State of Israel itself, according to the Declaration, was declared on the basis of 'natural and historical rights' and on the basis of the November 1947 partition resolution of the UN, it was also supposed to be based 'on the precepts of liberty, justice and peace', as 'taught by the Hebrew prophets'. The Declaration added that the state 'will uphold the full social and political equality of all its citizens, without distinction of race, creed or sex' – but not nationality (Kimmerling 1999: 339-63).

The 'War of Liberation', which led to the creation of the State of Israel on 78 per cent of historic Palestine (and not the 55 per cent according to the UN partition resolution), resulted not in 'equality for all citizens' 'as taught by the Hebrew prophets' but in the destruction of much of Palestinian society, and much of the Arab landscape, in the name of the Bible, by the Zionist Yishuv, a predominantly European settler community that emigrated to Palestine in the period between 1882 and 1948. The 1948 War was presented by the Zionist leadership in messianic terms as a 'miraculous clearing of the land' and as another 'War of Liberation' modelled on the Book of Joshua. The question is: from whom was the land 'liberated'? From the British, whose colonial administration in Palestine after 1918 had alone made it possible for the growth of the European Jewish settlement against the will of the overwhelming majority of Palestinians? Or from its indigenous inhabitants, who had tilled the land and owned the soil for many centuries[45] and for whom the Bible had become an instrument mandating expulsion (Prior 2002: 44-5).

From the territory occupied by the Israelis in 1948, about 90 per cent of the Palestinians were driven out – many by psychological warfare and/or military pressure and a very large number at gunpoint. The war simply provided the opportunity and the necessary background for the creation of a Jewish state largely free of Arabs. It concentrated Jewish-Zionist minds, and provided the security, military and strategic explanations and justifications for purging the Jewish state and dispossessing the Palestinian people (Masalha 1992, 1997, 2003). Today some 70 per cent of the Palestinians are refugees; there are over 4 million Palestinian refugees in the Middle East and many more worldwide. In 1948 a minority of Palestinians – 160,000 – who remained behind, many of them internally displaced, became second-class citizens of the State of Israel, subject to a system of military administration by a government that confiscated the bulk of their lands.

The conquest narrative of the Old Testament contains the legend of the Israelites, under the leadership of Joshua, sacking the city of Jericho and killing its inhabitants, after the city walls came tumbling down 'miraculously'. Central to the conquest narrative of the Zionist leadership was the 'miraculous clearing of the land' in 1948. Following the 1948 conquest Ben-Gurion and other leaders invented several foundational myths, including the myth of 'no expulsions', the myth of 'self-defence' and the Haganah slogan/myth of 'purity of arms' (see below). The myth of 'no expulsion' was echoed by the first United States ambassador to

Israel, James McDonald, who told of a conversation he had with the president of Israel, Chaim Weizmann, during which Weizmann spoke in 'messianic' terms about the 1948 Palestinian exodus as a 'miraculous simplification of Israel's tasks'. McDonald said that not one of Israel's 'big three' – Weizmann, Prime Minister David Ben-Gurion and Foreign Minister Moshe Sharett – and no responsible Zionist leader had anticipated such a 'miraculous clearing of the land' (MacDonald 1951: 160-61). The available evidence (based on mountains of Israeli archival documents), however, shows that the big three had all enthusiastically endorsed the concept of 'transferring' the Palestinians in the 1937-48 period and had anticipated the mass flight of Palestinian refugees in 1948, referred to by Palestinians as the Nakba (catastrophe).

In the official Zionist rendition of the 1948 war the events are presented as a battle between a Jewish David and an Arab Goliath. Central to key narratives in Israeli culture is the myth which depicts the Israel-Palestine conflict as a 'war of the few against the many'. Since the early twentieth century Zionist historiography has based this narrative of the 'few against the many' on the biblical account of Joshua's conquest of ancient Palestine, while mainstream Israeli historians continue to portray the 1948 war as an unequal struggle between a Jewish David against an Arab Goliath, and as a desperate, heroic and ultimately successful Jewish struggle against overwhelming odds.[16] The European Zionist settlers brought with them to Palestine the 'few against the many' narrative – a widespread European cultural myth which has appeared in many variations, including the American western cowboy variation of the early twentieth century (Gertz 2000: 5). Turning the Jewish faith into secular ideology, Israeli historians and authors have adopted and reinterpreted biblical sources and myths and mobilised them in support of post-1948 Israeli objectives (Gertz 2000: 5). The few who overcame the many by virtue of their courage and absolute conviction were those European Zionist settlers who emulated the fighters of ancient Israel, while the many were those Palestinians and Arabs who were the embodiment of various ancient oppressors. The Zionist struggle against the indigenous Palestinians was thus portrayed as a modern re-enactment of ancient biblical battles and wars, including David's slaying of Goliath, the Hasmonean (Maccabean) uprising against ancient Greece, and the Jewish wars against the Romans, with the zealots' last stand at Massada in 73 AD and the Bar-Kohkva revolt sixty-seven years later (Gertz 2000: 5).

While the David and Goliath version of the Israel–Palestine conflict continues to gain hegemony in the Western media, since the late 1980s, however, many of the myths that have come to surround the birth of Israel have been challenged by revisionist Israeli historians, including Flapan (1987), Morris (1987), Pappé (1992), Shlaim (1996a, 2000; Rogan and Shlaim 2001). Furthermore, the new and recent historiography of Palestine-Israel has shown that the 1948 Palestinian catastrophe was the culmination of over half a century of often secret Zionist plans and, ultimately, brute force. The extensive evidence shows a strong correlation between transfer discussions, their practical application in 1948 and the Palestinian Nakba. The primary responsibility for the displacement and dispossession of three-quarters of a million Palestinian refugees in 1948 lies with the Zionist-Jewish leadership, not least David Ben-Gurion. The work of revisionist Israeli historians contributed to demolishing some of the long-held Israeli and Western misconceptions surrounding Israel's birth. Containing remarkable revelations based on Hebrew archival material, their studies throw new light on the conduct of the Labour Zionist founding fathers of the Israeli state.

The new historiography of Israel-Palestine shows that in reality throughout the 1948 war, the Israeli army outnumbered all the Arab forces, regular and irregular, operating in the Palestine theatre. Estimates vary, but the best estimates suggest that on 15 May 1948 Israel fielded 35,000 troops whereas the Arabs fielded 20-25,000.[47] Moreover, during the war imported arms from the Eastern bloc – artillery, tanks, aircraft – decisively tipped the military balance in favour of Israel. During the second half of 1948 the Israelis not only outnumbered but also outgunned their opponents. While 'the Arab coalition facing Israel in 1948 was one of the most deeply divided, disorganised and ramshackle coalitions in the history of warfare, the final outcome of the war was not a miracle but a reflection of the underlying Arab-Israeli military balance'.[48] Furthermore, since 1948 the Arab-Israeli military imbalance has been illustrated by the fact that Israel (with US backing) has developed the fourth most powerful army in the world and has become the only nuclear power in the region.

Ben-Gurion's 1948 war against the Palestinians was a form of politi-cide.[49] Ben-Gurion entered the 1948 war with a mindset and premeditation to expel Palestinians. On 19 December 1947, he advised that the Haganah, the Jewish pre-state army, 'adopt the method of aggressive defence; with every [Arab] attack we must be prepared to respond with a decisive blow: the destruction of the [Arab] place or the expulsion of the residents along with the seizure of the place' (Ben-Gurion 1982: 58). There is also plenty of evidence to suggest that as early as the beginning of 1948 his advisers counselled him to wage a total war against the Palestinians, and that he entered the 1948 war with the intention of expelling Palestinians.

Plan Dalet, a straightforward document, this Haganah plan of early March 1948 was in many ways a blueprint for the expulsion of as many Palestinians as possible. It constituted an ideological-strategic anchor and basis for the destruction of Arab localities and expulsion of their inhabitants by Jewish commanders. In conformity with Plan Dalet, the Haganah cleared various areas completely of Arab villages.

The general endorsement of transfer schemes and the attempt to pro-mote them secretly by mainstream Labour leaders, some of whom played a decisive role in the 1948 war, highlight the ideological intent that made the 1948 refugee exodus possible. Ben-Gurion in particular emerges as both an obsessive advocate of compulsory transfer in the late 1930s and the great expeller of the Palestinians in 1948 (Masalha 1992; Morris 1987; Flapan 1987; Segev 1986; Pappé 1992; Shlaim 1996a; Rogan and Shlaim 2001). In 1948 there was no need for any Cabinet decision to drive the Palestinians out. Ben-Gurion and senior Zionist military commanders, such as Yigal Allon, Moshe Carmel, Yigael Yadin, Moshe Dayan, Moshe Kalman and Yitzhak Rabin, played a key role in the expulsions. Everyone, at every level of military and political decision-making, understood that the objective was a Jewish state without a large Arab minority.

There is plenty of evidence to suggest that a policy of mass expulsion was adopted and carried out in 1948. Aharon Cohen, who in 1948 was the director of the Arab Department of Mapam, wrote a memorandum dated 10 May 1948:

> There is reason to believe that what is being done ... is being done out of
> certain political objectives and not only out of military necessities, as they
> [Jewish leaders] claim sometimes. In fact, the 'transfer' of the Arabs from

the boundaries of the Jewish state is being implemented ... the evacuation/ clearing out of Arab villages is not always done out of military necessity. The complete destruction of villages is not always done because there are 'no sufficient forces to maintain garrison'. (Cohen 1948)

Yosef Sprintzak, who in 1948 was secretary general of the Histadrut, stated at a debate at the Mapai Centre on 24 July 1948, which was held against the background of the Ramle-Lydda expulsions of 12–13 July (see below):

There is a feeling that faits accomplis are being created. ... The question is not whether the Arabs will return or not return. The question is whether the Arabs are [being or have been] expelled or not. ... I want to know, who is creating the facts [of expulsion]? And the facts are being created on orders. (Morris 1990: 42–3)

Sprintzak added that 'a line of action [has been adopted] of expropriating and of emptying the land of Arabs by force' (Morris 1990: 42–3).

With the 1948 war, Prime Minister Ben-Gurion and the Zionist leadership succeeded in many of their objectives. Above all, they created a vastly enlarged Jewish state (on 77 per cent of historic Palestine) in which the Palestinians were forcibly reduced to a small minority. The available evidence shows that the evacuation of some three-quarters of a million Palestinians in 1948 can only be ascribed to the culmination of Zionist expulsion policies and not to mythical orders issued by the Arab armies. Israeli historian Benny Morris's *The Birth of the Palestinian Refugee Problem* (1987) explodes many Israeli myths surrounding the 1948 exodus. Morris assesses that of 330 villages whose experience he studied, a total of 282 (85 per cent) were depopulated as a result of direct Jewish attack.

Ben-Gurion, who was personally responsible for many of the myths surrounding 1948, had this to say in the Israeli Knesset debate of 11 October 1961:

The Arabs' exit from Palestine ... began immediately after the UN resolution, from the areas earmarked for the Jewish state. And we have explicit documents testifying that they left Palestine following instructions by the Arab leaders, with the *Mufti* at their head, under the assumption that the invasion of the Arab armies at the expiration of the Mandate will destroy the Jewish state and push all the Jews into the sea, dead or alive.[50]

Ben-Gurion was propagating two myths: (a) there were orders from the neighbouring Arab states and the Hajj Amin Al-Husseini, the *Mufti* of Jerusalem, for the Palestinians to evacuate their homes and lands on the promise that the Arab armies would destroy the nascent Jewish state; (b) that those armies intended to 'push all the Jews into the sea, dead or alive'. Ben-Gurion gave no attribution for this phrase, nor did he claim that it was a quotation from an Arab source. Since the Second World War the Shoah had been used as a legitimiser of Zionism. However, the phrase 'push all the Jews into the sea' – a highly emotive phrase invoking images of the Holocaust, though adapted to a Mediterranean setting – has since acquired extraordinary mythical dimensions as it is constantly invoked by Israelis and Zionists in order to justify the policies of Israel towards the Palestinians as well as the continuing occupation of the West Bank, Gaza and East Jerusalem.[51]

Although Ben-Gurion and his commanders did not drive the Palestinians into the sea, they did drive them from their homes and villages and ancestral lands and from Palestine into squalid refugee camps. The irony of Ben-Gurion's 'chilling phrase' should not escape us. He demanded deference for a fictitious intention on the part of the Palestinians and Arabs[52] while denying his own direct and personal involvement in the very real expulsion of the Palestinians.

Lydda and Ramle

From the territory occupied by the Israelis in 1948-49 about 90 per cent of the Palestinians were driven out, many by psychological warfare and/or military pressure. A very large number of Palestinians were expelled at gunpoint. A major instance of 'outright expulsion' is the widely documented case of the twin towns of Lydda and Ramle in July 1948. More than 60,000 Palestinians were expelled, accounting for nearly 10 per cent of the total exodus. Ben-Gurion and three senior army officers were directly involved: Yigal Allon, Yitzhak Rabin and Moshe Dayan. Shortly before the capture of the towns, Ben-Gurion met with his army chiefs. Allon, commander of the Palmah, the Haganah's elite military force, asked Ben-Gurion, 'What shall we do with the Arabs?' Ben-Gurion answered (or, according to one version, gestured with his hand), 'Expel them.' This was immediately communicated to the army headquarters and the expulsion implemented (Morris 1986b: 91).

Morris writes:

> At 13.30 hours on 12 July ... Lieutenant-Colonel Yitzhak Rabin ... issued the following order: '1. The inhabitants of Lydda must be expelled quickly without attention to age. They should be directed to Beit Nabala ... Implement immediately.' A similar order was issued at the same time to the Kiryati Brigade concerning the inhabitants of the neighbouring town of Ramle, occupied by Kiryati troops that morning. ... On 12 and 13 July, Yiftah and Kiryati brigades carried out their orders, expelling the 50–60,000 remaining inhabitants of and refugees camped in and around the two towns. (Morris 1990: 2)

In the case of Nazareth, Ben-Gurion arrived only after its capture. On seeing so many Palestinians remaining *in situ*, he angrily asked the local commander, 'Why are there so many Arabs? Why didn't you expel them?' (Bar-Zohar 1977: 776).

The Haganah and the Myth of 'Purity of Arms'

The view that the Bible provides Jews with a title deed to the 'Land of Israel' combined with European Zionism's self-perception as morally superior to the indigenous inhabitants of Palestine, was echoed in the myth of 'purity of arms' – a slogan initially coined by the Haganah/Palmah in early 1948. In the period between the mid-1930s and 1948, the Yishuv Labour leadership had embraced the concept of 'transfer' while quietly pondering the question of whether there was a 'more humane way' of expelling the indigenous Palestinians. In *Land and Power: The Zionist Resort to Power* (1992), Anita Shapira shows that already during the Great Palestinian Rebellion of 1936–39 the Zionist leadership abandoned the slogan of *havlaga* – a restrained and proportionate response – and legitimised the use of terror against Palestinian civilians; the Zionist nationalist end justified the means (Shapira 1992: 247–9, 350).

More crucially, however, the 'War of Independence' proved that engineering mass evacuation was not possible without perpetrating a large number of atrocities. According to Israeli military historian Arieh Yitzhaki, about ten major massacres (of more than fifty victims each) and about one hundred smaller massacres were committed by Jewish forces in 1948-49. Yitzhaki argues that these massacres, large and small, had a devastating impact on the Palestinian population by inducing and precipitating the Palestinian exodus. Yitzhaki suggests that in almost every village there were murders. Another Israeli historian, Uri Milstein, corroborates Yitzhaki's assessment and goes even further to suggest that each battle in 1948 ended with a massacre: 'In all Israel's wars, massacres were committed but I have no doubt that the War of Independence was the dirtiest of them all.'[53] Both Israeli 'new historiography' and Palestinian oral history confirm that in almost every Palestinian village occupied by the Haganah and other Jewish militias during the 1948-49 war atrocities – such as murders, execution of prisoners and rape – were committed (Finkelstein 1995: 110-12; Prior 1999c: 208-9).

Moreover, the most striking result of the new historiography of Israel-Palestine is that the discourse has shifted away from the orthodox Zionist interpretation of the Deir Yasin massacre as 'exceptional'. The focus of study is no longer so much on the terrorism carried out by the Irgun Tzvai Leumi (National Military Organisation), the military arm of Betar Zionism, and Lehi irregular forces before and during the 1948 war, but on the conduct of the mainstream Haganah/Palmah and Israeli Defence Force (IDF). At issue are the roles and involvement of the Haganah and the Israeli army in the numerous atrocities carried out in 1948. Sharif Kanaana of Birzeit University places the massacre of Deir Yasin and the evacuation of Arab West Jerusalem in 1948 within the framework of what he terms the Zionists' 'maxi-massacre pattern' in their conquest of large Palestinian cities: Jewish attacks produced demoralisation and exodus; a nearby massacre would result in panic and further flight, greatly facilitating the occupation of the Arab city and its surrounding towns and villages (Kanaana 1992: 108).

Deir Yasin was the site of the most notorious massacre of Palestinian civilians in 1948, a massacre which became the single most important contributory factor to the 1948 exodus, a powerful marker of the violence at the foundation of the State of Israel. On 9 April, between 120 and 254 unarmed villagers were murdered, including women, the elderly and children. (The number of those massacred at Deir Yasin is subject to dispute. The widely accepted death toll has been that reported in the *New York Times* of 13 April 1948: 254 persons.) There were also cases of rape and mutilation. Most Israeli writers today have no difficulty in acknowledging the occurrence of the Deir Yasin massacre and its effect, if not its intention, of precipitating the exodus. However, most of these writers take refuge in the fact that the massacre was committed by 'dissidents' of the Irgun, then commanded by Menahem Begin[54] (who would later become prime minister of Israel), and Lehi, then co-commanded by Yitzhak Shamir (who also would later become prime minister of Israel), thus exonerating Ben-Gurion's Haganah, the mainstream Zionist military force. Recently published Hebrew material, however, shows that: (a) in January 1948, the *mukhtar* (head man) of Deir Yasin and other village notables had reached a non-aggression agreement with the Haganah and the neighbouring Jewish settlements of Giva't Shaul and Montefiori; (b) the Irgun's assault on the village on 9 April had the full backing of the Haganah commander of Jerusalem, David Shaltiel, who not only chose to break his agreement with the villagers but also provided rifles and ammunition for the Irgunists; (c) the Haganah contributed to the assault on the village by providing artillery cover; (d) a Haganah intelligence officer in Jerusalem, Meir Pa'il, was dispatched to Deir Yasin to assess the effectiveness and performance of the Irgun forces (Masalha 1988: 122-3).

Although the actual murders of the non-combatant villagers were carried out by Lehi and the Irgun, the Haganah must share responsibility for the slaughter. The atrocity was fiercely condemned by liberal Jewish intellectuals, most prominent of whom was Martin Buber, who wrote repeatedly to Prime Minister David Ben-Gurion about the massacre. But apparently Ben-Gurion did not reply. According to Israeli historian Benny Morris, Ben-Gurion was at that very time explicitly sanctioning the expulsions of the Palestinians (Morris 1987: 113-15). More significantly, the recently published Israeli material shows that Deir Yasin was only one of many massacres carried out by Jewish forces (mainly the Haganah and the IDF) in 1948. Recent research shows that the Palestinians were less prone to evacuate their towns and villages in the second half of the war. Hence the numerous massacres committed from June 1948 onwards, all of which were geared at forcing mass evacuation.

In 1948, al-Dawayma, situated in the western Hebron hills, was a very large village, with a population of some 3,500 people. Like Deir Yasin, al-Dawayma was unarmed. It was captured on 29 October 1948 without a fight. The massacre of between eighty and a hundred villagers was carried out at the end of October 1948, not in the heat of the battle but after the Israeli army had clearly emerged victorious in the war. The testimony of Israeli soldiers present during the atrocities establishes that IDF troops under Moshe Dayan entered the village and liquidated civilians, throwing their victims into pits. 'The children they killed by breaking their heads with sticks. There was not a house without dead.' The remaining Arabs were then shut up in houses 'without food and water' as the village was systematically razed:

> One commander ordered a sapper to put two old women in a certain house ... and blow up the house. ... One soldier boasted that he had raped a woman and then shot her. One woman, with a newborn baby in her arms, was employed to clear the courtyard where the soldiers ate. She worked a day or two. In the end they shot her and her baby.

A variety of evidence indicates that the atrocities were committed in and around the village, including at the mosque and in a nearby cave, that houses with old people locked inside were blown up, and that there were several cases of the rape and shooting of women (Masalha 1988: 127-30; Morris 1987: 222-3; Khalidi 1999).

Clearing the Galilee

The evidence surrounding the Galilee expulsions shows clearly the existence of a pattern of actions characterised by a series of massacres designed to intimidate the population into flight. On 29-31 October 1948, the Israeli army, in a large military campaign named Operation Hiram, conquered the last significant Arab-held pocket of the Galilee. According to new Israeli archival material uncovered by Benny Morris, commanding officers issued expulsion directives: 'There was a central directive by Northern Command to clear the conquered pocket of its Arab inhabitants' (Morris 1999: 70). Moreover, the operation was 'characterised by a series of atrocities against the Arab civilian population' (Morris 1995: 55).

On 6 November 1948, Yosef Nahmani, director of the Jewish National Fund office in the eastern Galilee between 1935 and 1965, toured the newly conquered areas. He was accompanied by Immanuel Fried of Israel's

minority affairs ministry, who briefed him on 'the cruel acts of our soldiers', which Nahmani recorded in his diary:

> In Safsaf, after ... the inhabitants had raised a white flag, the [soldiers] col-
> lected and separated the men and women, tied the hands of fifty-sixty *fellahin*
> [peasants] and shot and killed them and buried them in a pit. Also, they raped
> several women. ... At Eilabun and Farradiya the soldiers had been greeted with
> white flags and rich food, and afterwards had ordered the villagers to leave,
> with their women and children. When the [villagers] had begun to argue ...
> [the soldiers] had opened fire and after some thirty people were killed, had
> begun to lead the rest [towards Lebanon]. Where did they come by such a
> measure of cruelty, like Nazis? ... Is there no more humane way of expelling
> the inhabitants than such methods? (Morris 1999: 73)

The following is only a partial inventory of other IDF massacres committed in the Galilee in 1948: Safsaf, Jish, Sa'sa', Saliha, 'Eilabun, Majd
al-Kurum, Deir al-Asad, al-Bi'ene, Nasr al-Din, 'Ayn Zaytun, al-Tantura,
Lydda, Tel Gezer, Khisas, Qisarya, Kabri and Abu Shusha.

Erasing Villages and Deleting Historic Palestine: Biblical Naming and the Hebraicisation of Palestinian Geography

In 1948 more than half of the Palestinians were driven from their towns
and villages, mainly by a deliberate Israeli policy of 'transfer' and ethnic
cleaning. The name of Palestine disappeared from the map. To complete
this transformation of the country, in August 1948, a de facto 'Transfer
Committee' was officially (though secretly) appointed by the Israeli Cabinet to plan the Palestinian refugees' organised resettlement in the Arab
states. The three-member committee was composed of 'Ezra Danin, a
former senior Haganah intelligence officer and a senior foreign ministry
adviser on Arab affairs since July 1948; Zalman Lifschitz, the prime
minister's adviser on land matters; and Yosef Weitz, head of the Jewish
National Fund's land settlement department, as head of the committee.
The main Israeli propaganda lines regarding the Palestinian refugees
and some of the myths of 1948 were cooked up by members of this official Transfer Committee. Besides doing everything possible to reduce
the Palestinian population in Israel, Weitz and his colleagues sought in
October 1948 to amplify and consolidate the demographic transformation
of Palestine by:

- preventing Palestinian refugees from returning to their homes and villages;
- destroying Arab villages;
- settling Jews in Arab villages and towns and distributing Arab lands among Jewish settlements;
- extricating Jews from Iraq and Syria;
- seeking ways to ensure the absorption of Palestinian refugees in Arab countries and launching a propaganda campaign to discourage Arab return.

Apparently, Prime Minister Ben-Gurion approved of these proposals, although he recommended that all the Palestinian refugees be resettled in one Arab country, preferably Iraq, rather than be dispersed among the neighbouring states. Ben-Gurion was also set against refugee resettlement in neighbouring Transjordan (Morris 1986a: 522-61).

An abundance of archival documentation shows a strong correlation between the Zionist transfer solution and the 1948 Palestinian Nakba. By the end of the 1948 war, hundreds of villages had been completely depopulated and their houses blown up or bulldozed. The main objective was to prevent the return of refugees to their homes, but the destruction also helped to perpetuate the Zionist myth that Palestine was virtually empty territory before the Jews entered. An exhaustive study by a team of Palestinian field researchers and academics under the direction of Walid Khalidi details the destruction of 418 villages falling inside the 1949 armistice lines. The study gives the circumstances of each village's occupation and depopulation, and a description of what remains. Khalidi's team visited all except fourteen sites, made comprehensive reports and took photographs. The result is both a monumental study and a kind of memorial. It is an acknowledgement of the enormous suffering of hundreds of thousands of Palestinian refugees (W. Khalidi 1992).

Of the 418 depopulated villages, 293 (70 per cent) were totally destroyed, and 90 (22 per cent) were largely destroyed; 7 survived, including 'Ayn Karim (west of Jerusalem), but were taken over by Israeli settlers. A few of the quaint Arab villages and neighbourhoods have actually been meticulously preserved. But they are empty of Palestinians (some of the former residents are internal refugees in Israel) and are designated as Jewish 'artistic colonies' (Benvenisti 1986: 25; Masalha 2005). While an observant traveller can still see some evidence of the destroyed Palestinian villages, in the main all that is left is a scattering of stones and rubble.

The names of Palestinian villages were deleted from the map and the Arabic names of geographical sites were replaced by newly coined Hebrew names, some of which resembled biblical names. In his recent book, *A History of Modern Palestine*, Israeli historian Ilan Pappé remarks:

> [W]hen winter was over and the spring of 1949 warmed a particularly frozen Palestine, the land as we have described ... – reconstructing a period stretching over 250 years – had changed beyond recognition. The countryside, the rural heart of Palestine, with its colourful and picturesque villages, was ruined. Half the villages had been destroyed, flattened by Israeli bulldozers which had been at work since August 1948 when the government had decided to either turn them into cultivated land or to build new Jewish settlements on their remains. A naming committee granted the new settlements Hebraized [*sic*] versions of the original Arab names: Lubya became Lavi, and Safuria Zipori ... David Ben-Gurion explained that this was done as part of an attempt to prevent future claim to the villages. It was also supported by the Israeli archaeologists, who had authorized the names as returning the map to something resembling 'ancient Israel'. (Pappé 2004a: 138-9)

The destruction of Palestinian villages and the deletion of the demographic and political realities of historic Palestine and the erasure of Palestinians from history centred on key issues, the most important of which is the contest between a 'denial' and an 'affirmation' (Said 1980). The deletion of historic Palestine was designed not only to strengthen the newly created state but also to consolidate the myth of the 'unbroken link' between the days of Joshua and the Israel state.

In the post-1948 period several Israeli leaders adopted Hebrew names. for instance, Moshe Shertok (born in Russia in 1894), who became foreign minister in 1948, chose to Hebraicise his last name to Sharett in 1949; Golda Meyerson (born Golda Mabovitch in Kiev in 1898) Hebraicised her last name to Meir, only after she became foreign minister in 1956; two Israeli prime ministers, Yitzhak Yezernitsky (born in eastern Poland in 1915) became Yitzhak Shamir, and Ariel Sharon was born (in Palestine in 1928) Ariel Scheinermann to Shmuel and Vera (later Hebraicised to Dvora), immigrants from Russia. Earlier during the Mandatory period, David Green became David Ben-Gurion and Yitzhak Shimshelevitz (born in the Ukraine in 1884) became Yitzhak Ben-Tzvi. But the post-1948 project concentrated mainly on the Hebraicisation of Palestinian geography and the practice of naming events, actions, places in line with biblical terminology. The Hebraicisation project deployed renaming to construct new places and new geographical identities related to supposed biblical places. The new Hebrew names embodied an ideological drive and political attributes that could be consciously mobilised by the Zionist hegemonic project (Peteet 2005: 153–72).

The official project began with the appointment of the Governmental Names Committee (Va'adat Hashemot Hamimshalteet) by Prime Minister Ben-Gurion in July 1949. Ben-Gurion had visited the Negev in June and been struck by the fact that no Hebrew names existed for geographical sites in the region. The 11 June 1949 entry for his War Diary reads: 'Eilat ... we drove through the open spaces of the Arava ... from 'Ein Husb ... to 'Ein Wahba ... We must give Hebrew names to these places – ancient names, if there are any, and if not, new ones!' (Ben-Gurion 1982, vol. 3: 989). The Committee, which included members of the Israeli Exploration Society and some leading Israeli biblical archaeologists, concentrated in its initial efforts on the creation of a new map for the Negev (Abu El-Haj 2001: 91–4). Throughout the documents produced by the Committee, there were reported references to 'foreign names'. The Israeli public is called upon 'to uproot the foreign and existing names' and in their place 'to master' the new Hebrew names. Most existing names were Arabic names. The committee for assigning Hebrew names in the Negev held its first meeting on 18 July and subsequently met three times a month for a ten-month period, and assigned Hebrew names to 561 different geographical features in the Negev – mountains, valleys, springs and waterholes – using the Bible as a resource. Despite the obliteration of many ancient Arabic names from the Negev landscape, some Arabic names, such as Seil 'Imran, became the similar-sounding Nahal 'Amram, apparently named after the father of Moses and Aaron; the Arabic Jabal Haruf ('Mount Haruf') became Har Harif ('Sharp Mountain'), Jabal Dibba ('Hump Hill') became Har Dla'at ('Mount Pumpkin'). After rejecting the name Har Geshur for the people to which David's third wife belonged, as a Hebrew appellation for the Arabic Jabal Ideid ('Sprawling Mountain'), the committee decided to call it Har Karkom ('Mount Crocus'), because crocuses grow in the Negev.[55] However, the sound of the Arabic name Ideid was retained in the nearby springs, which are now called 'Beerot Oded' ('the Wells of Oded'), possibly after the biblical prophet of the same name.[56] The committee report of March 1956 stated:

> In the summarized period 145 names were adopted for antiquities sites, ruins and tells: eight names were determined on the basis of historical identification, 16 according to geographical names in the area, eight according to the meaning of the Arabic words, and the decisive majority of the names (113) were determined by mimicking the sounds of the Arabic words, a partial or complete mimicking, in order to give the new name a Hebrew character, following the [accepted] grammatical and voweling rules. (quoted in Abu El-Haj 2001: 95)[57]

Throughout the country the Hebraicisation project included renaming Muslim holy men's graves and holy sites as Jewish and biblically sounding ones. 'In the fifties and sixties', Meron Benvenisti writes,

> the location and 'redemption' of holy men's graves was in the hands of the religious establishment – especially the Ministry of Religions – and of Ashkenazi Haredi groups. ... According to an official list, issued by a group known as the Foundation of the World and appended to a book [entitled *Jewish Holy Places in the Land of Israel*[58]] published by the Ministry of Defence, there are more than 500 Jewish holy places and sacred graves in Palestine (including the Occupied Territories). Many of these, albeit not the majority, are former Muslim sites. (2002: 282)

Among the many Judaised Muslim holy places were two sites, Nabi Yamin and Nabi Sama'an, located in the centre of the country, one kilometre east of the Jewish town of Kfar Saba – itself named after a Palestinian village destroyed in 1948. Until 1948, Benvensiti writes, these two sites were

> sacred to Muslims alone, and the Jews ascribed no holiness to them. Today they are operated by ultraorthodox Jewish bodies, and members of the religion from which they were taken do not set foot there, despite the fact there is a large Muslim population in the area. (Benvenisti 2002: 276-7)

The tomb of Nabi Yamin was renamed the grave of Benjamin, representing Jacob's youngest son, and Nabi Sama'an became the grave of Simeon. Jewish women seeking to bear offspring pray at the grave of Benjamin:

> The dedication inscriptions from the Mamluk period remain engraved on the stone walls of the tomb, and beside them hang tin signs placed there by the National Center for the Development of the Holy Places. The clothes

embroidered with verses from the Qur'an, with which the gravestones were draped, have been replaced by draperies bearing verses from the Hebrew Bible. (Benvenisti 2002: 277)

Digging up the Bible: Biblical Archaeology, Settler Colonialism and Military Conquest

The role of colonial archaeology in justifying South African apartheid has been described elsewhere (Hall 1984: 455–67). In contrast, however, although a great deal has been written about the role of Israeli ethno-centric biblical archaeology in confirming the legitimacy of the Zionist claim, little attention has been paid to the role of the biblical paradigm of 'promised land–chosen people' and biblical archaeology in providing the ideological justification for the expulsion and dispossession of the Palestinians. However, while the colonial attitudes of European and North American academics and archaeologists towards former colonies of the West began to be re-evaluated in the post-colonial period, the 'Israelis, by contrast, chose to maintain the colonial tradition with only minor changes' (Benvenisti 2002: 304). Biblical archaeology in Israel has always been an obsession and the convergence between biblical archaeology and Zionist settler colonialism has always loomed large, but became most pronounced after the post-1967 conquests. Paradoxically, however, while Israeli biblical archaeology has remained central to secular Zionism, most orthodox Jews in Israel were and still are indifferent to its findings (Elon 1997b: 38).

In Israel the ancient history and archaeology of Palestine are arranged 'to emphasize the Jewish connection to the land, adding designations such as the biblical, Hasmonean, Mishnaic, and Talmudic periods' (Benvenisti 2002: 300). The country's archaeological chronology is generally arranged in periods named after its 'foreign conquerors': Roman, Byzantine, early Arab, Crusader, Mamluk, Ottoman and British. These designations and the division of the Arab-Muslim rule of 1,400 years into periods, in order to make it look 'shorter' than the ancient 'Jewish rule over the Land of Israel', is designed

> to portray the history of the country as a long period of rule by a series of foreign powers who had robbed it from the Jews – a period that ended in 1948 with the reestablishment of Jewish sovereignty in Palestine. It was thus possible to obscure the fact that the indigenous Muslim Arab population

was part and parcel of the ruling Muslim peoples and instead to depict the history of the local population – its internal wars, its provincial rulers, its contribution to the landscape – as matters lacking in importance, events associated with one or another dynasty of 'foreign occupiers'. (Benvenisti 2002: 300)

Thus wars of conquest were central to Israeli archaeology. Moreover, secular Israeli politicians have tended to use the Bible during and after wars of conquest. In November 1956 when the Sinai peninsula was conquered during the Anglo-French-Israeli collusion and initiation of the Suez war, the Israeli attack on the Egyptian army was described by Ben-Gurion as a return to roots (Sternhell 1998: 336). Ben-Gurion's views of the biblical borders are found in his 1972 book *Ben-Gurion Looks at the Bible*: 'In days of old our neighbors were Egypt and Babylon' (Ben-Gurion 1972: 4). In 1956 Ben-Gurion explained to the Israeli parliament the political and military reasons for Israel invading Sinai. In spite of being an atheist, proud of his complete disregard for the commandments of the Jewish religion, he pronounced in the Knesset on the third day of that war that the real reason for it was 'the restoration of the kingdom of David and Solomon' to its biblical borders; at this point in his speech most Knesset members rose spontaneously and sang the Israeli national anthem (Shahak 1994: 8–9). The Gulf of Sharm al-Shaykh was now called Mifratz Shlomo (Gulf of Solomon) and Ben-Gurion declared the whole war to be a 'new Sinai revelation' – a historical repetition of the (mythical) national birth at Mount Sinai (Sternhell: 1998: 336–7). However, as a realist and pragmatic Labour expansionist, Ben-Gurion argued, in his public debates with maximalist Zionists who sought a Jewish state from the Nile to the Euphrates, for the need to distinguish between 'biblical and historical rights' and the necessity of achieving internationally recognisable borders (recognised by the Western powers) for the State of Israel.[59]

Ben-Gurion was credited with many Zionist projects. Among these are: making the Book of Joshua central to Zionist politics and Israeli political culture, and deploying the biblical narrative and biblical archaeology in the service of Israeli state policies. Ben-Gurion was instrumental in making the study of the Book of Joshua a major component of the school curriculum in Israel; he initiated the conducting of Bible quizzes in 'Israel and the Jewish Diaspora'; he participated in conferences on rather uncritical biblical archaeology and initiated a regular nationalist Bible study circle in his official residence.[60] The ideological and political overtones of Israeli court archaeology have long been recognised (Elon 1997b; Abu El-Haj 2001; Zerubavel 1995; Silberman 1982, 1989, 1997; Meskell 1998; Kapitan 1999). Although archaeology and antiquities have been used in other countries to weld the social bonds and nationalist consciousness essential to building modern nations (Smith 1991; Anderson 1991; Shanks 1992), archaeology in Israel has always been a political and academic obsession, driven partly by the Ben-Gurion axiom 'the Bible is our Mandate'. Its 'finds' have been used in virtually all Israeli national symbols, from the State Seal to medals and postage stamps (Elon 1997b: 37). Inevitably its sites and 'finds' were bound to be used by Ben-Gurion and others to prove Jewish historical roots and common descent, rights to Palestinian territories, and overall the superiority of Zionist claims (Abu El-Haj 2001: 166-7, 180). In her 1995 book *Recovered Roots: Collective Memory and the Making of Israeli National Tradition*, the Israeli-American historian Yael Zerubavel highlights the role that biblical archaeology played in shoring up the fiction of modern Israeli identity and reinforcing Zionist claims to the land of Palestine by creating a (mythical) continuity between the modern State of Israel and 'biblical Israel' through large, government-funded excavation projects:

> Archaeology thus becomes a national tool through which Israelis can recover their roots in the ancient past and the ancient homeland. To participate in the archaeological excavation ... is to perform a patriotic act of bridging Exile to reestablish the connection with the national past and authenticate national memory. (Zerubavel 1995: 59)

In the post-1948 period heavily politicised, massive Israeli government-sponsored excavation projects were carried out by leading members of the first generation of Israeli archaeologists, the most important of whom were professors Benjamin Mazar (1906–1995) and Yigael Yadin (1917–1984), the latter an army general who carried out large excavations at Massada, Hazor and Meggido from the 1950s to the 1970s. Both archaeologists chose to Hebraicise their last name. Benjamin Mazar was born Benjamin Maisler in Poland and was educated in Germany; after he emigrated to Palestine in 1929 he Hebraicised his name to Mazar. Yigael Yadin was born Yigael

Sukenik in 1917 to archaeologist Eleazar Lipa Sukenik, who emigrated from Russia to Palestine in 1911.

In the post-1967 period Israeli claims of exclusive control over Jerusalem benefited greatly from the 'discoveries' of Mazar and other court archaeologists (see also Talhami 2000: 113–29). Mazar, the father of the Israeli branch of biblical archaeology, was president of the Hebrew University, and Yadin was the head of the Institute of Archaeology of the Hebrew University, the oldest university department of archaeology in Israel, established by the Yishuv in 1926. After 1948 Mazar continued the nationalist project of digging up the Bible – a project started by American archaeologist William Foxwell Albright (1891–1971) during the Mandatory period.[61] In 1943 he joined the faculty of the Hebrew University of Jerusalem, where he served as Professor of Biblical History and Archaeology of Palestine from 1951 to 1977. During the Mandatory period he served as secretary of the Jewish Palestine Exploration Society, renamed after 1948 the 'Israel Exploration Society'. Mazar earned a formidable academic reputation through leadership of the Israeli branch of biblical archaeology, combining a traditional Zionist account of biblical history with archaeological evidence. Extensive excavations under the direction of Mazar were undertaken in the southwestern corner of the Muslim al-Haram al-Sharif (Temple Mount) in 1968–78. The site became accessible to Israeli archaeologists after the occupation of the Old City in 1967 and the excavations were undertaken by the Hebrew University of Jerusalem and the semi-official Israel Exploration Society. As we shall in Chapter 7, much of the work undertaken by Mazar has been discarded by a growing number of academics and new archaeologists, who view the 'united kingdom' of Judah and Israel as a piece of fiction.

In Israeli popular imagination, the hero of the 'Six Day War' was Ben-Gurion's protégé, the charismatic Defence Minister Moshe Dayan, who, perhaps more than any other Israeli official, typified Labour territorial expansionism in the post-1967 era. He was a renowned military leader and politician, whose influence over Israel was considerable (Slater 1991: vii–viii, 208, 279; Golani 1998: 5, 195, 199). In 1956 Dayan was chief of staff, leading the Israeli army to, and in, the 1956 Suez war. General Dayan, who was an 'amateur archaeologist' and wrote a book entitled *Living with the Bible* (*Lehyot 'Im Hatanch*, 1978), and did more than any other Labour establishment figure to popularise the concept of Greater Israel and to begin the actual integration of the newly occupied West Bank and Gaza into Israel proper. It was also Dayan who, upon arriving at the Wailing Wall (*Hait al-Mabka* in Arabic, or the 'Western Wall' of the temple according the Jewish tradition), in the Old City of Jerusalem, on the war's fourth day, uttered the widely publicised words: 'We have returned to all that is holy in our land. We have returned never to be parted again' (in Sachar 1976: 673; also Sprinzak 1991: 40). On another occasion that followed the 1967 war, during an emotional ceremony for the burial of Jewish casualties of 1948 on East Jerusalem's Mount of Olives, Dayan repeated the same vision of Greater Israel, a revived vision which was also symbolically illustrated by the title of his 1969 book, *A New Map, Other Relationships*:

> Our Brothers who fell in the War of Independence – we have not abandoned your dream and we have not forgotten your lesson. We have returned to the Temple Mount, to the cradle of our people's history, to the inheritance of the Patriarchs, the land of the Judges and the fortress of the Kingdom of the House of David. We have returned to Hebron and Shechem [Nablus], to Bethlehem and Anatot, to Jericho and the crossings of the Jordan at Adam Ha'ir. (Dayan 1969: 173)

Zionism's ongoing demographic battle with the indigenous Palestinians has always been a battle for more land and less people, or (as some Labour Zionist leaders put it in the post-1967 period) a battle for 'maximum land and minimum Arabs' (Masalha 1997, 2000). General Dayan epitomised this politically pragmatic, demographically racist Labour Zionism in the post-1967 period. He was appointed defence minister on the eve of the 1967 war and retained this powerful post until 1974. He was the most famous and typical exponent of Israeli post-1967 expansionism and the de facto integration of the occupied territories into Israel. Dayan instituted a policy of 'creeping annexation', a process by which Israeli administration, jurisdiction and law gradually, incrementally and draconianally were imposed on the West Bank and the Gaza Strip, in ever-expanding areas, yet without a comprehensive act of legal annexation. That process, also described as de facto annexation, is seen in the actual transformation of the demographic and physical realities of the 'Administered Territories of Judea and Samaria'. 'Living together in Judea and Samaria' had been repeatedly used by Dayan since June 1967 as a euphemism to express Israel's determination to hold on to the West Bank and Gaza.

The 1967 war not only reopened the question of Israel's borders but also rekindled mass interest and excitement in the so-called 'whole Land of Israel'. The influence of the biblical narrative in the secular intentions of Labour Zionism, including biblical conquests as narrated in the Book of Joshua, had always been evident. In the wake of the 1967 conquests, Israeli author Amos Elon writes, the daily Hebrew press was filled with 'maps of Joshua's, Solomon's and Herod's conquests on both sides of the Jordan [river], and with argumentative articles proclaiming Israel's right to the whole of Palestine', irrespective of the wishes of its Palestinian inhabitants (Elon 1997a: 46).

According to Elon, Jewish 'biblical borders' included Sinai and the Syrian Golan Heights. Apparently he was upset by the Dayan declaration that Israel's 'historical borders' included only the West Bank (Elon 1997a: 46). Zionist Israelis advanced their claims of Jewish rights to the whole land based on security or economic or demographic or religious considerations. And so the contest over 'biblical Israel' and its boundaries continued. There were many reasons why the expansionist sentiments of Greater Israel were sharply reawoken in the post-1967 period. First, the claims of 'Jewish historical rights in the whole Land of Israel' had a deep basis in mainstream secular Labour Zionism. Second, the spectacular and manifold consequences of the 1967 military successes underlined the success of Zionism and the creation of a dynamic, powerful and expansionist settler society. Third, the mobilisation of neo-Zionist, Jewish fundamentalist political and social forces in Israel was highly effective. Fourth, according to Amos Elon, the territory of Israel prior to the 1967 conquests, though rich in Roman, Byzantine, Nabatean, Crusader and Muslim historical sites, actually had almost no historical monuments testifying to an ancient Jewish past. The pre-1967 territory never embraced the ancient territory of the Hebrews – who were peoples of the Hills – but rather, according to the Bible, that of their plainlands enemies, the Philistines, as well as the Negev of the Edomites and 'Galilee of the Gentiles' (Elon 1997a: 46).

The 1967 conquests suddenly brought the vast mythic repertoire of the Old Testament and its biblical sites of 'Judea', Hebron and Jericho under Israeli control. It would be illuminating to compare the irredentist drive for Greater Israel in the post-1967 period with some of its central European equivalents – nations which were born in the nineteenth or the early twentieth century and are committed to the recovery of their 'unredeemed national territories' which are populated by still more national groups. But it would also be illuminating to compare the religious messianism of the post-1967 period with the First Latin Crusade (1096–99). In the euphoric and feverously messianic environment of post-1967, Amos Elon writes,

> Tombs of renewed Hebrew prophets and kings, all said to be absolutely authentic, as well as Saul's own throne and Samson's alleged cave were all discovered almost daily by enthusiastic and amateur archaeologists. The new discoveries also included tombs of minor biblical figures such as Abner, King Saul's chief of staff, and the prophet Nathan (the discoveries were reminiscent of similar finds during the First Crusade – for example, the discovery of the holy lance at Antioch and the recognition of Baldwin I of the cup of the Last Supper among the booty at Caesarea). (Elon 1996: 92)

Dayan never took academic courses in archaeology (Slater 1991: 161). However, during three decades between 1951 and 1981, he obsessively collected a vast collection of antiquities acquired through illicit excavations; in addition he bought, exchanged and sold antiquities in Israel and abroad. He turned his Tzahala Tel Aviv house into an archaeological garden (Dayan 1976a: 125; Ben-Ezer 1997: 122–3). One Israeli hagiographer commented thus on Dayan's collection: 'the precious relics in the garden, as well as in his house, have made ancient Israel, Egypt, Mesopotamia and the Mediterranean Islands an inseparable part of his daily thoughts' (Teveth 1972: 202).

Dayan seldom spoke explicitly about his obsession with antiquity, but much can be read between the lines of his book *Living with the Bible* (1978). The most famous incident of his digging activities took place at Azur near Tel Aviv in 1968, when he was badly injured by a landslide while robbing a burial cave, and hospitalised for three weeks (Kletter 2003). Most of Dayan's looting was done in areas conquered after 1967 and under his own military rule. It is even claimed that Dayan ordered a training exercise with soldiers practising entrenching at a known antiquity site, so that once the exercise was over he could go and look for antiquities. Other IDF commanders began to follow Dayan in collecting and stealing antiquities.[62]

Dayan's army colleague Professor Yigael Yadin, who served from 1949 to 1952 as the second chief of staff of the army, was one of the founding fathers of Israeli archaeology. He was a military advisor to Prime Minister Levi Eshkol in 1967 and dominated Israeli archaeology from the 1950s to the 1970s. Yadin's life has been described by Professor Neil Asher Silberman in *A Prophet from amongst You: The Life of Yigael Yadin, Soldier, Scholar and Myth-Maker of Modern Israel*. Under Yadin archaeology in Israel was not strictly an academic activity but 'a means of communication 'between the people and the land' (Silberman 1993). For Yadin, like Ben-Gurion, biblical archaeology and biblical history were a kind of civic religion (Elon 1997b: 39). Commenting on his own mobilised archaeology, Yadin wrote in the Israeli army journal *Bamahane* of March 1969:

> Everyone feels and knows that he is discovering and excavating findings and artefacts from the days of his fathers. And every finding bears witness to the connection and covenant between the people and the land. ... As far as Israel is concerned, it seems to me that the factor I mentioned – the search and building of the connection to the people and the land – must be taken into consideration. [Archaeology] in my view reinforces the Hebraic conscious-ness, let us say – the identification and the connection with ancient Judaism and Jewish consciousness. (quoted in Sabbagh 2006: 90)

In 1962–63 Yadin was put in command of the excavation of Massada, a hilltop fortress where some 1,000 Jewish warriors had 'committed suicide' rather than surrender to the Romans in AD 73. The mythical narratives produced by Yadin's excavations at Massada fed into what Zerubavel (1995: 214) refers to as the 'master commemorative narrative that highlights their members' common past and legitimizes their aspiration for a shared destiny'. One of the outcomes of Yadin's biblical archaeology was the emergence of Massada – a mountaintop Hellenistic–Roman fortress site in the southern desert near the Dead Sea – as Israel's main secular-nationalist military shrine, a place where Israeli army recruits were assembled to take an oath of allegiance in dramatic night-time ceremonies – this despite complaints on the part of critical biblical scholars that evidence for a mass suicide was lacking and that there was reason to believe that ancient accounts of the event were actually falsified.[63]

After the 1967 war Dayan started to buy antiquities on a large scale in shops in the West Bank and Gaza, mainly in Jerusalem (Dayan 1986:142).

Dayan was a robber of antiquities, who had never acquired nor showed the slightest interest in acquiring scientific knowledge, such as methods of excavation, dating, stratigraphy. As a deeply secular man, religion was not important for Dayan. He associated all antiquities with the biblical narrative. Raz Kletter, of the Israel Antiquities Authority, writes:

> At first, Dayan was helped by family members, but soon he became involved with amateur and professional robbers, dealers and smugglers. I have documented 35 sites where evidence of robbing and illegal digging by Dayan exists. No doubt, this is only the tip of the iceberg, but it testifies to the scale and temper of his activities. The distribution of sites fits his arena of activities, first in the south when he commanded the southern front, then in whole Israel until 1967, later extending to the Occupied Territories. I present a sample of four of the robbed sites. (Kletter 2003)

Dayan robbed antiquities, lied about it, abused his high position by using army personnel and material for his private aims; he sold antiquities, and did not pay income tax on the profits he made.[64] His illicit digging activities and his eclectic collection were put on display in the Israel Museum in Jerusalem in April 1985. His Israeli critics complained that he corrupted in his archaeological activities the whole archaeology of Israel.[65] Some liberal Israelis criticised the Israel Museum for displaying stolen antiquities, and for buying them for so much money (Segev 1986: 61-2). But leaders of archaeological research institutions and Israeli took no action. Dayan apparently was given free rein by Ben-Gurion, Israel's first prime minister. After many private complaints about Dayan's activities, Ben-Gurion concluded that Dayan should not be allowed to dig illicitly, but should be allowed to 'go after the plough' and pick up 'stray' antiquities (Kletter 2003). Other Israeli army commanders started to cultivate their own collections.

The 1967 Conquests, Population Transfer and the Holy City of Jerusalem

All Palestinian areas conquered by Israel in June 1967 experienced immediate and substantial out-movements of Arab residents, both of the native population and of those Palestinian refugees who had been driven out from present-day Israel in 1948-49. Among the first to go were the inhabitants of the three ancient villages of 'Imwas (Emmaus of the New Testament) Yalu and Bayt Nuba, situated near the Green Line in the Latrun area north-west of Jerusalem.[66]

On 31 December 1997 the Hebrew daily *Haaretz* revealed the details of an extraordinary conversation that took place between General Narkiss and the Israeli army's chief rabbi, Shlomo Goren (later to be Ashkenazi chief rabbi of Israel from 1973 to 1983), in June 1967. Narkiss recalled in an interview that only a few hours after the Old City was captured by the Israeli army he was urged by Rabbi Goren to blow up the Dome of the Rock.

> The paratroopers wandered around the plaza [on the Temple Mount] as if in a dream ... Rabbi Shlomo Goren was among them. I was alone for a moment, lost in thought, when Rabbi Goren approached me. 'Uzi', Rabbi Goren said, 'Now is the time to put 100 kg of explosives into the Mosque of Omar [the Dome of the Rock] so we may rid ourselves of it once and for all' ... I said to him, 'Rabbi, enough.' He said, 'Uzi, you will go down in history if you do this.... This is an opportunity that can be taken advantage of now, at this moment. Tomorrow it will be too late.' ... I said, 'Rabbi, if you don't stop, I'll take you to jail.' ... He simply walked away silently. He was completely serious.[67]

Also on 31 December 1997 Israel's army radio played a recording of a speech Rabbi Goren made in 1967 to a military convention, in which he said the following about the Dome of the Rock and the al-Aqsa Mosque: 'Certainly we should have blown it up. It is a tragedy that we did not do so.'[68] Whether or not the third holiest shrine of Islam came close to being blown up by Israeli paratroopers immediately after it was captured in June 1967 remains an open question. However, in the 1980s members of a militant Jewish group (Hamahteret Hayehudit) were arrested and put on trial for plotting to blow up these shrines. Clearly the destruction of these shrines remains a most vivid fear for Palestinians and Muslims and an ambition for most extremist Jewish fundamentalists in Israel.

The June 1967 war began suddenly and ended quickly. In the course of hostilities and in the immediate aftermath of the June 1967 war, with its rapidly changing circumstances, and particularly given the fact that most Western governments applauded the overwhelming Israeli victory, Defence Minister Dayan and other army generals (including 'Uzi Narkiss, Haim Hertzog and Shlomo Lahat) found an ideal opportunity to drive out tens of thousands of Arabs from their villages, towns and refugee camps in the West Bank and Gaza Strip. Among the first evictees were the residents of the ancient al-Magharbeh quarter in the Old City of Jerusalem. They were turned out of their homes on 11 June, two days after the capture of East Jerusalem by the Israeli military, after three hours' notice.[69] Apparently the quarter was completely demolished because it was located immediately adjacent to the southern part of the Wailing Wall, the Western Wall of al-Haram al-Sharif (the Noble Sanctuary). Its inhabitants, about 135 families (some 650-1,000 persons), were the beneficiaries of an ancient and important Islamic Waqf foundation originally established in 1193 by al-Malik al-Afdal, the son of Salah al-Din. Its obliteration in June 1967 resulted also in the destruction of several historic religious sites (including two mosques, two *zawiyas* and a great number of endowed residences) which the quarter contained.[70]

Narkiss (a Labour Party man who later became director general of the Jewish Agency's (JA) Department of Immigration and Absorption and in 1995 chairman of the Agency's Department of Information) also commanded the troops who captured Jerusalem and clearly approved of the order to evict the al-Magharbeh quarter (Masalha 2003: 189-95).

The Old City of Jerusalem was captured by the Israeli army on 7 June 1967. In his book *Jerusalem: A City without a Wall*, 'Uzi Benziman, a prominent journalist of the daily *Haaretz*, described in detail the circumstances surrounding the destruction of this Muslim quarter (Benziman 1973). The story began on 7 June, while Israeli paratroopers were advancing through the alleys of the Old City. An engineering corps officer in the Central Command, Eytan Ben-Moshe, approached Shlomo Lahat, a senior military officer in the Central Command and the designated military governor of Jerusalem (and subsequently mayor of Tel Aviv) and proposed the demolition of a building used as a 'public toilet', which was part of the al-Magharbeh quarter and adjacent to the Wailing Wall. In fact, Defence Minister Dayan had already requested from Lahat, before the latter had arrived in Jerusalem, 'to clear pathways' to the Wailing Wall so that 200,000 Jews would be able to visit during the forthcoming feast of Shavuoth (Pentecost) (Benziman 1973: 37-8). This seemed to suggest that the original idea to level at least part of the quarter came from Dayan. Furthermore, according to Benziman's account, several senior

Israeli commanders in the Jerusalem district (including 'Uzi Narkiss, the commanding general of the Central Command, Shlomo Lahat and Haim Hetrzog) as well as Dayan, the mayor of West Jerusalem Teddy Kollek, and former prime minister David Ben-Gurion were all involved, one way or another, either in the initial decision or in the actual implementation of the systematic operation to destroy the Arab quarter.

To begin with, Lahat approved of Ben-Moshe's idea and sent the demolition plan to 'Uzi Narkiss (who also gave the orders to bulldoze the three Arab villages of Bayt Nuba, 'Imwas and Yalu, see above). Moreover, on 8 June Ben-Gurion, accompanied by Teddy Kollek and Reserve Colonel Ya'acov Yannai, director of the National Parks Authority, visited the Wailing Wall. Both Ben-Gurion and Kollek were strongly in favour of the removal of Arab buildings adjacent to the Wailing Wall (Benziman 1973: 38). Kollek, who had long been closely associated with Ben-Gurion and who had been elected mayor of West Jerusalem in 1965, appeared to have played a central role in the formulation and implementation of the decision to demolish the al-Magharbeh quarter. He apparently also informed the minister of justice, Ya'acov Shimshon Shapira. The latter replied: 'I am not certain of the legal position, but what should be done – do it quickly, and let the God of Israel be with you' (Benziman 1973: 40). In addition to Defence Minister Dayan, who represented the civil authority as well as approving and controlling the conduct of the field commanders, and, as we shall see, oversaw the progress of the demolition, Shapira's answer suggests at least some indirect and tacit ministerial approval of the action.

However, the actual order to evict the quarter and destroy its houses was given by Shlomo Lahat, then the commander of Jerusalem, with the express approval of 'Uzi Narkiss, commanding general of the Central Command, whose approval was given at a meeting with Lahat on 9 June. On the following day, Saturday 10 June, Mayor Kollek assembled a group of 'experts' at his apartment to discuss basic information about the Wailing Wall and the al-Magharbeh quarter. The group included Dan 'Max' Tanai, the engineer of the National Parks Authority; the historian and archaeologist professor Michael Avi-Yonah; Ya'acov Yannai; Aryeh Sharon, Chairman of the National Parks Authority; Ya'acov Salman, deputy military governor of East Jerusalem and Lahat's assistant. Kollek explained to the participants the reasons for this urgent meeting:

The al-Magharbeh quarter adjacent to the Wailing Wall must be demolished. The responsibility for executing the plan will be in the hands of the National Parks Authority in order to give the matter as far as possible an unofficial character. The department of antiquities in the ministry of education and the Israel Defence Force are not interested in involvement, publicly, in the execution of the plan, although they both bless it and will accord it practical assistance. (Benziman 1973: 41)

Kollek put Tanai in charge of executing the operation, possibly seeking to bestow upon it a civilian legitimacy. Central to the planning and mode of procedure by Kollek and his technical 'experts' was the need to act speedily in order to stave off internal criticism and potential obstruction and avoid attracting too much attention by the foreign media. At noon (10 June) Kollek and his colleagues proceeded to the area of the Wailing Wall and decided on the spot to bulldoze the entire Arab quarter with the aim of creating a vast plaza for the 'Western Wall' which was big enough to hold at least a hundred thousand people (Benziman 1973: 40-41; Elon 1996: 93). Kollek also got in touch with several Jerusalem construction companies and asked them to make earth-moving equipment available and undertake the demolition task as 'a donation to the city' (cited in Ben-Dov, Naor and Aner 1983: 163).

While the actual demolition job was partly assigned to a civilian body called the Guild of Builders and Contractors, the Israeli army, particularly its Central Command's engineering corps, rendered the needed assistance. Sometime during the afternoon or the evening of the same day (10 June) an army officer went from one house to another ordering the residents of the quarter to move out. When many families refused to leave their homes, an army unit moved in and evicted the bulk of the inhabitants by force. Meanwhile two bulldozers and other heavy equipment were assembled by the engineering corps, and those in charge of the operation sought to complete the whole work on the night of 10-11 June. Commenting on this driven urgency by those responsible for the deed, Benziman explained:

Those who were presiding over the destruction of the [Arab] neighbourhood assumed that their action was motivated neither by security [considerations] nor by mere town planning. They were driven that night by an almost mystical feeling: that, in their eyes, they were the representatives of the Jewish people, who came to assert [Jewish] sovereignty over its most sacred site ... the fate of

135 Arab families, who were the victims of these desires, was of no concern to them. (Benziman 1973: 42)

The speed with which the Israeli authorities sought to carry out the levelling of the Arab residential houses was also evident in the fact that in the same evening one demolished wall of a house revealed an unconscious, badly injured, middle-aged Arab women. By midnight she was dead.

The head of the OC Central Command, 'Uzi Narkiss, came to the site in the early morning of Sunday 11 June, and ordered that the levelling be completed speedily. More men and heavy equipment were brought in. In the afternoon of the same day Defence Minister Dayan appeared on the site. He also ordered Lahat to complete the levelling of the quarter very quickly (Benziman 1973: 43), possibly in order to prevent foreign journalists seeing the remains of the destroyed Arab quarter. In fact only muted internal questioning of the levelling of the quarter was made by the minister of religious affairs, as well as by Prime Minister Levi Eshkol himself, who asked Narkiss on the telephone: 'Why are residential houses being demolished?' The ministry of religious affairs, in particular, appeared to be concerned that the action could tarnish Israel's image abroad (Benziman 1973: 45-6). However, backed by the powerful defence minister (Dayan) – who conducted the June 1967 war with great independence – Narkiss and Lahat managed easily to ignore the criticism and pursued the policy of levelling and forcible evacuation with and without the approval of the civilian authorities. Benziman believed that

> The policy of evacuation and demolition continued only for several days after the [Israeli army] entrance into the city within the walls. It was executed at the initiative of middle military echelons and with the tacit approval of senior level command. There was lack of communication between the civil authorities and the military government; in practice the latter exercised civilian functions. The military echelon, on its own responsibility, encouraged the Arab residents to get out of Jerusalem and other cities in the West Bank and to go to the East Bank [of Jordan]. (Benziman 1973: 45)

The evicted residents of the al-Magharbeh quarter were dispersed in West Bank villages close to Jerusalem (such as Shu'fat, Bayt Hanina and Silwan) as well as in the Muslim quarter of the Old City of Jerusalem. None of the Israeli government ministries was prepared to accept responsibility for the demolition of the quarter, and no attempt was made to offer the

evictees alternative accommodation (Dumper 1994: 116). Like the eviction of the three large villages in the Latrun area, this removal should
be seen as an internal expulsion rather than transfer out of the occupied
territories. However, it is extremely important to remember that these
cases of internal expulsion had a psychological effect on the 1967 exodus
from the West Bank to Jordan, helping (almost certainly) to precipitate
and encourage further exodus out of the country, especially in the first
few weeks following the war.

The levelling of the al-Magharbeh quarter was only the beginning of
the sweeping changes carried out by Israel – changes designed to wrest
control of the Old City and make it, eventually, an exclusively Jewish
area. On 17 June 1967 at 4 a.m. the Israeli army ordered the inhabitants
of the former Jewish quarter and the surrounding houses to leave the
premises within twenty-four hours. Apparently this measure affected
several hundred Palestinian families who, according to the 1967 *Jerusalem
Diary of Sister Marie-Therese*, could be observed all day carrying their
belongings through the alleys of Jerusalem. Some of them were able to
find refuge with relatives and friends. But the majority had to leave the
town.[71] In the Old City's Jewish quarter and its surrounding districts, some
4,000 Palestinians were evicted to make possible the reconstruction of a
vastly enlarged and completely 'Jewish' quarter, excluding its former Arab
residents.[72] The destruction of the al-Magharbeh quarter should be seen as
part of a wider internal debate that took place during and after the 1967
war about the future of the Muslim shrines in the Old City of Jerusalem,
particularly the third holiest site of Islam: the al-Aqsa Mosque and the
Dome of the Rock. The Zionist deployment of the Old Testament in the
post-1967 period with the aim of driving Palestinians out of Jerusalem
and the continuing threats to the Muslim shrines in Jerusalem will be
discussed in subsequent chapters.

2

Biblical Prophecy and Christian Imperialism: Christian Zionism, Armageddon Theology and the Battle for Jerusalem

Christian support for Jewish 'Restoration' to Palestine, on biblical, theological or political grounds, preceded secular Jewish Zionism by nearly four centuries and paved the way for the latter's rise in the late nineteenth century. Indeed the Zionist dream of establishing a Jewish state in Palestine was nurtured and shaped by Christian Zionists long before Israel was established in 1948. Although the term 'Zionism' was first coined in the late nineteenth century, Christian Zionism and the idea that the creation of a Jewish state in Palestine would lead to the fulfilment of biblical prophecies were deeply rooted in post-Reformation Europe.

The historical roots of Christian Zionism have been examined by many authors (Sizer 2004: 27-105; Tuchman 1982; Sharif 1983; Wagner 1995; Halsell 1986; Culver 1995; Murray 1971; Toon 1970; Rausch 1979; Cohn-Sherbok 2006). Three important works on the subject are: Barbara Tuchman's *Bible and Sword: England and Palestine from the Bronze Age to Balfour* (originally published in 1956) and Regina Sharif's *Non-Jewish Zionism: Its Roots in Western History* (1983), and Stephen Sizer's *Christian Zionism: Road-map to Armageddon?* (2004). Tuchman looked at a large body of literature, demonstrating the historical roots of England's fascination with the Jews and the idea of 'Zion', while Sharif offers the first and best critical analysis of Christian Zionism, surveying its historical, theological and political dimensions. Several scholarly works on the attitudes of Christian Zionists towards the State of Israel, Jerusalem and the indigenous inhabitants of Palestine have also been written (Prior and Taylor 1994; Cragg 1992; Idinopulos and Thomas 1991; Walker 1994; Halsell 1986; Haddad and Wagner 1986; Ruether and Ruether 2002; Sizer 2004). Other critical scholars have emphasised what they saw as the invention of the 'heretical' tradition of Christian Zionism, whose principal ideas contravene New Testament teaching, arguing that the New Testament had declared the fulfilment of Old Testament prophecies and had degeographised faith, and that within the scope of Christian theology there was neither meaning nor need for Jewish Restoration to Palestine (Matar 1989: 52-70, 1999: 149-50; Sizer 2004).

Bishop Kenneth Cragg and Professor Rosemary Radford Ruether have shown that modern Christian Zionism and Western colonialism, with its lingering effects still reverberating in the Middle East, were, and still are, based directly upon the most primitive and savage elements of Old Testament Hebrew tribalism, of 'promised land–chosen people' theology. Ruether sums up the basic tenets of modern-day crusading Christian Zionism – tenets which are based on the following interconnected propositions:

> (1) God gave the Jews all of the land of Palestine as a promised land in Biblical times, and this divine donation of land gives Jews today a permanent and unconditional right to occupy all of this land, regardless of people who have been living there historically (i.e. the Palestinians); (2) as preparation for the events that will culminate world history, all the Jewish people must return to the land, resettle all of it, rebuild the temple; and (3) the founding of the State of Israel and Jewish settlement of the land are fulfillments of Biblical prophecy which will usher in the final days of judgment and redemption. This will be completed when the Jews are converted to (evangelical Protestant) Christianity. The battle of Armageddon will then take place, killing the enemies of God (unbelievers, Communists, Muslims). The saints (including the converted Jewish elect) will be raptured to heaven when God cleanses the earth of evil doers. Then those saints will descend to a purified earth and enjoy millennial blessing. (Ruether 1998: 118-19)

Dr Stephen Sizer argues that 'Christian Zionism distorts the Bible and marginalizes the universal imperative of the Christian message of equal grace and common justice' (2004: 259). The supremacist nature of Christian Zionism was highlighted by Bishop Cragg, who observes that the biblical paradigm of 'promised land–Jewish chosenness' can only be interpreted as either ethnic exclusivism or political chauvinism:

> It is so; God chose the Jews; the land is theirs by divine gift. These dicta cannot be questioned or resisted. They are final. Such verdicts come infallibly from Christian biblicists for whom Israel can do no wrong – thus fortified. But can such positivism, this unquestioning finality, be compatible with the integrity of the Prophets themselves? It certainly cannot square with the open peoplehood under God which is the crux of New Testament faith. Nor can it well be reconciled with the ethical demands central to law and election alike. (Cragg 1992: 237–8)

The Historical Roots of Christian Zionism: The Protestant Reformation and Prophetic Politics

Christian Zionism was a product of the Protestant Reformation and Christian biblicism (following James Barr (1977: 6), the term 'biblicism' is used here to describe a position which maintains that the Bible is the sole source for Christian theology). The sixteenth-century upheavals in Western Latin Christianity witnessed major shifts in attitude of European Christians towards their own identity and the invention of new Christian traditions. Furthermore, the emergence of militant 'nationalist' monarchies in Spain, Portugal, France, Holland and Britain made the 'nation', rather than the universal European Christian community, the new focus of European identity. These Christian nations were engaged in wars with each other that mingled religious rivalry, created by the Reformation, with trade competition and for colonies in Africa, Asia and the Americas. As Rosemary and Herman Ruether put it, central to the invention of a new Christian tradition was

> The Idea of the 'New Israel' [which] was shifted from a universal religious community, the Christian church, to the nation as an 'elect people,' commissioned by God to defend the true faith (whether Catholic or Protestant) and evangelize the 'heathen'. (Ruether and Ruether 2002: 70)

In Britain and later in the United States, Christian fundamentalists began to interpret history written in the framework of the biblical

'Israelite history', using Hebrew Bible texts such as Joshua's conquest of the Canaanites, and to identify themselves as the inheritors of the ancient 'Israelites' – the 'New Israel' – God's chosen people who were destined to play a strategic role in the world. The nationalising of the (Christian) New Israel and the racialising of the Jews in European thought were also added by the new biblicist scholarship of the Reformation and Renaissance (Ruether and Ruether 2002: 70–71). Protestants of the reformed tradition, in particular, saw the Hebrew Bible as the source of all truth, including political truth. This invented tradition created a new identification between 'biblical Israel' and the nationalised and racialised Christian New Israel (Ruether and Ruether 2002: 70–71).

The biblical paradigm of 'promised land–chosen people' is central to both Christian Zionism and Protestant fundamentalism, which is also often associated with the idea of biblical literalism. But, as James Barr has shown, not all Protestant fundamentalists 'take the Bible literally'. For many of them the debate is not about the *literality* of the Bible, but rather its *inerrancy*; for them the Bible does not contain error; 'In order to avoid imputing error to the Bible fundamentalists twist and turn back and forth between literal and non-literal (symbolic, metaphoric, transferred) exegesis' (Barr 1973: 168). However, for Protestant fundamentalists of the post-Reformation period, James Barr writes,

> the Bible is more than the source of verity for their religion, more than the essential source or textbook. It is part of the religion itself, indeed it is practically the centre of the religion, the essential nuclear point from which lines of light radiate into every particular aspect ... the Bible is a verbalized, 'inscripturated' entity, the given form of words in which God has made himself known, and thus the Bible equally enters into all relations, its words cannot be quoted too often, its terms, cadences and lineaments are all to be held dear. While Christ is the divine Lord and Saviour, the Bible is the supreme religious symbol that is tangible, articulate, possessable, accessible to men on earth. (Barr 1977: 36)

Regina Sharif highlights the importance of the Protestant Reformation for the emergence of modern non-Jewish Zionist doctrines:

> To the Christian mind in Protestant Europe, Palestine became the Jewish land. The Jews became the Palestinian people who were foreign to Europe, absent from their Homeland, but in due time were to be returned to Palestine. ... Manifestations of early non-Jewish Zionism were thus neither isolated

incidents nor espoused only by religious eccentrics and outsiders.... A vo-
luminous religious literature on the role and the destiny of the Jews spread
rapidly during the 17th century and, by its millenarian nature, never fell
out of vogue. Many millenarians were rebuked, persecuted and sometimes
even executed for their heretical beliefs. Nevertheless, their writings helped
to entrench the notion of a Jewish Restoration to Palestine. It was not long
until the more practical questions, as to when and how Restoration was to
take place, began to gain importance. (Sharif 1983: 13, 29)

Other historians have also traced the origins of Christian Zionism to
specific historical events and theological developments taking place in the
post-Reformation period, and also crucially, to the revivalist, millennialist, fundamentalist and apocalyptic eschatology which was fairly popular
between the seventeenth and nineteenth centuries in Europe and America
(Sizer 2004). Since the sixteenth century Christian prophetic politics and
pre-millennialist thinking have become popular towards the end of each
century (Wagner 1995: 88).

The British Library houses one of the oldest documents on Christian
Zionism in the English language: *Apocalypsis Apocalypseos* ('A Revelation
of the Revelation'), a monograph of less than fifty pages, was written in
1585 by a millennialist Anglican priest, Thomas Brightman (1562-1607),
described as the father of the 'Restoration of the Jews', who also predicted
the imminent conversion of the Jews to Christianity (Sizer 2004: 28-9;
Wagner 1995: 85). Donald Wagner, executive director of Evangelicals for
Middle East Understanding and a leading authority on Christian Zionism,
writes: 'To my knowledge, *Apocalypsis* is the first Christian publication
in English that calls for the creation of a Jewish state in Palestine in order
to fulfill biblical prophecy' (Wagner 1995: 85).[1]

Brightman also believed that 'the rebirth of a Christian Israelite nation'
would become the 'centre of a Christian world.' (Sizer 2004: 29). As is
common to early millennialist, fundamentalist and apocalyptic writings
concerning 'end-times' prophetic politics, Brightman's pamphlet argued
that the 'restoration' of the Jews to Palestine was necessary if England
was to be blessed by God when history enters its latter days and the
prophetic texts of the Old Testament's Book of Daniel are fulfilled (Sizer
2004: 28-9).

In 1621 Sir Henry Finch, a prominent British lawyer and Member of
Parliament, developing Brightman's biblical prophecy further, wrote a

book entitled *The World's Great Restauration* in which he suggested that European Jews should be encouraged to assert claims to Palestine:

> Where Israel, Judah, Zion and Jerusalem are named [in the Bible] the Holy Ghost meant not the spiritual Israel, or the Church of God collected of the Gentiles or of the Jews and Gentiles both ... but Israel properly descended out of Jacob's loynes. The same judgement is to be made of their returning to their land and ancient seats, the conquest of their foes. ... The glorious church they shall erect in the land itself of Judah. (quoted in Sizer 2004: 29)

Apparently Brightman drew a hostile reaction from the Church establishment and was forced to take his views and his followers underground (Wagner 1995: 86). Restorationism, however, remained the general belief of some Protestant fundamentalists, such as in a large-scale 'end-times' conversion of the Jewish people to Christianity. Such ideas were often used in support of Christian Zionism, which had a long tradition that began with the Protestant idea of Restoration, but had initially demanded the conversion of the Jews as a first step towards the Palestine goal. The nineteenth century witnessed major efforts at Christian–Jewish reconciliation in Europe (Rausch 1979, 1993), and subsequently Christian Zionism began to revise its restorationist doctrine, suggesting that the conversion might happen after restoration. As we shall see, by the late nineteenth century conversion had been largely dropped as a necessary requirement for Anglo-American Christian Zionism; the latter had instead become generally identified with a Jewish 'return' to Palestine.

While the Anglo-American fundamentalist Puritans were deeply influenced by the Hebrew Bible, the revival of Christian prophetic premillennialism during 1790–1800 was particularly marked on both sides of the Atlantic; its popularity in the nineteenth century, according to Donald Wagner, was

> a direct result of the turmoil Europeans felt in the wake of the French and American revolutions coupled with the approach of a new century. The British, like Europeans on the continent, began to feel that their world was falling apart. People turned away from new secular philosophy and political answers and embraced a more fundamentalist form of Christian teachings that included a revived form of prophetic interpretations of the Bible. In this troubled and uncertain climate, Christian Zionism began to take root. (Wagner 1995: 88)

Nineteenth-century Prophetic Politics and British
Colonial Interests: The Christian Zionist Lobby
and the Road to the Balfour Declaration

Ideas centred on the Bible's prophecy and 'Jewish restoration' to Palestine remained largely dormant until the rise of European secular nationalism in the nineteenth century – in the context of post-Enlightenment illiberal romantic nationalism, which coincided with the full bloom of British and French imperialism. Napoleon's invasion of Egypt in 1798 and his foray into Palestine had important consequences for the modern history of biblical scholarship and romantic orientalism – consequences which are beyond the scope of this study (see Said 1978: 76–7). A year after the invasion, the French imperial armies were camped outside Acre. Napoleon issued a letter offering Palestine as a homeland to the Jews under a French colonial protectorate (Guedalla 1925: 45–55). The project was stillborn because Napoleon was defeated and forced to withdraw from the Near East, but his colonial ideas took root in nineteenth-century Britain.

A combination of Protestant religious and imperialist considerations drove some Britons to produce Christian Zionist novels, to set up exploration societies and to advocate the 'restoration of the Jews to Palestine' in public and in private.[2] Furthermore, a succession of archaeological discoveries in the Near East, military adventurism, and a growing number of travelogues fired the imagination of Protestant missionaries, European officials and Arabist scholars and led to the direct involvement of European powers in the Holy Land (Shepherd 1987; Osband 1989). This European obsession with the archaeological past was marked by a decided contempt for the indigenous people of Palestine and life in modern Palestinian villages and towns.

At the height of the British Empire and the Victorian era, prophetic politics of biblical regeneration and restoration went hand in hand with increasing British colonial involvement in the 'Orient'. The Holy Land in the nineteenth century was an attractive target for several European nations which were flexing their colonial muscles around the globe. The region was ready for Western penetration, particularly while the Ottoman Empire was showing signs of political and economic disintegration. The race for a European national presence and colonial commercial interests in the East, and in the Holy Land in particular, was masked by scholarly activities and Oriental Studies (Said 1978). Coinciding with the European 'scramble for Palestine', various sectors of the Western academy, and most of the Western Christian Churches, displayed an increasing interest in Palestine. Invariably foreign interest took the form of establishing Christian institutions – the Turkish reforms after the Crimean War (1853-56) granted equal rights, including property rights, to non-Muslims – thereby uniting Christian missionary endeavour with national influence. The interests of God and country ran parallel. The British moved early,[3] and soon were emulated by the Russians,[4] Germans,[5] Austrians (Wrba 1996) and others, marking the beginning of extensive Western influence in Palestine, an influence which the Turks feared might be a prelude to attempting to recover Palestine as a Christian state.[6] Such was the degree of Western penetration that the Austrian consul, the Count de Caboga, reported in 1880 that Jerusalem had become a European city, and Captain (later General Sir) Charles Warren (1840-1927), of the British Royal Engineers and one of the key officers of the British Palestine Exploration Fund, who was sent to map the biblical topography of Jerusalem and investigate 'the site of the temple', noted:

> [British] King Consul [James Finn] rules supreme, not over the natives of the city, but over strangers; but yet these strangers for the most part are the rightful owners, the natives, for the most part, are usurpers. (Shepherd 1987: 127-8)

The Palestine Exploration Fund (PEF), which was founded in 1865 by a group of academics and clergymen, most notably the Dean of Westminster Abbey, Arthur P. Stanley, also worked closely with the British military establishment. With offices in central London, the Palestine Exploration Fund today is an active organisation which publishes an academic journal, the *Palestine Exploration Quarterly*. In addition, the PEF presents public lectures and funds research projects in the Near East. According to its website, 'Between 1867 and 1870 Captain Warren carried out the explorations in Palestine which form the basis for our knowledge of the topography of ancient Jerusalem and the archaeology of the Temple Mount/Haram al-Sherif'; 'In addition to his explorations on, under, and around the Temple Mount/al-Haram al-Sherif, Warren surveyed the Plain of Philistia and carried out a very important [military] reconnaissance of central Jordan.'' Both Warren and the long-serving and famous British consul, Finn, who was a biblicist Zionist involved with the Mission to the Jews (Shepherd 1987: 110), and who apparently 'literally burrowed' beneath Jerusalem to chart the 'original dimensions' of the Temple Mount; his biblical archaeology and topography remain basic data for some archaeologists of today (Shepard 1967: 195).

After his Palestine explorations Warren was sent to South Africa, taking up military and administrative posts in the Cape Colony and fighting in the Boer War. Warren, a keen Freemason and Master of the First Lodge, wrote in 1875 a treatise entitled *The Land of Promise*, in which he proposed that a colonial organisation similar to the East India Company – which had been dissolved in 1858 – should undertake the colonisation of Palestine with Jews under the protection of one or more or the imperial powers (cited in Gorenberg 2000: 80).

Protestant Zionists and British imperialists believed that a 'Jewish Palestine' would be convenient for a British protectorate there along the main route to India. From the late nineteenth century to the middle of the twentieth century three famous British prime ministers were closely associated with 'Gentile Zionism' in Britain: Benjamin Disraeli ('Benjamin of Israel') (1804-1881), who was successful in securing for imperial Britain the control of the Suez Canal; David Lloyd George (1863-1945), whose government issued the Balfour Declaration of 1917; and Sir Winston Churchill, who for nearly half a century in and out of office was devoted to political Zionism and the British Empire (Sykes 1973: 45, 52, 207). Both Disraeli and Lloyd George were fascinated by the theories of amalgamation or affinity between Christianity and Judaism (Anderson 2005: 60). Lloyd George, a Protestant Zionist, was once quoted as saying: 'I was taught far more history about the Jews than about the history of my own people' (quoted by Stein 1961: 142), and Disraeli was baptised a Protestant, but remained fascinated by his Jewish background. Describing Protestant Christianity as 'completed Judaism', he – like many Christian Zionists – delighted in describing himself as the 'missing page' between the Old and New Testaments (Johnson 1993: 324). Disraeli's civilising Christian imperialism combined patronising attitudes towards the Jews with imperialist foreign policies towards the Middle East – policies which he justified by invoking paternalistic and racist theories which saw imperialism as a manifestation of what Britain's imperial poet, Rudyard Kipling, would refer to as 'the white man's burden'.[8] Following in the footsteps of European imperialists, before the First World War some Zionist leaders (notably Theodor Herzl in his Zionist novel *Altneuland*), conceived the reality of Palestine, and the material benefits European Jewish colonisation would bring to Palestine, to be similar to the supremacist concept of the 'white man's burden'. During the Mandatory period, however, it became clear to the Zionist leadership that a systematic dislocation and 'transfer' of the indigenous inhabitants of Palestine was the *conditio sine qua non* of the Zionist enterprise (Wiemer 1983: 26; Masalha 1992).

In the late nineteenth century the British Christian Zionist lobby included establishment figures such as the seventh earl of Shaftesbury (1801–1885), Lord Lindsay (Crawford 1847: 71), Lord Manchester, George Eliot, Holman Hunt and Hall Caine. Shaftesbury (Anthony Ashley Cooper), a Tory member of the House of Commons, and subsequently of the Lords,[9] was, in particular, the most ardent propagator and lobbyist of the restoration of 'God's ancient people', as he styled the Jews (Tuchman 1982).[10] Shaftesbury and the influential circle he dominated were under the influence of the 'End of Times' prophetic politics – messianic politics based on the Old Testament's Book of Daniel – which they believed would be fulfilled by the 'literal return' and 'Restoration' of the Jews to Palestine.

The massive growth of Christian Zionism in Victorian Britain (Bar-Yosef 2003: 18–44) was illustrated by Byron's *Hebrew Melodies*, Disraeli's novel *Tancred* and George Eliot's novel *Daniel Deronda* (Prior 1997a: 115). Written in 1876, Daniel Deronda became a Victorian classic, and subsequently Zionist Jews in Russia found the novel hugely inspiring and turned it into their 'Zionist Bible' (al-Raheb 1985: 64). In the pessimistic Victorian age Christian Zionist prophetic politics was fixated with the fulfilment of the messianic prophetic texts of the Hebrew Bible, especially the Book of Daniel. Perhaps it is no surprise that the hero of Eliot's *Daniel Deronda*, the first Zionist novel in the history of Western fiction, is a Jew called Daniel. Daniel, adopted son of an aristocratic Englishman (perhaps a reference to Shaftesbury), becomes fascinated with Jewish traditions when he meets an ailing Jewish philosopher named Mordecai. Providentially, Daniel then discovers that he is himself Jewish. Of course this is also about Mary Ann Evans (1819–80), who wrote under the pen name George Eliot, discovering she was a Christian Zionist. Another novel inspired by the Hebrew Bible was Disraeli's *Tancred*. The following, inspired by the Book of Judges, is taken from Disraeli's novel:

> The most popular poet in England is the Sweet Singer of Israel. Since the days of the heritage, there never was a race who sang so often the odes of David as the people of Great Britain. It was the 'sword of the Lord and of Gideon' that won the boasted liberties of England; and the Scots upon their hillsides achieved their religious freedom chanting the same canticles that cheered the heart of Judah amid their glens.

In the nineteenth century the Western rational secularism of the eighteenth century was replaced by romantic nationalism (Anderson 1991: 17-21) and biblicist prophetic politics were constructed as an antidote. As Tuchman suggests, Christian Zionism, romantic biblicism and nineteenth-century anti-rationalism were all part of the same creed:

> For now the pendulum had swung back again, after the Hellenic interlude of the eighteenth century, to the moral earnestness of another Hebraic period. Eighteenth-century Skepticism had given way to Victorian piety, eighteenth-century rationalism was once again surrendering to Revelation. ... Whenever Christians returned to the authority of the Old Testament they found it prophesying the return of its people to Jerusalem and felt themselves duty-bound to assist the prophecy. (Tuchman 1956: 179)

Bible-bashing Lord Shaftesbury was a myth-maker. Pushing zealously the myth of a ubiquitous and perennial Jewish diaspora longing to 'return', on 4 November 1840 he placed an advertisement in the *Times*:

> RESTORATION OF THE JEWS: A memorandum has been addressed to the Protestant monarchs of Europe on the subject of the restoration of the Jewish people to the land of Palestine. The document in question, dictated by a peculiar conjunction of affairs in the East, and other striking 'signs of the times,' reverts to the original covenant which secures that land to the [Jewish] descendant of Abraham. (quoted in Wagner 1995: 91)

Shaftesbury was directly responsible for the propagandistic slogan 'A country without a nation for a nation without a country',[11] later to be become a key Zionist-Jewish myth: 'A land without a people for a people without a land' (Masalha 1997; Hyamson 1950: 10, 12). Assessing the

significance of his lobbying efforts on the fortunes of the biblicist Zionist
movement in Britain, Wagner writes:

> One cannot overstate the influence of Lord Shaftesbury on the British politi-
> cal elites, church leaders, and the average Christian layperson. His efforts
> and religious political thought may have set the tone for England's colonial
> approach to the Near East and in particular the holy land during the next
> one hundred years. He singularly translated the theological positions of
> Brightman, Henry Finch, and John Nelson Darby [the father of modern
> premillennial dispensationalism: see below][12] into a political strategy. His
> high political connections, matched by his uncanny instincts, combined to
> advance the Christian Zionist vision. (1995: 92)

Some British colonial officials residing in the region and several British
Members of Parliament continued to lobby for 'Jewish restorationism'
throughout the second half of the nineteenth century and this lobbying
intensified towards the end of the century as British imperialist interests
in the Middle East increased. In 1841 Charles Henry Churchill, a British
resident of Damascus and a zealous advocate of the establishment of a
Jewish state in Palestine, wrote a letter to the British Jewish philan-
thropist Moses Montefiore, stating: 'I consider the object to be perfectly
obtainable. But, two things are indispensably necessary. Firstly, that the
Jews will themselves take up the matter unanimously. Secondly, that the
European powers will aid them in their views.'[13] In 1880 F. Laurence
Oliphant (1829-1888), MP, novelist and evangelical Christian, a follower
of Shaftesbury, published a book entitled *The Land of Gilead* (named after
the biblical 'land of Gilead'),[14] in which he presented a plan of 'Jewish
restoration' and a detailed project for Jewish settlement east of the River
Jordan. He urged the British Parliament to assist Jewish immigration
from Russia and Eastern Europe to Palestine. Not surprisingly he also
advocated that indigenous Palestinian Arabs be removed to reservations
like those of the indigenous inhabitants of North America[15] (Sharif 1983:
68) – or hinting at the Bantustan concept later developed by South Africa
(Sharif 1983: 68; Wagner 1995: 93).

Until the mid-eighteenth century, by and large, Western orientalists
were biblical scholars, students of the Semitic languages and Islamic
specialists (Said 1978: 50). In the nineteenth century Laurence Oliphant,
Lord Shaftesbury and George Eliot – who wrote under the influence of and

herself contributed to the growth of a new romantic literary orientalism
in the West (Said 1978: 18) – were typical of British pro-Zionist authors
and novelists. Their impulse was towards biblically framed questions
and romantic orientalism with virtually no reference to the rights of the
indigenous inhabitants of Palestine. British Christian Zionism of the nineteenth century was obsessed with the prophetic texts of the Book of Daniel.
George Elliot's novel *Daniel Deronda* was central to the evolution of British
romantic literary writings. This biblically framed discourse entails both the
shaping of history, 'so that this history now appears to confirm the validity
of Zionist claims to Palestine, thereby denigrating Palestinians claims'
(Said 1980: 8), and the Zionist legitimisation of Zionist colonisation in
Palestine – a process that did not end with the creation of Israel in 1948, but
intensified after 1967. The Palestinians had to be dispossessed in order to
be civilised. However, it was in the capital cities of the West that Christian
biblicists deployed their colonialist rhetoric of the civilising mission and
argued that Palestine was largely 'a land without a people', empty and
uncultivated, inhabited by backward 'natives'.[16] Christian Zionists, Lord
Shaftesbury in particular, were associated with liberalism, reforms and
philanthropy; by contrast, their enemies – the indigenous inhabitants of
Palestine, and Arabs and Muslims in general – were associated with oriental
despotism, ignorance, fanaticism and backwardness.

In his *Orientalism* (1978) Edward W. Said subjected Western 'Oriental
Studies' to a devastating critique and exposed the underlying presumptions
of the discipline. He also concluded that biblical studies were part of and
an extension of the Western orientalist discourse, which had been constructed without any 'oriental'/Arab/Muslim reader in view. For Said, in
this biblical–orientalist discourse the indigenous inhabitants of Palestine
were presented as incapable of unified action and national consciousness.
The biblical scholars, following in the footsteps of the Western orientalists,
concentrated on historical and archaeological questions. In *The Question
of Palestine*, which came out two years after *Orientalism*, Said also tried
to explain the erasure of Palestinians from history. For him, the deletion
of the reality of Palestine centred on three key issues. The first is the
representation of Palestine, the Palestinians and Islam in the West. In this
regard, Said's book *Covering Islam* (1981) should be treated as the third
part of a trilogy which includes *Orientalism* (1978) and *The Question of*

Palestine (Said 1980; Ashcroft and Ahluwalia 2001: 125). For Said, the representations of Islam in the West are an important part of the question of Palestine because they are used to silence the Palestinians, the majority of whom are Muslims (Said 1980; Ashcroft and Ahluwalia 2001: 128). The second is the 'contest between an affirmation and a denial'. The third is Western orientalist attitudes towards Arabs and Islam, Western racial prejudices and, especially, the Western narrative of a contest between the 'civilising' forces of the Zionist European settlers and the 'uncivilised', 'treacherous' and degenerate oriental Arabs (Said 1980: 25-8).

The interplay between British war and imperial interests, Jewish Zionist lobbyists and Christian Zionist prophetic politics would lead to the Balfour Declaration of 1917 (Anderson 2005: 1, 57-8). The key to understanding the contribution of Britain to the twentieth century's Palestinian catastrophe lies in the intensity with which some British Christian restorationists embraced the project of a 'Jewish homeland' in Palestine; the way in which the Bible, 'divine rights and divine promises' were seen by the likes of British Prime Minister Lloyd George and his foreign secretary, Arthur James Balfour (who issued the Balfour Declaration); and generally the extraordinary appeal political Zionism had in the West. Although the Balfour Declaration was partly motivated by Great War calculations, it was not issued in an ideological vacuum. Its content reflected the Christian Zionist prophetic politics which became deeply rooted in nineteenth-century nationalist Protestant Britain (Verete 1970: 48-76).[17] This all meant that, from the beginning, the reality of Palestine and the Palestinians lay outside Western and Zionist conceptions of the 'Jewish homeland' in Palestine. Furthermore, as Edward Said argued, the 'site of the Zionist struggle was only partially in Palestine'; the crucial site remained until 1948 in the capital cities in the West, while the reality of Palestine and 'the native resistance to the Zionists was either played down or ignored in the West' (Said 1980: 22-3). By removing the struggle from the Middle East, the Palestinians (and Arabs) were prevented from representing themselves and were deemed incapable of representing themselves; '[T]hey cannot represent themselves; they must be represented' (quoted in Said 1980).[18] A major success of the Christian and Jewish Zionists has been their ability to occupy the space from which they were all to represent and explain the Arabs to the West:

[The] Zionists took it upon themselves as a partially 'Eastern' people who had emancipated themselves from the worst Eastern excesses, to explain the Oriental Arabs to the West, to assume responsibility for expressing what the Arabs were really like and about, never to let the Arabs appear equally with them as existing in Palestine. This method allowed Zionism always to seem both involved in and superior to the native realties of Middle Eastern existence. (Said 1980: 26)

Applying theories of contemporary literary deconstruction based on the works of Said, Derrida and Freud, Irish scholar John McDonagh has suggested that these supremacist attitudes towards the realities of Palestinian existence were partly derived from age-old Western prejudices towards the ancient 'Philistines' – a highly cultured, seafaring people who had settled in Canaan during the thirteenth and twelfth centuries BC and who had given their name to 'Palestine'. The biblical 'Philistines' have, for centuries, suffered under the weight of their relentlessly negative portrayal in the books of the Old Testament. McDonagh showed that, surrounded by biblical myths from Goliath to Delilah, in the West the Philistines have personified the intrinsically evil *Other* in the narrative myth of the Israelites. Their name, in particular, has entered the lexicon of mute shame, ranking alongside the Barbarians as the personification of the *Outsider* (McDonagh 2004: 93-4).

The Philistines were destined to play out the role of scapegoats in the biblical narrative used for sustaining the myth of the existence of the Israelite nation. Their name has been used from biblical times to the present day to distinguish between those who have set the cultural and political agendas and those who have stood irredeemably outside the ideologies which were propagated to facilitate the rationalisation of the 'nation's' space. In the Bible the Philistines became the archetypal Other, whose sole function in the text was to plot the destruction of civilisation, and whose activities provided justification for the expansion of the Israelites. The Philistines – not unlike the modern Palestinians – had become the Other as a result of the challenge they posed to the burgeoning collective Hebrew identity, within the parameters established by the biblical narrative. The 'ignorant' and 'demonic' Philistines, then, fulfilled a role in the construction of the great colonial edifice of Otherness that was later to be played by, among others, Arabs and Muslims, Africans, Indians, Aboriginals, this role furthermore ironically played out to tragic effect by the Jews themselves over centuries of persecution in the West (McDonagh 2004: 93-4).

In 1917 the interplay between Jewish Zionist lobbyists (especially Chaim Weizmann, 1974-1952), British Empire interests, First World War considerations and Christian Zionism brought about the famous Balfour Declaration which promised a 'Jewish homeland' in Palestine. Then an imperial world power, Britain gave sanction for the first time to the Zionist campaign for possession of Palestine. This highly controversial document, dated 2 November, was issued by Foreign Secretary Arthur James Balfour (later Lord Balfour), in the form of a letter to a prominent British Jewish supporter of the Zionist movement, Lord Rothschild, declaring British support for political Zionism:

> Her Majesty's Government views with favour the establishment in Palestine of a national home for the Jewish people, and will use their best endeavours to facilitate the achievement of this object, it being clearly understood that nothing shall be done to prejudice the civil and religious rights of the existing non-Jewish communities in Palestine, or the rights and political status enjoyed by Jews in other countries. (Quoted in Said 1980: 3)

For centuries – and for more than eighty years of political Zionism – the Palestinian Arabs were an absolute majority in Palestine. Balfour was fully aware of this fact when, on 11 August 1919, he expressed his typically colonialist views with frankness when he wrote:

> Zionism, be it right or wrong, good or bad, is rooted in age-long traditions, in present needs, in future hopes, of far profounder import than the desires and prejudices of the 700,000 Arabs who now inhabit that ancient land. ... The idea of planting a [European] minority of outsiders upon an indigenous majority population, without consulting it, was not calculated to horrify men who had worked with Cecil Rhodes or promoted European settlement in Kenya. (quoted in Talmon 1965a: 248, 250)

In 1925 Balfour visited Palestine and was a key guest of honour at the opening of the Hebrew University of Jerusalem. He was greeted enthusiastically by the leadership of the small European Zionist Yishuv (settlement) in Palestine, while the majority of indigenous inhabitants of Palestine welcomed him with black flags.

During the Mandatory period (1920-48) several other passionate British 'Gentile Zionists' worked tirelessly for the international Zionist movement; the niece of Arthur Balfour, Blanche Dugdale ('Baffy') worked in the Political Department of the London office of the Jewish Agency, alongside Chaim Weizmann. In her biography of her uncle she noted that 'Balfour's interest in the Jews and their history was lifelong, originating in the Old Testament training of his mother, and his Scottish upbringing' (Dugdale 1936: 433). In her diary Dugdale vividly describes Weizmann's diplomatic activities in London, while comparing and contrasting these with Old Testament images – 'the walls of Jericho have fallen, fallen!' (Sykes 1973: 207)

The great anti-colonial Palestinian rebellion of 1936–39 was crushed with the expertise of a British military strategist and Christian Zionist bible-basher, Colonel Charles Orde Wingate and his Special Night Squads. Wingate, an enthusiastic convert to 'Gentile Zionism', trained the Field Companies (FOSH),[19] an elite strike force established as the commando arm of the Labour Zionist Haganah force in 1937 mainly to combat the Palestinian uprising. By March 1938 FOSH had 1,500 trained soldiers, armed with British weapons, divided into thirteen regional groups. From its headquarters at the Jewish kibbutz settlement of 'Ein Harod, in Marj Ibn 'Amer (Jezreel valley), Wingate's Special Night Squads conducted swift raids on Palestinian villages. Wingate, who was subsequently killed (in 1944) in a plane crash in Burma, where he led a guerrilla force fighting the Japanese, was later described in Israel as one of 'founders' of the Israeli army (Sykes 1973: 182–3). Ron Grossman, writing in the *Chicago Tribune* on Israel's fiftieth anniversary, summed up Wingate's legacy under the title 'Remembering One of Israel's Founding Fathers – A Protestant Scotsman':

> He spent scarcely three years in the land that was then part of the British empire and known as Palestine. Yet he developed tactics that remained the combat philosophy of Israel's armed forces today. He also tutored many who became its famed commanders, including (Moshe) Dayan and Yigal Allon, whose elite strike force, the Palmah, utilised Wingate's trademark aggressively mobile tactics to win the 1948 War of Independence.[20]

Grossman goes on to describe Wingate's commitment to the Zionist project:

> Wingate also had a special feeling for the Bible, keeping his own well worn copy always at hand. When stumped by a strategic problem, he would turn to

the Book of Judges. There he would find inspiration in the account of Gideon, the great general of ancient Israel and, like Wingate, a master of hit-and-run guerrilla tactics. That attachment to the Scriptures inspired Wingate with a feeling for Palestine's Jewish inhabitants that set him apart from other British military officers.[21]

In 1957 Israel's National Centre for Physical Education and Sport, the Wingate Institute, was inaugurated and named in honour of Orde Charles Wingate.

Proving the Veracity of the Bible: Digging up the Bible under British Mandate

The political and ideological premisses of Israeli archaeology can be traced to the very foundations of the Western discipline of biblical archaeology in Palestine which developed in the late nineteenth and early twentieth centuries, simultaneously with European imperial competition for influence in the Near East (Silberman 1982). The Eurocentric obsession with historical roots, the evidence for the Bible and the biblical paradigm has been discussed by many authors (Prior 1997a; Whitelam 1996; Lemche 1991). The first biblically oriented topographical study of Palestine was carried out in 1838 by two American scholars, Dr Edward Robinson and Eli Smith, who identified scores of 'biblical sites' on the basis of modern Arabic place-names (Silberman 1997: 66). At the end of the nineteenth century, archaeologist Sir William Matthew Flinders Petrie began to explore the large number of mounds, or tells (*tall* in Arabic), as possible 'biblical sites' (Herzog 2001 72–93). From its beginning, the Western discipline was established 'to prove the veracity of Scripture'. The main push behind archaeological research in Palestine was the country's relationship with the Old and New Testaments. This drive to authenticate the Bible also determined the choice of archaeological sites; the first excavators in Jericho and Nablus (Shechem) were biblical researchers who were looking for the remains of the cities mentioned in the Bible (Herzog 2001: 72–93, 1999: 6–8). Biblical archaeology also became an index of diplomatic prestige for the European powers in their scramble for the Holy Land.

One of the shaping events in biblical historiography was the story of how the land was seized from the Canaanites by the Israelite tribes led by

Joshua. Under the British Palestine Mandate this biblical paradigm and the land conquest narrative dominated Western biblical archaeology, which gathered momentum with the activity of William Foxwell Albright (1946), an American academic from Johns Hopkins University, who then came to epitomise 'Oriental Studies' in the West (Long 2003: 141). The son of a Christian priest, Albright arrived in Palestine in December 1919, at the age of 28, to begin his postgraduate research as the Thayer Fellow of the American School in Jerusalem; the following year he became director of the school, a position he held between 1920 and 1929 and again from 1933 to 1936. Albright began excavating in Palestine in the 1920s. His declared position was that biblical archaeology was the scientific means to refute the critical claims against the historical veracity of the biblical stories (Long 1997), particularly those of the Julian Wellhausen school in Germany.[22] For several decades Albright and his students would deploy linguistics and biblical archaeology to authenticate the historicity of the Hebrew Bible. The Wellhausen school of biblical criticism, which had developed in Germany in the second half of the nineteenth century, challenged the historicity of the biblical stories and claimed that biblical narrative was articulated during the Jewish Babylonian exile – the later reconstruction of events being made with a theological purpose. Albright, for his part, believed that the Bible is a historical document which reflected the ancient reality. As a biblicist Zionist, he was convinced that the ancient remains of Palestine would provide proof of the historical truth of the events relating to the Jewish people: their 'rights' to the land; the period of the patriarchs; the Canaanite cities that were 'destroyed' by the Israelites as Joshua conquered the land; the boundaries of the twelve tribes, and so forth (Herzog 1999: 6–8).

During the Mandatory period large-scale excavations were conducted by Albright and his students to create a reliable history of the Bible. These Western archaeologists brushed aside the historical and contemporary social realities of Arab and Muslim Palestine in favour of the biblical paradigm; for them the Palestinian uprisings raging in the late 1920s and 1930s meant little 'in comparison to the eternal verities' of the Bible (Long 2003: 143). Their efforts to rewrite the history of Palestine and to exclude the indigenous inhabitants of the land contributed to the overall Zionist project, with disastrous consequences for the Palestinian quest

for self-determination during the Mandatory period. For the Albright-
ians Palestine was simply a 'biblical space' and the cradle of the 'Judeo-
Christian tradition' – a landscape created by Old Testament declarations
of God's purposes and promises, a space to be excavated and recovered
through archaeology and relived through Jewish political restoration to
Palestine (Long 2003: 140, 143-6); archeology laid bare the birthplace of
the Bible, Albright wrote in 1922, the

> land where the sacredest of human possessions came into being, and [where]
> hardly a mile of its surface is not hallowed by Biblical associations. In the
> illustration, elucidation, and, if need be, confirmation of this masterpiece
> of world literature archaeology justifies itself finely.[23]

In the same year Albright wrote in the *Bulletin of the American Schools
of Oriental Research*:

> These unassuming mounds among the hills of Ephraim and Benjamin are of
> greatest interest to us ... They represent authentic monuments of the Israelite
> past. Every stone and potsherd they conceal is hallowed by us by association
> with the great names of the Bible. We can think of the tells which mark
> ancient Mizpah and Gibeah without a thrill as memory calls up the shade of
> Samuel, and the heroic figure of Saul.[24]

Adopting a virtually fundamentalist approach to archaeology, Albright
and his pupils based the sites of excavation on biblical names: Megiddo (the
site of the biblical Armageddon), Lachish, Gezer, Shechem (Nablus), Jericho, Jerusalem, Ai, Giveon, Beit Shean (Baysan), Beit Shemesh, Taanach
and Hazor (Herzog 1999: 6-8), the last the site of the ancient Canaanite
city-state mentioned in the book of Joshua, the same city whose subsequent
excavation later became a major landmark in the history of mobilised
Israeli archaeology (Silberman and Small 1997: 21).

In 1949 Albright wrote that only 'a few diehards among older scholars'
had not accepted the essential historicity of the patriarchal traditions in
the light of archaeological data, and that it was no longer fashionable to
view those traditions as artificial creations by the scribes of the monarchic
period (1949b: 3). He repeated this statement fourteen years later (1963:
1-2). Until the early 1970s biblical archaeology was convinced that the
Bible accurately reflected the material world where it developed. Studies
such as *The Archaeology of Palestine* (1949) and *The Biblical Period from*

Abraham to Ezra (1949a, 1963) by Albright, *A History of Israel* (1980) by John Bright, *The Land of the Bible* (1967) by Yohanan Aharoni, and *Archeology in the Holy Land* (1960) by Kathleen Mary Kenyon used archaeology to demonstrate the historical accuracy of the Bible. These political histories uncritically accepted the biblical traditions as reliable reflections of past events. The Western archaeologists involved were not on the margins of archaeology, but rather prominent figures in their field; for instance, Dame Kathleen Kenyon (1906–1978), who conducted extensive excavations at Jericho from 1952 until 1958, was the eldest daughter of Sir Frederic Kenyon, a biblical scholar and later director of the British Museum.[25] She was the first female president of the Oxford Archeological Society and contributed to the foundation of the Institute of Archaeology of University College London. In 1962 Kenyon was appointed Principal of St Hugh's College, University of Oxford.

During the same Albrightian period, similar arguments were formulated by the Hebrew archaeology of the Yishuv, whose links to the archaeology of the State of Israel and Jewish nation-building have been discussed elsewhere (Abu El-Haj 2001; Elon 1997a: 35–47; Silberman 1989). After 1948 a nationalist Hebrew archaeology became a cornerstone of an Israeli civic religion, testifying to Jewish claims to the land (Rose 2004). But the new state-driven Israeli archaeology did not emerge in a vacuum. By the 1960s attempts had already begun to separate the archaeology of ancient Palestine from biblical and theological studies. As we shall see in Chapter 7, broadly speaking the collapse over the last two decades of the historicity of the narrative described in the Hebrew Bible, Iron Age I, has been the result of several factors, including the emergence of new archaeological evidence, literary criticism and a post-colonial critique of biblical studies.

The 1967 War and the Rise of 'Crusading' American Fundamentalism

In the early twentieth century, following the devastating toll of the First World War, and then the 'Great Depression', American evangelical fundamentalism appeared to be more preoccupied with refuting critical biblical theories and theological liberalism in the USA and less with political

Zionism and prophetic politics. This situation radically changed after the 1967 war, which was a turning point for American evangelism and Jewish religious nationalism. The war marked a significant watershed for evangelical Christian interest in Israel and Zionism. With the occupation of East Jerusalem and the West Bank – while liberal Protestant organisations such as the World Council of Churches increasingly distanced themselves from Zionism – Israeli expansionist policies fuelled enthusiasm among conservative American evangelicals. Moreover, while in the nineteenth century the Holy Land was reimagined and constructed by the expertise of British restorationists and prophetic biblical scholars for the benefit of the British imperial project, since 1948 the Holy Land has been appropriated and constructed by the expertise of Israeli orientalists for the benefit of both the Israeli colonial project and the American empire. The success of the representations of the Palestinians by both biblical and orientalist Zionists (both Christian and Jews) effectively suppressed the Palestinian capacity for self-representation.

Karen Armstrong (1988: 377) traces in modern Christian Zionism evidence of the Western legacy of the Crusades. Christian fundamentalists have, she argues, 'returned to a classical and extreme religious crusading'. Of course the Latin Crusaders were – like Christian Zionists of the post-Reformation period – religious fundamentalists. The idea of Muslim (or Jewish) control of the Christian holy places in Jerusalem was anathema to them. They attacked Muslims, persecuted Jews, and declared a 'holy war' against all manner of people. Historians have examined in detail the lasting impact of the Latin Crusaders and have traced the devastating consequences of the sacralising of medieval European military designs to claim the Holy Land for the church and get rid of 'infidels' – that is, Muslims and Jews (Runciman 1954; Armstrong 1988). As Pope Urban II put it in 1095, 'wrest the land from the wicked race'.[26] For the Crusaders, Muslims and Jews had no 'religious rights' in Jerusalem. They also looked down on the Orthodox Church and wanted its leaders out of the way. The conquest of Jerusalem by the Crusaders on 15 July 1099 started a new period of terror against Muslims and Jews, all of whom were driven out of the city, their mosques and synagogues destroyed. The city became exclusively Christian. The al-Aqsa Mosque, the third holiest shrine in Islam, and the Dome of the Rock were turned into Christian churches.

The Templars took over the al-Aqsa Mosque, and the Dome of the Rock was consecrated as the 'House of the Lord' in 1142, with a gilded cross placed above the dome; the Holy Sepulchre, which was renewed and enlarged, was entrusted to the Hospitallers (Cragg 1992: 102). Roy H. May, Jr, writing in *Joshua and the Promised Land*, notes:

> During the Middle Ages, European Christians launched military campaigns to take the Holy Land from the Muslims. Early on the Crusaders took Jericho. Following the example of Joshua 6, they marched around the city led by clergy carrying sacred banners and pictures of Christian saints. When the walls did not fall down as expected, they attacked and overran the city. Then they massacred the inhabitants. Jews were locked in their synagogue and burned alive. Even some of the Crusaders were horrified by the slaughter.[27]

Such religious arrogance and the consequent extermination of the Jewish and Muslim inhabitants of Jerusalem by the European Crusaders unleashed a spiral of barbaric savagery which has fermented for a thousand years, each side locked in what Armstrong calls 'a murderous triangle of hatred and intolerance' (Armstrong 1988: xii). Bishop Kenneth Cragg draws some important conclusions about the effect of the Latin Crusades (1095–1291) on the 'eastern' psyche:

> Whatever the problematics of the Arab Christian East of the Greek associa-tion, those of the Latin West were, for the most part, blatant and malign. They had to do not with the subtleties and strife of theology but with arrogance and intrusion. The western, Latin Rome saw the Christian East in terms of juridical dominance and ecclesiastical power.... The Crusades became an enduring symbol of malignancy as well as heroism, of open imperialism and private piety.... They left noble piles of architecture on the eastern landscape but seared the eastern soul. They gave Arab Muslims through every succeeding century a warrant of memory to hold against Christian Arabs as, by association, liable to pseudo-Arabness or worse.
>
> What the crusaders did to the eastern psyche, Muslim and Christian, long outlived their tenure of the Latin Kingdom of Jerusalem.... The image of them is one that no century since has been able to exorcise. (Cragg 1992: 23)

The crusading kingdom in Jerusalem lasted eighty-eight years from 1099 to 1187, when Salah al-Din (Saladin) recovered the city from the Latins. His *qadi*, al-Fadil, however, paid a generous tribute to the physical legacy of the expelled crusaders:

Islam received back a place which it had left almost uninhabited, but which the care of the unbelievers had transformed into a paradise garden. ... Those accused ones defended with lance and sword this city which they had rebuilt with columns and slabs of marble, where they had founded churches and palaces of the Templers and the Hospitallers ... houses as pleasant as their gardens which made them look like living trees. (quoted in Cragg 1992: 101)

After the eviction of the Crusaders from the Holy Land in 1291, Christians were compelled to translate their conception of Jerusalem from early to a *heavenly* one. The Crusaders not only unleashed a huge conflict with Islam, but also set in motion a great earthly contest between the Eastern and Western churches for control of the holy places, above all the Holy Sepulchre in Jerusalem and the Church of the Nativity in Bethlehem. Unable to agree among themselves, the squabbling Christian sects agreed in 1289 to hand over the keys of the Church of the Holy Sepulchre to a Muslim family for safekeeping (Wasserstein 2002: 9). This Muslim family still has the keys to the Holy Sepulchre. When the last Crusader fortress in Palestine, at Acre, fell in 1291, the main Latin institutional presence in Palestine was that of the Franciscans, who had first arrived in 1217. In the early fourteenth century the Pope appointed them to the 'Custody of the Holy Land' (*Custodia Terrae Sancta*). This stronghold of Roman Christianity fought major battles with the Eastern Churches over control of the holy places in Jerusalem. This fight carried on into modern times; it is still going on. This struggle between the various Christian denominations over control of the holy places dominated many aspects of Christian life in Jerusalem, but was also linked with the diplomatic rivalry of the great powers (Russia, France, Britain) in relation to the city. For both Christians and Jews, in many ways, the holy city was at once a symbol of unity and the fault line of deep internal schisms and differences (Wasserstein 2002: 9).

Many scholars have observed that the combination of the founding of the State of Israel in 1948, the capture of Jerusalem and the West Bank in 1967, and the defeat on both occasions of the combined Arab armies, all contributed to the rise in America of prophetic politics. These events increasingly came to be seen as significant fulfilment of biblical prophecy by a new crusading generation of evangelical American and European fundamentalists (Ruether and Ruether 2002; Anderson 2005). For example, Jerry Falwell did not begin to speak about modern-day Israel until after Israel's 1967 military victory. James Price and William Goodman wrote:

> Falwell changed completely. He entered into politics and became an avid supporter of the Zionist State ... the stunning Israeli victory made a big impact not only on Falwell, but on a lot of Americans. ... Remember that in 1967, the United States was mired in the Vietnam war. Many felt a sense of defeat, helplessness and discouragement. As Americans we were made acutely aware of our own diminished authority, of no longer being able to police the world or perhaps even our own neighbourhoods ... [m]any Americans, including Falwell, turned worshipful glances toward Israel, which they viewed as militarily strong and invincible. They gave their unstinting approval to the Israeli take-over of Arab lands because they perceived this conquest as power and righteousness. ... Macho or muscular Christians such as Falwell credited Israeli General Moshe Dayan with this victory over Arab forces and termed him the Miracle Man of the Age, and the Pentagon invited him to Vietnam and tell us how to win that war.[28]

In July 1967, shortly after the war, Billy Graham's father-in-law, L. Nelson Bell, the editor of *Christianity Today*, a highly influential organ of American conservative evangelicalism, appeared to express the sentiments of many American evangelicals when, in an 'editorial', he wrote: 'That for the first time in more than 2,000 years Jerusalem is now completely in the hands of the Jews gives a student of the Bible a thrill and a renewed faith in the accuracy and validity of the Bible.'[29]

The concentration on 'earthly political Jerusalem' is central to post-1967 pro-Zionist Christian fundamentalism. For Christians the sanctity of Jerusalem derives wholly from the events associated with the life, death and resurrection of Jesus. The city witnessed the birth of the faith. For Christians – even for those who have not visited Jerusalem – places such as the Via Dolorosa, the Mount of Olives, the Garden of Gethsemane conjure up very powerful images. Of course devotion to the 'sacred geography' of Jerusalem is a phenomenon also found in Islam and Judaism.[30] Although Jerusalem was not founded by Jews, Christians or Muslims – it is one of the oldest cities on earth, founded by the Jebusites, who belonged to a Canaanite tribe, about 5,000 years ago – the city, for different reasons, become central to the 'sacred geography' of the three Abrahamic faiths (Armstrong 1996: xiv). Such is the symbolic power of this ancient city that its future status poses a major obstacle to a comprehensive regional peace in the Middle East. Furthermore, the religious attitudes towards the 'sacred geography' of Jerusalem – the Jewish, Christian and Muslim 'holinesses' of the city – have evolved historically and will continue to do so, under ever-changing social and political conditions (Wasserstein 2002).

The emerging Christian faith generally detached itself from the old biblical paradigm of the centrality of 'promised land' and 'chosen people' (Cragg 1992: 239), although for Christianity – as for Judaism – throughout history tension existed between the concept of *heavenly, spiritual* Jerusalem and the reality of *earthly, physical and political* Jerusalem. Historically speaking, however, there is no evidence to suggest that Christians attached any particular sanctity to Jerusalem until the fourth century and it is only then that we find the first recorded account of a Christian pilgrimage to Jerusalem (Wasserstein 2002: 7). Until the fourth century we encounter two distinct theological views of Jerusalem among Christians. The first view is represented by St Jerome (337–420 AD) who, in the fourth century, went on pilgrimage to the Holy Land and spent the last thirty-four years of his life in a monastery in Bethlehem. St Jerome argued that Jerusalem was part of the Christian faith, 'to adore where His feet have stood and to see the vestiges of the nativity, of the Cross, and of the passion'. The second view was represented by St Gregory of Nyssa (also in the fourth century AD), who wrote to a disciple, 'When the Lord invites the blest to their inheritance in the Kingdom of Heaven, he does not include a pilgrimage to Jerusalem among their good deeds.' Also, in contrast to the views of Eusebius (*c.* 260–341 AD), Bishop of Caesarea in Palestine, the 'Father of Church History, Cyril of Jerusalem (*c.* 320–386 AD) maintained that the 'prerogative of all good things was in Jerusalem'. Either way, the turning point in the conception of the 'sanctity' of Jerusalem was the fourth century. Recent scholarship has actually focused on the struggle in the fourth century within the church between those who affirmed the 'sanctity' of Jerusalem and those who tended to play it down. P.W.L. Walker cites the dismissive views of Eusebius regarding Jerusalem's 'holiness'; his opinion derived partly from competition between Jerusalem and Caesarea. But Walker also argues that the 'dismissive view' was born of a desire to combat an incorrect emphasis on the 'physical earthly Jerusalem' (Wasserstein 2002: 7). From the fourth century onward, however, 'holy Jerusalem' became the dominant view of the Church (Walker 1994: 351; Wasserstein 2002: 7).

Under the Byzantine Emperor Constantine, the triumph of the Christian theological view of Jerusalem's 'holiness' was an outcome not only of debate among the Church Fathers but also of the political triumph of the Emperor Constantine, who ruled Jerusalem from 324 AD. The famous journey of his mother Helena to Jerusalem, to identify the sites of the Crucifixion and resurrection, marked a radical turning point in the church history of the city. The Church of the Holy Sepulchre (known to the Byzantines as the Church of the Resurrection, or Anastasis) was erected over the tomb at Constantine's command and inaugurated in 335 AD, replacing the temple of Aphrodite at the same location.[31] Like so many other holy places and shrines in Jerusalem, the Holy Sepulchre from its very outset gave physical expression to a competitive religious spirit – in this case between Christianity and paganism. With Helena's visit, Jerusalem became firmly established as a centre of veneration and pilgrimage for Christians. The Christian glorification of Jerusalem and external financial support for religious intuitions all date back to the Byzantine period (Wasserstein 2002: 7).

In the early Muslim period, in the seventh century, the Christians formed a majority of the population in the city; there was even a Christian governor of the province of Jerusalem. On Christmas Day 800 AD, the coronation day of Charlemagne in Rome, the new emperor was reported to have received the key to Church of the Holy Sepulchre and the flag of the holy city as a token of respect from the patriarch of Jerusalem (and according to one account from the Abbasid Caliph Harun al-Rashid himself). While the city was under Muslim rule, Charlemagne and his son Louis built many new Christian institutions in Jerusalem (Wasserstein 2002: 7). There was a certain amount of competition between Muslims and Christians over construction work in Jerusalem: in 827 AD, some Muslims complained that Christians had built a bigger dome over a church than that over the Muslim Shrine of the Dome of the Rock (Wasserstein 2002: 7). But the latter, an Islamic masterpiece erected by the Umayyad Caliph 'Abd al-Malik with the skills and crafts of Christian artisans, remained the most exquisite edifice in the city. The magisterial splendour of the Dome of the Rock, as Bishop Cragg remarks, was an index to such approximation by conquerors to the conquered taking place in all the spheres to which architecture belong – art, prestige, identity, faith, and perpetuity.

Perhaps the prime purpose of the Dome of the Rock lay in serving notice on Christianity that a suppression was under way. Its splendor would certainly outshine the Church of the Resurrection hard by. The choice of Jerusalem for its site could hardly be misread nor the import of its quality. The calligraphy, moreover, from the Quran had largely to do with the passages incriminating Christology and the doctrine of the Trinity and underlining the role of Jesus as prophet and as exemplary 'Muslim'. The scribes and ceramicists of Christendom were thus employed to join the issues between the caliph and patriarch ... The Dome of the Rock was in this way the sign and the herald of *Dar al-Islam* [the House of Islam], the realm of displaced creed and of the replaced power and the shape of their interaction. (Cragg 1992: 53-4)

The rise of highly influential Christian Zionism in the USA was particularly noticeable in the 1980s and 1990s. The collapse of the Soviet Union, the rise of radical Islam, the first American-led Gulf War against Iraq (1990-91), and the approaching third millennium fuelled a fervent rhetoric among north American premillennial dispensationalists, while the same anti-Arab prejudices and orientalist stereotypes continued. Some call American Christian dispensationalist fundamentalists the 'Armageddon Lobby'; others have referred to them as the 'Christian AIPAC' (Haija 2006: 75-95). Biblical *Armageddon* incorporates the Hebrew name *Megiddo*, referring to the plains of Esdraelon and Megiddo, an area in Palestine south-east of Haifa stretching towards Nazareth, north of the Carmel mountain range. For the dispensationalists the biblically predicted Battle of Armageddon, the final battle between the forces of light and darkness (Barr 1977: 190), signals the end of this age and the beginning of the earthly reign of Jesus Christ. Barr writes:

Dispensationalism is a totally fundamentalist scheme. Liberal and critical analysis lie almost entirely below its horizon. While 'orthodox' fundamentalism is very busy in polemics against modern criticism, once we get to the dispensationalist world we are in a very different atmosphere: here liberal and critical perceptions scarcely need to be combated, because they scarcely exist ... Dispensationalism ... though it may say with general fundamentalism that the Bible is in principle a human book as well as divinely-inspired holy scripture, in fact goes a good deal farther in treating it as a direct transcript of the divine will ... the surface markings of the biblical texts are a direct transcript of God's will and future plans. (Barr 1977: 197-8)

During the 1980s, under the Reagan administration, there was an upsurge in evangelical Christian Zionism and dispensationalist prophetic politics. The growth in political readings of the books of Daniel and Revelation seemed to encourage belligerency in US foreign policy, even to provide ideological legitimation for unleashing nuclear war as a step in 'God's plan for the end of the world' (Halsell 1986).[32] In her book *Prophecy and Politics: Militant Evangelists on the Road to Nuclear War*, Grace Halsell, who was a White House speechwriter under Lyndon Johnson, observes:

> Convinced that a nuclear Armageddon is an inevitable event within the divine scheme of things, many evangelical dispensationalists have committed themselves to a course for Israel that, by their own admission, will lead directly to a holocaust indescribably more savage and widespread than any vision of carnage that could have generated in Adolf Hitler's criminal mind. (1986: 195)

The Reagan administration, closely aligning itself with the Israeli Likud government, enabled the evangelical Christian Zionists to expand their political influence in Washington DC. The first Bush administration, which proclaimed after the Gulf War and the collapse of the Soviet Union in 1991 the 'New World Order' led by America, however, remained restrained in its support for the evangelical Zionists. According to Wagner there are a number of evangelical Christian Zionist leaders even more right wing than Jerry Falwell and Pat Robertson, who in the 1980s had direct access to President Reagan and the White House. Among them are Terry Risenhoover and Doug Krieger, who in the early 1980s were the prime movers providing support for the 'Temple Mount Faithful', a radical Israeli organisation based in Jerusalem. Both evangelical Christian Zionists and the Temple Mount Faithful support the destruction of the Dome of the Rock and al-Aqsa Mosque and the rebuilding of the Third Jewish Temple; for fundamentalist evangelicals, however, these acts are necessary for the return of Jesus.[33] The Likud Israeli government, for its part, was keen on exploiting to the full this Christian–Zionist coalition and in the spring of 1991, following the Gulf War, the Israeli Ministry of Tourism hired the fundamentalist musician Pat Boone – described by 'Guided Group Tours of Israel' as 'Entertainer, Christian Ambassador for Tourism to the Evangelical Community'[34] – to promote pilgrimages in

North America through a series of advertisements in evangelical journals and on television (Wagner 1992).

Typically, contemporary Christian Zionist lobbyists – like their British nineteenth-century counterparts Shaftesbury and Oliphant – are completely oblivious to the consequences of Zionism and its biblical paradigm for the indigenous inhabitants of Palestine. They are completely in denial about the Palestinian Nakba of 1948. They blindly subscribe to one major tenet: they see the founding of the State of Israel in 1948 as highly significant, even signalling the end of 2,000 years of 'Jewish exile'. Christian Zionists – like Jewish Zionists – equate 1948 as another 'Exodus', a return to the 'promised land' in fulfilment of biblical prophecy and Divine blessing. Of course this theological interpretation of the historical events surrounding the founding of the secular State of Israel in 1948 is highly controversial. To begin with, both peoples, the Israeli Jewish settlers and the indigenous Palestinian Arabs, not only claim the same land, but endow the same locations with different place names and religious significance. Both peoples also promote rival and contradictory nationalist histories of the 1948 events, with the Israelis celebrating their independence and the Palestinians mourning their Nakba. Therefore it is difficult for both Western tourists and Christian pilgrims visiting the Holy Land to maintain a neutral position. As British scholar Glenn Bowman has observed, most tourists, in accord with the Israeli Ministry of Tourism, call the land 'Israel', but in United Nations terminology the land is 'Israel and the Occupied Territories'. This variance in nomenclature reflects a deeper issue of identity; Israel with the area it occupied in the 1967 war constitutes a deeply, and violently, divided country (Bowman 1991: 121–34).

Christian Zionism, the Israel Lobby and Armageddon: The Shaping of US Policy on Israel–Palestine

There are a number of similarities between nineteenth-century British and twentieth-century American attitudes to Israel. In both, as the international power brokers of their day, religion and politics became inextricably entwined. In the closing decades of the nineteenth and the early twentieth century, there was a convergence of British strategic colonial interests and Christian Zionism within significant segments of the intellectual and political intelligentsia. Likewise current American foreign policy in the Middle East largely coincides with that of the powerful Christian Zionist lobby (Chomsky 1983). Both parties, now as then, favour a strong and dominant pro-American presence in the Middle East, whether for pragmatic reasons of military strategy, or because it conforms to their particular eschatology. Among a consensus of American Christian fundamentalist leaders, these twin motives, religious and political, are unashamedly connected and intrinsic to a predicted apocalyptic scenario, which one writer has gone so far as to describe as 'Operation Desert Storm II' (Dyer 1991: 232).

Clearly the Christian Zionist lobby, with its influence among powerful elites in the United States, has become a major factor in US policy towards the Middle East – a policy whose centrepiece since 1967 has been the US relationship with Israel. Since 1973, Washington has provided Israel with a level of support dwarfing that given to any other state. Israel has been the largest annual recipient of direct economic and military assistance since 1976, and is the largest recipient in total since World War II, to the tune of well over $140 billion (in 2004 dollars). Israel receives about $3 billion in direct assistance each year, roughly one-fifth of the foreign aid budget.[35] The Christian Zionist lobby is also a major component of the 'Israel Lobby'. In an important recent article in the *London Review of Books* two US scholars, John Mearsheimer and Stephen Walt, of Chicago and Harvard universities respectively, argued that US Middle East policy derives almost entirely from the activities of the 'Israel Lobby', which exerts a 'stranglehold' on this policy and inhibits public debate of the issue. The Israel Lobby is described by Mearsheimer and Walt as follows:

> The Lobby includes prominent Christian evangelicals like Gary Bauer, Jerry Falwell, Ralph Reed and Pat Robertson, as well as Dick Armey and Tom DeLay, former majority leaders in the House of Representatives, all of whom believe Israel's rebirth is the fulfilment of biblical prophecy and support its expansionist agenda; to do otherwise, they believe, would be contrary to God's will. Neo-conservative gentiles such as John Bolton; Robert Bartley, the former *Wall Street Journal* editor; William Bennett, the former secretary of education; Jeane Kirkpatrick, the former UN ambassador; and the influential columnist George Will are also steadfast supporters.[36]

The Christian Zionist lobby includes the following advocacy organisations based in Washington DC: Christians' Israel Public Action Campaign, The International Christian Embassy in Jerusalem, Christian Coalition, Southern Baptist Convention, Bridges for Peace, Jerusalem Friendship Fund, Jerusalem Prayer Team, Stand With Israel, Christian Broadcasting Network, International Fellowship of Christians and Jews, Family Research Council, Council for National Policy, and Christians for Israel/USA (Salaita 2006: 170).

In America the 'Israel Lobby' realised the potential significance of wooing the political endorsement of the powerful 50-60 million evangelical block-vote through their evangelical leadership and through evangelical television personalities, most of whom are Christian Zionists (Salaita 2006: 170). In the 1980 presidential elections, 80 per cent of US evangelicals supported the conservative wing of the Republican Party, and Ronald Reagan in particular (Wagner 1992). In 2000 George W. Bush received roughly 50 million votes – 30 million of them from evangelical Christians, of whom approximately 15 million were dispensationalists. The percentage of Christian Zionists voting for Bush in 2004 was similar (Salaita 2006: 170). The faith of Bush is seen in his frequent incorporation of the Scriptures into his speeches, in his personal commitment to biblicist Zionism, and in his sympathy for Christian fundamentalism (Mansfield 2003). His civilising Christian imperialism and Middle East policies are powerfully shaped by a Christian supremacist vision, oil imperialism and the belief that an American-Israeli alliance is central to US domination of the Middle East.

Earlier in May 2002, following the Israeli army's re-invasion and re-occupation of the West Bank, *Time* magazine published an article under the title: 'Right's New Crusade: Lobbying for Israel', which stated: 'Today the most influential lobbying on behalf of Israel is being done by a group not usually seen as an ally of the largely Democratic Jewish community: Evangelical Christians.'[37] In 1976-77 several events occurred simultaneously which had the effect of accelerating the influence of Christian Zionism as a political phenomenon in America. A religious and political marriage was consummated between American Zionist organisations, the Israeli leadership and Christian fundamentalists.[38] In 1977 the Likud Party under Menahem Begin came to power on an expansionist Zionist platform using biblical phraseology to justify the settlement of the West Bank. It was Begin, for example, who intensified the colonisation of the occupied territories, and insisted on the use of biblical terms such 'Judaea and Samaria' to justify the occupation and colonisation of the West Bank.[39]

Although fundamentalist sermons through Sunday school lessons and Bible reading have influenced the belief of a large number of evangelical Christians in the USA, the actual dispensationalist doctrine or Armageddon theology appear to have influenced smaller but highly active groups (Anderson 2005: 41). However, with this in mind, in 1979, the Israeli government honoured Jerry Falwell with the Jabotinsky Award in appreciation of his support of Israel. They also provided him with a Lear jet to assist in his work on their behalf.[40]

American prophetic politics is not confined to hard-line evangelicals and the Christian right; it was also propagated by leading moderate evangelicals such as President Jimmy Carter, who, in 2002, was given the Nobel Peace Prize for his commitment to non-violent problem-solving. In 1977, Carter, a Southern-born Baptist and Democrat, became America's first evangelical president. His presidency was a catalyst for evangelical political activism in the 1970s, laying the basis for its key role in American political life under three successive US presidents, including Ronald Reagan, and the two Bush presidents. Carter, the first American president to place American evangelism at the centre of the American political agenda, also applied his biblical beliefs to US policy towards Israel–Palestine (Carter 1985). In a speech in 1978 he explained how he saw the State of Israel as

> A return at last, to the Biblical land from which the Jews were driven so many hundreds of years ago ... The establishment of the nation of Israel is the fulfilment of Biblical prophecy and the very essence of its fulfilment.[41]

In another speech, this time given before the Israeli Knesset in March 1979, Carter dwelt on the special relationship between America and Israel, stressing how

> It has been and it is a unique relationship. And it is a relationship that is indestructible, because it is rooted in the consciousness and the morals and the religion and the beliefs of the American people themselves ... Israel and the United States were shaped by pioneers – my nation is also a nation of

immigrants and refugees – by peoples gathered in both nations from many lands ... We share the heritage of the Bible.[42]

President Carter made several trips to the Middle East, where he met both Israeli and Palestinian leaders. His recollection of those meetings demonstrates a certain political naivety, especially when faced with the reality of the denial of basic human rights among the Palestinians under Israeli occupation; although out of office, and especially more recently, he has shown greater sensitivity to Palestinian rights. But more crucially his conservative evangelical roots were evident in the fact that following the failure of the Camp David agreements to solve the issue of Palestine, he came to believe the Israel–Palestine conflict could not be solved by the intervention of the international community, or pressure from the America administration, Israel's chief sponsor, but only by internal Israeli changes effected by the Israeli electorate alone (Carter 1985: 60).

Carter's eventual downfall was, in part, due to the loss of the evangelical fundamentalist block vote and the support of the Christian right. The religious conservatives within the USA ultimately used their power to replace Carter with President Ronald Reagan, who more carefully articulated their religious and political agenda. The Christian pro-Israeli forces came to play a major role in the post-Carter era, and the Reagan presidency itself publicly subscribed to a premillennial dispensational theology. These groups centred on Evangelicals Concern for Israel (including well-known figures such as Pat Boone and Vernon Grounds); and on the Moral Majority as a political campaigning organisation under Jerry Falwell. With a sympathetic administration, the Christian right groups all combined to give a considerable boost to the Israel Lobby in the USA.

The election of President Reagan in 1980 ushered in not only the most pro-Israel administration in history but gave several Christian Zionists prominent political posts. In addition to the president, those who subscribed to a futurist premillennial theology and Christian Zionism included Attorney General Ed Meese, Secretary of Defense Casper Weinberger, and Secretary of the Interior James Watt. Evangelical Christian Zionist televangelists and writers were given direct access to the president and to Cabinet members, Falwell, Christian Zionist televangelist Mike Evans and author Hal Lindsey among them (Wagner 1992). 'White House Seminars' became a regular feature of Reagan's administration, bringing

Christian Zionists into direct personal contact with national and congressional leaders. In a personal conversation reported in the *Washington Post* in April 1984, Reagan told the chief Israeli lobbyist, Tom Dine:

> You know, I turn back to the ancient prophets in the Old Testament and the signs foretelling Armageddon, and I find myself wondering if – if we're the generation that is going to see that come about. I don't know if you've noted any of these prophecies lately, but believe me they certainly describe the times we're going through.[13]

For Christian fundamentalists such as Falwell, America is seen as the great redeemer, its role in the world providentially and politically preordained (Lienesch 1993: 197). The two nations of America and Israel are like Siamese twins, linked not only by common self-interest but more significantly by similar religious foundations. Together they were perceived to be pitted against an evil world dominated by communist and Islamic regimes antithetical to the values of America and Israel (Simon 1984: 63-4, 71-2).

Traditionally, US policy has dwelt with the issue of Jerusalem by the continued presence of an embassy in Tel Aviv and a consulate in Arab East Jerusalem. The East Jerusalem consulate is the most interesting US diplomatic mission in the Middle East. It represents the Arabist front line against the pro-Israel section of the State Department, as represented by the US embassy in Tel Aviv, forty-five minutes away with no crossing points in between. The consulate building in Arab East Jerusalem was a rebuke to the State of Israel. It was, to all intents and purposes, an American embassy located on territory controlled by the Israeli government. But the consulate did not recognise the Israeli government in Jerusalem; nor did it primarily deal with Israelis. Its main purpose was to deal with Palestinians in Jerusalem and the West Bank under Israeli military rule. Because the United States did not recognise Jerusalem as Israel's capital, the consulate tried to insist that when the US ambassador to Israel visited Jerusalem from Tel Aviv he should not fly the American flag on the hood of his limousine. Jerusalem was the consulate's turf, not the embassy's. The consulate in East Jerusalem, a graceful old stone building near the medieval Arab souk, was Arab, while the embassy, situated on a noisy and garish street in the heart of Jewish Tel Aviv, clearly was not. A war raged between the two installations (Kaplan 1993: 193).[14] Although

George Bush promised to move the American embassy to Jerusalem, in reality his administration successfully deflected congressional pressures in favour of relocation.

Dispensationalist Perspectives on Jerusalem: Armageddon Theology and the Building of the Third Temple

Proponents of contemporary Christian Zionism insist that the movement is mandated in both Old and New Testaments, which, they claim, are the source of their motivation (Wagner 1995: 97-113).[45] Christian Zionists – like their Jewish counterparts – talk about the 'unbroken chain of Jewish presence' in the city, from the earliest times to the rise of Zionism in the late nineteenth century. While Jerusalem was central in the religious imagination, this was never in fact translated into political, social, economical, demographic, cultural and intellectual realities. Indeed, Jerusalem was never a major centre for Judaism during the last 2,000 years. Religiously, of course, the city has been at the heart of Jewish religious thought and symbolism. Its 'holiness' for Jews derives from the perception that it was the site of the temple (Wasserstein 2002: 3-4). Hal Lindsey, one of the most influential US Christian Zionist fundamentalists and the 'Father of the Modern-Day Bible Prophecy Movement', wrote:

> Long ago the psalmist predicted the final mad attempt of the confederated Arab armies to destroy the nation of Israel. … The Palestinians are determined to trouble the world until they repossess what they feel is their land. The Arab nations consider it a matter of racial honour to destroy the State of Israel. Islam considers it a sacred mission of religious honour to recapture Old Jerusalem. (Lindsey 1983: 38-9)

It is important politically for the Israelis and Christian Zionism to predicate a constant and enduring Jewish presence in the city for 2,000 years (Wasserstein 2002: 2). Bernard Wasserstein, a distinguished British Jewish historian, argues that the historical evidence for this claim is highly questionable. He explains that Jews were even forbidden to enter the city throughout the period of Roman and Byzantine rule. Although some Jewish pilgrims appear to have visited Jerusalem, there is no evidence of a Jewish community in Jerusalem for five centuries between the second and seventh centuries (Wasserstein 2002: 2). The traditional anti-Jewish view was reflected in the writings of the 'Father of Church History', Eusebius, metropolitan bishop of Caesarea (260-339 AD), who believed that Jerusalem could be rebuilt only with the 'Second Coming' of Jesus Christ, tried to account for 'why the Second Temple was destroyed':

> from that time seditions and wars and mischievous plots followed each other in quick succession, and never ceased in the city and in all Judea until finally the siege of Vespasian overwhelmed them. Thus the divine vengeance overtook the Jews for the crimes which they dared to commit against Christ.[46]

The belief in the 'Second Coming' of Christ was a major component of Christian thought and central to writings of early Christian theologians – but these writings have little to do with the doctrine of modern premillennialist dispensationalism, described below (Anderson 2005: 26), which lays considerable emphasis on the advent of Christ. (Barr 1977: 190-207).

Ironically, in the light of the fact that the current conflict over the city is mainly between Israeli Jews and predominantly Muslim Palestinians, it was only after the Arab conquest in 638 AD, when Muslims took over the city, that Jews were allowed to return to Jerusalem. In fact for most of its history, Christianity has had a worse record of persecuting Jews: with the Crusades, the Inquisition, the bloody religious wars of the sixteenth and seventeenth centuries, meaning that Europe saw far more blood spilt for religion's sake than did the Muslim world. A number of documents found in the Cairo *geniza* (a storeroom for old religious manuscripts, uncovered at the end of the nineteenth century) record the financial contribution of rich Jews in Egypt and Sicily towards the support of poor Jews in Jerusalem and the maintenance of a synagogue next to the Wailing Wall (Wasserstein 2002: 2), which, of course, is adjacent to the Muslim holy shrines the al-Aqsa Mosque and the Dome of the Rock situated on al-Haram al-Sharif (the Nobel Sanctuary) – the area situated in the south-east of the Old City, known in Hebrew as Mount Moria, supposedly the site of the Second Jewish Temple. Israeli architect Tuvia Sagiv argues that the total destruction of the Second Temple by Titus, the massive building programme by Hadrian and the cutting off of Jews from the city of Jerusalem all caused confusion in the identification of the site of the Temple. Thus, it was written in the third century AD that the Jews of Babylon could not identify the sight of the Temple.[47]

Jerusalem was central to the spiritual identity of Muslims from the very beginning of their faith. When the Prophet Muhammad first began to preach in Mecca in about 612 AD, according to the earliest biographies, he had his converts prostrate themselves in prayer in the direction of Jerusalem. Thus Jerusalem acquired a unique status as the first *Qibla* (direction of prayer) of Islam.[48] When the Muslims conquered the city, they identified the area as the 'Temple Mount', cleared the rubbbish that had gathered, and identified it as 'Solomon's Temple'. As the Quran states, it was to al-Aqsa that the Prophet Muhammad was carried on his 'Night Journey' from Mecca; and from the Rock of Abraham (in the Dome of the Rock), the patriarch of Islam and Judaism, the Prophet 'ascended' to the seventh heaven (*al-Israi wal-mi'iraj*). On this Quranic basis the al-Aqsa Mosque and the Dome of the Rock, the most beautiful of all Muslim shrines, were built on the site of 'Solomon's temple' (Gragg 1992: 52–3). According to Sagiv, with Muslim identification of the area as 'Solomon's temple', an error was begun (Gorenberg 2000: 74): European Christians, travellers, and later investigators all claimed that the walls of the al-Haram al-Sharif were the remnants of the Jewish Temple Mount. For many Christians, Muslims and Jews the identification of the Moriah Mount as delineated by the walls of the Temple Mount has become a fundamental principle which needs no proof.[49]

However, the fact that for centuries Muslim rulers allowed the Jewish community to build and maintain a Jewish synagogue next to the third holiest shrine of Islam is striking. For different reasons, however, both Israeli Jews and Palestinians prefer to gloss over the historical fact that Jewish and Muslim 'holy places' and holy spaces coexisted side by side in the city.[50]

The arguments put forward by dispensationalist Christians concerning Israel–Palestine rehash not only some of the official Israeli propaganda line on Jerusalem but the rhetoric of Jewish supporters of Greater Israel. The dispensationalists argue: (a) The Islamic claim to Jerusalem, including its claim to the 'Temple Mount', is in direct contradiction to the 'biblical and historical significance of the city and its holiest site', and this claim is of later religio-political origin rather than arising from any Quranic text or early Muslim tradition. (b) Because of the 'sovereign purposes of God for the City', Jerusalem must remain 'undivided, under Israeli sovereignty', the capital of Israel only, and all nations should so concur and place their embassies in Jerusalem. (c) The truths of God are sovereign and it is written that the 'Land which He promised to His People is not to be partitioned'. (d) It would be wrong for the nations to recognise a Palestinian state in any part of 'biblical *Eretz Yisrael*'. (e) The Golan Heights are part of 'biblical Israel' and are a 'vital strategic asset necessary for the security and defense of the entire country' – Greater Israel. (f) Christian theology which does not recognise the 'ongoing biblical purposes for Israel and the Jewish People' is doctrinal error. (g) Christians should seek to encourage and assist in the continuing process of 'Return of the Exiles to Eretz Israel' – and indeed tens of millions of dollars have been raised by Christian Zionist organisations in the USA and Europe and donated to Jewish settlers in the West Bank (Salaita 2006: 171).

There is, of course, a basic difference between Jewish and Christian fundamentalisms and mainstream and fundamentalist Muslim attitudes on the question of the shrines in the Old City. Palestinian Muslims in occupied East Jerusalem are on the defensive, struggling against the creeping Judaisation of the Old City (Masalha 1997: 229–30) and seeking to preserve the religious and prayer *status quo* on al-Haram al-Sharif,[51] while Jewish and Christian fundamentalists are on the offensive, running joint and well-funded campaigns in both Israel and the USA for the building of the Jewish Third Temple on al-Haram al-Sharif. The latter seek to alter the situation of the Muslim shrines radically, something which could result in a local and global conflagration.

For some Christian fundamentalist evangelicals, in particular, the 'Battle for Jerusalem' is the 'End of Days Battle of Armageddon'. Apparently in the USA some 60 million evangelical Christians adhere to this apocalyptic eschatology. In the 'Battle for Jerusalem', Christian fundamentalists have found common ground with Jewish religious radicals and hard-line Zionists. The fundamentalists share five tenets: (a) belief in the 'sanctity' of the modern State of Israel; (b) support for Greater Israel and Zionist territorial expansionism, including Jewish sovereignty over the 'Whole Land of Israel'; (c) support for exclusive Jewish sovereignty over Greater Jerusalem; (d) the desire for, and indeed the determination to build, the Third Temple on the site of the Muslim shrines at al-Haram al-Sharif; and (e) a general hostility towards Islam – including the claim that Muslims worship a different God from that of Jews and Christians – which is perceived as a common enemy.[52]

It is important to note that such views are confined to fundamentalist circles, foreign alike to Palestinian and mainstream international Christianity. Furthermore, Palestinians – both Christians and Muslims – see these views as the violation of their fundamental human right to exist autonomously in the land of their birth and forefathers.

Fundamentalist 'End-time' Eschatology: Pro-Zionist or Anti-Semitic and Genocidal?

Disturbingly also, the secular–sacred package of the State of Israel, Jerusalem and the 'Third Temple', the Second Coming of Christ, and the 'end-time' Battle of Armageddon have all become central to 'dispensationalist' Christian fundamentalist belief and aspiration (see Gunner 2003: 35–50). Dispensationalism is one of the most influential theological systems within the evangelical church today. Largely unstudied until recently, it has increasingly shaped the presuppositions of American fundamentalist, evangelical, Pentecostal and charismatic thinking concerning Israel and Palestine over the past 150 years (Gerstner 1991: ix). Dispensationalist fundamentalists hold that there are several ages of God's history. Each age is a *dispensation* from God. The ages are named after Old Testament figures such as Adam, Noah, Abraham, Moses and others. These ages are followed by the Christian or 'church age', which culminates in the messianic and 'New Heaven and New Earth' ages.[53] The emphasis on the theory of historical *dispensations* can be traced back to John Nelson Darby (1800–1882), the founding father of modern premillennial dispensationalism. Darby was at first a Church of England clergyman and later a main founder of the Plymouth Brethren movement. Darby who believed that the church was hopelessly corrupt and authoritarian, founded what would become a widespread prophetic movement, and insisted that these *dispensations* were irreversible, speculating that the Church would soon be replaced on earth by a revived national Israel (Sizer 2004). His dispensationalist theology, which has become central to contemporary Christian

Zionism, represented a radical departure from historic Christian doctrine, by dividing biblical and human history into distinct *periods* – in his case seven – which he called *dispensations*, representing different succeeding systems of relations between God and man (Darby 1962; Wagner 1995: 88–81). Like Darby, most modern dispensationalists divide history into seven epochs, beginning with 'creation' and ending with the kingdom of Jesus (the Millennium), which is to follow the 'Battle of Armageddon' (Barr 1977: 1991–2; Wagner 1992).

There is, of course, a variety of interpretations among Christian fundamentalists and some of them tend to be both 'pro-Zionist' and, at the same time, deeply 'anti-Semitic'.[54] However the trends we describe here are broadly shared by Christian fundamentalists. For pro-Zionist 'dispensationalist' fundamentalists, in particular, the 'Battle for Jerusalem' is also the key to their theory of the 'End Times' (Hagee 2001: 132). A critical element of this doctrine is the unshakable belief in the *inerrancy* of the Bible. The Scriptures, representing the word of God, provide a 'road map', not for peace in the Middle East, but for future turbulence. Moreover, the Bible prophesies a Second Coming by Christ. There is some disagreement as to whether the Second Coming would be precipitated by humankind's positive advances and achievements, or by its failings. In either case, the 'signs of the times' are invariably bad news – political conflict in the Middle East, religious apostasy, increased wickedness, earthquakes, plagues and widespread misfortune.

The first event in the redemptive process is the *Rapture*, whereby faithful Christian believers would be 'caught up together to meet the Lord in the air'. The rest of humanity will be left behind to endure the 'tribulation', a series of terrible calamities that will last for seven years, under the direction of the 'Antichrist'. In the course of the tribulation, the Antichrist will force people to wear 'the mark of the beast' and will desecrate the 'Third Temple' in Jerusalem. The Second Coming of Christ and the Battle of Armageddon, and the tribulation will be followed by the millennium and the Last Judgement. Those who are redeemed will be granted eternal bliss, while the wicked will be condemned to eternal punishment. The Righteous, who will meet the Lord during the Rapture, will presumably avoid all this tribulation, and the key to their salvation and selection for the Rapture will be unwavering adherence to the scriptures.

According to Jeff Halper, Coordinator of the Israeli Committee Against House demolitions (ICAHD), what is deeply anti-Semitic in this apparently pro-Zionist doctrine is the fact that it is predicated upon the outcome of Armageddon, where, among other horrendous outcomes, not only will the State of Israel be completely wiped out as a political entity but most Jews would be killed.[55] Gershom Gorenberg, in his book *The End of Days: Fundamentalism and the Struggle for the Temple Mount*, writes:

> I've listened ... to American evangelical ministers who insist on their deep love for Israel and nevertheless eagerly await apocalyptic battles on Israel's soil so terrible that the dry river beds will, they predict, fill with rivers of blood. I also came to realize that the center of my story had to be the Temple Mount. What happens at that one spot, more than anywhere else, quickens expectations of the end in three religions. And at that spot, the danger of provoking catastrophe is greatest. (Gorenberg 2000: 6)

A similar assessment was offered by Rosemary Ruether:

> This extraordinary theology, while ultimately anti-Jewish and genocidal, places these fundamentalist Christians on the side of the most militant of Jewish fundamentalist settlers who desire to settle all of the land, expel all Palestinians, and destroy the Muslim holy buildings on the Temple Mount in order to rebuild the temple, founding a strictly observant Torah state. (Ruether 1998: 119)

Although many liberal Israelis, like Halper, were critical of this basically anti-Semitic theology, in the mid-1990s, under the influence of the then Prime Minister Benyamin Netanyahu, the Israeli government was enthusiastically canvassing the support of Christian Zionists. Exploiting the association of 'Armageddon theology' and the apocalypse with biblical Megiddo, in 1996 Israeli planners and architects, with Netanyahu's encouragement, began creating a three-dimensional 'virtual Megiddo'. While some Israeli critics described it as 'Apocalypso', Israeli officials were keen to capitalise on the millions of additional visitors 'expected to flock to mark the end of the millennium in gloomy style'.[56]

There is currently one critical element missing from the 'end-time' theological package: there is no temple in Jerusalem. Consequently, the Jews, despite the obvious irony, must construct it on the 'Temple Mount' (al-Haram al-Sharif) in order that the followers of the Antichrist may desecrate it, in accordance with whose understanding of the fulfilment of 'biblical prophecy'. Hal Lindsey, 'the Father of the Modern-Day Bible Prophecy Movement' (Lindsey 1995), is a prolific writer, with at least eighteen books dealing directly or indirectly with the 'end-time' theology, his own radio and television programmes, seminars, Holy Land Tours, and by subscription, his monthly *Countdown Magazine* and *International Intelligence Briefing*. In *The Late Great Planet Earth* Hal Lindsey had this to say:

> Obstacle or no obstacle, it is certain that the [Third] Temple will be rebuilt. Prophecy demands it. ... With the Jewish nation reborn in the land of Pales-tine, ancient Jerusalem once again under total Jewish control for the first time in 2600 years, and talk of rebuilding the great Temple, the most important sign of Jesus Christ's soon coming is before us. ... It is like the key piece of a jigsaw puzzle being found. ... For all those who trust in Jesus Christ, it is a time of electrifying excitement. (Lindsey 1970: 56–8)

This most influential of Lindsey's book has been described by the *New York Times* as the first 'Non-fiction Bestseller of the Decade'. It has gone through more than a hundred printings, with sales by 1993 in excess of 18 million in English, with a further 30 million copies sold in thirty-one foreign editions (Marsden 1991: 77; Lienesch 1993: 311. Lindsey's latest publisher, Western Front, is more conservative, referring to 'a dozen books with combined world sales of more than 35 million' (Lindsey 1995: back cover). Despite dramatic changes in the world since its publication in 1970, the book remains in print in its original unrevised form. Lindsey has subsequently become a consultant on Middle Eastern affairs to both the Pentagon and the Israeli government.[57]

Lindsey's particular kind of reading of history, coloured by a literalist exegesis of selected biblical scriptures, is dualistic, dogmatic, trium-phalist, apocalyptic and confrontational. Lindsey's last but one book, *The Final Battle* (1995), includes the statement on the cover 'Never before, in one book, has there been such a complete and detailed look at the events leading up to "The Battle of Armageddon".'[58] Lindsey, like some other Christian and Jewish fundamentalists, believes that the Muslim Dome of the Rock must be destroyed and the 'Third Jewish Temple' built in order to ensure the return of Jesus.[59] He argues that the world is degenerating and that the forces of evil manifest in godless communism and radical Islam are the real enemies of Israel. He describes in detail the events leading to the great battle at Megiddo between the massive Russian, Chinese and African armies that will attempt but fail to destroy Israel. He and others like Louis Goldberg, a professor of Theology and Jewish Studies at the Moody Bible Institute, offer detailed illustrated plans ostensibly showing future military movements of armies and naval convoys leading up to the Battle of Armageddon (Goldberg 1982: 172; also Lindsey 1970: 155). Lindsey writes:

> These will merely hasten the return of Jesus Christ as King of the Jews who will rule over the other nations from the rebuilt Jewish temple on the site of the destroyed Dome of the Rock in Jerusalem ... Jerusalem will be the spiritual centre of the entire world ... all people of the earth will come annually to worship Jesus who will rule there. (Lindsey 1983: 31–48, 165)

One of the reasons Christian fundamentalists appear so enthusiastic about such a terrible scenario may have to do with their hope of the secret rapture. Just before the final conflagration, they believe, Jesus will

> 'rapture' true Christians into the upper air, while the rest of humankind, was being slaughtered below. 144,000 Jews would bow down before Jesus and be saved, but the rest of Jewry would perish in the mother of all holocausts. (Mahoney 1992: 2)

The Moody Bible Institute and Dallas Theological Seminary have played no small part in promoting a fundamentalist and Zionist eschatology among thousands of American ministers and missionaries (Walvoord 1962, 1974; Dyer 1991, 1993).

A Critique of Christian Zionism

Dr Stephen Sizer and Professor Donald Wagner, two leading experts on dispensationalist writings, have highlighted the predominance of militaristic and apocalyptic terminology in the titles of popular books written by Christian Zionists since the 1980s. These include: Hal Lindsey, *The 1980s: Countdown to Armageddon* (1981), *Israel and the Last Days* (1983), *The Road to Holocaust* (1989), *The Final Battle* (1995) and *The Apocalypse Code* (1997); Dave Hunt, *Peace, Prosperity and the Coming Holocaust* (1983); Billy Graham, *Approaching Hoofbeats, The Four Horsemen of the Apocalypse* (1983) and *Storm Warning* (1992); John F. Walvoord,

Armageddon, Oil and the Middle East Crisis (1974); Moishe Rosen, *Beyond the Gulf War: Overture to Armageddon* (1991); Edgar C. James, *Arabs, Oil and Armageddo*n (1991a) and *Armageddon and the New World Orde*r (1991b). These authors are representative of apocalyptic dispensational-ism, or what Don Wagner calls 'Armageddon Theology'. Andrew Walker has described this as 'PMT' or 'Premillennial Tension'. 'We're counting up to the year 2000 and there's a strong apocalyptical anxiety'.[60] Another indication of how seriously American fundamentalists take the military aspect of their apocalyptic scenario can be seen from the content of the itinerary followed by Jerry Falwell on his Friendship Tour to Israel in 1983. The tour included meetings with senior Israeli government and military officials and an 'On-site tour of modern Israeli battlefields ... Official visit to an Israeli defence installation ... strategic military positions, plus experience first hand the battle Israel faces as a nation.'[61]

Many Christian fundamentalists find common ground with many fun-damentalist Jews and hard-line secular Zionists. Their ideologies are founded upon biblically authorised land theft and slaughter. To such fundamentalists the existence of the Palestinians, including a Palestinian Christian church, is either ignored completely or maligned as theologically liberal and spiritually dead, an irrelevance in the inexorable movement of world history towards the imminent return of the Jewish Messiah. Since their fate and that of the entire world is at stake, Christian fundamental-ists and the Christian right in the USA are committed to supporting and protecting Greater Israel and exclusive Israeli domination of Jerusalem at all costs. This alliance between fundamentalist Christian Zionists and Israeli Jewish fundamentalists (and hard-line secular Zionists) has serious implications for interfaith and communal relations in the Holy Land (and elsewhere). The new 'war on terror' provides for more immediate and direct expressions of Christian Zionist animosity towards any and all who stand between militant Zionism and their dreams of and desire for 'rapture', heavenly release, on a schedule of their own making.

Since the setting up of the International Christian Embassy (ICEJ) in Jerusalem in 1980 the city has seen a hugely active international move-ment. The ICEJ, which employs an international staff of fifty and has rep-resentatives in over eighty countries, operates from Edward Said's former family home in West Jerusalem (Salaita 2006: 171), and was established at a time when other governmental embassies were being moved out of Jerusalem to Tel Aviv in protest at Israel's unilateral annexation of East Jerusalem. Among other things, the work of the ICEJ specifically includes promoting Christian Zionist pilgrimages, and the imposition of a Zionist narrative and Israeli political agenda on pilgrimage itineraries. ICEJ offers unconditional support for exclusive Israeli sovereignty over the city and the Judaisation of Arab Jerusalem (Middle East Council of Churches 1988).

Since the 1980s, the ICEJ has become the driving force behind a coalition of Christian religious and political Zionist organisations, frequently exploited by the Israeli government whenever a sympathetic Christian viewpoint is needed to enhance their own policies, and rebut Western criticism. For example, in October 1996, Israeli Prime Minister Netanyahu spoke at the 'Jerusalem 3000 years' rally organised by the ICEJ in Jerusalem to support Israeli policies in the city. This rally followed the provocative opening of an underground tunnel by the Israelis through the Muslim Quarter in the Old City, and Netanyahu was cheered when he insisted the tunnel would be kept open.[62] Six years later, on 21 September 2002, some 2,500 Christian Zionists from a dozen countries gave an ovation to another Israeli prime minister, Ariel Sharon, in the annual Feast of Tabernacles celebration organised by the ICEJ in Jerusalem. Sharon told the largely evangelical crowd that 'names of places in Israel had remained unchanged for 3,000 years' and that Pope John Paul II, prior to his visit to Jerusalem in 2000, had told Sharon that Jerusalem was holy to Jews, Christians and Muslims, 'but it was promised only to the Jews'.[63]

Critics of the ICEJ and evangelical Zionism have argued that their doctrine has aggressively imposed an aberrant expression of the Christian faith and an erroneous interpretation of the Bible which is subservient to the political agenda of the modern State of Israel: dispensationalism is being used today to give theological justification to what the United Nations regards as racism and the denial of basic human rights; it supports the ethnic cleansing of Palestinians from their historic lands; endorses the building of Jewish settlements in the occupied territories; incites religious fanaticism by supporting the rebuilding of a Jewish Temple on Mount Moriah; dismisses moderate Jewish opinion willing to negotiate land for peace; and advocates an apocalyptic eschatology likely to become a self-fulfilling prophecy. Other critics have argued that Christian biblicists have failed to recognise the reality in Palestine–Israel; they have distorted the Bible and marginalised the universal imperative of the Christian Gospel, ultimately ignoring the sentiments of the overwhelming majority of indigenous Christians (Chapman: 2002: 284–5). Inevitably indigenous Palestinians Christians and the Middle East Council of Churches, which represents the indigenous and ancient Eastern Churches, have also been highly critical of the activities of American dispensationalists. The Middle East Council of Churches declared in 1988:

> [The dispensationalists] ... force the Zionist model of theocratic and ethno-centric nationalism on the Middle East ... [ignoring] ... the movement of Christian unity and inter-religious understanding which is promoted by the churches in the region. The Christian Zionist programme, with its elevation of modern political Zionism, provides the Christian with a world view where the gospel is identified with the ideology of success and militarism. It places its emphasis on events leading up to the end of history rather than living Christ's love and justice today. (Middle East Council of Churches 1988: 13)

Religion and religious groups, however, can also bring conflict resolution and peace to the Holy Land. In all three faiths, religion has also engendered pacifism and pacifist trends. Among the Jerusalem-based religious groups promoting non-violent struggles for peace and justice are Clergy for Peace and Rabbis for Human Rights. Christianity, for instance, through its doctrine of pacifism, has advanced religious ethics in warfare. In addition to 'love our neighbour as ourselves', Christ's Sermon on the Mount instructs followers to 'love your enemies and pray for your persecutors' (Matt. 5: 38–46). Over the years, the involvement of groups such as the Quakers and Pax Christi in the struggle for a just peace in Israel–Palestine has derived from a pacifist tradition. The same non-violent tradition has had a major impact on Palestinian liberation theology. Leading Palestinian Christian theologians based in Jerusalem have promoted non-violent struggle for peace and justice and reconciliation between the three faiths. Dr Naim Ateek, the founder of Sabeel and a leading critic of Christian Zionism, believes that Christian crusading, in the Middle Ages and now, involved holy wars fought by the Western Church that perverted religion, for which Eastern Christians have paid dearly and continue to suffer (Ateek 1989). For Eastern Christians, he holds, the way of non-violence is 'their tradition, their Gospel milieu, their heritage'. The challenge for all religious groups in the Holy Land – as well as for religious politics in Jerusalem – is to develop a pluralistic, democratic and humanist mode of existence based on equality for all the citizens of Israel–Palestine and the recognition of shared principles, values and interests amid acknowledged religious and political differences.

PART II

From the Secular to the Sacred

3

From Secularism to Messianism:
The Theology and Geopolitics
of Neo-Zionism, 1967–2006

The Impact of the 1967 War

Political Zionism emerged in Europe in the late nineteenth century as a basically secular movement, with non-religious and frequently anti-religious dispositions. Although the Jewish Bible was always in the background as a support, the Jewish state would not be a theocracy. In the nineteenth century the Zionist programme was generally opposed by both wings of Judaism, orthodox and reform, as being anti-religious (by the Orthodox) and contrary to the universal of Judaism (by Reform Jewry). Indeed the founding fathers of modern Zionism and the State of Israel were almost all of them atheists or religiously indifferent, although their legitimisation of the Zionist enterprise in the biblical narrative and record was always a powerful driving force to gain international support. However, since its establishment in 1948 the Israeli state, which had been built mainly by atheist Zionists, has undergone a slow but constant process of clericalisation and orthodoxisation, with leading Labour Zionists and founding fathers of the state (notably David Ben-Gurion) seeking an alliance with religious Zionism – thus cementing the alliance between the sword and the Torah, between the secular establishment of Zionism and the Zionist religious parties (Cygielman 1977: 28–37). This partnership between the ostensibly secular Labour Zionism and the declared forces of religious nationalism, Zeev Strenhell observed, was much deeper than appeared on the surface (Sternhell 1998: 335).

Furthermore, since the 1967 conquests radical religious Zionism, often described in Hebrew as the 'messianic' force or religious fundamentalist trend, has transposed Theodor Herzl's political Zionism from an altogether secular aspiration to create the sovereign 'state for the Jews' (*Der Juden-staat*) to the process apocalyptic redemption of the 'whole Land of the Bible' (Prior 1997b, 1999a: 67–102, 1999b; Masalha 2000: 105-62, 2003a: 85-117). Although the deeply secular Herzl had been little concerned with the exact location of the 'Judenstaat' and the scope of its boundaries, the Zionist messianic force has been inspired by maximalist territorial expansionism. This continuing process of clericalisation of the Israeli state, which has been accelerated in recent decades, has serious implications for interfaith relations and religion and the state in Israel–Palestine. Yet, as Israeli sociologist Baruch Kimmeling has argued, the shift was bound to take place from the moment secular Zionist leadership invented a tradition, retitling and reimagining Palestine as the 'Land of Israel':

> [Zionism] has to repeatedly explain to itself and to the international community why it chose Palestine, the land retitled as 'The Land of Israel', as its target-territory for settlement ... it was chosen out of ideological-religious motives. This fact not only turned the Zionist project into ... an essentially religious project, which was not able to disconnect itself from its original identity as a quasi-messianic movement. The essence of this society and state's right and reason to exist is embedded in symbols, ideas and religious scriptures – even if there has been an attempt to give them a secular re-interpretation and context. Indeed, it was made captive from the beginning by its choice of a target-territory for immigration and a place for its nation building. For then, neither the nation nor its culture could be built successfully apart from the religious context, even when its prophets, priests, builders and fighters saw themselves as completely secular.[1]

This major shift from secular to messianic Zionism was reflected in the findings of a public opinion poll conducted in the late 1990s, and cited by Kimmerling. It showed, inter alia, that a majority of 55 per cent of the Jewish population of Israel believed in the absolute basis of the faith in the (mythological) biblical story that the Torah (Matan Torah, in Hebrew) was given to Moses on Mount Sinai – only 14 per cent rejected it outright as a historical reality. Furthermore, 68 per cent believed that the Jewish people were a 'chosen people' – only 20 per cent rejected this ethnocentric belief. Some 39 per cent believed in the coming of the Messiah (but they were not asked about the time of his coming); only 14 per cent had some doubts about this and only 32 per cent completely rejected the very messianic idea (Kimmerling 1999: 339-63). In the 1980s even the leader of the secular Labour Party, Shimon Peres, was undergoing a process of orthodoxisation. Israeli media reports and pictures showed him going to the Wailing Wall after being sworn in as prime minister and head of the National Unity government in September 1984; then he was observed taking Talmud lessons from a chief rabbi – although these displays of piety elicited some ridicule and derision in the secular press (Beit-Hallahmi 1992: 136).

The spectacular rise of neo-Zionist messianism was partly the outcome of the 1967 war, a watershed in the history of Israel which had a profound effect on the country's religious and secular camps (Masalha 1997, 2000: 105-62). Even for many secular Israelis who were indifferent to religion or even opposed it, the capture of East Jerusalem and the West Bank represented a conversion of almost mystical proportions: 'Religious and "secular," Right and Left, fathers and sons, still felt that they shared historical and cultural rights based on the sanctity of the Jewish heritage [of the Bible]' (Sternhell: 1998: 335). Israel's astounding victory created a sense of triumphalist history among many non-believing Israeli Jews who saw the capture of the old city of Jerusalem as a 'sign from Heaven'.[2] This triumphalist feeling brought to prominence fundamentalist Zionism and gave rise to messianic Zionism, or neo-Zionism, which generated feverish Jewish fundamentalism, whose rise contributed to exacerbating Israel's schizophrenic cultural identity and the division between the secular and religious camps in the country.[3] In the wake of the war, and the rise of radical religious Zionism, the role of the biblical narrative within Zionist ideology and Israeli settler colonialism increased significantly. Radical religious Zionism has since developed into a major political and cultural force, with a considerable influence on the attitudes, commitments and votes of a large number of religious and secular Israelis. Its organised focus is the settlement movement of Gush Emunim ('the Bloc of Faithful'), the most influential Jewish fundamentalist movement in the country, which also activates the entire panorama of neo-Zionist and secular ultra-nationalists, including some of Israel's most powerful secular right-wing leaders (Lustick 1988: ix, 12–16, 153).

Messianic Zionism in Israel, in its various shades, emphasises both the 'holiness' and the 'territorial wholeness' of 'biblical *Eretz Yisrael*' (Land of Israel). In constructing neo-Zionist ideology, national identity is not simply a socio-cultural phenomenon but a geopolitical and territorial ideal (Lustick 1987: 118–39). This is reflected in the popular slogan: 'The Land of Israel, for the People of Israel, according to the Torah [Bible] of Israel.' As the late Rabbi Tzvi Yehuda Kook, the spiritual leader of Jewish messianism, put it: 'The Land was chosen before the people.' Hanan Porat, one of the most influential leaders of Gush Emunim, echoed this view:

> For us the Land of Israel is a Land of destiny, a chosen Land, not just an existentially defined homeland. It is the Land from which the voice of God has called to us ever since that first call to the first Hebrew: 'Come and go forth from your Land where you were born and from your father's house to the Land that I will show you.' (Lustick 1987: 127)

Although there is a variety of Jewish religious radical groups in Israel, they invariably envisage a theocratic regime for Israel based on the *halacha* (Jewish religious law) and spurn universal, humanistic and liberal values. For them Zionism and the State of Israel are divine agents (Ravitzky 1996). The theology of the Israeli messianic force is based on four major components: (a) messianic fervour related to the belief in the 'sanctity' of Greater Israel; (b) the building of the Temple on the site of the Muslim shrines in occupied East Jerusalem; (c) the ethos of a religious utopia, reflecting the desire to build a theocratic Jewish state based on the *halacha*, as a substitute for Western-style liberal democracy; (d) the establishment of Jewish political sovereignty over the 'whole Land of Israel' (Gorny 1994: 150–51).

Moreover, the creation of the State of Israel in 1948 and the conquest ('liberation') of additional territories in the 1967 war are both perceived as constituting part of the divine process of messianic redemption – a process that, according to Jewish fundamentalists, should not be stopped or altered by any elected government of Israel (Newman 1994: 533).

The theology of the messianic current generally conceives a radical and sharp distinction between Jew and non-Jew in the Holy Land and assumes basically antagonistic relations between them. For Jewish fundamentalists, the conflict with 'gentiles' over Jerusalem, and even war against them, is 'for their own good', because this will hasten messianic redemption (Lustick 1988: 120). For Jewish fundamentalists, who embrace the supremacist notion of Jews as a divinely 'chosen people' (*'am segula*), the indigenous Palestinians are no more than illegitimate tenants and squatters, and a threat to the process of messianic redemption; their human and civil rights are no match for the divine legitimacy and the religiously ordained duty (or *mitzvah*) of 'conquering, possessing and settling the Promised Land'. Rabbi Tzvi Yehuda Kook, in particular, promoted a racist doctrine of the Jews as a divinely chosen 'superior race', while the Palestinian Arabs were an inferior 'race' (Rachlevsky 1998: 392-3); 'The distinction between Yitzhak [the father of the Jews, according to the Hebrew Bible] and Ishmael [the father of the Arabs] is a clear racial distinction', Kook wrote (Rachlevsky 1998: 406).

For Kook and his disciples, Israel must continue the ancient biblical battles over settlement of the 'Land of Israel', to be won by a combination of religious faith and military might. The devotion of an increasingly powerful trend to the exclusive possession of Greater Jerusalem and the Holy Land, and to messianic redemption, has effectively turned Palestinian East Jerusalem – illegally occupied and unilaterally annexed to Israel after 1967 – into resident aliens in their own city. The same theology spawned Jewish terrorism in East Jerusalem and the West Bank from the late 1970s through the 1980s and 1990s. This Jewish terrorism has been reflected in, among others, the activities of *Hamahteret Hayehudit* (the Jewish Underground) and 'Terror against Terror' of the early 1980s; the Hebron massacre in February 1994; and the assassination of Prime Minister Yitzhak Rabin on 4 November 1995. The continuing rise of the Zionist messianic force is bound to have serious implications for community and national and interfaith relations in the Middle East.

The Rise of Middle-class Ashkenazi Jewish Fundamentalism in Israel

Several Israeli scholars who have documented the ongoing process of clericalisation in Israel since 1948 and the rapid growth of messianic

Zionism since 1967, have observed a strong element of religious coercion. Already in 1965 a prominent Israeli historian, Ya'acov Talmon, observed the major role played by the religious establishment in the Israeli state and society:

> In Israel today, the Rabbinate is rapidly developing into a firmly institutionalized Church imposing an exacting discipline on its members and facing the general body of laymen as a distinct power. This is not a religious development, but, ironically enough, the outcome of the emergence of the [Jewish] State. The latter has given birth and legitimacy to an established Church. (Talmon 1965a, cited in Tamarin 1973: 37)

Professor Talmon pointed out that none of this has roots in Jewish tradition or the Jewish Diaspora. The theocratic elements in Israeli state and society are often explained in terms of the problems of coalition politics, but the socio-political and cultural reasons run much deeper. Such a theocratic development is hardly surprising in a society in which some basis must be established – in state ideology, cultural attitudes, and law – to distinguish the privileged and dominant Jewish population from the non-Jewish citizens of Israel (Chomsky 1975: 37-8).

However, until 1967 religious Zionism remained relatively pragmatic in its demand to apply the *halacha* within Israel as well as in foreign affairs. Since 1967, as several Israeli scholars – including Yehoshafat Harkabi, Yesha'ayahu Leibowitz, Ehud Sprinzak, Avi'ezer Ravitzky and Uriel Tal – have pointed out, militant religious Zionism has become central to Israel's domestic and foreign policies. Moreover, the relationship between Jewish religion and Zionist state policies has become increasingly more intertwined: a radical fundamentalist theology is deployed in the service of settler colonial policies, and Zionist nationalist policies implement Jewish religious commandments (*mitzvot*) and Jewish theocracy (Harkabi 1986: 207). Furthermore, the Zionist messianic force is inspired by maximalist territorial annexationism (Lustick 1988: 107; Shaham 1979; Elitzur 1978: 42-53). Michael Neumann, a professor of philosophy at Trent University in Ontario, Canada, wrote:

> [the late Professor] Israel Shahak [of the Hebrew University of Jerusalem] and others have documented the rise of fundamentalist Jewish sects that speak of the greater value of Jewish blood, the specialness of Jewish DNA, the duty to kill even innocent civilians who pose a potential danger to Jews, and the

need to 'redeem' lands lying far beyond the present frontiers of Israeli control. Much of this happens beneath the public surface of Israeli society, but these racial ideologies exert a strong influence on the mainstream. So far, they have easily prevailed over the small, courageous Jewish opposition to Israeli crimes. The Israeli government can afford to let the fanatical race warriors go unchecked, because it knows the world would not dare connect their outrages to any part of Judaism (or Zionism) itself. As for the dissenters, don't they just show what a wonderfully democratic society Israel has produced?[4]

On the whole, the rise of radical neo-Zionism in Israel – unlike the variety of Islamic fundamentalism in Palestine – is not the product of socio-economic or political marginalisation.[5] It is, rather, a middle-class phenomenon and the product of state policies, the influence of Zionist elites, and coalition politics. This can be seen in the following six aspects.

1. *The role of the Ashkenazi religious establishment*   The single most influential ideologue of Ashkenazi fundamentalism was Rabbi Tzvi Yehuda Kook (1891–1982), who was the head of the large Merkaz Harav Yeshiva in Jerusalem. His father was the Chief Ashkenazi Rabbi of the Jewish community in Mandatory Palestine between 1920 and 1935, Rabbi Avraham Yitzhak HaCohen Kook (1865–1935). The latter ('HaRav', or 'Rabbi Kook the elder'), a prolific author, was the founder of the Zionist religious and messianic ideology. He was a key figure in accommodating the ideology of secular Zionism to classical Jewish orthodoxy, and is held in great regard not only by religious messianics but also by many secular Zionists. He established the foundation of the Chief Rabbinate of Israel, the Rabbanut, and Israel's national rabbinical courts, Batei Din, which work in coordination with the Israeli government, having jurisdiction over much law relating to marriage, divorce, conversion and education. He also built political alliances between the secular Labour Zionist leadership and followers of religious Zionism. He believed, according to his ideo-theological system, that the secular and even anti-religious Labour Zionist settlers of the pre-state period were part of a grand divine scheme of building up the physical land, laying the groundwork for the ultimate messianic redemption of world Jewry. The Kooks (father and son) were key figures in Israel's Ashkenazi (religious and secular) establishment (Lustick 1988: 8, 12–15; Schnall 1985: 15). Their demand that the *halacha* guide official policies towards the Palestinian population is widely accepted in religious circles and parties in Israel.

Moreover, because of its middle-class Ashkenazi origins, the powerful settlement movement of Gush Emunim has been the most successful extraparliamentary movement to arise in Israel since 1948, and has had a profound influence upon the Israeli political system (Lustick 1988: 8, 12–15; Schnall 1985: 15). Its practical settlement of the West Bank has been the main vehicle of the political success of Jewish fundamentalism inside Israel. In *The Ascendance of Israel's Radical Right* (1991) Sprinzak writes:

> Gush Emunim has changed since the 1970s. From a messianic collective of young true believers who thought they could change the world by concentrated spirituality and pioneering devotion, it has become a movement of dozens of settlements, thousands of settlers, with financial assets and material interest. It has added a maturity and skepticism to its early spontaneity and messianic craze. But Gush Emunim is still a very dynamic force, by far the most viable component of the radical right. It may also be the most effective social movement that has emerged in Israel since 1948. (Sprinzak 1991: 107)

2. *Middle-class Ashkenazi elite politics*   The Gush Emunim radical settlers and activists are mostly highly educated Ashkenazi, middle-class and professional Israelis who have close, and often personal, ties with Israel's ruling elites, traditional ruling parties and powerful figures in the Likud and the National Religious Party (NRP, or Mafdal). The same messianic settlers perceive themselves as continuing the process of early 'pioneering Zionism', particularly within the field of establishing new Jewish settlements. For much of the larger camp of the Israeli right and the supporters of Greater Israel, Gush Emunim now fulfils the role that the elites of the kibbutz movement fulfilled for Labour Zionism in the pre-state period (Sprinzak 1991: 107). And, like early Zionist settlers in Palestine, who engaged in actual 'redemption' of land (*geulat haadamah*) and the creation of irreversible 'facts', the Gush Emunim settlers have invariably had a disproportionate impact on the official policies of successive Israeli governments. The Gush settlers' disproportionate impact on official policies stemmed also from their dogged religious determination, as well as from their dynamism and practical pursuit of their objectives.

3. *State funding*   The nationalist-religious *yeshivot* (talmudic seminaries and high schools) of the NRP and its religious youth movement, Bnei 'Akiva ('Sons of 'Akiva') – which gave birth to Gush Emunim – are funded by the state's Ministry of Education.

4. *Yeshivat Merkaz Harav and the Militarised Hesder Yeshivot in the occupied territories* Yeshivat Merkaz Harav in Jerusalem, which has been the focus of the neo-Zionist messianic movement in Israel, is closely associated with the West Bank fundamentalist settlers. Though founded by Rabbi Avraham Kook, it was his son, Rabbi Tzvi Yehuda Kook, who turned it into a political platform for messianic neo-Zionism immediately after 1967, when he came out publicly against any territorial concessions, and emerged as the spiritual head of the settler movement, attracting thousands of supporters for strident, apocalyptic messianic redemptionism. His disciples founded, and currently run, several major *yeshivot* in the occupied territories, which also function as *hesder yeshivot* for the Israeli army – virtually all of their students serve in military units. These included Yeshivat Birkat Moshe in the settlement of Ma'alei Edumim, founded in 1977, which has become one of the army's premier *hesder yeshivot*; Yeshivat 'Ateret Cohanim, founded in 1978 in the heart of the Old City of Jerusalem, just 'opposite the Temple Mount', is headed by Rabbi Shlomo Aviner, its activities focused on rebuilding the Temple; its students also serve in the Israeli army; and Yeshivat Hakotel (the 'Western Wall' Yeshiva), which was founded in the early 1970s, also in the Old City of Jerusalem. Other militarised Hesder Yehivot in the occupied territories were Yeshivat Nir in the settlement of Kiryat Arba'a and Yeshivat Har-Ezion in the settlement of Alon Shevut, both of which were founded in the 1970s.

5. *Coalition politics* Clearly a large measure of the rise in Jewish religious radicalism in Israel has been due to both elite and coalition politics, and in particular to the symbiotic relationship that the religious fundamentalists have forged with secular right-wing Israeli elites, especially the leaders of the Likud. The Likud – unlike Labour Zionism – had no strong settlement movement of its own. Consequently after May 1977 the practical expertise and settlement zeal of thousands of messianic settlers provided the Likud administrations with an indispensable resource in the implementation of their annexationist policies (Lustick 1988: 8–9). Formally established in February 1974 and wielding tremendous influence over Likud administrations, the religious settler movement has played a key role in establishing

dozens of illegal Jewish settlements in Greater Jerusalem and throughout the occupied West Bank.

Seen as a natural successor to the Whole Land of Israel Movement – a predominantly Zionist secular and territorially expansionist movement founded immediately after 1967 – the Gush Emunim movement underwent several stages of development. Its roots, however, are embedded in the post-1967 reality. It had evolved into an organised and dynamic force of Jewish settlers from the youth branch of the NRP, a party which, in the last three decades, has epitomised the rise of the nationalist-religious messianic force in Israeli politics.[6] Until 1967, the NRP's main interest had been in advocating legislation of a religious nature and its role in Israeli external affairs had been limited. However, in the post-1967 period, the NRP became dominated by its young guard: those elements committed ideologically to the practical settlement by Jews of the 'whole Land of Israel' and its permanent incorporation into the State of Israel. Although the NRP remained a coalition partner of the pragmatic ruling Labour Party until 1977 its commitment to Greater Israel and its close identification with Gush Emunim meant that its natural partnership lay with maximalist Revisionist Zionism, with the Likud and Israel's secular radical right.

6. *Israeli plans to colonise the occupied Palestinian territories*   In 1967, after the occupation of the West Bank and Gaza Strip, Israel immediately began an intensive campaign of colonisation. In 1967 Israel unilaterally annexed East Jerusalem and took over the outer zone of the Arab city. Since then Israel has confiscated additional Palestinian land and has transferred Palestinian citizens in a drive to Judaise Arab Jerusalem. Attempts have also been made to change the demographic character of the Palestinian territories radically by taking over Palestinian land and isolating population centres.

If the 1967 war conquests provided the initial impetus for the emergence of Zionist religious radicalism in Israel, Likud's assumption of power in May 1977 helped to consolidate radical Judaism in the country, giving the Gush Emunim settlers an enormous boost. From 1977 through the early 1980s it became public knowledge that the Gush Emunim movement enjoyed the crucial support of Prime Minister Menahem Begin, of the agriculture minister and chairman of the Ministerial Committee on Settlement and later Defence Minister, Ariel Sharon, and the army chief of staff Raphael Eitan (*Le Monde*, 19 June 1980). Under Likud, settlement activities in areas densely populated by Arabs acquired official authorisation and were carried out as government policy. New settler groups were assisted in establishing numerous settlements throughout the West Bank in accordance with blueprints prepared jointly by Gush Emunim and the Settlement Department of the World Zionist Organisation under its new co-chairman, Likud appointee Matityahu Drobless. Since 1977, the principal financial support of the settlement movement and its activities has been the Israeli government, the World Zionist Organisation and the Jewish Agency (Rubinstein 1982: 157-9; Newman 1982, 1985). These official bodies provided the Jewish settlers with material resources; and the Israeli army gave them weapons and explosives, and protected them, while ensuring the Arab population remained defenceless. In this context, Michael Neumann, a professor of philosophy at Trent University in Ontario, Canada, wrote a remarkable essay in July 2002 entitled 'What's So Bad about Israel?'

> [The] Israeli settlement policy, quite apart from its terrible effect on Palestinians, is outrageous for what it represents: a careful, deliberate rejection of peace, and a declaration of the fixed intention to dispossess the Palestinians until they have nothing left. And something else has changed. Israel could claim, as a matter of self-interest if not of right, that it needed the pre-1967 territory as a homeland for the Jews. It cannot say this about the settlements, which exist not from any real need for anything, but for three reasons: to give some Israelis a cheap deal on housing, to conform to the messianic expectations of Jewish fundamentalists, and, not least, as a vengeful, relentless, sadistically gradual expression of hatred for the defeated Arab enemy. In short, by the mid-1970s, Israel's crimes were no longer the normal atrocities of nation-building nor an excessive sort of self-defense. They represented a cold-blooded, calculated, indeed an eagerly embraced choice of war over peace, and an elaborate plan to seek out those who had fled the misery of previous confrontations, to make certain that their suffering would continue.[7]

With thousands of full-time devotees (Aronoff 1985), Gush Emunim fundamentalists' real power lies in the organization's extensive settlement network, its thousands of highly devoted and motivated settlers, its dozens of illegal settlements established in the West Bank, and in the Golan Heights since 1967,[8] with their huge financial and material assets, and above all in the activities of its leading personalities in all the political parties of the right. Gush Emunim has drawn crucial support from the Likud, the NRP, Tzomet, Moledet, Tehiya, Matzad and Ihud Leumi. Knesset members of these parties identified with Gush Emunim objectives and openly campaigned for their implementation. In 1987, members of the Knesset faction Matzad, all of whom were closely identified with Gush Emunim, succeeded in capturing key positions within the NRP. Furthermore, several leading Gush Emunim personalities, including Hanan Porat, Rabbi Eli'ezer Waldman and Rabbi Haim Druckman, have been Knesset members (Joffe 1996: 153).

In August 2005 the Israeli government forcibly evacuated 7,500 Jewish settlers from the (small and hugely overcrowded) Gaza Strip, in an attempt to concentrate on the colonisation of the much bigger area of the West Bank. In fact the colonisation process has never been halted: today a visitor to West Bank can see the result of these settlement policies, with colonies scattered all over the area. The current settlement emphasis is on three areas:

- Greater Jerusalem: to create demographic facts in order to frustrate any Palestinian claims to Jerusalem.
- Along the West Bank's western edges: to make the return to the 1967 borders practically impossible, and to make the settlement blocs closely integrated with Israel, with settlers commuting to work inside Israel.
- The Jordan valley: for its perceived importance to Israel's 'security' as well as for its valuable agricultural resources.

In reality, the growth of settlements in the West Bank is designed to promote the formation of large blocs which will continue to expand and swallow ever greater areas of Palestinian land.

The Bible and 'Kookist' Theology

The teachings of the Kooks (father and son) integrated the traditional, passive religious longings for the land with modern, secular, activist and expansionist Zionism, giving birth to a new comprehensive theology of Jewish nationalist-religious messianism (Jones 1999: 11-14; Prior 1997b:

20-21; Aran 1997: 294-327). 'Kookist' ideo-theology saw the 1967 war and the occupation of the Old City of Jerusalem as a turning point in the process of messianic redemption and the deliverance of *Eretz Yisrael* from what it termed the *Sitra Achra* (literally the 'evil [i.e., Arab] side') (Jones 1999: 12). Tzvi Kook himself rushed with his biblical claims towards the West Bank immediately after the 1967 conquests:

> All this land is ours, absolutely, belonging to all of us, non-transferable to others even in part ... it is clear and absolute that there are no 'Arab territories' or 'Arab lands' here, but only the lands of Israel, the eternal heritage of our forefathers to which others [the Arabs] have come and upon which they have built without our permission and in our absence. (in Schnall 1984: 19; Leor 1986)

Kook's politics were described by the Israeli journalist David Shaham as 'consistent, extremist, uncompromising and concentrated on a single issue: the right of the Jewish people to sovereignty over every foot of the Land of Israel. Absolute sovereignty, with no imposed limitations'; 'From a perspective of national sovereignty', he [Kook] says, 'the country belongs to us.'[9] Immediately after the 1967 war, Rabbi Kook demanded the annexation of the Occupied Territories, in line with explicit *halacha* provisions.[10] He also said at a conference after 1967:

> I tell you explicitly ... that there is a prohibition in the Torah against giving up even an inch of our liberated land. There are no conquests here and we are not occupying foreign land; we are returning to our home, to the inheritance of our forefathers. There is no Arab land here, only the inheritance of our God – the more the world gets used to this thought the better it will be for it and for all of us. (in Pichnik 1968: 108-9)

These statements were made in the presence of over one thousand people, including the Israeli President Zalman Shazar, ministers, members of the Knesset, judges, chief rabbis and senior civil servants (in Pichnik 1968: 108-9).

For the followers of Rabbi Kook, continuing territorial expansion, combined with the establishment of Jewish sovereignty over the entire, biblically described Land of Israel, and the building of the Temple in oc-cupied East Jerusalem, are all part of implementing the divinely ordained messianic redemption. Rabbi Shlomo Aviner, a Paris-born Jew and the chief rabbi of the 'Ateret Cohanim yeshiva in East Jerusalem's Old City

– a fundamentalist group campaigning to rebuild the Jewish Temple on the al-Haram al-Sharif (the Noble Sanctuary) (Aviner 2000) – called for further territorial expansionism beyond the current Occupied Territories: 'Even if there is a peace, we must instigate wars of liberation in order to conquer additional parts of the Land of Israel' (Aviner 1982: 110).

The Bible, the Verdict of Amalek and 'Counter-Jihad'

The indigenous Palestinians are viewed by radical rabbis as temporary alien residents, and as a population living, at best, on sufferance. The same rabbis deny that a Palestinian nation existed and strongly oppose the idea of Palestinian rights in Jerusalem. According to them, there is no need to take into consideration the Arab residents, since their residence in the city for hundreds of years was prohibited and was based on theft, fraud and distortion; therefore now the time has come for the Arab 'robbers' to depart. As Rabbi Aviner explains:

> To what can this be compared[?] It resembles a man entering his neighbour's house without permission and residing there for many years. When the original owner of the house returns, the invader [the Arab] claims: 'It is my [house]. I have been living here for many years'. So what? All of these years he was a robber! Now he should depart and pay housing rent as well. A person might say: there is a difference between a residence of thirty years and a residence of two thousand years. Let us ask him: Is there a law of limitation which gives a robber the right to his plunder? ... Everyone who settled here knew very well that he was residing in a land that belonged to the people of Israel. Perhaps an Arab who was born here does not know this, nonetheless the fact that a man settled on land does not make it his. Legally 'possession' serves only as evidence of a claim of ownership, but it does not create ownership. The Arabs' 'possession' of the land is therefore a 'possession that asserts no right'. It is the possession of territory when it is absolutely clear that they are not its legal owners, and this possession has no legal and moral validity. (Aviner 1983: 10)

In a similar disposition Rabbi Tzvi Yehuda Kook, who apparently inspired Aviner's apologia, wrote:

> We find ourselves here by virtue of our forefathers' inheritance, the foundation of the Bible and history, and there is no one that can change this fact. What does it resemble? A man left his house and others came and invaded it. This is exactly what happened to us. There are those who claim that these

are Arab lands here. It is all a lie and falsehood. There are absolutely no Arab lands here. (Kook 1982: 10)

The imagery of the homecoming Jew and the Arab invader permeates the writings of a variety of spiritual leaders and ideologists of Jewish fundamentalism, particularly the radical extremists, and implies that the Jew has the right to evict the 'alien' Arab 'invader'. Moreover these ideologues interpret the Zionist assertion of 'historical rights' to the land as meaning that the very fact of Arab residence on, and possession of, the land is morally flawed and legally, at best, temporary; therefore the Arabs must evacuate the land in the interests of the 'legal owners' of the country, and depart.

Palestinian resistance to the extension of Jewish sovereignty, according to many Jewish fundamentalists, will result in their uprooting and destruction. The late Rabbi Meir Kahane, who acquired a reputation for defining the outer limits of both right-wing politics and Jewish fundamentalism in Israel, was a major contributor to the rise of militant messianic theology in Israel in the post-1967 period. After Kahane's assassination in New York in 1990, his funeral in Jerusalem was attended by two Israeli Cabinet ministers, two deputy ministers, and by the Chief Sephardi Rabbi, who urged the mourners to 'follow in Kahane's ways' (Elon 1997a: 197). Kahane, unlike some of the rabbis of Gush Emunim, made little distinction between Palestinian Christians and Palestinian Muslims. His racist public campaign thrived on media publicity, concentrating on the Palestinian citizens of Israel, and not just those of the Occupied Territories. Kahane declared on another occasion, 'No non-Jews can be citizens of Israel', seeking to rescind the citizenship status currently given to Palestinian Christians and Muslims inside the Green Line; if the Arabs refuse to accept the (*halacha*) status of *ger toshav* (paying 'tribute' and living in 'servitude'), 'We'll put them on trucks and send them over the Allenby Bridge ... we'll use force. And if they fire at our soldiers, we'll kill them' (in Tessler 1986: 31).

Rabbi Kahane and other loosely associated rabbis frequently referred to the Palestinians as the 'Amalekites' or the 'Canaanites' of today. Although some refer to the local Arabs as 'Ishmaelites' and to the circumstances under which biblical Abraham expelled Ishmael, many prefer to use Joshua's destruction and subjugation of the Canaanites as a model for the determination of Israeli policy towards the contemporary 'Arab problem' of Greater Israel. Reflecting on the appropriate policy for Jews to adopt towards the Palestinians, Rabbi Tzvi Yehuda Kook cited Maimonides to the effect that the Canaanites had three choices – to flee, to accept Jewish sovereignty or to fight – implying that the decision by most Canaanites to resist Jewish rule justified their destruction (Kook 1982: 19). According to the Old Testament, the Amalekites were an ancient nomadic people, who dwelt in the Sinai desert and southern Palestine, regarded as the Israelites' inveterate foe, whose 'annihilation' became a sacred duty and against whom war should be waged until their 'memory be blotted out' forever (Exod. 17.16; Deut. 25.17-19).

Although the biblical stories mention that the Amalekites were finally wiped out during the reign of Hezekiah in the 8th century BC, Rabbinical literature dwells on Amalek's role as the Israelites' permanent arch enemy, saying that the struggle between the two peoples will continue until the coming of the Messiah, when God will destroy the last remnants of Amalek. Some of the religious radicals insist on giving the biblical commandment to 'blot out the memory of Amalek' an actual contemporary relevance in the conflict between Israelis and Palestinians. In February 1980, Rabbi Yisrael Hess, the former Campus Rabbi of the religious university of Bar-Ilan, published an article in the student bulletin *Bat Kol*, the title of which, 'The Genocide Commandment in the Torah' (in Hebrew, *Mitzvat Hagenocide Batorah*) leaves no place for ambiguity. The article ends: 'The day is not far when we shall all be called to this holy war, to this commandment of the annihilation of Amalek' (Hess 1980). In fact, the association of the Palestinians with the ancient Amalekites was made in a book written in 1974 by Rabbi Moshe Ben-Tzion Ishbezari, the rabbi of Ramat Gan.[11] Hess quotes the biblical commandment according to which he believes Israel, in the tradition of Joshua from biblical times, should act: 'go and strike down Amalek; put him under the ban with all that he possesses. Do not spare him, but kill man and woman, baby and suckling, ox and sheep, camel and donkey' (Hess 1980; 1 Samuel 15.3). Hess adds:

Against this holy war God declares a counter jihad ... in order to emphasise that this is the background for the annihilation and that it is over this that the war is being waged and that it is not a conflict between two peoples ... God is not content that we annihilate Amalek – 'blot out the memory of Amalek'

– he also enlists personally in this war ... because, as has been said, he has a personal interest in this matter, this is the principal aim. (Hess 1980)

Citing Hess's article, Amnon Rubinstein, a Knesset member then representing the centrist Shinui Party and a lecturer in Law at Tel Aviv University, commented:

Rabbi Hess explains the commandment which instructs the blotting out of the memory of Amalek and says that there is not the slightest mercy in this commandment which orders the killing and annihilation of also children and infants. Amalek is whoever declares war on the people of God. (Rubinstein 1980: 125)

Rubinstein points out that 'no reservation on behalf of the editorial board, the students or the University was made after publishing this article which was also reprinted in other newspapers' (Rubinstein 1980: 179). However, a subsequent issue of *Bat Kol* (no. 2, 16 April 1980) carried two articles written by Professor Uriel Simon and Dr Tzvi Weinberg severely criticising the article of Rabbi Hess. Clearly for Hess Amalek is synonymous with the Palestinian Arabs, who have a conflict with Israeli Jews, and they must be 'annihilated', including women, children and infants. His use of the Arabic term *jihad* leaves no doubt as to whom such a war of 'annihilation' should be waged against.

These disturbing ideas were not confined to Rabbi Hess, for whom the Palestinian Arabs are the 'Amalekites of today' who 'desecrate the Land of Israel'. In his *On the Lord's Side* (1982) Danny Rubinstein has shown that this notion permeates the Gush Emunim movement's bulletins. Thus, Nekudah of 29 August 1980 carried an article written by Gush Emunim veteran Haim Tzoriyah, entitled 'The Right to Hate', which reads: 'In every generation there is an Amalek. The Amalekism of our generation finds expression in the deep Arab hatred towards our national revival in our forefathers' land.' The same notion propagated by the messianic trend regarding the equiparation of the Palestinians with the Amalekites was widely discussed in the Israeli daily press and even on television. It was also criticised in moderate religious circles.[12] But it was the late Professor Uriel Tal, a prominent biblical scholar at Tel Aviv University, in a study in the early 1980s, who did more than any one to expose the 'annihilationist' notions preached by the rising messianic force in Israel. Professor Tal, who had also done extensive research on anti-Semitism between the two world wars, concluded that these messianic doctrines were similar to ideas common in Germany during the Weimer Republic and the Third Reich. The gist of Tal's research was presented to an academic forum at Tel Aviv University in March 1984 and was subsequently widely publicised in the Hebrew press and in Israeli journals.

Tal pointed out that the totalitarian messianic force refers to the Palestinian Arabs in three stages or degrees:

1. the reduction of the Palestinians in Jerusalem and the West Bank to the *halacha* status of 'resident alien';
2. the promotion of Arab 'transfer' and emigration (Nisan 1986);
3. the implementation of the commandment of Amalek, as expressed in Rabbi Hess's article 'The Commandment of Genocide in the Torah' – in other words, 'annihilating' the Palestinian Arabs (Uriel Tal in *Haaretz*, 26 September 1984: 27; Kim 1984; Peri 1984; Rash 1986: 77).

Like Uriel Tal, many liberal Israelis found the resurgence of this messianic and anti-Arab trend a chilling prospect, as the Israeli political scientist Yoram Peri remarked in 1984:

> The solution of the transports and the trucks is not the end of the story. There is a further stage which the proponents of racist Zionism do not usually refer to explicitly, since the conditions for it are not ripe. But the principles are there, clear and inevitable. This is the stage of genocide, the annihilation of the Palestinian people. (Peri 1984)

Religious Zionist figures sought to legitimise discussions of mass Arab 'transfer' and ethnic cleansing. In October 1987, a prominent office-holder from the religious right, Yosef Shapira, a former member of the NRP and a Morasha minister in the Cabinet of Yitzhak Shamir, referred to 'transfer' as a reasonable and viable solution, suggesting that a sum of $20,000 should be paid for a Palestinian family ready to leave permanently (Sprinzak 1991: 346 n20). In support of his proposal, Shapira cited a survey his party conducted among rabbis in the West Bank and Gaza Strip, in which 62 per cent responded that 'we must force them to do so by any means at our disposal and see in it an exchange of population'; 13 per cent favoured the encouragement of voluntary emigration (*Nekudah*, November 1987: 37). In the same year, an article entitled 'In Defence of the Transfer', published in *Nekudah* of 14 April 1987, Moshe Ben-Yosef wrote:

> It is kosher to discuss the idea of transfer, and even to put it into effect.... It is kosher not only because its is an 'actual solution', but also because it is required for the vision of the whole Land of Israel. ... The idea of transfer has deep roots in the Zionist movement.

Gush Emunim's main organ, *Nekudah*, has been assiduously popularis-ing the 'transfer' idea since its first appearance in December 1979. By 1986 its circulation had reached 10,000 copies, sent to subscribers in the Occupied Territories and in Israel, including public institutions as well as public and academic libraries. *Nekudah* also appears in pamphlet form with a circulation of 50,000 (Benvenisti 1986: 160). The November 1987 issue of *Nekudah* discusses the results of a recent questionnaire on 'security matters' conducted among rabbis, Yeshiva students and directors in the settlements of 'Judea', 'Samaria' and Gaza. Some 86 per cent of the respondents to the questionnaire from the Tzomet Institute in Elon Shvut settlement supported the imposition of collective punishment – on a refugee camp, *hamulah* or family – for Arab inhabitants; 64 per cent were of the opinion that the collective punishment should be expulsion; 77 per cent believed that 'Arab emigration should be encouraged'; while 85 per cent thought that the death penalty should be imposed on Arab 'terrorists'.[13] Yisrael Harel, a Gush Emunim activist and the editor of *Nekudah*, wrote in January 1988: 'half a year ago, 90 per cent of people would have objected to transfer. Today 30 to 40 per cent would argue that it's not a dirty word or an inhuman policy. On the contrary, they would argue it's a way to avoid friction'.[14] David Rosentzweig of Kidumim wrote in an article in *Nekudah* in December 1983:

> We should urge them [the Arabs] to get out of here. The Arab public must feel that the land (really the land) is being pulled from under its feet ... the very fact of their presence endangers our life every day.... For our own safety there is no place for the Arabs with us in this country ... we must seek a new and revolutionary way to deal with the Jewish–Arab conflict.[15]

A prominent leader of the NRP, Rabbi Yitzhak Levy, a founder of Matzad (the Religious Zionism Camp), an extreme-right faction within the NRP, who has previously made clear his opposition to allowing Israeli Arab

Knesset members the right to vote on the Oslo Accords of 1993 and who (according to the daily *Haaretz* of 25 February 1998) was reputed to have supported 'exiling Arabs' in the Occupied Territories to other Arab states (Jones 1999: 19) is also known to be close to former Sephardic Chief Rabbi Mordechai Eliyahu, another advocate of Greater Israel, who has called for the rehabilitation of Yigal Amir, Yitzhak Rabin's assassin (Jones 1999: 19). In 1983, while serving as Sephardi Chief Rabbi, Eliyahu had sponsored a conference with Ateret Cohanim Yeshiva on the rebuilding of the Third Temple in Jerusalem. He believes that the Third Temple would descend from heaven amids flames of fire; at that point the Muslim shrines, the Dome of the Rock and the al-Aqsa Mosque would be burnt and the Third Temple built in their place (Ronel 1984: 12).

Israeli journalists who have covered East Jerusalem and the West Bank for over three decades provide some of the best accounts of the ideology of the settlers' movement and its anti-Arab racist concepts, as well as amply documenting its violence in the Occupied Territories (Grossman 1988). In his seminal work on Gush Emunim, Danny Rubinstein concludes that the majority of the Gush Emunim settlers are in favour of expelling the Arab population. He describes the anti-Arab feelings that permeate the Gush Emunim meetings and provides excerpts from the settler movement's pamphlets and bulletins: 'Hatred of the [Arab] enemy is not a morbid feeling, but a healthy and natural phenomenon'; 'The people of Israel have a legitimate national and natural psychological right to hate their enemies'; 'The Arabs are the Amalekites of today'; 'the aim of the settlements in the Nablus area is 'to stick a knife in the heart of the Palestinians' (Rubinstein 1982: 90–93, 151). For the right-wing religious fundamentalists Jewish sovereignty over the 'whole Land of Israel' was divinely ordained, since the entire land had been promised by God to the Jewish people. Moreover, for many settlement leaders, particularly religious figures and extremist rabbis, the ideological conflict with the Palestinian Arabs had its roots in biblical injunctions, regarding the Amalekites (see 1 Samuel 15.2–3), as we have seen. At least some leading rabbis have interpreted this biblical injunction to justify not only the expulsion of local Arabs but also the killing of Arab civilians in the event of war (Aronson 1990: 289).

In 1980 the Gush Emunim movement's Department of Information published an article written by Dr Yisrael Eldad, a supporter of a 'Greater

Israel from the Nile to the Euphrates', recommending that the best course of action would be to bring about large-scale Arab emigration through the deliberate creation of economic hardship in the West Bank and Gaza. Similar views have been expressed at every level of the Gush Emunim movement by both leaders and rank-and-file members, most of whom are religious extremists. Elyakim Ha'etzni of Kiryat Arba'a, a prominent secular figure in the settlers' movement who later became a Tehiya Party Member of the Knesset and was until the early 1950s a member of the Mapai Party, spoke at a conference of the settlers attended by fifty leading activists from settlements in the occupied territories held in Moshav Bnei-Tal in the Gaza Strip in 1980 – a few weeks after the maiming of the West Bank mayors – to discuss the future of Arab–Jewish relations in *Eretz Yisrael*. According to the account of the conference, published by the official Gush Emunim bulletin *Hamakor* (August 1980), Ha'etzni stated:

> We must get rid of the real obstacle to peace, which is the Hashemite royal house, and we must not leave Amman [after the IDF has occupied it] except in exchange for an agreement stipulating the elimination of the Hashemite royal house and the elimination of the refugee problem. We must help the Palestinian Arabs to set up their own state on the East Bank of the Jordan.... The Arabs living on the West Bank, in Judea and Samaria, and in the Galilee and the Negev will then elect the Jordanian Parliament, and the Jews settled on the East Bank will elect the Knesset.[16]

David Grossman, a correspondent of the *Jerusalem Post* covering the West Bank, described a meeting of Gush Emunim in the settlement of Alfei Menashe at which Ha'etzni urged the authorities to take steps against PLO activities and any one who opposed the settlement policies. Grossman writes: 'I make out the words "expulsion", "closure", "imprisonment", "death penalty", "destruction", and for a short, mad moment I see Haetzni [sic] prancing happily through a West Bank completely emptied of people' (Grossman 1988: 207).

In 1987 Dr Mordechai Nisan, a senior lecturer at the Hebrew University and a supporter of Gush Emunim, attempted to legitimise the transfer solution with ample documentation of previous Zionist leaders' support for such a solution. After reviewing Zionist transfer ideas and proposals from Herzl to Ben-Gurion, Nisan quotes several statements made by leading

Israeli politicians and Knesset members (including Yitzhak Rabin, then prime minister; Haim Hertzog, then president; Michael Dekel, a former deputy defence minister (Likud); Meir Cohen-Avidov, a former deputy speaker of the Knesset; and Yuval Neeman, then leader of the Tehiya Party and former minister of science) (Nisan 1986: 117-19, 200). Nisan states that 'the idea of transferring the Arabs from the Land of Israel has not left the national agenda in Israel, in recent years books were written proposing explicitly the removal of the whole Arab population or at least most of it, from the Jewish state, in order to safeguard it from the Arab danger which is becoming stronger.' All these statements, books and articles in the Hebrew press in support of transfer 'are a few signposts which, perhaps, indicate a tendency in the Israel public to raise forcefully this ancient idea ... it seems to me that the time makes the idea relevant and vital now' (Nisan 1986: 119, 200).

Nisan went on to question the very possibility of Arab–Jewish coexistence, as is characteristic of so many of the supporters of neo-Zionism and Greater Israel. His justification of Arab removal rests on explicitly racist premises – echoing the strident arguments of Rabbi Meir Kahane; for example, 'it is likely that a sharp and extreme solution will be raised as a remedy to the Arab plague that afflicts the country. The idea of removing the Arabs from the western Land of Israel [i.e., Palestine] radiates hope and arouses interest in the face of the hopelessness that the governments of Israel have shown in the recent period'. Nisan spells out three advantages for Israel 'if the country were to be emptied of the Arab inhabitants':

- 'The internal security problem would disappear.'
- 'The Arab claim over the land of Israel would loose its validity, and the Jewish people would be able to enjoy exclusive sovereignty without contestation' over the country.
- 'The danger of assimilation, the blurring of the state being solely a Jewish state, mixed marriages etc., all these would disappear as a threat to the Zionist/Jewish domination of Greater Israel.... These advantages in the security, political and cultural field would certainly contribute to the strengthening of the State of Israel and its turning into a more comfortable secure, quiet and Jewish place. The extreme solution of removing the Arabs from the country is surely tempting in

its simplicity and its anticipated results of spoils (or gains). It appears as a positive and pragmatic measure that could solve once and for all the bitter conflict and thereby secure a good life for the people of Israel. ... Is it a secret that among very many Jews in Israel this is the solution that has settled deep in their heart? Every person who is deeply-rooted in the life of Israel, with its problems and dreams, knows this at first hand', Nisan concludes (Nisan 1986: 108).

For messianic Zionists, the Palestinians face the same predicament as the Canaanites of the Bible and have little choice but to leave their native land (Prior 2003: 26-9). Hence the approval of Jewish terrorism by Nisan is the logical and practical conclusion of the ideo-theology of Greater Israel and is a political instrument designed to force the Arab population into evacuation (Nisan 1990/91: 139-41). With the rise of Jewish fundamentalism and the radical messianic force in Israel in the last two decades, many far-reaching ideas, such as 'annihilating the Amalekites of today', have entered mainstream Zionist religious thinking. Inspired by a fundamentalist interpretation of the Old Testament scriptures, especially the books of Exodus, Deuteronomy and Joshua, their discourse presents ethnic cleansing as not only legitimate, but as required by the divinity. It has already been shown that the idea of 'ethnic cleansing', or 'transferring' the Palestinians, is widely supported by nationalist religious groups as well as by the Gush Emunim movement, both leaders and members. If the very idea of Arab residence in Palestine is based on 'theft', is morally flawed and is legally only temporary, according to the religious fundamentalists, then the logical conclusion is Arab removal. Rabbi Yisrael Ariel bluntly and explicitly demands expelling the Palestinians, as necessitated by Jewish religious commandments:

> On the one hand there is a commandment of settling *Eretz Yisrael*, which is defined by our sages of blessed memory also as the commandment of 'inheritance and residence' – a commandment mentioned many times in the Torah. Every young student understands that 'inheritance and residence' means conquering and settling the land. The Torah repeats the commandment 'You shall dispossess all the inhabitants of the land' tens of times, and Rashi [Rabbi Shlomo Yitzhaki, a paramount Bible and Talmud commentator in the eleventh century] explains that 'You shall dispossess – you shall expel'. The Torah itself uses the term 'expulsion' a number of times such as: 'Since you shall expel the inhabitants of the country with my help'. The substance of

this commandment is to expel the inhabitants of the land whoever they may be. ... This is also the opinion of Rashi in defining the commandment. In the same Talmudic passage which mentions the commandment pertaining to the land, Rashi interprets: 'Because [of the commandment] to settle *Eretz Yisrael* – to expel idolaters and to settle [the people of] Israel there'. Thus according to Rashi the commandment to settle [the land] aims at the expulsion of the non-Jew from *Eretz Yisrael* and that it be settled with Jews. (Ariel 1980)

The theology of the messianic Zionists, including the fundamentalist notion of the 'Amalek of today', found an echo in an article published by the chief military rabbi of the IDF Central Command, Rabbi Avraham Semel (Avidan), who, according to Professor Amnon Rubinstein, gave *halacha* justification for the 'murder of non-Jewish civilians including women and children, during war' (Rubinstein 1980: 124). Another soldier, who was also a yeshiva student, asked his rabbi about the subject of *tohar haneshik* (the 'purity of arms'). From the answer of the rabbi the soldier concluded: 'During war I am permitted or even obliged to kill every male and female Arab that happens to be in my way. ... I must kill them even if this involves complication with the military law' (Rubinstein 1980: 124). Professor Rubinstein (who in his book *From Herzl to Gush Emunim and Back Again* cites many references by the spiritual mentors of Gush Emunim to the Arabs as the 'Amalek of today') wrote critically in an article in *Haaretz* daily on 3 February 1983:

> We are dealing with a political ideology of violence. It is needless to show how this ideology is expressed in the way the Arabs are treated. The Rabbis of Gush Emunim – except for the few brave ones ... publicly preach incitement to kill Arab civilians, and those who kill civilians, and are caught and brought to court, are later amnestied by the Chief of Staff [General Raphael Eitan], who believes in the use of violence that the Arabs understand'. Those who think that it is possible to differentiate between blood and blood are wrong. The verdict on 'Amalek' can easily be extended to the enemies within, the traitors.

Rubinstein wrote his article against the background of the attacks carried out by the extreme right on the Peace Now demonstrators and the increasing violence in Israeli political life in general, as well as the resurgence of the far right and national religious chauvinists. There is good reason to suggest that the greater the role of the Jewish *halacha* in the political life of Israel becomes, the more vigorously this messianic force will demand that the Palestinian Arabs be dealt with according to halachic regulations, including the imposition of the status of 'resident alien' on them; the insistence on diminishing Arab numbers by making life more difficult still; the revival of the command to 'blot out the memory of Amalek' and the insistence that the Palestinians are the 'Amalekites of today', to be dealt with by annihilation; the assertion that the killing of a non-Jew is not a murder.

The Geopolitics of the Neo-Zionist Messianic Force: *Milhemet Mitzvah* and Territorial Expansionism

Although at present the colonisation drive is confined to the Occupied Territories, according to the late Ehud Sprinzak, a renowned expert on Jewish fundamentalism,

> When Gush ideologues speak about the complete [whole] Land of Israel they have in mind not only the post-1967 territory, but the land promised in the Covenant (Genesis 15) as well. This includes the Occupied Territories – especially Judea and Samaria, the very heart of the historic Israeli nation, and vast territories that belong now to Jordan, Syria and Iraq. (Sprinzak 1991: 113)

Traditionally Transjordan – where, according to biblical myths and legends, the Israelite tribes of Reuven, Menashe and Gad were supposed to have resided – has been the primary focus of Gush Emunim's expansionist ambitions (Lustick 1988: 107). Although other expansionist aspirations in numerous directions across the Fertile Crescent have also been openly expressed. In the judgement of the late Rabbi Tzvi Yehuda Kook, the destined borders of the Jewish state will stretch broadly across the whole area: Transjordan, the Golan Heights, the 'Bashan' (the Jabal Druze region in Syria) are all part of the 'Land of Israel' (Shaham 1979). Echoing the same geopolitical ambitions, Yehuda Elitzur, one of the most influential scholars in Gush Emunim, considered the 'promised land' and 'patriarchal' boundaries as extending to the Euphrates river, southern Turkey, Transjordan and the Nile Delta; the lands that Israel is required eventually to conquer, 'redeem', 'inherit' and settle include northern Sinai, Lebanon and western Syria, the Golan Heights, and much of Transjordan (Elitzur 1978: 42-53).

Israel's military invasion of Lebanon in 1982 encouraged many religious Jews to discuss '*halachic* imperatives' towards territorial expansion in the direction of Lebanon, whatever the price. They claimed large tracts of Lebanon to be the domain of the biblical tribe of Asher. Beirut was even Hebraicised to Beerot – Hebrew for 'well'. Members of the Israeli army's rabbinate issued a leaflet which quoted the 'inheritance of Asher' in the Book of Joshua (Shindler 2002a: 155). In September of that year the Gush Emunim journal *Nekudah* published 'a study' of Yehuda Elitzur, claiming that the most serious distortion of Israel's borders was in the north – in Lebanon (Lustick 1988: 107). The following month a paid advertisement of Gush Emunim in support of the invasion of Lebanon asserted that south Lebanon was part of *Eretz Yisrael* and that the 1982 war 'brought back the property of the tribes of Naftali and Asher into Israel's boundaries' (Talmon 1965a: 37). In the same month Jewish fundamentalists reiterated the claim in a book entitled *This Good Mountain and the Lebanon*. Rabbis Ya'acov Ariel, Dov Leor and Yisrael Ariel, as well as other fundamentalists, declared southern Lebanon to be the lands of the (mythologised) biblical tribes of Zevulon, Asher and Naphtali. Yisrael Ariel went even further by asserting that the boundaries the Land of Israel included Lebanon up to Tripoli in the north, Sinai, Syria, part of Iraq and even part of Kuwait.[17] In the same month he called for the annexation and settlement of most of Lebanon with its capital Beirut to Israel, at any price:

> Beirut is part of the Land of Israel – about that there is no controversy, and Lebanon being part of the Land of Israel we must declare that we have no intention of leaving. We must declare that Lebanon is flesh of our flesh, as is Tel Aviv and Haifa, and that we do this by right of the moral power granted to us in the Torah. Our leaders should have entered Lebanon and Beirut without hesitation, and killed every single one of them. Not a memory or a trace should have remained ... We should have entered Beirut at any price, without regard to our own casualties, because we are speaking of the conquest of the Land of Israel ... We should immediately divert the waters of the Litani to the Jordan [river]. (*Nekudah*, 12 November 1982: 23)

Forty American rabbis who had been brought to the hills surrounding Beirut to view the Lebanese capital besieged and bombarded by the Israeli army declared that Operation Peace for Galilee was, Judaically, a just war and a *milhemet mitzvah* – a 'commandment war' or an obligatory war – a war which resulted in the death of some 20,000 Palestinians and

Lebanese. Following the invasion of Lebanon, a leading American Jewish scholar, Rabbi J. David Bleich, suggested that a verse from the biblical Song of Songs (4:8) supported the acquisition of southern Lebanon. Bleich interpreted this as another step towards complete redemption (Shindler 2002a: 155). The Ashkenazi Chief Rabbi of Israel, Shlomo Goren, went even further and, following Maimonides (see Chapter 5), cited three categories of obligatory wars: Joshua's battle to clear the 'land of Israel', when biblical Israelites crossed into Canaan; the battles against the Amalekites, who became the symbolic biblical enemies of the Israelites down the centuries; and the contemporary war in Lebanon (Shindler 2002a: 156). The Lubavitcher Rebbe, the Hasidic leader who held court in Brooklyn and popularised the messianic idea, fiercely opposed Israel's partial withdrawal in 1985 from southern Lebanon, describing the area as Israel's 'North Bank' which allegedly had been part of the biblical Land of Israel (Shindler 2002a: 193).

Back in 1982, shortly before Israel's invasion of Lebanon and immediately after Israel's evacuation of the settlement of Yamit in northern Sinai, leading Gush Emunim figures, such as Beni Katzover and Rabbis Moshe Levinger and Haim Druckman, formed an organisation called Shvut Sinai ('Return to Sinai'), dedicated to campaigning for the reconquest of Sinai by Israel and Jewish rule over it (Lustick 1988: 61). Two years later, in 1984, Ya'acov Feitelson, a Tehiya Party member and the former mayor of Ariel, the largest Jewish settlement in the northern part of the West Bank, echoed the same Jewish imperial vision of a Jewish state stretching across the entire Arab East:

> I am speaking of a tremendous vision. We are only in the infancy of the Zionist movement ... Israel must squarely face up to the implementation of the Zionist vision – a vision that has not changed since the days of Herzl. As is known, Herzl never indicated what the borders of the state were to be ... in his time the settlement [by Jews] of the Syrian desert was discussed. I say that Israel should establish new cities throughout the entire area. I mean really the whole area of the Middle East, without limiting ourselves. We should never say about any place: here we stop. (*Koteret Rashit*, 14 November 1984: 23)

In the same year, Rabbi Eli'ezer Waldman expressed opposition to the idea then propagated by Likud leaders, such as Ariel Sharon and Yitzhak Shamir, that Jordan has become the Palestinian homeland. Waldman and the majority of Gush Emunim opposed any final agreement to relinquish the East Bank of Jordan to non-Jewish rule (Lustick 1988:107).

This geopolitical vision of territorial expansion across the region can only be ensured by military campaigns and 'wars of liberation'. In fact the actual settlement drive in the West Bank is viewed and planned as nothing less than a military campaign. Military might, war and warfare are desired and often eagerly sought by many neo-Zionist groups. War simply represents a time of testing, a sign of strength – a necessary means by which the will of Providence is worked out. Territorially ambitious rabbis and leaders of Gush Emunim share the same attitude to war. Within Gush Emunim, war, leading to Jewish rule over the 'whole Land of Israel', is a central component of the purgative process that will bring about messianic time. Emphasising expansion by military means, Rabbi Tzvi Kook advised the following:

> We are commanded both to possess and to settle [the land]. The meaning of possession is conquest, and in performing this *mitzvah*, we can perform the other – the commandment to settle ... We cannot evade this commandment ... Torah, war, and settlement – they are three things in one and we rejoice in the authority we have been given for each of them. (Kook 1982: 19)

In a similar vein Rabbi Shlomo Aviner writes:

> We have been commanded by the God of Israel and the creator of the world to take possession of this entire land, in its holy borders, and to do this by wars of defence, and even by wars of liberation. (Lustick 1988: 106)

Hanan Porat, a leading Gush Emunim figure, spoke in 1982 in terms of practical preparations for future opportunities that will arise:

> We must prepare ourselves in terms of our consciousness and by establishing new settlement nuclei, to settle those portions of the Land of Israel that today are still not in our hands ... nuclei for the Litani area [in south Lebanon], Gilead, Transjordan, and Sinai. (*Nekudah* 43, 12 May 1982: 17)

Conclusion

In the political culture of the post-colonial world order, Israel is a society plagued by the problem of identity politics and deep cultural divisions (Kimmerling 1999: 339-63). On the liberal Israeli side, many authors have voiced strong criticism over messianic Zionism and pointed to the violent activities of groups such as Jewish Underground and TNT as an inevitable consequence of the philosophy and activities of Gush Emunim (Shahak and Mezvinsky 1999; Evron 1995: 223-41; Shlaim 2000; Elon 1997a). But the reluctance of the state in general and the Likud administrations in particular to punish those settlers who have murdered Palestinian civilians, as exemplified by the delayed publication of, and subsequent reticence over, the Karp report on settler violence against Palestinians, has only encourage militant Gush Emunim settlers and their radical right-wing supporters, who are determined to drive the Palestinians out one way or another. The same reticence over settler violence against Arabs has doubtless also encouraged those Jewish fundamentalists who are prepared to use violence against those they perceive to be dovish Israeli Jews.

In the 1990s the Oslo process and the Israeli-Palestinian agreements clearly shocked the messianic forces, including the rabbis and leaders of Gush Emunim, and brought to the surface the deep divisions that had been developing within Israeli society in response to the peace talks with the Palestinians. The establishment of the Palestinian Authority in Gaza and the West Bank, the appearance of armed Palestinian police, and the sight of Palestinians waving their flags all constituted clear evidence of the weaknesses of the messianic vision of a quick redemption.

In recent years the messianic rabbis have even turned their hatred on 'Jewish traitors', whose treason has spoiled God's plan and influenced many Israelis to disregard the divine commandments and to follow those who are prepared to give away parts of the 'sacred' land. Expressing the deep divisions within society and echoing religious Zionism's traditional hostility towards the symbols of Christianity in the Holy Land, Rabbi Yair Dreyfus, an articulate settlement leader, declared:

> The true Jews, desirous to live as Jews, will have no choice to separate themselves in ghettos. The new, sinful Canaanite-Palestinian state [Israel after Oslo] will soon be established upon the ruins of the genuine Jewish-Zionist state ... God may even make war against this polluted throne of his. The Jews who lead us into that sin no longer deserve any divine protection. ... Our leadership will walk a Via Dolorosa before it understands that we are commanded to resist the [secular] state of Israel, not just its present government. (in Shahak and Mezvinsky 1999: 89)

Having organised themselves into a militant, well-disciplined, private army, with the encouragement of successive Israeli governments, and having always regarded themselves as being subject to divine and halachic laws and above the conventional laws of the state as far as the 'biblical lands' are concerned, the Gush Emunim settlers represent the severest challenge to any Israeli government that might consider ceding West Bank territory to Palestinian sovereignty. Moreover, as Jewish fundamentalist theology spreads in Israel, with its mystical and fanatical attacks on rationalism and democracy, the repercussions for inter-ethnic and inter-faith relations in the Holy Land at large is a major concern. There is good reason to fear that the greater the role of the *halacha* in the political life of Israel, the more vigorously these fundamentalists will demand that the Palestinians, Muslim and Christian, be dealt with according to halachic regulations, including the imposition of the status of 'resident alien' on them, thereby making life even more difficult for the Palestinians.

4

Jewish Fundamentalism, the Bible and the 'Sacred Geography' of Jerusalem: Implications for Inter-faith Relations

Devotion to some 'sacred geography' is a phenomenon shared by all faiths and cultures. Historians of religion argue that it is one of the earliest such manifestations. A 'sacred geography', of which 'mountains' often are a part, has more to do with the spiritual life of a faith. The notion of 'sacredness' is also bound up with the notion of God. It seems to answer a profound human need. Sacred geography, like God, involves also the bestowal of meaning on a life which is not infrequently mundane and even boring, offering both value and hope (Eliade 1958: 368, 1959: 373). The notion of the 'sacred space' can inspire contradictory emotions: fear, awe, calm, peace, pain, dread, compelling moral activity (Armstrong 1996). Although Jerusalem was not founded by Jews, Christians or Muslims, it is one of the oldest cities on earth, apparently founded by the Canaanites about 5,000 years ago. According to the Hebrew Bible the city was known as 'Jebus', and the term 'Jebusites' is used in the Bible to describe the 'pre-Israelite' inhabitants of Jerusalem who are identified as belonging to a Canaanite tribe. The books of Genesis (10:16; 15:21) and Exodus (3:8,17; 13:5) mention the Jebusites as one of seven peoples doomed to destruction. But, as we shall see in Chapter 7, in the opinion of most modern archaeologists and biblical scholars the Jebusites, Canaanites and Israelites were not distinct or separate ethnicities. Archaeologists and biblical scholars now question the historicity of the Hebrew Bible, and its account of the capture of Jerusalem by David they consider to be totally fictional. However, the city, for different reasons, became central to the 'sacred geography' of the three Abrahamic faiths. Furthermore, religious attitudes towards the 'sacred geography' of Jerusalem – the Jewish, Christian and Muslim 'holinesses' of the city – have evolved historically and will continue to do so, under ever-changing social and political conditions.

Religiously the city of Jerusalem has been at the heart of Jewish religious thought and symbolism. Its 'holiness' for Jews derives from the perception that (a) it had the site of the temple; (b) it was the subject of lamentation down the ages; (c) Jews faced Jerusalem when they prayed; (d) the Torah, Halacha, Haggada, Tefilla, Kabbala, and so on, all celebrated the city's ancient history and mourned its devastation; and (e) Jerusalem was also the focus of messianic hope (Wasserstein 2002: 3-4).

While Jerusalem was central in the religious imagination, this did not translate into political, social, economical, demographic, cultural and intellectual realities. Indeed, Jerusalem has not been a major centre for Judaism over the last 2,000 years. Nevertheless, Jewish fundamentalists talk about the 'unbroken chain of Jewish presence' in the city, from the earliest times to the rise of Zionism in the late nineteenth century.

It is important politically for the Israelis to uphold the claim of a constant and enduring Jewish presence in the city. Bernard Wasserstein, a distinguished British Jewish historian, argues that the historical evidence for this claim is highly questionable. He explains that Jews were even forbidden to enter the city throughout the period of Roman and Byzantine rule. Although some Jewish pilgrims appear to have visited Jerusalem, there is no evidence of a Jewish community in Jerusalem for five centuries between the second and seventh centuries (Wasserstein 2002: 2).

The arrival of the Crusaders ensured that the Jewish presence therein would, again, be interrupted. When they captured Jerusalem in 1099, the Jewish as well as the Muslim community was once again thrown out of the city. Only after 1260, under the Muslim Mamluke Sultans of Egypt, did Jews slowly begin to return to the city. But then a conflict began to simmer between the Jewish community and local Christians over holy places on Mount Zion. After 1516, under Ottoman Muslim rule, the Jewish settlement in the city was secure, and we see some demographic growth. In the seventeenth century, the estimated Jewish population of the city was 1,000, about 10 per cent of its inhabitants. Moreover, until the mid-nineteenth century, the Jewish community in Jerusalem remained very small; relatively poor, and largely dependent on charity and financial support from Jews outside Palestine. Indeed for four centuries of Ottoman rule, the main intellectual and religious centre of Jewish life in Palestine was not Jerusalem, but the city of Safad in Galilee (Wasserstein 2002: 2). For such historical reasons, the Zionist claim of an 'unbroken chain of Jewish presence in the city' is no more than a myth. Indeed, for nearly 700 years after the destruction of the Second Temple there is no evidence of a Jewish community, and for many centuries between the second and the nineteenth centuries, Jewish settlement in Jerusalem was patchy. Although theologically, religiously and symbolically Jerusalem remained central in the Jewish religious imagination, politically, socially, economically, demographically and even culturally and intellectually Jerusalem was not a major centre for Judaism. Only for a short period, some forty years only, was Jerusalem the capital of the ancient Israelite monarchy (see von Waldow 2004).

Nevertheless, Jewish fundamentalists continue to propagate the two interrelated myths of Jerusalem as the 'united eternal capital of Israel', and of the 'unbroken chain of Jewish presence' in the city. Not only do they emphasise Judaism's strong bond with the city, but they claim unbroken Jewish presence in the city for the last 5,000 years.[1] The fundamentalist perspective of Jewish fundamentalists is ahistorical, and indeed mythical.[2] For them religious 'holiness' is not a historically evolving phenomenon, but rather something which exists above and outside history.[3]

Historically various factors made Jerusalem 'holy' also to Muslims. The actual Arabic name of the city is 'Al-Quds', the Holy. The 'holiness' of Jerusalem in the Muslim tradition is religious at heart, focused on al-Aqsa Mosque and the Dome of the Rock. As the Quran states, it was to al-Aqsa that the Prophet was carried on his Night Journey from Mecca, and from the rock that he ascended to the seventh heaven (*al-Israi wal-mi'iraj*). Today Muslims insist that the entirety of al-Haram al-Sharif (including the Dome of the Rock and the al-Aqsa Mosque, and the open squares between the shrines) are all sacred ground. Some Palestinian Muslims further assert that there is no archeological evidence for the Jewish Kingdom founded by King David, and that no trace of Solomon's Temple has been found. The Kingdom of Israel is not mentioned in any contemporary text but only in the Bible. It is quite likely, therefore, that it is merely a myth.[4]

Secular and religious Israelis are little different. They discount the story of the Prophet Muhammad's ascent to heaven from al-Haram al-Sharif – a narrative that lies at the heart of the Muslim devotion to al-Quds (Armstrong 1996: xviii). They ascribe political and administrative motives only to Muslims (and Christians), and not at all to themselves. They deny any religious or theological motivation behind the construction of the Muslim shrines, and assert that the building the Dome of the Rock by the Umayyad Caliphs was purely politically motivated. Writing in *Middle East Quarterly*, Daniel Pipes, American-Jewish author and supporter of the Israeli right wing, and perhaps best known in the USA for his promotion of Campus Watch in US universities, had this to say:

> The first Umayyad ruler, Mu'awiya, chose Jerusalem as the place where he ascended to the caliphate; he and his successors engaged in a construction program – religious edifices, a palace, and roads – in the city. The Umayyads possibly had plans to make Jerusalem their political and administrative capital; indeed, Elad finds that they in effect treated it as such. But Jerusalem is primarily a city of faith, and, as the Israeli scholar Izhak [sic] Hasson explains, the 'Umayyad regime was interested in ascribing an Islamic aura to its stronghold and center'. Toward this end (as well as to assert Islam's presence in its competition with Christianity), the Umayyad caliph built Islam's first grand structure, the Dome of the Rock, right on the spot of the Jewish Temple, in 688–91. This remarkable building is not just the first monumental sacred building of Islam but also the only one that still stands today in roughly its original form.[5]

It should be pointed out that similar attitudes towards the al-Aqsa Mosque and other Muslim shrines in Jerusalem are propagated by both Jewish religious fundamentalists and secular Zionists-attitudes. Typically, Jewish fundamentalist perspectives on the Muslim shrines consist of:

• Theologically and religiously they deny any significance of Jerusalem in Islam, and reject Muslim religious 'holiness' in Jerusalem, and Muslim religious rights in the city.

- Socially and politically, they assert that Islam – and Christianity as well-has only a loose and insignificant bond with Jerusalem; Muslims, Arabs and Palestinians, they say, have no attachment to the city, and they deny that Jerusalem was ever a cultural or scholarly centre for Palestinians or Muslims.[6]
- They deny that Jerusalem ever had a role in the life of the Prophet.
- They ascribe purely political motives to Muslims in the sanctification of the city: the Umayyad Caliphs, for political reasons, forced the city of Jerusalem to assume a role in the life of the Prophet Muhammad; the 'sanctification' of Jerusalem in Islam was based exclusively on the Umayyad political and building programmes in the city, etc.[7]
- The 'Furthest Mosque' (*Al-Masjid al-Aqsa* of the Quran) they claim, is merely a figure of speech. They deny the basis for associating the 'al-Aqsa Mosque' with Jerusalem.
- They assert, by way of contrast and conclusion, that the Jewish faith has altogether stronger and more deeply rooted bonds with Jerusalem.

Both radical Jewish nationalists and religious fundamentalists argue that the current struggle for a Palestinian state, with East Jerusalem as its capital, contains a trace of the claim that Jerusalem is holy to Islam. They claim, however, that the historic record shows that the actions and circumstances on which the Muslim claim is based are not very holy at all. Rather, Jerusalem has been imbued artificially with Muslim sacredness, through 'wordplay and administrative sleight of hand', which, of course, means that there are no genuine 'holy' places for Islam in Jerusalem.[8] Such positions are yet another reflection of Israel's deeply rooted politics of denial (Masalha 2003).

Building the Temple and the Muslim Holy Shrines

One of the most salient aspects of the Arab–Israeli conflict in the last thirty years has been the growing power of exclusivist fundamentalism within the three 'Abrahamic faiths' (Appleby 1997; Aran 1997: 294-327; Shahak and Mezvinsky 1999), and the focus of religious conflict in the Holy Land on the question of Jerusalem. There are some similarities between the Jewish, Christian and Muslim religious fundamentalist attitudes on 'sacred Jerusalem' – we deal with differences below:

- The issue of Jerusalem is explosive partly because the city has acquired a powerful mythical status in all three. Each side has many 'myths' of the 'sacred geography' of Jerusalem. The recourse to this mythology is linked to what psychologists might describe as 'self-perception', or, 'inner truth'. Many Muslims, Christians and Jews are wrapped up in all kinds of mythology about Jerusalem and the whole notion of 'sacredness' is bound up with themselves, their perception of reality, their search for meaning and perhaps their own identity (Armstrong 1996).
- A key element in the fundamentalism of the faiths – as in other fundamentalist movements of other faiths – is the adherents' belief that they possess special and direct access to transcendental truth, to the future course of events and their understanding of them.
- The faith and ideological dedication of the believer across the three faiths are the decisive factors, and these are couched in *absolute, rather than historically evolving, terms.*
- The holy texts, representing the word of God, provide a road-map for the future, guiding the continuing struggle toward redemption.
- For religious fundamentalists, history is God's means of communication with his people. Political trends and events contain messages that provide instructions, reprimands and rewards. Thus, political and historical analysis is equivalent to the interpretation of God's will.
- Fear is a common thread that weaves radical religious movements together. Although it is not the only motivating factor behind political violence, it is virtually always there. Religious fundamentalists fear that the young will abandon the synagogues, churches, mosques for physical and material gratification.
- Religious fundamentalists of all creeds also share some common traits and motivations with those secular radical nationalists who engage in political violence.
- Perhaps the most disturbing situation is the convergence of fundamentalist interests across the faiths, creating the potential for a global holy war.
- No less disturbing is the virtual equiparation, within some circles of Jewish and Christian fundamentalism, with 'Ground Zero' of Jerusalem's al-Haram al-Sharif/Temple Mount.

There is, of course, a basic difference between mainstream and fundamentalist Muslim attitudes on the question of the shrines in the Old City. Palestinian Muslims in occupied East Jerusalem are on the defensive, struggling against creeping Judaisation of the Old City (Masalha 1997: 229-30) and seeking to preserve the religious and prayer status quo on al-Haram al-Sharif,[9] while Jewish and Christian fundamentalists are on the offensive, running joint and well-funded campaigns in both Israel and the USA for the building of the Jewish temple on Al-Haram Al-Sharif. The latter seek to alter the situation of the Muslim shrines radically, something which could result in local and global conflagration. For some Christian fundamentalist evangelicals, the 'Battle for Jerusalem' is the 'End of Days Battle of Armageddon'.

Christian fundamentalists find common ground with fundamentalist Jews and hard-line secular Zionists. Since their fate and that of the entire world is at stake, Christian fundamentalists and the Christian right in the USA are committed to supporting and protecting Greater Israel and exclusive Israeli domination of Jerusalem at all costs. This relatively new and unusual alliance between fundamentalist Christian Zionists and Israeli Jewish fundamentalists (and hard-line secular Zionists) has serious implications for interfaith and communal relations in the Holy Land (and elsewhere).

Rights of Occupancy and Residency in Jerusalem

For radical Jewish fundamentalists the presence of non-Jews in Jerusalem is morally and politically irrelevant, when compared to the national right of the Jews to settle and possess the 'holy' city, 'the eternal possession of the Jewish people alone' (Nisan 1983, in Chomsky 1983: 444 and 470 n3). The messianic rabbis see the Palestinians' very residence in the Holy Land as marking them off as criminals, and imply that Israel's failure to clear out the Palestinian Muslims and Christians from Jerusalem completely is a transgression of the *halacha* (Harkabi 1986 :212). The same rabbis have demanded that the Palestinians should be at least discouraged from living in Jerusalem. They repeatedly cite the following from Maimonides' *Mishneh Torah*: 'Jerusalem is more sacred than other towns surrounded by a wall ... no place allowed in it for *ger toshav*' (Ben Mainom 1985: 46-7).

Rabbi Shalom Dov Wolpo, who bases his views on both Maimonides and the opinions of the Brooklyn-based Rabbi from Lubavich (the late Rabbi Schneerson, the head of the Habbad Hassidic movement) emphasises that not even a '*ger toshav*' can live in Jerusalem – how much less Christians and Muslims who are not included in this category:

> According to *halacha* it is forbidden for a gentile to live in Jerusalem, and in accordance with the ruling by Maimonides it is forbidden to permit even a ger toshav in Jerusalem. ... True, this applies when Israel has a strong hand, but today, too, although it is not possible to expel them by force, this does not mean that we have to encourage them to live there. (Wolpo 1983: 146)

Rabbi Wolpo adds:

> If they [the Israeli leaders] had declared at the time of the occupation of Jerusalem and the territories [in June 1967] that they were going to leave alive the residents and give them financial compensation, but they must cross immediately to Trans-Jordan, they [the Arabs] would have been thankful for this until today ... yet what did the [Israeli] leaders do [?]: they left the Arabs in their location ... but from the beginning they should have removed them from here. (Wolpo 1983: 145 n4)

Some influential rabbis have demanded that the Arabs, Muslims as well as Christians, should be removed from, or at least discouraged from living in, Jerusalem.[10] Rabbi Eli'ezer Waldenberg, the Israel Prize winner for 1976, stated:

> I, for example, support the application of the *halacha* prohibition on gentiles living in Jerusalem, and if we should apply the halacha, as it should be, we would have to expel all the gentiles [Arabs] from Jerusalem and purify it absolutely. Also we must not permit the gentiles to be a majority in any of Israel's cities (in Rubinstein 1980: 123).[11]

Waldenberg implies not only the expulsion of the Arabs from Jerusalem but also from Nazareth, Nablus, Hebron, Ramallah, etc. The Palestinians, who should only be given the status of resident alien, must be reduced to a small minority.

The leader of the NRP, Rabbi Yitzhak Levy – a founder of Matzad (the Religious Zionism Camp), an extreme right faction within the NRP – had made clear earlier his opposition to allowing Israeli Arab Knesset members the right to vote on the Oslo Accords of 1993. According to *Haaretz* (25

February 1998) he also supported 'exiling Arabs' in the Occupied Territories to other Arab states (Jones 1999: 19). Rabbi Levy is also known to be close to former Sephardic Chief Rabbi Mordechai Eliyahu, a leading advocate of the building of the temple in Jerusalem, who has called for the rehabilitation of Yigal Amir, Yitzhak Rabin's assassin (Jones 1999: 19; Aviner 2000: 9-10). In 1983, while still serving as Sephardi Chief Rabbi, Eliyahu had sponsored a conference with 'Ateret Cohanim' Yeshiva on the rebuilding of the Temple (see also below). He believes that the Temple would descend from heaven amidst flames of fire – at that point the Muslim shrines, the Dome of the Rock and al-Aqsa Mosque, would be burnt, and the Temple built in their place (in Ronel 1984: 12).

These fundamentalist ideas, which in the past were marginal, are becoming increasingly close to the centre of political thinking. For instance, 'Ovadia Yosef – the politically relatively moderate former Chief Rabbi of Israel, and spiritual mentor of the orthodox religious party of Shas, which was in the government of Ehud Barak – ruled that the New Testament should be burned because Christianity is a form of idolatry.[12] The practical effect of this ruling was revealed in the Hebrew daily *Ma'ariv* in June 1985, when New Testament copies found in the library of the base of the army Chief Education Officer were burned by the military Rabbi of the base.[13] Three weeks later *Ma'ariv* reported that the influential Knesset Foreign Affairs and Defence Committee had referred to the incident and one of its members (MK and Rabbi Haim Druckman) had justified the New Testament burning.[14] The implication of these ideas and actions are crystal clear: if Christian Arabs are practising a form of 'idol worship' and if the Palestinians, Christians and Muslims, are to be discouraged from living in Jerusalem and are to be subjected to the Torah laws of 'resident alien' – a status that is extremely unlikely to be acceptable to the Palestinians – expulsion becomes a logical conclusion.

'Ateret Cohanim, the Temple, and Judaisation of the Old City of Jerusalem

Since 1967 much Israeli settlement activity has been undertaken to 'redeem' East Jerusalem's Old City from its Christian and Muslim inhabitants. The Old City, however, has remained predominantly inhabited by Palestinian Muslims and Christians, despite creeping 'Judaisation': already in 1967, in the Old City's Jewish quarter and surroundings, some 4,000 Palestinians were evicted to make possible the reconstruction of a vastly enlarged and completely Jewish quarter (Masalha 1997: 81). In 1981, Israel's High Court, to preserve the ethnic purity of the Old City's Jewish quarter, ruled that non-Jews could not buy property there (Friedman 1992: 99). Both the Muslim and Christian quarters of the Old City – in sharp contrast to the Jewish quarter – have remained religiously mixed: according to Israel's *Statistical Yearbook* of 1988, for example, 3,900 Christians and 700 Muslims lived in the Christian quarter.

In December 1978, a group of orthodox Jews and disciples of Rabbi Tzvi Yehuda Kook announced they had set up a yeshiva in the Muslim quarter of the Old City, calling it 'Ateret Cohanim, 'the Priestly Crown'. 'Ateret Cohanim was formed to publish and distribute material concerning 'the priesthood and functions of the Temple', and 'to acquire in any manner whatsoever, and especially by grant, gift lease or purchase, land, rooms or houses [in Arab East Jerusalem]'. Its members state openly that they want to prepare the way for the Messiah by 'redeeming' the Old City stone by stone, until they have transformed Jerusalem into a holy city in the service of the Third Temple. They also justify the expulsion of Palestinian Muslims and Christians by invoking Maimonides, who said that that after the Messiah comes, only Jews will be permitted to live in Jerusalem (Friedman 1992: 118). Since the 1980s, Friends of 'Ateret Cohanim in the United States have donated millions of US dollars. Some of the money has come from right-wing Christian evangelicals (Friedman 1992: 111), who, as we have seen, view the activities of Jewish Israeli fundamentalists as the prelude to the Second Coming of Christ. 'Ateret Cohanim officials stated that most of the money collected in the USA goes to its subsidiary, the 'Jerusalem Reclamation Project', founded in the early 1980s, whose primary purpose is to purchase Arab property in East Jerusalem.

The activities of 'Ateret Cohanim have included the takeover of the St John's Hospice in the Old City, just a few metres from the Church of the Holy Sepulchre. On 11 April 1990, during the Easter Holy Week and Passover, 150 armed Jewish settlers affiliated with 'Ateret Cohanim moved into the seventy-room hospice. The hospice is owned by the Greek Orthodox Church, but had been leased since 1932 to an Armenian, Martyos

Matossian. This somewhat elusive man rented hospice rooms to Arab families and European pilgrims, but already by 1980 the Greek Orthodox Church had been trying to evict him. On 28 June 1989, Matossian sublet the building for $3.5 million to a mysterious Panamanian company called SBC Ltd, which turned over the building to the Jewish settlers. The settlers renamed the site Neot David, put up a Star of David and invited Israeli minister Ariel Sharon to visit the site. The Israeli Housing Ministry, which had been quietly helping 'Ateret Cohanim to purchase Arab property in the Old City since 1986, had covertly channelled $1.8 million to a subsidiary of the Jewish National Fund (JNF). The JNF company then passed on the money to subsidise the purchase of the sublease to the Panama-based SBC (Friedman 1992: 99-110).

The encroachment by Jewish fundamentalist settlers into the Christian quarter, culminating in the purchase of the hospice, erupted into a huge controversy in Israel and the West. On 27 April 1990, all the major Christian churches in Israel and the Occupied Territories closed and rang funeral peals in protest. It was the first time that the Church of the Holy Sepulchre had been closed in eight hundred years. In New York, Cardinal O'Connor denounced the takeover as an 'obscene' plot to acquire Christian property in the Holy Land. In Jerusalem the Greek Orthodox Church argued that the sublet to SBC was illegal. The Church's claim was subsequently upheld by an Israeli court, which then ordered the settlers to vacate the property but permitted twenty security and 'maintenance employees' (actually settlers of 'Ateret Cohanim) to remain in the building pending litigation. The settlers and their families are still living in the hospice (Friedman 1992: 100).

Direct Action and Violence: Muslim Shrines and the Temple Mount-related Groups

The fundamentalist theology of the Israeli messianic force is not confined to doctrines and sermons. From the outset, the ideas of the Jewish messianics began to accommodate and even sacralise the use of violence as a proactive means of forestalling any moves that might retard the 'messianic process' of territorial 'redemption' and land conquest. From the beginning of the occupation, and especially since the late 1970s, the settlers – whose theology grants them the divine right to Judaise the territories and who reject the very existence of the Palestinians – were deliberately seeking to foster clashes between Arabs and Jews, and to create conditions that would precipitate a gradual Arab depopulation. Many supporters of the violent groups live among Jewish settlers on the West Bank. One of these zealots was Dr Baruch Goldstein, of the Kiryat Arba settlement, adjoining Hebron, who carried out the massacre of twenty-nine Muslim worshippers at the Ibrahimi mosque in Hebron on 24 February 1994 (McDowall 1994: 123). After the Hebron massacre the two groups associated with Kach were banned. Nevertheless, prominent figures of these groups continued to receive funds from supporters in the USA and resurfaced in other groups such as Eyal (Joffe 1996: 151), one of whose members, Yigal Amir, assassinated Prime Minister Yitzhak Rabin on 4 November 1995. No'am Federman is currently active in the Committee for Safety on the Roads, a right-wing pressure group led by a former Tehiya Member of Knesset whose *raison d'être* is to keep the West Bank roads safe for passage by Jewish settlers and whose members have been accused of acts of violence against Palestinians (Joffe 1996: 151-2).[15]

After 1977, with the encouragement of successive Likud-led governments, the militant settlers in the West Bank and Gaza Strip effectively organised themselves into a private and highly motivated army. In 1979, at the behest of the army Chief of Staff, General Raphael Eitan, the settlers were integrated into regular reserve units responsible for patrolling the streets of local Arab towns and villages (Zucker 1983: 51-2; Lustick 1988: 66). With weapons, ammunition and training readily available, and a sympathetic political climate created by superhawks Chief of Staff Eitan and Likud Defence Minister Ariel Sharon, attacks on Arab civilians and Arab property became commonplace. From 1980, and through 1984, the Israeli press reported more than 380 attacks against individual Arabs, of whom 23 were killed, 191 injured and 38 abducted. Hundreds more attacks were directed at Arab property, cars, homes and shops. Forty-one attacks on Muslim and Christian institutions were also recorded (Lustick 1988: 66; Abu Shakra 1985: 15). In 1981, Yehuda Litani of *Haaretz* warned: 'The West Bank settlers constitute military units.... They will disrupt any political move towards concessions to the Arabs.... Their well-stocked ammunition stores in the West Bank will be of great help in this struggle.'[16]

Having organised themselves into a militant, well-disciplined, private army, and having always regarded themselves as being subject to divine laws and above the conventional law of the state, so far as *Eretz Yisrael* is concerned, the Gush Emunim-type settlers would represent the severest challenge to any Israeli government that might consider ceding West Bank territory to Arab sovereignty.

Gush Emunim also harboured a whole range of violent groups which either planned or had actually carried out attacks against Arab civilians. These militant groups included Kach; Temple Mount-related groups; Terror Against Terror (TNT), a shadowy group or groups related to Kach which claimed responsibility for attacks against Palestinians in East Jerusalem, Christian missionaries in Jerusalem, and dovish Israeli Jews; and the Sicarites, a group which vowed to avenge tit-for-tat the stabbing of Jews by militant Palestinians (Joffe 1996: 153; Lustick 1988: 67). Gush Emunim also had ties with Kach, the Temple Mount Faithful and the 'Ateret Cohanim group, which has apparently on various occasions tried to blow up the two mosques on the al-Haram al-Sharif, so as to herald the building of the Jewish Temple (Joffe 1996: 153; Shragai 1995).

From 1967 and through the mid-1980s at least five separate Temple Mount-related groups, with an estimated membership of 1,500, sought to change (sometimes violently) the status quo on the site of the al-Haram al-Sharif. Their objectives ranged from building a Jewish synagogue on the site to restricting the Muslim access area, and even replacing the Muslim shrines with a rebuilt Temple. In the late 1990s, a Miami-based American Jewish millionaire, Dr Irving Moskowitz, offered $12 million for Jewish groups seeking to replace the Muslim shrines with a rebuilt Temple.[17] More recently former director of Israel's General Security Service (Shen Bet) Avi Dichter had this to say: the dream of these radical fundamentalists – to blow up the Temple Mount in Jerusalem, one of the most important holy sites in the Muslim world – 'should give us sleepless nights'; 'Jewish terror is liable to create a serious strategic threat that will turn the Israeli–Palestinian conflict into a conflict between thirteen million Jews and a billion Muslims all over the world'.[18]

Already in May 1980, the Israeli police had discovered a plot to blow up al-Aqsa Mosque. A large cache of explosives was unearthed on the roof of a yeshiva in the Old City. Those involved included two soldiers with links to Gush Emunim and Kach. In March 1983, several dozen yeshiva students and soldiers from Kiryat Arba and Jerusalem were arrested after they were found digging under the mosques. Equipped with weapons, shovels and diagrams of the underground passageways, they seemed to have planned to seize the site and hold public prayer services there. Leading Gush Emunim figures, including Hanan Porat, Moshe Levinger and Ele'ezer Waldman, had prior knowledge of the operation, and expressed support for the conspirators' objectives. On the night of 27 January 1984, another group of Jewish religious zealots was reported in the immediate vicinity of the Muslim shrines. The group managed to escape, leaving behind thirty pounds of explosive, fuses, detonators, and twenty-two grenades (Lustick 1988: 68–69).

In 1983, the so-called 'Lifta Gang' came closer than any other Jewish fanatical group in succeeding to carry out its plot to blow up the Muslim Mosques on al-Haram al-Sharif (Shragai, 1995: 172). However, by far the best organised effort to destroy the al-Aqsa Mosque and the Dome of the Rock was planned by a secret group of Gush Emunim leaders and activists known in the Hebrew press as *Hamahteret Hayehudit* (the Jewish Underground). The plot to blow up the Muslim shrines in January 1984 was developed carefully and systematically over several years. It involved a group of twenty-five men from Jewish settlements on the West Bank and the Golan Heights, including an army officer with a high level of expertise in explosives, and ammunition stolen from the Israeli army sufficient to carry out the operation (Lustick 1988: 69).

Haggai Segal, a prominent Gush Emunim settler from 'Ofra on the West Bank, who had served three years in prison for his part in the car-bomb attacks on the two West Bank mayors in June 1980, said several years later:

> You can't make a big roundup and put them on buses, but you must make conditions bad for the Arabs – and if they continue the war [*intifada*], you must make them leave. I drove by the American consulate in East Jerusalem yesterday and saw a long line of Arabs waiting to get visas. The situation is very hard for them now, and it must get harder. (Friedman 1992: 80)

The discovery of the activities of the Jewish Underground organisation in the mid-1980s showed again that the ideas of the messianic trend were not confined to sermons and doctrinal exhortations. On 2 May 1985, the

Jerusalem Post published an article by David Richardson which pointed out that at least seven rabbis, among them the prominent spiritual guide of Gush Emunim, were privy to the violent campaign conducted by the Jewish Underground. According to the article, a statement confirming this was given to the Jerusalem police by the accused leader of the underground group, Menahem Livni, and his 27-page affidavit was presented to the Jerusalem District Court on 1 May 1985. These rabbis included the above-mentioned Rabbis Tzvi Yehuda Kook, 'Ovadia Yosef and Shlomo Aviner, as well as Rabbi Moshe Levinger, a prominent veteran leader of Gush Emunim, and the founder of the first Jewish settlement in Hebron (1968) and of the adjoining Kiryat Arba settlement, and Rabbi Eli'ezer Waldman (a Tehiya MK at the time), Rabbi Yo'ezer Ariel and Rabbi Dov Leor. Wald-man, Ariel, Leor and Levinger all took part in a meeting at which it was discussed and unanimously decided upon to wage a widespread campaign of violence against the inhabitants of the Occupied Territories.

In fact, support for an amnesty for these Underground members did not come only from the religious camp. On 19 June 1985, a public opinion poll conducted by *Haaretz* daily revealed the following results: 52.6 per cent of those interviewed supported an immediate release without trial; 4 per cent supported pardon after the trial; 35.5 per cent opposed a pardon; the remaining 7.9 per cent expressed no opinion. A reputed 'moderate' rabbi, Rabbi Likhtenstein, who heads a yeshiva in the Occupied Territories, voiced his opinion that these Jewish Underground members – though they should receive some punishment – should not receive the same penalty meted out to a Jew convicted of murdering another Jew, because the soul of a non-Jew had a different value from that of a Jew (Shahak 1988: 3). The former Ashkenazi Chief Rabbi, the late Shlomo Goren, an enthusiastic Temple Mount advocate, also expressed sympathy for the Underground members. And MK Yuval Neeman, Minister of Science in the Shamir government, who supported Arab 'transfer', defended the Underground network as acting in self-defence (Inbari 1984: 10–11).

Likewise the relatively light punishment of the Jewish Terror Against Terror (TNT) network in 1984 did nothing to discourage settlers' violence, which aims at precipitating an Arab exodus. Nor did it help when leading Israeli politicians described the convicted murderers as basically 'good boys' who acted in self-defence, or those convicted murderers had their sentences reduced, or were pardoned by the president, after the intervention of leading rabbis. Sixty prominent Israeli rabbis, including the two former Chief Rabbis, 'Ovadia Yosef and Shlomo Goren, intervened on behalf of, and supported the release of, the TNT detainees,[19] whom General Yehoshafat Harkabi, of the Hebrew University of Jerusalem, described in 1984 as

> Serious people who occupy high positions among their public ... they have a rational state of mind and their chief motivation stems apparently from the awareness that annexation of the West Bank together with its Arab population would be disastrous and tantamount to national suicide – unless that population were thinned out and made to flee by terrorism. This reasoning is not moral, but it stems from the rational conclusion of the policy that aims at annexation. Such terrorism is neither a 'punishment' nor a deterrent; it is a political instrument.[20]

Conclusion

In Jerusalem, religious, theological and historical claims matter. For religious fundamentalists (Jewish, Muslim and Christian), however, these claims are the functional equivalent to the deed to the city and have direct operational consequences. In large measure, the question of Jerusalem is religious: the ancient city has sacred associations for Jews, Muslims and Christians alike – although Christians today no longer make an independent political claim to Jerusalem. Furthermore both Palestinian Muslims and Israeli Jews insist on sovereignty over their overlapping sacred areas: al-Haram al-Sharif/Temple Mount. In part, the question of Jerusalem is practical: Palestinians insist that occupied East Jerusalem should serve as the capital of their state, something the Israelis are loathe to accept. The construction of nationalist myths centred on the holy places of Jerusalem has become central to nation-building of both Israelis and Palestinians. The deployment of spurious scholarship, often by secular Zionist authors (such as Daniel Pipes and Yitzhak Hasson) in support of Jewish fundamentalist claims and attacking other theological and historical claims is designed to provide justification for Israeli de-Arabisation policies in Jerusalem (Masalha 1997: 229-30). Jewish fundamentalism's propagation of the myth of the Jewish connection and attachment to Jerusalem is the most powerful one: Judaism made Jerusalem a holy city over five thousand years ago, and through all that time there was a Jewish political and territorial presence in the city. Although theologically, religiously and symbolically Jerusalem remained central to Judaism, politically, socially, economically, demographically and even culturally and intellectually Jerusalem was not a major centre for Judaism. Only for a short period, some forty years, was Jerusalem the capital of the ancient united monarchy of Israel and Judah.

Moreover as Jewish fundamentalist theology spreads in Israel, with its mystical and fanatical attacks on rationalism and democracy, its repercussions for inter-ethnic and inter-faith relations in the Holy Land at large is a major concern. On a practical, policy-oriented level, it is important to point out that the intensification of Israeli de-Arabisation policies in and around the Old City of Jerusalem – with its 'sacred geography' – led to the eruption of the 'al-Aqsa Intifada' (uprising) in September 2000, thus unleashing an unprecedented wave of violence that went far beyond the bloody clashes which followed the opening of the 'archaeological tunnel' near the al-Aqsa Mosque in September 1996, where riots resulted in dozens killed. Both the opening of the tunnel and Ariel Sharon's highly provocative tour of al-Haram al-Sharif on 28 September 2000 – which were aimed at tightening Israeli control over the centre of the holy city, particularly around the Islamic shrines – have brought Israel into open war with the Palestinians, resulting in the deaths and injuries of thousands. However, the current al-Aqsa Intifada will not be sufficient to bring an end to the massive violation of human and religious rights in occupied East Jerusalem. In late 2005 Ehud Olmert replaced ailing Prime Minister Sharon, first as acting prime minister and leader of the new Kadima Party, and then, several months later, in April 2006, as prime minister. As mayor of Jerusalem in the 1990s, Olmert oppressed the Palestinian inhabitants of the city and intensified the process of de-Arabisation. He pressed for opening the 'archaeological tunnel' near the Muslim shrines and encouraged American Jewish right-wing millionaires to build Jewish settlements in the middle of unilaterally annexed Arab districts and pushed for the building of the Apartheid Wall that cuts up Arab neighbourhoods.[21]

There have been recent protests in Israel against the continuing desecration of Muslim holy sites in the city; on 10 April 2006 the daily *Haaretz* published a petition signed by dozens of Israeli and Palestinian lecturers in which they protested against the intention of the Simon Wiesenthal Institute to build a 'Museum of Tolerance' on the site of the Muslim cemetery in Mamilla in Jerusalem. Qadi Ahmad Natour, President of the Muslim Sharia Appeals Court in Israel, had written earlier in March:

> we hope that the initiators of the Tolerance Museum project will understand that they cannot trample the emotions of millions of Muslims in Israel and around the world and will decide by themselves on canceling the project in this location.[22]

On 16 April, Knesset member Meir Purush, of the orthodox Yahdut Ha'Torah party, added his voice to the protest:

> The desecration of the Muslim cemetery in Mamilla is a form of ugly racism which may, God forbid, place in danger the obliteration of Jewish cemeteries around the world. Where is our responsibility? ... For years ultra Orthodox Jewry is waging a principled struggle against the destruction of graves in the Land of Israel. The respect for their remains is dear to us and even touches the essence of our souls. More than once we have protested against the disrespect of archaeological explorations when graves are discovered. The same disrespect and lack of comprehension is evident now regarding the unfortunate decision to open graves and remove skeletons in the Muslim Cemetery in Mamilla. We must stop the building now in the initial stage of building.[23]

In the opinion of this author, the international community has an obligation and duty, under international law and due to the unique international status of Jerusalem – a *corpus separatum* under UN Partition Resolution of 11 November 1947 – to enforce the humanitarian provisions of the Fourth Geneva Convention, not to mention the scores of UN resolutions with the aim of protecting peoples under occupation. The international community could and should intervene to protect the Palestinian Muslim and Christian residents of Jerusalem and their holy places and persuade the right-wing Israeli government to abandon its support for Jewish fundamentalist groups operating in the Old City of Jerusalem, and indeed abandon its own plans to de-Arabise East Jerusalem.

5

Reinventing Maimonides:
From Universalist Philosopher to
Neo-Zionist Messianic, 1967-2006

This chapter focuses primarily on two distinct and mutually antagonistic strands of Jewish fundamentalism in Israel. The first is represented by the Jewish-Zionist fundamentalist or nationalist-religious camp (also known as the 'messianic' camp), and the second by the ultra-orthodox rabbis and non-Zionist religious parties of the Haredim, both Sephardi and Ashkenazi. I shall explore the doctrinal differences and disputes between these two fundamentalist strands over the 'messianic doctrine' and their impact on Israeli foreign and domestic policies. We shall see how the two main currents, militant Zionist and orthodox non-Zionist, invoke the theological orthodoxy and conservative interpretation of the Jewish *halacha* of the celebrated medieval philosopher and theologian Moses Maimonides (1135-1204) to justify their respective attitudes.

Maimonides' halachic orthodoxy was particularly illustrated in his approach to Christianity, which was similar to the views common to Jewish theologians in medieval Muslim Spain. He described Christianity as *'avoda zara* ('strange worship', or 'false worship') and a form of 'idolatry'. We shall see that his religious orthodoxy was the product of a distinct historical setting, and must therefore always be located, studied and understood within its proper medieval context. It will be seen that modern radical Jewish fundamentalists manipulate his insights as they view Christianity in the Holy Land today. We shall examine the rise of such hostile attitudes to Christianity (its symbols and churches) and Christians in the Holy Land, shared by the Zionist religious camp and the rabbis of the ultra-orthodox Haredim in the post-1967 period, discuss its ideo-theological roots, and assess its impact in Israel and on inter-faith relations in Israel and Palestine.

Rather than presuming to offer new insights into Maimonides' theology or the Jewish religion, or offering a new interpretation of classical Jewish religious attitudes towards the Palestinian Christians, the primary concern here is to explore the religious fundamentalism embraced by highly influential segments of the various religious camps in Israel. In citing traditional and medieval Jewish sources (especially Maimonides' writings and theology) one is conscious that they are widely cited by both orthodox Haredi Jews and Israeli–Jewish religious nationalists.

Maimonides: Universalist or Nationalist?

The struggle between neo-Zionist messianics and Arab nationalists over Maimonides, as he is now commonly known, is one of the most extra-ordinary episodes of intellectual conflict in modern times. Maimonides is widely recognised as Judaism's greatest theologian. A popular Jewish saying, 'From Moses to Moses there was none like Moses [Maimonides]', expresses the eminent position he has long held in Jewish estimation. In 1985, conferences were held in Israel and among Jewish communities in the West to commemorate the 850th anniversary of his birth. These meetings dealt with his intellectual contribution and considered its relevance for contemporary Jewish thought and practice.

Maimonides, however, was never merely a Jewish philosopher in some narrow sense. He was, rather, a distinguished medieval rationalist philosopher, and the most illustrious example of the golden age of Arabo-Islamic-Judaic symbiosis in the eleventh and twelfth centuries. Indeed, modern Arab historians have not only tended to portray Maimonides as a product of the Arabo-Islamic-Jewish culture of the Middle Ages but have also assessed his work within the wider context of the chronicles of Arab history itself. In *History of the Arabs*, Philip Hitti, while acknowledging Maimonides'

Jewish background, included him in the distinguished group of 'Spanish Arab physicians who were physicians by avocation and something else by vocation', and called him Abu 'Imran Ibn Maymun in the Arabic form of his name. 'For first place after Ibn Rushd [Averroes, 1126-1198] among the philosophers of the age the only candidate is his Jewish contemporary and fellow Cordovan ... Maimonides ..., the most famous of the Hebrew physicians and philosophers of the whole Arabic epoch' (Hitti 1956: 576, 584-5). More recently several Arab authors and academics describe Musa Ibn Maymun as an Arab-Muslim thinker and philosopher (Omran 1980: 18, 23-4; *Time*, 23 December 1985).

Ironically, in present-day Israel Maimonides has become the hero of messianic Zionism and anti-Arab religious fundamentalism. Yet Maimonides' medieval orthodoxy and contemporary Israeli–Jewish fundamentalism have completely different historical contexts and settings. He was neither an Arab nationalist nor a Jewish (Zionist) nationalist; he was a man of his own medieval period and of the Arabo-Judaic rationalist tradition. To begin with, the religious relationship of medieval diaspora Jews to the land had little to do with either modern and contemporary Jewish nationalism, or secular or religious Zionism. Religious Zionism and Gush Emunim in particular have made the sanctity of the 'whole land of Israel' a central tenet of their doctrine and a prime object of their religious passion.[1]

Yet for Maimonides the 'land of Israel' was of itself no different from other lands. It was distinctive, but only because it was sanctified by the commandments and by events of Israelite history. Since neither territory nor land demarcated the cultural identity of Diaspora Judaism, the land was not an object of passion for him. His medieval theology had little to do with modern Zionist nationalism or feverish religious messianism. His theology, which preceded Zionist nationalist ideas by 700 years, reflected a confident Jewish religious and social identity away from the 'land of Israel'; returning to, and colonisation of, the 'land of Israel' did not constitute the great hope of the Jewish people. Flourishing Jewish identity and culture were safeguarded in an accommodation with the Arab-Muslim civilisation. Born in Muslim Spain, Maimonides passed through the land on his way to Muslim Egypt and lived his entire life in the Diaspora (Prior 1999c: 56-7). For him the Jewish relationship to the 'land of Israel' resembled the Muslim relationship to Hijaz and the holy cities of Mecca and Medina.

There is neither a unified Jewish fundamentalist discourse in Israel nor a monolithic attitude towards Maimonides. Both doctrinally and politically, Israeli religious fundamentalists are not a homogeneous group, and their interpretation and use of Maimonides' theology vary from one group to another, for political and ideological reasons. Both the National Religious Party (NRP or Mafdal) and Gush Emunim represent fundamentalist Jews who are not Haredim (the name, which means 'fearing', i.e. 'God-fearing', refers to those ultra-orthodox Jews who object to modern innovations). Let us first examine Maimonides within his proper medieval context.

The Medieval Context: Maimonides and the Golden Age of Arabo-Islamic-Judaic Symbiosis

Europeans called him Maimonides, the Arabs Musa Ibn Maymun, and in rabbinical literature he is named the Rambam, an acronym of Rabbi Moshe ben Maimon. He is generally recognised as Judaism's greatest theologian and halachic authority (Leibowitz 1987: 68). He also distinguished himself as an astronomer, as a physician and above all as a rational philosopher, and he became the most illustrious example of the Arabo-Islamic-Judaic symbiosis of the late Middle Ages. Today he is generally recognised as both the most important codifier of Jewish law and one of the most radical philosophers of the Islamic world. Perceived as the pinnacle of Jewish scholarship and sagacity over the ages, Maimonides was linked in Jewish folk sayings to Moses himself. Moses gave the Torah and Maimonides gave the Torah Mishneh, the second or additional legal code, by which orthodox Jews have conducted their normative religious life for the last 800 years. In the modern era, Maimonides became a hero in Reform Judaism also.

Maimonides was born in 1135 in Cordoba, the capital of Muslim Spain, ruled by the Umayyad caliphs – by far the most enlightened country in Europe. It was a magnificent seat of culture, philosophy and science. His family left the country in the aftermath of the conquest of Cordoba by the Islamic sect al-Muwahhid (Almohades), and lived some time in Fez in Morocco. When in his thirties, he emigrated to Fustat, south of Cairo, where he lived for most of his life. He died in 1204. It is believed that he served as the court physician to Saladin and his son al-Malik al-Aziz (Hitti 1956: 584; Lewis 1973: 166–76). Classical orthodox Judaism and Arabo-Islamic culture were the contexts within which Maimonides worked, although most accounts of his thought are unduly influenced by his Jewish background and fail to do justice to the outstanding part he played in the development of medieval Arabic thought and culture and Islamic civilisation (Leaman 1990). Although he was an orthodox rabbi and the leader of his community, it would be misleading in philosophical terms to think of him as a specifically Jewish philosopher. Of far more importance is the influence of the rationalist and universalist tradition of philosophy in the Islamic world. He was a member of a distinguished group of thinkers in the Islamic world who took on board the methodology of Aristotle and applied it to difficult conceptual issues in interesting and perceptive ways (Leaman 1990: x). Maimonides was highly influenced by the philosophical doctrines of Ibn Sina (Avicenna) and Al-Farabi, two of the great rationalist medieval Muslim philosophers, and his philosophy was a grandiose attempt at a synthesis between the Jewish faith (a monotheistic 'revealed' faith) and rational Greek–Arabic Aristotelian philosophy.

Maimonides, his son Abraham, Sa'adya Gaon and many other famous Jewish personalities were the product of the golden age of the 'Arabo–Judaic culture' of the Middle Ages and the embodiment of its rational flowering (Goitein 1974: 70-71, 93). For the medieval Muslims, Jews and Christians were 'People of the Book' (*Ahl al-Kitab*) and as such entitled to religious tolerance and protection within the Islamic community under the covenant (*dhimma*). Islamic doctrine proudly proclaimed its Judaeo-Christian descent, and the Quran, while introducing significant modifications into the biblical narrative, affirmed Islam's adherence to classical Abrahamic orthodoxy (Quran 2.113, 135-6). In the Middle Ages as a whole the position of Jews under Arab Islam was far better than that of the Jews in medieval Christian Europe (Goitein 1974: 84). The medical professional in Muslim countries was held in high esteem and Jewish doctors are known to have been court physicians to caliphs and other Muslim rulers in practically every Muslim country. Reading Arabic sources on the history of medicine, for example, Ibn Abi 'Usayba, a colleague of Abraham, Maimonides' son and successor, was impressed by the spirit of true fellowship which bound together the doctors of various denominations of that time (Goitein 1974:

70–71). An observant Jew and a famous doctor, Maimonides was a good example of Jews' ability to reach the highest government posts in Muslim countries. His descendants occupied the office of *nagid* (in Arabic *ras al-millah*), the head of the Jewish community in Egypt, for nearly two centuries.

The Guide of the Perplexed: Maimonides' Arab Philosophy and Jewish Theology

The golden age of Arabo-Islamic civilisation linked Hellenic–Roman antiquity with modern times. Its dominant religion was Islam, its language was Arabic. Arabic had ceased to be an ethnic language and had become the language of a civilisation. Jews and Christians unhesitatingly used it even while expounding topics sacred to their co-religionists. Cambridge historian and orientalist Erwin Rosenthal states:

> The talmudic age apart, there is perhaps no more formative and positive period in our long and chequered history than that under the empire of Islam from the Mediterranean to the Indian Ocean. ... The basic tenets of Judaism, its formative concepts and ideas, were combined into a system intended to sustain the Jews, to demonstrate their distinctiveness, to secure survival and to instil hope and expectancy of redemption. The form of this exposition was largely borrowed from Muslim theology and religious philosophy. Even the newly-developing codification of the *Halachah* and the Responsa-literature of the Gaonin owe their form to Muslim patterns. (Rosenthal 1961: ix–xi)

Maimonides' philosophy and theology, in particular, drew freely and copiously from Muslim patterns and he must have regarded Islam as being from the flesh and bone of Judaism (Goitein 1974: 130). Under Islam the Jewish *dhimmi* was not equal to the Muslim. But the *dhimmi* was permitted to maintain his religious and cultural autonomy, and Maimonides' theology is an illustrious example of Arab Judaism, and of the fact that Judaism within Islam was a self-assured, autonomous culture despite, and possibly because of, its intimate connection with its Arabo-Islamic environment. Maimonides' generally positive attitude towards Islam is often contrasted with his relative hostility towards Christianity, which together with the Greek New Testament was perceived to be at variance with orthodox Jewish religious culture, while Islam and the Quran, within the context of the Arabo-Jewish symbiosis of the time, were perceived as closely related to Judaism.

Tolerant Muslim pluralism and linguistic integration laid the ground for an extraordinary intellectual symbiosis in which Muslims, Jews and Christians joined together in the discovery, study, imitation and illustration of Hellenistic philosophy, in what Franz Rosenthal called 'the classical heritage of Islam' (1975; also Epstein 1990; Rajwan 1968: 31-42). This intellectual renaissance created a new theology (*kalam* in Arabic; *mutakallimun*, theologians) designed to make religious law and philosophy coincide: to rationalise divine Revelation and show that it was in harmony with logic and the natural order. The most basic aspect of the Arab-Jewish symbiosis was the fact that the great majority of the Jews adopted the Arabic language, while Hebrew not only retained its position as a second and literary language, but also experienced an unprecedented revival. Writing in literary Arabic, Maimonides justified it thus: 'Any one who knows the three languages, Hebrew, Aramaic and Arabic, knows that they are only three branches of one and the same language' (in Halevi 1987: 61). The acquisition of the Arabic language by the Jews meant also their adoption of Arab ways of thinking and forms of literature as well as Muslim religious notions. Arabic was used by Jews for all kinds of literary activities, not only for scientific and other secular purposes, and also for expounding and translating the Bible or the Mishnah, for theological and philosophical treatises, for discussing Jewish law and ritual, and even for the study of Hebrew grammar. For letter-writing and other purposes, a more colloquial form of Arabic, interspersed with Hebrew words and phrases, was used (Halevi 1987: 131-2).

The Judaic–Arabic symbiosis is reflected in the history of the translation of the Jewish Bible into Arabic. Originally, the reason for this activity was the endeavour to provide by these translations an authoritative interpretation of the texts, in particular in theological matters (e.g. the inculcation of a spiritual–abstract conception of the human-like qualities attributed to God in the Bible). That is why the most famous of the classical translations, which superseded all the others in popular usage, that of Saʿadya Gaon – a linguist, philosopher and theologian of Egyptian origin who became Gaon, the spiritual head of the Jewish community in Baghdad (d. 942) – was called his *Tafsir*, 'commentary'. In order to avoid misunderstanding, Sa'adya wrote also a famous Arabic commentary on the Bible. His Arabic translation of the Bible, Goitein writes, 'became a sacred text, which was copied, and later printed, beside the Hebrew original and the old Aramaic version. This procedure was followed even in the latest standard of the Pentateuch for Yemenite Jews printed in Tel Aviv in 1940' (1974: 135).

Writing in Arabic and using Arabic methods and terminology, Jewish scholars assiduously explored and described the Hebrew Bible and the Mishnah. For the first time, the pronunciation, the grammar and the vocabulary of Hebrew were studied scientifically. Thus Hebrew and Hebrew Bible studies became a disciplined and well-organised means of expression under the influence of the Arabic language of Arabo-Islamic culture (Goitein 1974: 136; Halevi 1987: 134-6).

Islam saved the Jewish theology of the Talmud from disintegration and gave it a new content, in the image of Islam and the image that Islam had of Judaism. In Muslim theology, Maimonides found a model of a renaissance for Arab Judaism that Islam encouraged and cultivated. With the exception of *Mishneh Torah*, his code of Jewish law, all of Maimonides' major works were written in Arabic, although some were printed in Hebrew characters by simple transliteration from one alphabet to the other in order to get round the Islamic ban on missionary activity by the 'Peoples of the Book' in Ayyubid Egypt. But despite this device his works were read and discussed by theologians of all faiths.

The philosophical work that is considered Maimonides' magnum opus, *The Guide of the Perplexed* (in Arabic, *Dalalat al-Hairin*), was studied and used copiously by Jews, Christians and Muslims. It was also taught by Muslim lecturers to Jewish audiences who were less familiar with the philosophical and scientific thinking of the time (Goitein 1974: 146). In *Jews and Arabs: Their Contacts through the Ages*, Goitein writes:

> *The Guide of the Perplexed* is a great monument of Jewish–Arab symbiosis, not merely because it is written in Arabic by an original Jewish thinker and was studied by Arabs, but because it developed and conveyed to large sections of the Jewish people ideas which had so long occupied the Arab mind. (1974: 146-7)

In *The Guide of the Perplexed* Maimonides debates with Al-Farabi and the *mutakallimun* and with the Karaites whom he fought with all the authority of his rabbinical position. *The Guide of the Perplexed* deals with the apparent contradictions between the study of philosophy and science and a person's continued adherence to religious beliefs and practices. Maimonides' translator into Hebrew, his contemporary Yehuda Ibn Tibbon, explained in the preface (written in Provence) that all these great works could only have been written in Arabic, since they used Arabic concepts for which no words existed in Hebrew (Halevi 1987: 73-5). Subsequently Samuel Ibn Tibbon (*c.* 1165-1232), a translator and philosophical commentator on the Bible, became famous for his accurate and faithful rendition of the work from the Arabic into Hebrew, under the title *Moreh Nebuchim*.

Maimonides' theological innovation was in the codification of Jewish law. He created a new literary form for the codification of Jewish law, of which his own work, the *Mishneh Torah*, was the peak. The creation of a new Arabo-Hebrew legal style is one of the highlights of Maimonides' work. Enlightened though he was, Maimonides reclaimed a traditionalist Talmudist theology for which science was in the service of religious piety. He was politically opposed to the materialist and dialectical theologies of the Abbasids, though he was intellectually formed by them. Although attempting to synthesise rationalist philosophy and religion, Maimonides' two monumental works, *The Guide of the Perplexed* and *Mishneh Torah*, apparently represent the disparate concerns of Maimonides the orthodox rabbi and Maimonides the universalist philosopher.

The Crusades may have contributed to strengthening the Arabo-Jewish solidarity of the Middle Ages in the face of the encroachment of Christian Europe. At the time of the First Crusade (1096-1102) Jews living in Jerusalem shared the same terrible fate as the Muslims when the city fell to the Crusaders. One medieval Muslim chronicler reported that the Crusaders burned the 'Church of the Jews'. Another gave more detail: 'They collected the Jews in the "Church" and burnt it down with them in it. They destroyed shrines and the tomb of Abraham – on him be peace – and they took the *mihrab* of David peacefully' (in Hillenbrand 1999: 66). Apparently medieval Muslim scholars did not view the Jews living under Islam with the same suspicion which they harboured on occasions towards Middle Eastern Christians, who might, rightly or wrongly, have been suspected of siding with their co-religionists, the Crusaders (Hillenbrand 1999: 66-8).

Theology, of course, differs from religion itself. It involves reflection on both the content and the institutions of religion. The central tenet of Maimonides' theology is the doctrine of the divine. His medievalist doctrine of theo-centricity (God as the centre) contrasts with what is called in modern times 'religious humanism' or 'ethical monotheism', since any modern humanistic and moralistic world-view is of necessity anthropocentric (with man at the centre). For Maimonides, who recognised only God as the true being and ascribed no value or significance to man except in his knowledge of God, morality had no intrinsic value, but only an instrumental significance. He regarded morality as a means required by man for the purpose of making him free for his great aim, which is the knowledge of God (Leibowitz 1987: 59). For Maimonides' theology, the proof of God's existence is incomplete, unless it also establishes his absolute unity. In reflecting on this question, practically all Jewish philosophers and theologians of the Middle Ages came to the conclusion that the unity of God necessarily implies that he must be incorporeal. This conclusion required them to set forth figurative or metaphorical interpretations of the many biblical passages that ascribe bodily characteristics to God. Maimonides devoted such attention to the arguments for God's unity and incorporeality. He began his *The Guide of the Perplexed* with an elaborate and comprehensive effort to refute all literal interpretations of passages in the Bible that speak of God as having corporeal features. Within his medieval context Maimonides – who had no experience of living in a European Christian country – was bound to be hostile to the Trinitarian concept of God which he associated with Christianity. Though Christian theologians interpreted the Trinity as a doctrine of one God in three persons, Maimonides perceived it as a denial of the divine unity. Most Jewish anti-Trinitarian polemics before and after Maimonides were directed against Christianity (Fox 1971: 671-2).

Maimonides, as befitted a great rational philosopher, was tolerant by nature. But his theological orthodoxy reflected the Jewish thought of his time. Some of his formulations contain offensive statements and precepts directed specifically against Christianity. But his theological orthodoxy can only be understood within its historical setting. As the product of a rational philosophy and a tolerant culture, Maimonides significantly lowered the barrier separating Jew and non-Jew. He often referred to the rabbinical dictum of Jews engaging in normal social relations with non-Jews 'in order to pursue the ways of peace'. He also quoted biblical verses like 'His [God's] mercy is on all creatures', in order to incorporate all of humanity within the range of Jewish obligations towards others (Nisan 1992: 170). Ironically, however, in spite of his being one of the most distinguished thinkers of the Arab and Islamic worlds, Maimonides has become the hero of religious Zionists and Jewish fundamentalists in modern Israel. In the post-1967 period, in particular, his theological orthodoxy has been widely used and abused by an array of Jewish fundamentalist groups and parties.

Messianic Zionism and the Reinvention of Maimonides

For orthodox Jews the *halacha* is binding, and Jewish religious ordinances have absolute validity. Moreover, many orthodox Jews and Israeli (messianic) religious nationalists claim to find justification for their attitudes towards the Palestinians, often referred to as 'Arabs living in Israel', in Maimonides' theology. For many Israeli Jewish fundamentalists, Maimonides' orthodoxy and his medievalist interpretation of the *halacha* are the starting point of their politico-religious conceptions of the Arab–Israeli conflict. For Israeli–Jewish messianics, the Jewish halachic system reflected in Maimonides' formulations elevated the status, rights and life ('blood') of Jew above non-Jew. Reinterpreting radically some of Maimonides' rational formulations, many mystical Jewish fundamentalists in Israel seek the establishment of a Jewish theocracy over the entire, biblically defined land of Israel, and the rebuilding of the Temple in Jerusalem, as part of implementing divinely ordained messianic redemption.

In post-1967 Israel, the general tendency to quote selectively and misleadingly from Maimonides' theology derives from a neo-Zionist messianic ideology which conceives a radical and sharp distinction between Jew and non-Jew, and assumes a basically antagonistic relation between them. For Israeli messianics, Jewish conflict with 'gentiles', and even war against them, is 'for their own good', because this will hasten messianic redemption (Lustick 1988: 120). The neo-Zionist messianics, furthermore, have deployed both the Bible and Maimonides to articulate religious arguments for justifying Israeli wars of expansion. Ashkenazi Chief Rabbi of Israel from 1973 to 1983, Shlomo Goren (who, as the Israeli army's chief rabbi in June 1967, supported privately the blowing up of the al-Aqsa Mosque in Jerusalem, used Maimonides to justify the Israeli invasion of Lebanon in 1982.

Maimonides adopted an Aristotelian universalist conception of the nature of the human soul. Moreover, his philosophical position committed him to a variety of unpopular Jewish positions: he played down the special character of the Jewish people, and affirmed that the difference between Jew and non-Jew was theological rather than essential. He denied that Jews benefited from special divine providence and prophecy. He extended an unusually welcoming hand to proselytes. He defined 'who is a Jew' in terms, first and foremost, of faith commitment, as opposed to national, racial or ethnic affiliation (Kellner 1991: 6, 59–64).

Neo-Zionist messianics envisage a theocratic regime for Israel based on the *halacha*, and spurn universal, humanistic and liberal values. In contrast to Maimonides' core sentiments, the ideo-theology that guides Gush Emunim, which is shared by many others in the Zionist religious-nationalist camp, embraces the supremacist and essentialist notions of Jews as a divinely 'chosen people' (*'am segula*), and as the rightful owners of the 'promised land'. The indigenous Palestinians, on the other hand, are aliens and no more than illegitimate tenants and squatters on the land, and are a threat to the process of messianic redemption. Their human and civil rights are no match for the divine legitimacy and the religiously ordained duty (*mitzvah*) of 'conquering, possessing and settling the promised land'. For the Gush Emunim settlers in the West Bank, Israel must continue the ancient biblical battles over settlement of the 'Land of Israel', to be won by a combination of religious faith and military might. The devotion of an increasingly powerful trend to the total possession of 'the biblical land of Israel' and to messianic redemption has effectively turned the Palestinians into resident aliens on their own soil.

The Gush Emunim settlement movement finds justification for the annexation of the occupied territories, or at least a prohibition on with-drawal, in Maimonides' commentary, where he wrote in *Book of the Commandments*: 'We are commanded to inherit the land that God gave to Abraham, Isaac, and Jacob, and must not leave it in the hand of any other nation or desolate. ... We must not leave the land in their hands [the seven

Canaanite nations] or [in the hands of] any other people in any generation'
(Harkabi 1986: 208). While Maimonides' theology reflected a traditional
Diaspora cultural identity, Gush Emunim's neo-Zionist and revolutionary
ideology emphasises both the 'holiness' and the 'territorial wholeness' of
Eretz Yisrael expressed in modern Israeli settler colonialism.

In Gush Emunim's theology, Israeli–Jewish national identity is not just a
sociocultural reality but a geopolitical and territorial ideal. Israeli–Jewish
national identity is born both out of a cultural self-understanding and
out of the actual land that the Jews inhabit (Lustick 1987: 118–39). The
slogan of the movement reflects this: 'The Land of Israel, for the People
of Israel, According to the Torah of Israel.' As Rabbi Tzvi Yehuda Kook,
Gush Emunim's most influential ideologue, put it: 'The Land was chosen
before the people.' The Gush fundamentalist philosophy is based on several
components: messianic fervour related to the belief in the 'sanctity' of
Greater Israel; the establishment of Jewish sovereignty over the 'whole
Land of Israel' and the rebuilding of the Temple in Jerusalem (Gorny 1994:
150–51).

Maimonides' universalist tradition and his rationalist Arabo-Greek
philosophy synthesised with Jewish Diaspora orthodoxy stand in sharp
contrast to contemporary messianic Zionism and Jewish fundamentalism.
According to an international authority on Maimonides, the late Professor
Yesha'ayahu Leibowitz, an orthodox Jew and a foremost Jewish thinker of
his day, Maimonides does not ascribe great significance to the messianic
idea, although he does not ignore it, since it is an integral part of Jewish
tradition, religion and faith (Leibowitz 1987: 61).

Jewish Supremacy and the Halacha Concept of *Ger Toshav*

Since 1967, Israeli religious Zionists have debated whether Palestinians
residing in the 'land of Israel' could qualify for the halachic status of
ger toshav ('resident alien'). In line with this *halacha* concept, both
Palestinian Muslims and Palestinian Christians are viewed by some Jewish
religious nationalists, including many Gush Emunim rabbis, as temporary
'resident aliens', a population living, at best, on sufferance. While the
relatively moderate members of the NRP have categorised the Palestinians
as *gerei toshav*, the more radical Jewish fundamentalists pointed out that

biblical discussion of *ger toshav* refers only to non-Jews who adopt Judaism (Num. 10.14). They also pointed out that Maimonides had made it clear in his law code that the Torah concept of *ger toshav* refers to a 'righteous gentile' who becomes a Jew. That radical position is found in the book of Mordechai Nisan (1987), a senior lecturer at the Hebrew University of Jerusalem, and a leading fundamentalist intellectual. The halachic legal status of *ger toshav* is, according to Nisan, as follows: a non-Jew who accepts the Seven Noahide Laws, and joins the community of the Jewish people, who lives a rather free life, and enjoys a social standing above a man who is a slave to a Jew:

> The Gentile in Eretz-Israel who accepts the Seven Noahide Laws becomes a *Ger-Toshav* (a resident alien) and, according to Maimonides, enters the category of 'the righteous nations of the world'. This point is discussed in halachic literature and codified by Maimonides into Jewish Law. The concept of the *Ger-Toshav* refers to a person who has gone through the process of a partial conversion before a Rabbinic court of three. The *Ben-Hoah* assumes a more inferior and limited status if his acceptance of Torah is due to a rational decision alone, but not a Divinely fixed obligation. The *Ger-Toshav*, then, is positioned between the *Ben-Noah* and the Jew. He ascends to a level of social and religious performance, he goes through a stage of partial conversion, but limits himself to accepting just the Seven Commandments. The *Tosafot* commentary in the Talmud implies that this individual should go further and consider converting completely to Judaism. However, for the moment, the *Ger-Toshav* assumes a middle position in the Torah order within a Jewish-led society. 'The position of non-repentant Gentile remains inferior. He refuses to assume a higher life standard as set out by the Torah and rejects Jewish primacy in Eretz-Israel. Maimonides explicates that non-Jews (Bnei Noah) are to endure a lowly status compounded by elements of servitude and special taxes. (Nisan 1992: 163)

Nisan, who has elsewhere expressed rationalisation and endorsement of Jewish terrorism against the Palestinians of the occupied territories,[2] writes the following passages shedding further light on Jewish religious fundamentalism and the exclusionist premisses underpinning his 'transfer'/'ethnic cleansing' imperative:

> At the very dawn of Jewish history, contact with the Land of Israel established the principle that the presence of non-Jews in the country is morally and politically irrelevant to the national right of the Jews to settle and possess the Land. ... The Bible states the Jewish right regardless of non-Jewish presence. Much later, the Rabbinic sages expounded on the patriarchal promise and

articulated the following principle: ... Dwelling in the Land is the Jewish priority and it is in no way restricted, let alone nullified, by a non-Jewish majority population in any given part of the Land. This principle was later codified by Maimonides in his legal work, thus lending his outstanding halachic [religious legal] authority to this Abrahamic national imperative. ... [The view that questions the legitimacy of Jewish settlement in 'Judea' and 'Samaria'] is a direct denunciation of Abraham, the first Jew, the Father of the Jewish people ... [who] set the precedent and model for settling there in spite of the fact that the 'Canaanite was then in the Land'. The Jewish presence in the Land has always had to contend with, and at least partially overcome, an indigenous non-Jewish element in the Land. ... The land is the eternal possession of the Jewish people alone. (Nisan 1983, quoted in Chomsky 1983: 444, 470 n3)

In August 1984, Nisan, who supports the replacement of Israel's secular law by the *halacha*, repeated the same ideas in an article in *Kivunim* (an official organ of the World Zionist Organisation). Relying on a nationalised and racialised Maimonides, he argued that a non-Jew permitted to reside in the land of Israel 'must accept paying a tax and suffering the humiliation of servitude'. In *Toward a New Israel*, Nisan bemoans the traditional Jewish *dhimmi* status under Islam: 'the hallmark of the *dhimmi* condition was the precarious and pitiful nature of existence under Muslim rule. Subjugated to an inferior status, the Jew paid a special poll tax, the *jizya*' (Nisan 1992: 156). Yet in *Kivunim*, Nisan demands, supposedly in keeping with a religious text of Maimonides, that a non-Jew in Israel 'be held down and not [be allowed] to raise his head against Jews'. For Nisan, non-Jews must not be appointed to any office or position of power over Jews; if they refuse to live a life of inferiority, then this signals their rebellion and the unavoidable necessity of Jewish warfare against their very presence in the 'land of Israel' (Nisan 1984: 151–6; Harkabi 1986: 216–17).

For a supporter of Gush Emunim like Nisan, the struggle against the Palestinians is also part of a wider effort to reinterpret Jewish history and redeem Maimonides:

The struggle over Maimonides between Jews and Arabs is really an instance of the confrontation going back more than a millennium, as the Jewish people try to perpetuate their unique religious and national identity within the extensive Muslim/Arab homeland. An awareness of this historic confrontation conveys the profundity of the rejection of modern Zionism by modern Arab nationalism. (Nisan 1992: 173–4)

Other Gush Emunim supporters and rabbis deny that a Palestinian nation ever existed and strongly oppose the idea of Palestinian autonomy of any sort in the Occupied Territories.

The Debate on the Torah 'Genocidal' Theme

In modern times, a whole range of settler colonial enterprises have used the Bible. The biblical narrative has been deployed as the idea that provides moral authority for modern colonial conquests (Prior 1999a). The content of the biblical text is highly problematic; in the narrative of the Book of Exodus, there is an inextricable link between the extrication of the Israelites from slavery in Egypt and the divine mandate to plunder ancient Palestine and even commit genocide; the invading Israelites are commanded to annihilate the indigenous inhabitants of Canaan. In the Book of Deuteronomy (often described as the focal point of the religious history and theology of the Old Testament) there is an explicit requirement to 'ethnically cleanse the land' of the indigenous population of Canaan (Deut. 7.1-11; see also 9.1-5, 23, 31-32; 20.11-14, 16-18; Exod. 23.27-33) (Prior 1997b: 16-33, 278-84).

The deployment of the biblical text and the evocation of the exploits of biblical heroes in support of settler colonialism is deeply rooted in Zionism, although secular Zionists deny that the books of Exodus and Deuteronomy have any contemporary relevance to the fate of the Palestinian Arabs. But with the rise of religious Zionism since 1967 the narratives of Exodus have found an explicit relevance in contemporary Israel. Many Jewish fundamentalists, including Gush Emunim rabbis and political leaders, have routinely compared Palestinian Muslims and Christians to the ancient Canaanites or Amalekites, whose extermination or expulsion by the ancient Israelites was, according to the Bible, predestined by a divine design (Shahak and Mezvinsky 1999: 73). Although many rabbis refer to Palestinian Muslims as 'Ishmaelites' and to the circumstances under which biblical Abraham 'expelled' Ishmael, others prefer to use Joshua's destruction and subjugation of the Canaanites as a model for the application of Israeli policy towards the contemporary 'Palestinian problem'. For example, in April 1969, in a statement in *Mahanaim*, the journal of the Israeli Army Rabbinate, a certain Shraga Gafni cites biblical authority for driving the 'Canaanite peoples' from the land of Israel and explains the 'relevance' of the judgement of Amalek (1 Sam. 15) to the Palestinian Arabs:

> As to the Arabs – the element that now resides in the land is foreign in its essence to the land and its promise – their sentence must be that of all previous foreign elements. Our wars with them have been inevitable, just as in the days of the conquest of our possessions in antiquity, our wars with the people who ruled our land for their own benefit were inevitable. ... In the case of the enemies, who, in the nature of their being, have only one single goal, to destroy you, there is no remedy but for them to be destroyed. This is 'the judgment of Amalek'.

Reflecting on the appropriate attitude towards the Palestinian Arabs, Rabbi Yisrael Hess cites Maimonides and quotes the biblical commandment according to which he believes Israel, in the tradition of Joshua from biblical times, should act: 'Go and strike down Amalek; put him under the ban with all that he possesses. Do not spare him, but kill man and woman, baby and suckling, ox and sheep, camel and donkey'. Hess adds: 'Against this holy war God declares a counter *jihad* ... in order to emphasise that this is the background for the annihilation and that it is over this that the war is being waged and that it is not a conflict between two peoples ... God is not content that we annihilate Amalek – "blot out the memory of Amalek": he enlists himself personally in this war ... because, as has been said, he has a personal interest in this matter. This is the principal aim' (in *Bat Kol*, 26 February 1980; see also 1 Sam. 15.3).

Other Jewish fundamentalist leaders have argued that Palestinian Muslims and Christians face the choice between emigration or conversion to Judaism. Rabbi Yisrael Ariel, using and abusing Maimonides, justified the campaign of the Jewish Underground terrorist organisations, implying that the killing of an Arab was not murder (Ariel 1980).

Traditional Rabbinical Attitudes towards Christianity

The reasons for the historical tension between Christianity and Judaism are not to be sought merely in differences in religious beliefs and dogmas, which exist also in relation to all other religions. Nor can they be located in the long history of anti-Semitism and persecution of Jews in Christian countries, since anti-Semitism was the result rather than the first cause of

the tension between Christianity and Judaism. The situation is more com-
plicated. Jewish scholars often dwell on the negative attitudes to Judaism
on the part of Christians. The tension, they argue, is due essentially to the
Church's ambivalent position vis-à-vis Judaism. Christianity had a Jewish
beginning and, in virtue of the attachment to the (Hebrew) Bible (Old
Testament), natural ongoing links with Jewish thought. But Christianity
has become a distinct religion with its own concepts of salvation, forms of
piety, emotional and intellectual attitudes, and historical consciousness.
The ambivalence created by this sense of both relatedness and difference is
far from being resolved either in the Christian world or within Jewry and
the State of Israel. By conceiving of itself as the fulfilment of the promises
in the Bible (the Old Testament), the Church placed itself squarely on a
Jewish foundation: it was the consummation of the biblical promise. Jesus
was the promised Son of David – the Lord's Anointed (*Mashiah ben David*)
– and hence the Church was the 'true Israel' of God.

Rabbinical attitudes towards Christianity have been determined by
historical, social and religious factors. Christianity, after it had ceased
to be a Jewish 'heretical' sect, became a dominant religion, and assumed
its medieval Catholic form. This included the cultic use of images, which
were considered by Jewish philosophers and theologians in turn to be
'idolatrous'. The fact that for many centuries medieval Jewish philosophy
was influenced mainly by Muslim thought only exacerbated this conception: medieval Jewish theologians argued that Islam shared with Judaism
a conception of God that could be described as more monotheistic than
that of Christianity.

Rabbinical authorities debated whether the laws and injunctions concerning commerce and contacts with 'idolators' also applied to Christians.
To rabbinical authorities of medieval times the Christian world appeared
as the incarnation of Rome, symbolised by Edom and Esau, and as the
evil power bent on destroying Jacob. Occasionally Jewish thinkers would
suggest that Christianity, recognising the divine character of the Bible
and being less polytheistic than classical and primitive paganism, might
be a providential instrument used by God to bring the 'gentiles' gradually
nearer to true religion (Werblowsky 1971: 513-14).

Yet, in spite of the traditional attitudes of mistrust, there was always
a certain amount of mutual interest. Jewish thinkers, Maimonides in

particular, have influenced Christian theologians and biblical exegetes. The rabbinical theological evaluation of Christianity also had repercussions in the sphere of *halacha*, and the exigencies of the latter in turn influenced theoretical attitudes (Katz 1961). Rabbinical authorities saw valid distinctions between Judaism and Christianity, and criticised concepts such as the Trinity, the atoning sacrifice of the Messiah, the Son of God, on the cross, while Christians did not accept rabbinical interpretation as the authentic divine law.

The Halachic Concept of *'Avoda Zara*

Rabbinical hostility to Christianity is found in both orthodox Judaism and contemporary religious Zionism. The theological arguments stem from the focus of orthodox Judaism on the 'service of God and obedience to His commandments'. *'Avoda zara*, or 'idolatrous worship', is the grossest rejection of orthodox Judaism. In practice, the Jewish laws (*halacha*) dealing with *'avoda zara* covered all relations between Jews and Gentiles (Urbach 1974: 614-23). Orthodox Judaism was founded on a total rejection of *'avoda zara*.

The term *'avoda zara* is found frequently in the biblical text and Talmudic literature: for example, 'You shall have no other gods but Me' (Exod. 20.3); 'You shall not make for yourself a sculptured image, or any likeness of what is in the heavens above, or on the earth below' (Exod. 20.4); 'As for that image – its head was of fine gold, its breasts and arms were silver, its belly and its thighs of brass, its legs of iron, its feet part of iron and part of clay (Dan. 2.32-3); 'A drunkard who prays is as though he worships idols' (Talmud, *Berakhot*); 'When Jewish elders in Rome were asked: If God has no pleasure in an idol, why does He not make an end of it? They answered: If men worshipped a thing of which men had no need, He would make an end of it, but lo!, they worshipped the sun and the moon and the stars and the planets: shall God destroy His world because of fools?' (*'Avoda Zara* 4, 7); 'Of any sin spoken of in the Torah, if a man is told, "Commit it and you will not die"; let him commit it, save only idolatry, incest and bloodshed!' (Talmud, *Sanhedrin*); and 'Who denies idolatry is as one that avows the entire Torah' (Talmud, *Qiddushim*). One traditional definition of the term *'avoda zara* is that everyone who has not accepted the seven Noahide commandments is considered to be an idolator. However, in many contexts the term 'Gentile' is synonymous with 'idol worshipper' (Harkabi 1986: 221).[3] These are some of the historical origins of orthodox Judaism's traditionally stern position towards those it perceived as followers of *'avoda zara*. They must be destroyed lest they seduce Jews to follow their steps (Harkabi 1986: 221). Maimonides wrote:

> An affirmative precept enjoined for the destruction of any idol, articles and subsidiary to its worship, and everything made for its benefit. ... In the land of Israel, it is a duty actively to chase out idolatry until we have exterminated it from the whole of our country. Outside of the holy land, however, we are not so commanded; but only that whenever we acquire any territory by conquest, we should destroy all the idols found there. (Maimonides, *Halachot 'Avoda Zara Vehokot Hagoim*, in Harkabi 1986: 221)

Maimonides summed up the Jewish law on the treatment of idolators as follows:

> It is forbidden to show them mercy, as it was said, 'nor show mercy unto them' (Deuteronomy 7.2). Hence, if one see a heathen who worships idols perishing or drowning, one is not to save him... Hence you learn that it is forbidden to heal idolators even for a fee. But if one is afraid of them or apprehends that refusal might cause ill will, medical treatment may be given for a fee but not gratuitously. ... The foregoing rules apply to the time when the people of Israel live reviled among the nations, or when the Gentiles' power is predominant. But when Israel is predominant over the nations of the world, we are forbidden to permit a gentile who is an idolator to dwell among us. He must not enter our land, even as a temporary resident; or even as a traveller, journeying with merchandise from place to place, until he has undertaken to keep the seven precepts which the Noahides were commanded to observe. (in Harkabi 1986: 221-2)

Yet there is a fundamental difference between the medieval and the modern mind. Maimonides was a man of his time and tradition and his theological position on *'avoda zara* was first and foremost a product of the medieval mind. His theological position towards both Islam and Christianity reflected his medievalist approach. He generally regarded Ishmaelites or Muslims as monotheistic Gentiles in spirit and practice and exempted them from the category of idolators. But not so with the Christians: 'Christians are idol worshippers' (Maimonides, in Harkabi

1986: 222). In a letter to 'Ovadia the convert, Maimonides set forth the religious status of Muslims from the viewpoint of the Torah:

> These Ishmaelites [i.e. Muslims] are not idol worshippers at all, and it has been removed from their tongues and hearts, and they worship the exalted God as a unity, as is proper, a unity without defect. ... Regarding the unity of God they are not in error at all. (*Teshuvot Harambam* 1940: 726)

On the other hand, Christianity, according to Maimonides, was not a pure monotheistic faith, for, in it, while God is *one* in name, he is *three* in thought and conception, thus conflicting directly with halachic principles. Maimonides' anti-Christian prejudices reflected deeply rooted Jewish attitudes of medieval times. In his interpretation of the Mishnah he wrote: 'You should know that the Christian nation ... all of them are idolators' (Maimonides, in Harkabi 1986: 222).

In another *responsum* Maimonides throws light on his ambivalent view of both Christianity and Islam, and the differences between them from the viewpoint of the *halacha*:

> It is permissible to teach *mitzvot* to Christians and to attract them to our religion, but it is forbidden to do this with Ishmaelites based on what their faith teaches them, that this Torah is not of Heavenly origin. (*Teshuvot Harambam* 1937: 284-5)

We see, then, that Maimonides' views of both Christianity and Islam were complex. For example, while the Muslims rejected the sanctity of the first Five Books (the Pentateuch), considering them a forgery and therefore invalid as to their ideas and ways, Christians believe that the Torah text and its validity had never changed. Contemporary Israeli–Jewish fundamentalists display none of the nuances of Maimonides in regard to the two religions.

While virtually all Israeli–Jewish fundamentalists reject the notion of the 'Judeo-Christian tradition', which in the estimation of many Israeli secular and Western commentators constitutes the basis of Western civilisation, they differ over what distinctions are worth making between 'Gentiles' and 'Christians' (Lustick 1988: 120). In 1992 at a symposium organised by the Ministry of Religion on the subject 'Is Autonomy in the Holy Land Feasible for *ger toshavs* [resident aliens]?', Rabbi Shlomo Min-Harar had this to say: 'All Christians without exception hate the Jews and look forward to their deaths' (in Shahak and Mezvinsky 1999: 75–6). But the marked hostility among Israeli–Jewish fundamentalists towards Christianity and its followers in the Holy Land has little to do with the persecution of Jews in Europe or the Holocaust. Although anti-Semitism and the persecution of Jews in Christian Europe did contribute to anti-Christian attitudes, they are not the sole explanation. Sephardi Jewish rabbis, and to a lesser extent their followers who came from Muslim countries and had no experience of persecution by Christians, have expressed more open hostility towards Christianity and its symbols and sites in the Holy Land than have fundamentalist Ashkenazi rabbis and their Ashkenazi followers, who actually had experienced discrimination in Christian countries (Shahak and Mezvinsky 1999: 154).

Some fundamentalist rabbis, using a synthesis of messianic Kookist theology and a nationalised and racialised theology of Maimonides, make a clear distinction between Palestinian Christians and Palestinian Muslims. Several Gush Emunim rabbis, for instance, have made the distinction in discussions on Jewish relations with non-Jews living in the 'land of Israel', claiming that the Palestinians are 'unquestionably monotheistic', while the Christians' belief in the Trinity suggests they should be regarded as 'idol-worshippers' (Leor 1986: 21; see also *Nekudah*, 22 November 1985: 26). The same rabbis (using Maimonides) attack Christianity as a form of paganism and of idol-worshipping, which should be discouraged in the 'Land of Israel'. For Rabbi Kook decreed that Palestinian Christians were 'idol worshipping' and therefore should not be allowed to remain in the country; as for Palestinian Muslims, although they were not 'idol worshipping' they should only be allowed to live in the country if they accepted Jewish supremacy and sovereignty over the land unconditionally (Rachlevsky 1998: 406). A similar view was expressed by Rabbi Moshe Levinger of the Jewish settlement in Hebron, who has always referred to Palestinian Muslims as 'Ishmaelites' (never as Muslims, Arabs or Palestinians) who 'do not worship idols': 'Maimonides determined that Islam is not pagan, like Christianity. If there had been a crucifix here [in the Ibrahimi Mosque of Hebron], it would have been a different matter' (in Elon 1997a: 70). Other disciples of Kook, however, are no so generous: for them, both Muslims and Christian should be driven out (Rachlevsky 1998: 406).

Burning the New Testament

Jewish fundamentalist anti-Christian theology is increasingly encouraged by the centre of religious thinking in Israel. For instance, 'Ovadia
Yosef – ex-Sephardi Chief Rabbi of Israel and spiritual mentor of Shas
(an acronym for *Shomrie Torah Sephardim*, 'Sephardi Torah Guard-
ians', the party of the Sephardi Jewish Haredim, which wants Israel
to become a halacha state and which was represented in the cabinet
of Ariel Sharon 2003–05) – ruled that the New Testament should be
publicly burned because Christianity is a form of idolatry.[1] On 23 March
1980, following Rabbi Yosef's ruling, hundreds of copies of the New
Testament were publicly and ceremonially burned in Jerusalem under
the auspices of Yad Leakhim, a Jewish religious organisation subsidised
by the Israeli Ministry of Religions (Shahak 1994: 21). Another impact
of the same ruling was revealed in the Hebrew daily *Ma'ariv* in June
1985 when copies of the Old Testament found in the library of the army
base's chief education officer were burned by the military rabbi of the
base (*Ma'ariv*, 14 June 1985). Three weeks later *Ma'ariv* reported that
the Knesset Foreign Affairs and Defence Committee had referred to the
incident and one of its members (Rabbi Haim Druckman, a Member of
the Knesset and prominent supporter of Gush Emunim) had justified
the burning of the New Testament (*Ma'ariv*, 5 July 1985: 19). However,
some Jewish fundamentalists, for instance Moshe Ben-Yosef Hagar, were
against the burning of the Old Testament, but only because, indirectly,
Christian beliefs affirm the Jewish people's connection to the 'Land of
Israel' (*Nekudah*, 22 November 1985: 26).

The Doctrinal Dispute between Gush Emunim
and the Haredi Rabbis

The widespread use and abuse of Maimonides' theology in contemporary
Israel is also evident in the fact that the deployment of his theological
publications cuts across religious Zionist and non-Zionist parties and
rabbis, Sephardi and Ashkenazi rabbis, and modernist nationalist and
ultra-orthodox Haredi communities. Maimonides' enormous influence on
Haredi rabbis is hardly surprising, but their interpretation of his theology

is distinctly different from that of the nationalist religious 'messianics'. In some respects the Haredi communities in Israel are the most authentic expression of the Jewish religion in its classical form. The clash between Haredi orthodoxy and modern, largely secular, Zionism has been central to the evolution of orthodox Judaism in Israel. The ultra-orthodox also remain sworn enemies of the Rabbis Kook (father and son) (Aran 1997: 297-8), and continue to proclaim their opposition to Zionism. The roots of Haredi opposition to both secular and religious Zionism are found in the Talmudic literature in which Jews were obliged to take 'three oaths', of which two are critical in this context: (a) that Diaspora Jews should not rebel against non-Jews; and (b) that they should not emigrate to Palestine in large numbers 'before the right time' – that is, before the coming of the Messiah and God brings an end to the exile. Over the past fifteen centuries the vast majority of the most important Jewish rabbis have interpreted 'the three oaths' as making the ongoing exile of Jews a religious obligation (Ravitzky 1996). Until the nineteenth century influential European rabbis continued to warn against the massive immigration of Jews into Palestine, even with the consent of all the nations of the world, before the coming of the Messiah.

Modern Zionism rejected this fundamental tenet of orthodox (Haredi) Judaism. Political Zionism emerged at the end of the nineteenth century in a fierce struggle with orthodox Judaism, which was supported by most influential rabbis of the period. The reinvention of Maimonides as a 'nationalist religious Zionist' had to wait until after the establishment of the State of Israel. And it was only after 1967 that Maimonides became the patron saint of the Zionist religious camp (Shahak and Mezvinsky 1999: 19). In contrast, in spite of the enormous prestige Maimonides enjoys among orthodox and Haredi Jews as the first codifier of the *halacha* and as the leading theologian of Judaism, he remains suspect among the Haredim, mainly because his philosophy attempted to synthesise the Jewish faith and Greek-Arabic Aristotelian rational philosophy. Traditionally the greatest criticism had been levelled at *The Guide of the Perplexed*. Conservative and super-purist sages labelled it a heretical work. In 1230, a group of purists succeeded in persuading the Roman Catholic Church to burn *The Guide*. Some sages banned the work to all but mature Talmudists (G. Rosenthal 1990: xx-xxi). Nowadays most Haredi rabbis in Israel still keep *The Guide of the Perplexed* and other philosophical writings of Maimonides away from most of their people (Shahak and Mezvinsky 1999: 167 n17).

The nationalist religious rabbis of the NRP and Gush Emunim, in total disregard of the Haredi and orthodox rabbis' theology, assert that the messianic era, with its pre-eminence of the Torah in the World, has already begun. They maintain also that the 'three oaths' do not apply in messianic times, and that, although the Messiah has not appeared, a cosmic process called the 'beginning of redemption' has begun. During the beginning of these messianic times some of the previous religious laws should be disregarded and others should be changed. Thus the doctrinal dispute between the NRP and the Haredi rabbis has centred on the issue of whether Jews are living in normal times or in the period of the 'beginning of messianic redemption'. Other party political and personal rivalries have further fuelled the intense mutual hatred between the diverse fundamentalist groups of religious Jews, especially in the personal quarrels between their rabbis.

While the nationalist religious messianic camp has been expanding in Israel since the early 1970s, the political and electoral successes of the Haredi sects and parties in Israel came to public attention only from the 1988 general elections onwards. Until then members lived in generally self-sustained and residentially segregated areas of the cities. Haredi Judaism, despite its opposition to Zionism, has changed its stance since the late 1980s: it has demanded a leadership role, advocating a form of (non-Zionist) Jewish fundamentalism and insisting that both the domestic and the foreign policy of Israel be derived from the *halacha*. Becoming self-confident after their electoral gains in 1988, the Haredim strengthened their doctrinal opposition to secular and religious Zionism. In 1989, the two most influential Haredi rabbis in Israel, Rabbi Menahem Eli'ezer Shach and Rabbi 'Ovadia Yosef – the spiritual leaders of Degel Ha'Torah and Shas parties respectively – held an anti-Zionist convention in Bnei Brak, a town near Tel Aviv. Rabbi Yosef is head of the seven-member Mo'etzet Hachmei Ha'Torah (Council of Torah Sages) and the Lithuanian Rabbi Shach (1896–2001) was one of the leaders of Mo'etzet Gedolei Ha'Torah (Council of Great Torah Scholars). For many years Rabbi Shach had conducted a fierce personal, ideological and scholarly rivalry with the late Rabbi Menahem Mendel Schneerson, the messianic missionary rabbi who lived in New York and who was a controversial figure in Haredi circles (Rolef 1993: 371-2). In their speeches, which were published in the Haredi newspaper *Yated Neeman* (the weekly of Degel Ha'Torah party), Rabbi Shach and Rabbi Yosef addressed from a halachic perspective the issue of whether some areas of the 'land of Israel' should be given to non-Jews – that is, to Palestinians. They rejected the 'beginning of redemption' doctrine, affirming that the messianic time of redemption had not yet arrived, and that Jews still live in normal times. They also rejected the NRP view that, in accordance with the belief in the 'beginning of redemption', no land should be given to non-Jews, and that saving Jewish lives should be more important than holding on to parts of the 'Land of Israel' (*Yated Neeman*, 18 September 1989, in Shahak and Mezvinsky 1999: 19-20).

The two Haredi rabbis were lauded by Israeli liberals and peace activists for approving the concept of partial withdrawal from the Occupied Territories in order to avert war and save Jewish lives, but little attention was paid to other, no less significant, pronouncements made by the rabbis at the convention. For instance, Rabbi Yosef (who is renowned for his halachic erudition and for being an important political figure in Israel) acknowledged that in messianic times Jews would be more powerful than non-Jews and would then be obliged by the *halacha* to conquer the 'Land of Israel', and expel all non-Jews, and to destroy the 'idolatrous Christian churches'. Yosef stated:

> The Jews are not in fact more powerful than the non-Jews and are unable to expel the non-Jews from the land of Israel because the Jews fear the non-Jews ... God's commandment is then not valid ... Even non-Jews who are idolaters live among us with no possibility of their being expelled or even moved. The Israeli government is obligated by international law to guard the Christian churches in the land of Israel, even though those churches are definitely places of idolatry and cult practice. This is so in spite of the fact that we are commanded by our [religious] law to destroy all idolatry and its servants until we uproot it from all parts of our land and any areas that we are able to conquer ... Surely, this fact continues to weaken the religious meaning of the Israeli army's conquests [in 1967]. (in Shahak and Mezvinsky 1999: 20)

Rabbi Yosef, whose political pragmatism is often admired in Israel, has never concealed his anti-Christian theology: that Jews, when sufficiently powerful, have a halachic duty to expel the Christians from the Holy Land and destroy all their churches, but only if doing so would not endanger Jewish life (Shahak and Mezvinsky 1999: 20-21). This openly anti-Christian sentiment is also demonstrated by the fact that the term 'Red Cross', supposedly associated with Christianity, is prohibited from usage in the Haredi press (Shahak and Mezvinsky 1999: 33). Although Haredi rabbis continued to express doctrinal opposition to religious Zionism, and especially the doctrine of 'the beginning of redemption', they also continued to advocate a form of Jewish fundamentalism, with its visible hostility towards Christianity in the Holy Land.

The fundamentalist rabbis have sought to establish a Jewish theocracy in the 'whole land of Israel' with the rebuilding of the Temple in Jerusalem. They have also justified the expulsion of Palestinian Muslims and Christians by invoking Maimonides, who said that after the Messiah comes, only Jews will be permitted to live in Jerusalem (Shahak and Mezvinsky 1999: 18). Rabbi Meir Kahane (1932-1990, the founder of the Jewish Defense League in the United States and its Israeli counterpart the Kach ('Thus') movement, actually submitted to the Knesset a draft bill that would make the *halacha* ban on the residence of a *ger toshav* in Jerusalem the law of the State of Israel, but it was disqualified by the Knesset presidium on 3 December 1984 (Harkabi 1986: 212).

Conclusion

While Maimonides regarded both Islam and medieval Arab culture as coming from the flesh and bone of Judaism, and his philosophy and theology drew freely and copiously from Muslim patterns, Israeli–Jewish fundamentalists nevertheless use his writings selectively to justify their attacks on Arabo-Islamic culture and the Palestinians. Maimonides found in Muslim theology a model of a renaissance for Arab Judaism that Islam encouraged and cultivated. Much of his code of Jewish law and all of his major works were written in Arabic; his philosophical magnum opus, *The Guide of the Perplexed* and many of his other great works could only have been written in Arabic, since they used Arabic concepts for which no words then existed in Hebrew. Ironically, then, the tendentious use of Maimonides' theology by Jewish fundamentalists is designed largely to encourage the adoption of anti-Arab and anti-Muslim sentiments and policies.

The reinvention of one of the great symbols of Arabo-Muslim-Jewish understanding as a religious bigot is an extraordinary phenomenon that is a product of post-1967 Israel. Moreover, the fact that the reinvented Maimonides has become, in a peculiar way, the hero of 'messianic' Zionism and anti-Arab fundamentalism is indicative of the growing influence of fundamentalist currents on Israeli society. While Maimonides (who was not a Jewish philosopher in the narrow sense) embraced a universalist Aristotelian conception of the nature of the human soul, played down the special character of the Jewish people, and affirmed that the difference between Jew and non-Jew was theological rather than essentialist, racial or ethnic, he defined a 'Jew' in terms of commitment to faith, as opposed to national, religious or ethnic racial affiliation. The theology that guides Gush Emunim and other 'messianic' groups in Israel peddles the supremacist and essentialist notion of Jews as a divinely chosen 'race' (Rachlevsky 1998: 392–3) – 'chosen people' or *'am segula* in Hebrew – and as the rightful and exclusive owners of the 'promised land', a land, indeed, which ought to be 'ethnically and religiously cleansed'. The indigenous Palestinians, for their part, are aliens in this land; they are no more than illegitimate tenants and squatters, and a threat to the process of messianic redemption; their human and civil rights are no match for the divine legitimacy and the religiously ordained duty (or *mitzvah*) of 'conquering, possessing and settling the promised land'. The extraordinary reinvention of Maimonides' rationalist legacy as a form of deeply racist religious nationalism has been condemned by prominent scholars in Israel. Professor Yesha'ayahu Leibovitch, a distinguished religious orthodox scholar and former editor-in-chief of the *Encyclopaedia Hebraica* – who opposed the occupation immediately following the war in June 1967 – once described the militant messianic trend in Israel as 'Judeo-Nazism' (in Skutel 1983: 83).

Israeli–Jewish fundamentalists have exploited Maimonides' halachic orthodoxy for a variety of reasons, while deliberately ignoring the fact that his approach was the product of a distinct historical setting and medieval context. Rabbi Tzvi Yehuda Kook and his disciples also tended to focus on his medievalist approach to Christianity, which he described as *'avoda zara* ('strange worship' or false worship') (Rachlevsky 1998: 406), mainly in order to attack Palestinian Christians, who according to Kook should not be allowed to live in the country (Rachlevsky 1998: 406), burn copies of the New Testament and debate whether 'idolatrous' Christian churches should be completely banned in the Holy Land. One recent example of such anti-Christian sentiments is found in a statement by Rabbi Yair Dreyfus, an articulate settlement leader, who declared:

> The true Jews, desirous to live as Jews, will have no choice to separate themselves in ghettos. The new, sinful Canaanite-Palestinian state [Israel after Oslo] will soon be established upon the ruins of the genuine Jewish-Zionist state ... God may even make war against this polluted throne of his. The Jews who lead us into that sin no longer deserve any divine protection. ... Our leadership will walk a Via Dolorosa before it understands that we are commanded to resist the [secular] state of Israel, not just its present government. (in Shahak and Mezvinsky 1999: 89)

While the reinvention of Maimonides is symptomatic of the kind of intolerant new religious politics emerging in present-day Israel, the struggle over Maimonides is also about reclaiming the cultural heritage of Arabo-Judaism and the future of interfaith relations in Israel and Palestine. The fundamentalists' distortion of Maimonides' legacy is also aimed at undermining the notion that Judaism under Islam was an autonomous, self-confident culture based on a prosperous society, with intimate connections with its Arabo-Islamic environment. Moreover, while Maimonides – the most illustrious example of the golden age of Arabo-Islamic-Judaic symbiosis – contributed to religious tolerance and interfaith coexistence, and significantly lowered the barriers between Jew and non-Jew, the current distortion of his legacy of rationalism and Arabo-Judaism is the outcome of a deeply ingrained anti-Arab racism in Israel, and the denigration of the culture of Arab-Mizrahi Judaism, a denigration which permeates the process of the general brutalisation of society. There is also good reason to suggest that the further Jewish fundamentalism spreads, and the greater the role of the *halacha* in the political life of Israel, the more vigorously these fundamentalists will demand that the Palestinians, Muslims and Christians be dealt with according to halachic regulations, including the imposition on them of the status of 'resident alien'.

PART III

Invented Traditions and New Challenges

6

Palestinian Religious Nationalism,
Decolonisation and the Biblical Paradigm:
Hamas, Zionism and Resisting the Occupation

Modern political Islam emerged in the Middle East in the first half of the twentieth century largely as an anti-colonialist revivalist movement. It was part of what François Burgat terms the 'rocket of de-colonisation' (Burgat 2003: 49). In the wake of secular nationalist and pan-Arabist attempts at obtaining political and economic independence, political Islam of the post-1967 period was a popular revivalist movement seeking to gain cultural autonomy from the colonial West (Burgat 2003: 48-50). The traumatic defeat and abject failure of the secular Arab regimes in the 1967 war was a turning point for political Islam. The post-1967 period provided Islamic movements in the region with an excellent opportunity to spread the notion that political Islam was the only true path to victory in the struggle against Israeli occupation and Western hegemony (Ahmad 1994: 11). Furthermore, the failure of secular nationalist options, together with the inspiration provided by the Islamic revolution in Iran in 1979 and the highly effective operations of the Islamic resistance fighters of Hizbullah against the Israeli occupation of south Lebanon, significantly enhanced the popularity of Islamic groups within the occupied territories, especially in the Palestinian refugee camps of Gaza (Hroub 2000: 29-36). In the process of Islamic assertion with the objective of gaining cultural autonomy from the West, as well as the creation of an Islamic state in the longer term, a significant part of the moderate Islamists' political strategy was to work within the framework of civil society as they sought to (re)Islamise society 'from below' (Jensen 2006: 57-74).

A major challenge to Zionism and four decades of Israeli occupation came from Palestinian popular resistance and from the rise of political Islam in Palestine. Historically political Islam in Palestine has always had a strong Palestinian nationalist dimension (Budeiri 1995: 89-95; Hroub 2000; Khalidi 1997: 148-9). The anti-colonial nationalist dimension was always central to the Palestinian 'Islamic Resistance Movement', better known as Hamas (Arabic acronym for *Harakat al-Muqawama al-Islamiya*; also meaning 'enthusiasm' in Arabic), which was founded in early 1988, at the beginning of the first Intifada – the Palestinian uprising against Israeli occupation which lasted from late 1987 to 1993. In effect, Hamas developed in response to the widespread popular Palestinian uprising, which, for the first time since 1967, brought the centre of Palestinian resistance to the occupied West Bank and Gaza Strip. Contemporary political Islam in Palestine was also the product of socio-economic or political marginalisation. In Palestine radical Islamist groups such as Hamas and Islamic Jihad have been founded as opposition groups, based on socially and economically deprived and marginalised groups in Palestinian society, fighting against the mainstream, predominantly secular, PLO.

Since 1988 Hamas has advocated an 'Islamic state' in Palestine, thus combining its religious outlook with Palestinian nationalist aspirations. At the top of its agenda are resisting the occupation and liberating Palestine through armed struggle, establishing an Islamic state on its soil and reforming Palestinian society on the basis of Islamic law, *sharia* (Mishal and Sela 2000: vii). For Hamas the 'Islamic state' in Palestine would not be imposed on the Palestinians via a revolutionary process; rather it would be the result of a gradual, continuous, incremental process, achieved primarily by education, electoral reforms and social action 'from the bottom up' (Mishal and Sela 2000). Hamas's social activities have included the establishment of medical clinics, kindergartens, sports clubs, hospitals, schools and colleges, and many authors have acknowledged the importance of these institutions for Palestinians living under Israeli occupation and their contribution to the rise in popular support for Hamas

(Sahliyeh 1995; Mishal and Sela 2000; Milton-Edwards 1999; Jensen 2006: 57-8). In *The Palestinian Hamas*, Israeli scholars Shaul Mishal and Avraham Sela (2000) have this to say about Hamas's social roots in Palestinian society:

> A close scrutiny of Hamas's roots and record since its establishment at the outbreak of the Palestinian uprising (Intifada) ... reveals ... that ... [Hamas] is essentially a social movement. As such, Hamas has directed its energies and resources primarily toward providing services to the community, especially responding to its immediate hardships and concerns. As a religious movement involved in a wide range of social activities, Hamas is deeply rooted in the Palestinian society in the West Bank and Gaza Strip and thus aware of the society's anxieties, sharing its concerns, expressing its aspirations, and tending to its needs and difficulties. (Mishal and Sela 2000: vii)

The Palestinians have been one of the most secular of all Arab populations, with little history of sectarian politics or religious fundamentalism. However, in January 2006, eighteen years after its establishment, Hamas won a stunning victory in the Palestinian parliamentary elections, sweeping away Fatah's monopoly of power in the Occupied Territories and its control of the Palestinian Authority in free and fair democratic elections. Owing to the system of representation, Hamas actually received only 44 per cent of the popular vote but managed to become the majority party in the Legislative Council, having won 74 out of 132 seats in the election. The majority of Palestinians did not vote for Hamas, and did not give a mandate for imposing a fundamentalist-style theocracy on Palestine. Whatever the outcome, for most Palestinians these parliamentary elections were a historic step forward in democratic politics as voters turned out in unprecedented numbers, taking part for the first time in fiercely competitive multi-party elections. Also significant was the fact that these historic elections marked the end of a five-decade period during which the Palestinian national movement was dominated by secular, territorial nationalism, and the beginning of a new phase in Palestinian politics dominated by an Islamist political culture. It was extraordinary that, given the nature of Zionism, its mystical attachment to the Hebrew Bible and its radical transformation from a secular to a religious messianic ideology after 1967, the Palestinian secular nationalist orientation had persisted for so long (Cragg 1992: 247).

The Historical and Social Roots
of Political Islam in Palestine

Hamas was not born in a vacuum at the outbreak of the first Intifada, of course. Its religio-political outlook has been inherited from its predecessor, the Palestinian branch of the Muslim Brotherhood movement, founded in Egypt in 1928 by Hassan al-Banna. The historical roots of political Islam in Palestine go back to the Mandatory period. The Muslim Brotherhood movement first became involved in Palestine during the Great Palestinian Rebellion of 1936–39, during which 'Abd al-Rahman al-Banna, the founder's brother, went to Palestine to spread the Brotherhood's message (Hroub 2000: 14). The Muslim Brotherhood founded its first group in Jerusalem in May 1946, gained the endorsement of the then most influential Palestinian leader, Haj Amin al-Husseini, the Mufti of Jerusalem, and in the same year opened other offices in Palestinian cities, including Gaza, Jaffa, Haifa, Lydda, Ramleh (Hroub 2000: 14-17). During the 1948 Palestine War, Hassan al-Banna mustered three brigades of Egyptian volunteers to fight in Palestine.[1] These were joined by volunteers from within Palestine, from Jordan and from Syria, all fighting under the banner of the Brotherhood.

By the mid-1950s the Muslim Brotherhood had become the strongest political force in the Gaza Strip, where it advocated armed struggle. In the West Bank, however, it was closely allied with the Jordanian authorities and advocated non-violent resistance, which enabled it to be officially recognised by the Jordanian government. It participated in Jordanian government elections when other Palestinian nationalist movements boycotted them, as in 1962. It remained loyal to the Hashemite regime and King Hussein in particular.

The Zionist demographic battle with the indigenous inhabitants of Palestine has always been a battle for more land and fewer people (Masalha 1997, 2000). After the occupation of the West Bank and Gaza in 1967, Israel instituted a policy of 'creeping annexation', a process by which Israeli administration, jurisdiction and law gradually, incrementally and draconianly were imposed on the West Bank and the Gaza Strip, over ever-expanding areas, yet without a comprehensive act of legal annexation. That process of colonisation, also described as de facto annexation, is generally seen in the transformation of the demographic and physical realities of these areas.

After the 1967 war, the Muslim Brotherhood developed into one of the largest social movements in Palestinian society – a society still dominated by secular nationalism and led by the rising PLO. However, unlike the PLO, which developed active armed resistance to the occupation, the Brotherhood concentrated on developing its social infrastructure and organisation, with the advantage of being able to operate openly and without fear of Israeli reprisals. The period between 1967 and 1976 was marked by the meticulous construction of the Muslim Brotherhood's institutional and social infrastructure under the leadership of Shaykh Ahmad Yasin, later to become the founder and spiritual leader of Hamas (Mishal and Sela 2000: 26).

Interestingly, Israeli and foreign commentators, in particular, tend to highlight Israel's support for the Muslim Brotherhood in the 1970s and early 1980s – support which apparently was designed to undermine both Palestinian secular nationalism and the widespread support for the PLO in the Occupied Territories; Palestinian authors, on the other hand, who acknowledge that the Brotherhood avoided direct resistance to Israeli occupation during this period (Hroub 2000: 27), make no mention of any Israeli support for the Brotherhood.[2] In 1973 the Israelis, seeing the leader of the Muslim Brotherhood in Gaza, Shaykh Yasin, as the ideal counter to the more popular PLO, allowed him to set up a non-militant Islamic organisation, which he named the *al-Mujamma' al-Islami* (the Islamic Centre). Apparently this voluntary association, which was formally legalised in 1978 (Mishal and Sela 2000: 19), had some financial support from the Israeli government via its Military Governor in Gaza.

The Brotherhood subsequently grew in the teeming refugee camps of the Strip – the same camps which possessed the world's highest population density and which later provided fertile soil for communal activism informed by radicalised religiosity (Mishal and Sela 2000: 19). Some studies have shown that the socio-economic background of the members of Hamas – mostly from villages or refugee camps living on the peripheries of cities, students of the natural (rather than social) sciences, products of modernity, yet alienated from enlightenment – fuelled in them resentment and the will to organise resistance (Ahmad 1994: 25–8). Consistent with these socio-economic conditions, in impoverished Gaza the Islamic movement was at its strongest (Ahmad 1994: 28). However, as we shall see below, Yasin's politics continued to evolve and would take on a more radical complexion in the 1980s, especially after the outbreak of the Palestinian rebellion, contributing to the founding of Hamas, and its military wing, the 'Izzedin al-Qassam brigades. It is not entirely clear whether Yasin's main aim was to try to turn Palestinian activists away from the secular nationalist politics of the PLO; but the refugee camps of Gaza certainly welcomed the Islamic option as an alternative way to challenge both dispossession and poverty and life under Israeli occupation (Mishal and Sela 2000: 19).

Resisting the Occupation and the First Intifada: The Emergence of Hamas

In the 1970s and early 1980s the PLO and the secularist Palestinian resistance movement as a whole enjoyed widespread popularity. Its fortunes began to decline, however, following the Israeli invasion of Lebanon in 1982, when the Palestinian resistance groups were forced to leave their bases in the country. This decline of the PLO in the diaspora provided a fillip to the fortunes of the Muslim Brotherhood inside Palestine and brought to prominence specifically Islamic solutions to the Palestinian problem. The turn to political Islam in the Occupied Territories was also boosted by the ascendance in Israel of the radical religious right from the late 1970s onwards (Sprinzak 1977, 1991). After the coming to power in 1977 of the Likud national religious coalition, led by Menahem Begin, the right-wing government embarked on a large-scale Jewish settlement effort in the West Bank, in which Gush Emunim played a central role (Mishal and Sela 2000: 26).

In the 1980s Israel's attitude towards the activities of the Muslim Brotherhood remained somewhat relaxed. However, although many secular Palestinian nationalists were initially targeted after the revival of the deportation policy by then Defence Minister Yitzhak Rabin in August 1986, from early 1988 Islamic activists also became prominent among the deportees.[3] Israel even continued to categorise the Islamist movement as 'nonviolent' – that is, not engaged in active resistance to occupation

– even after the eruption of the first Intifada (Mishal and Sela 2000: 26). It was only in May 1989 that Israel began to arrest some of the leadership of Hamas, and by September 1989 Hamas had been declared illegal.

During the first two decades of occupation the Palestinians in the West Bank and Strip Gaza, after the traumatic 1948 Nakba and dispersion, adopted a strategy of clinging to their land (in Arabic *sumud*, steadfastness). However, Israeli settlement policies coupled with the intensification of Israeli repression led to the eruption of the Palestinian popular rebellion in late 1987. The word *Intifada* (from a root meaning 'to shake off') entered international discourse, denoting the Palestinian rebellion aiming to shake off twenty years of brutal occupation. The catalyst was an incident on 8 December 1987, when an Israeli truck ploughed into a Palestinian vehicle, killing four Palestinians and wounding nine others inside who were returning from work in Israel. The following day some 4,000 inhabitants of the Jabaliyah refugee camp in the Gaza Strip – from which most of the killed workers originated – protested at the killings, and youths began to throw stones. Within a short time the whole population of the West Bank and Gaza had erupted in protest against the twenty-year occupation. On the third day of the Intifada, 10 December, the mayor of Gaza, Rashad al-Shawwa, summed up the new mood among the Palestinians in an interview broadcast on Israeli radio:

> One must expect these things after twenty years of debilitating occupation. People have lost hope. They are frustrated and don't know what to do. They have turned to religious fundamentalism as their last hope. They have given up hoping that Israel will give them their rights. The Arab states are unable to do anything, and they feel that the PLO, which is their representative, has failed. (quoted in Shalev 1991: 13)

The Israeli response to the first Intifada was similar to previous answers to Palestinian resistance since 1967, only this time the scale of the repressive measures undertaken by the Israeli army was much greater. To crush the Intifada, the military authorities, under the direction of Defence Minister Rabin, imposed an unprecedented scale of collective sanctions. These included mass arrests and detentions; 'limb breaking' and beatings; opening fire at unarmed protestors, resulting in the death of 1,418 persons up to July 1995 and the wounding of tens of thousands of others; prolonged curfews and house demolitions; as well as administrative deportations. Of the 1,418 Palestinians who died as a result of Israeli repression, 260 were under the age of sixteen. In comparison, during the same period (1987–95) 297 Israelis died as the result of Palestinian attacks against Israelis.[4]

Israeli efforts to restore the status quo shocked the international community, and precipitated serious self-doubt among sections of the Israeli public. Moreover, the uprising gained widespread international sympathy for the Palestinians, and condemnation of the brutal Israeli occupation (Prior 1999c: 36). The day after the killing of the Palestinian workers by an Israeli truck, the leaders of the Muslim Brotherhood met to discuss how the situation could be used to promote wider demonstrations. The meeting was attended by Shaykh Ahmad Yasin, Dr 'Abdul-Aziz Rantisi, Shaykh Salah Shehadeh, Dr Ibrahim al-Yazuri, 'Issa al-Nashshar, Muhammad Sham'ah and 'Abed al-Fattah Dukhan (Hroub 2000: 39; Ahmad 1994: 51). During the second (al-Aqsa) Intifada, Yasin, Rantisi and Shehadeh were all assassinated by Israel; Yasin had already served a period in Israeli jail for ordering the killing of four alleged collaborators. Several days later the group issued a statement, which was distributed in Gaza on 12–13 December and in the West Bank on 14–15 December, calling for resistance to the occupation (Hroub 2000: 40). This was the first official communiqué of Hamas, although the group did not adopt that name until January 1988. Within a year (December 1987–December 1988), Hamas had issued some 33 leaflets, replete with nationalist religious rhetoric and imagery, in contrast to those distributed by the Unified Leadership of the Uprising – a secular coalition of Fatah, the Palestinian Communist Party, the Popular Front for the Liberation of Palestine and the Democratic Front for the Liberation of Palestine (Ahmad 1994: 51–2).

The Palestinian Intifada provided the perfect opportunity for the founding of Hamas, and in its turn the Islamic movement fuelled and galvanised the popular uprising. The interests of the two became closely intertwined (Ahmad 1994: 19–20). Although it was only after the eruption of the uprising that Hamas began to offer a serious challenge to the dominant nationalist trends of the PLO and Fatah, by the spring of 1993 the West Bank and Gaza Strip were hovering on the brink of an anti-colonial war, with military forms of resistance replacing the uprising's earlier peaceful mass protest, and with the armed struggle being led not by the PLO or Fatah but by Hamas (Usher 1999: 9). The Palestinian rebellion provided a new context for political Islam in Palestine, one in which Hamas struggled for the liberation of the West Bank and Gaza Strip and to convince the people of the correctness of its political, social and educational programmes. Initially, during the early days of the Intifada, the military wing of the Brotherhood operated underground,[5] and became the strongest Islamic resistance movement in the Occupied Territories, giving the first true challenge not only to the occupation authorities but also to the mainstream nationalist and left-wing secular factions (Usher 1999). By 1992, slogans in Gaza promoted Hamas as 'the sole legitimate representative of the Palestinian people', and in July of that year armed Hamas–PLO clashes in Gaza left three Palestinians dead. Hamas regarded the PLO (and Fatah) leadership, 'strutting around the world in a lavish style, while people lived in poverty in the camps', with disdain (Prior 1999c: 37).

On the regional and pan-Arab levels, Hamas was very careful during the Kuwait crisis of 1990–91 not to alienate any of the countries from which its funds came, especially Kuwait. It combined criticism of Iraq's invasion of Kuwait in 1990 with criticism of the United States, thus ensuring continued political and financial support from Iran. With the PLO's stance in favour of Iraq, the Gulf countries saw Hamas as an alternative to the PLO, with the result that much of the Arab and Muslim financial support for the PLO was transferred to Hamas. The Islamist regime in the Sudan provided some training for Hamas activists and Saudi Arabian funds, previously channelled to the PLO, now went to Hamas. According to a Birzeit University professor, Hamas needed the financial support of the Arab states to advance its goals, while the Arab states needed Hamas to assist in the weakening of the PLO, which did not always succumb to the dictates of Arab leaders (Ahmad 1994: 93). Apparently substantial funding came not only from Arab states but also from Europe and the United States (Ahmad 1994: 48–9). Financial support for Hamas also came from Iran, Saudi Arabia, the Gulf States, Sudan and Algeria. The departure of the Soviet Union from Afghanistan was a great boost to Islamic movements throughout the region. After the success of the mujahideen in Afghanistan, Birzeit scholar and a leading Palestinian expert on Hamas Ziad Abu-Amr wrote in 1993: 'Muslims throughout the world, including in Europe and the United States, are now offering support to the *mujahediin* of Palestine' (Abu-Amr 1993: 7). Furthermore, internationally the collapse of the Soviet Union in 1991 marked the defeat of Marxism, which was a blow to the Palestinian left. The collapse was interpreted by Arab Islamists as being due to its disavowal of the Islamic way of life. Although in Afghanistan the mujahideen were heavily dependent on American support for equipment, their eventual victory appeared to encourage the idea of the Islamist state and discourage secular nationalism. In the 1990s inside Palestine Hamas capitalised on the general decline of both the Palestinian left and the secular PLO.

The Mass Deportations of 1992 and the Rise of Hamas

By late 1992, five years into the Intifada, Hamas had become the strongest resistance movement in the Occupied Territories. In December 1992 the 'Izzedin al-Qassam Brigades, the military wing of Hamas (named after the charismatic preacher-turned-guerrilla-leader who died fighting the British in the 1935) ambushed four Israeli military personnel in Gaza and Hebron, and abducted Sgt Nissim Toledano, all in the same week. After the body of Sgt Toledano, a maintenance man serving his time as a border policeman, who was captured in broad daylight in Lydda, a mixed Arab and Jewish town, was discovered near the Inn of the Good Samaritan on 15 December, troops flooded into Gaza and the West Bank, arrested nearly 2,000 men and selected 413 for deportation, in conformity with plans previously discussed within the Israeli politico-military establishment (Masalha 1997: 127-8). On 16 December, the Rabin Cabinet decided unanimously, with the abstention of the justice minister, to expel the alleged Hamas supporters. No charge was proffered against any of them. Rabin's intentions, it appears, were to bypass the legal process altogether. It was only when civil rights lawyers protested that the matter went to the Israeli Supreme Court. The Rabin government also set a new record for the number of Palestinians served with expulsion orders on a single day, when an unprecedented 413 such orders were issued against the alleged members and leaders of Hamas.

The majority of these deportees came from the West Bank and the rest from Gaza. In terms of locality, the largest group came from the city of Gaza and the second largest from the city of Hebron. The deportees, who numbered around 250, included about 30 lecturers, mainly from the Islamic universities of Gaza and Hebron, about 20 doctors and 5 engineers. Also among the expellees were imams of mosques, clerks of the religious courts, administrators of the Muslim holy places, as well as employees of educational, health and welfare institutions – schools, kindergartens, clinics, kitchens for the needy, and aid organizations for the disabled, orphans and prisoners' families.[6] Evidently the deportees were overwhelmingly clerics, professionals and intellectuals. Dr Rantisi, by then well-known as a Hamas spokesperson in Gaza and one of the deportees, representing the group in south Lebanon, said that 108 of the men were imams, 10 were doctors, 18 were engineers, 18 had university doctorates, 25 were lecturers at the Islamic University in Gaza, and 250 held bachelor degrees.[7]

Since 1967 nothing had unified Palestinians more than expulsions and deportations. The Palestinian national struggle is based more on resistance to expulsion and insistence on the right to return than on any other particular ideological doctrine. To Palestinians, who had been traumatised by the mass displacements of 1948 and 1967, the large-scale deportations of 1992 seemed another signal that the threat of 'transfer' from the West Bank and Gaza had not diminished under the new centre-left coalition of Prime Minister Rabin. The expelled Palestinians dumped on Lebanese territory in flagrant violation of that country's sovereignty represented a new dimension to Israel's deportation policy and set a precedent in its ongoing demographic battle with the Palestinians, a battle for 'maximum land and minimum Arabs'. While security, a standard Israeli justification for deportations, was invoked, this 'mini- transfer' had more to do with the desire to remove as many Palestinians as possible from the West Bank and Gaza Strip. The mass expulsion was completely out of proportion; about 1,600 Palestinians were rounded up, over 400 of whom were handcuffed, blindfolded and transported to the Lebanese border in the middle of the night and told to walk, while soldiers fired shots over their heads. This was carried out in the middle of a harsh winter, without charge or due process, in retaliation for the killing of four Israeli soldiers.

The Israeli intention to break the administrative backbone of Hamas most certainly backfired with the expulsions into south Lebanon. In the weeks following the deportations, there was an unusual degree of unity among the Palestinians. This unity, however, masked major political divisions and discords over the peace talks with Israel – divisions which were soon exposed and even deepened following the Declaration of Principles signed between Israel and the PLO in September 1993. The portrayal of the 413 deportees, expelled by Israel and unwelcome in Lebanon, praying and studying on the icy hills of Marj al-Zuhour in southern Lebanon was an ongoing international embarrassment to Israel. The incident gained an unprecedented level of respect for the Palestinian Islamists and internationalised the Palestinian crisis considerably. Evidently the protracted crisis constituted a public relations coup for Hamas and contributed to the dramatic rise in the organisation's popularity in the Occupied Territories and the decline in the popularity of the pro-negotiations PLO camp. Both the 1992 mass deportations and the subsequent Oslo Accords of 1993 contributed to the emergence of a new and complex political situation in the West Bank and Gaza: armed resistance against the Israeli settlers was carried out largely by radical and popular Islamic organisations such as Hamas and the Islamic Jihad, while the mainstream pro-negotiations camp in charge of the new Palestinian Authority (PA) was now making strenuous efforts to curb this resistance (Masalha 1997: 127-8).

Opposition to the Oslo Accords and After

On 15 November 1988, in a significant move away from its goal of establishing a Palestinian state throughout historic Palestine, the Palestinian National Council (the 'parliament in exile') in Algiers declared that the 'State of Palestine' should exist side by side with the State of Israel. Chairman Yasser Arafat, furthermore, confirmed the PLO's recognition of Israel, its 'renunciation of violence', and its willingness to negotiate a peaceful settlement based on UN resolutions. By 20 January 1993 secret talks were taking place near Oslo between 'unofficial representatives' of Israel and PLO officials. The PLO's fortunes had fallen to the lowest point in its history by the summer of 1993. Largely due to its stand during the Gulf War of 1991, it was experiencing severe financial and administrative difficulties, and was unable to pay the families of the martyrs and even its own supporters. Already suffering from problems of fatigue and routinisation, its collapse was accelerated by external factors, including the demise of the Soviet Union and the rout of Iraq in the Gulf War, which had catastrophic consequences for the organisation. The PLO's belated support for Saddam Hussein led to its supply of money from the Gulf states being cut off, and the expulsion of many Palestinians from the Gulf. From being a state in the making it was struggling to keep open its missions around the world. By contrast, Hamas was rising in popularity, both because of its ideological purity and because of the success of its social work in the Occupied Territories. The PLO's betrayal of its pledge to suspend negotiations with the Israelis until the deportees had been repatriated further alienated Hamas and many Palestinians in the Occupied Territories (Prior 1999c: 39).

For Hamas the Oslo Accords were a historic act of treason, and it judged the PLO to be too inept and weak to pursue any real resolution of the conflict. Nevertheless, the PLO persisted in its intentions, and despite the massacre of twenty-nine worshipping Muslims at the Ibrahimi shrine in Hebron (25 February 1994), and Hamas-inspired suicide attacks in early April 1994, 4 May saw the signing in Cairo of the 'Agreement on the Gaza Strip and the Jericho Area' by Israeli Prime Minister Rabin and PLO Chairman Arafat. A Palestinian Authority (PA) headed by Arafat was formed on 12 May and took over the governing of Jericho city from the Israeli military authorities the following day. The PA held its first meeting in Tunisia on 26 May when it endorsed a political agenda for the interim self-rule period in the Gaza Strip and Jericho. The PA later shifted its headquarters from Tunisia to the Gaza Strip and Jericho. On 11 July 1994 Arafat arrived in Gaza City after decades in exile to settle permanently in the Palestinian territory. Palestinian self-rule, which was later extended to other parts of the West Bank, was derided by Palestinian secular and religious dissidents as 'catastrophic' and a 'negotiated surrender', reflecting the asymmetry of power of the negotiating parties. Gradually many Palestinians would come to regard Oslo as a process in which Israel was seeking to consolidate its grip on all historic Palestine and completely marginalise the Palestinians.

The Oslo process suffered a severe blow after the extrajudicial execution on 5 January 1996 of Yahya 'Ayyash, also known as 'The Engineer', one of the instigators of bomb attacks against Israel. The long-awaited Palestinian elections were duly held on 20 January without the participation of Hamas and the other Palestinian rejectionist parties. Arafat won 88 per cent of the vote in the presidential contest, while his party, Fatah, won 50 of the 88 seats on the Council. However, the euphoria of the election yielded almost immediately to Hamas-inspired suicide bombings in Jerusalem on 25 February (which left twenty-four dead) and elsewhere. Israel imposed draconian collective punishment on the Occupied Territories, this time supported by the Palestinian police. Israeli Prime Minister Shimon Peres threatened Arafat that Israeli troops would invade the PA's areas if Hamas were not dealt with, and the PA's policemen opened fire on Hamas supporters in Gaza on 18 November, killing thirteen. Although it considered the Palestinian Authority to be behaving like a policeman for Israel, Hamas, at the height of the Oslo process, had no appetite for being embroiled in a civil war (Prior 1999c: 41); its leadership simply appeared to be waiting for the PA to 'self-destruct' (Zahhar 1995: 81–8, 1998).

Hamas's pro-resistance and anti-negotiations stand, furthermore, was benefiting from the fact that after the Oslo Accords were signed, the Rabin government did its utmost to preserve and even strengthen all the Jewish settlements in the Occupied Territories (Masalha 1997, 2000). Furthermore, the 'internal closure' of both Gaza and the towns and villages of the West Bank confirmed the perception of many Palestinians that the Oslo Accord prefigured merely a Zionist corralling of the natives into South African-style Bantustans (Prior 1999c: 41). The security of Jewish settlers became central to the Israel–PLO negotiations. The Rabin government allocated $330 million for the completion of bypass roads connecting Jewish settlements to each other and to Israel proper. This ambitious project, with its huge budgetary allocation, together with the construction of settlements and infrastructure in and around Jerusalem, is expected to 'annex' more than 35 per cent of the West Bank to Israel. Israeli journalist Haim Baram, reporting from West Jerusalem in *Middle East International* of 23 June 1995, wrote:

> The first year after Oslo was euphoric, but then the ugly reality began to emerge: it has become absolutely clear that the Rabin government has no intention of dismantling the settlements; the process of releasing Palestinian political prisoners is agonisingly slow and certainly behind schedule; Israel plans to annex a great amount of land around Jerusalem and to create

irreversible facts which amount to actually taking over at least 35 per cent of the occupied West Bank; the repression in the occupied territories continues unabated, including the official and semi-official use of torture and the fascist-style operation of the death squads. This was the case before Oslo, but the illusion that a new era has dawned has been dashed.[8]

The Triumph of Pragmatism:
Hamas, Ceasefire and Electoral Triumph

Hamas was the first Palestinian group to use suicide bombers in the 1990s as a tactic of resisting the occupation. But Palestinian suicide bombing, as a product of brutal Israeli occupation, was always a policy of desperation. Furthermore, Hamas only embarked on suicide-bombing campaigns as a response to extreme provocations by Israelis, such as the Hebron massacre of 1993. As an Israeli political scientist observed: Hamas only resorted to this atrocious type of terrorism after 1994, when Baruch Goldstein, an Israeli physician and army reserve captain, massacred 29 Palestinians in the Hebron shrine.[9] According to Israeli sources, between October 2000 and April 2006 Hamas carried out 51 suicide attacks, killing 272 Israelis. Islamic Jihad and the al-Aqsa Martyrs Brigade carried out 34 each, killing 98 and 80 Israelis respectively. During the same time almost 5,000 people, the vast majority of them Palestinians, were killed by the Israeli army.[10]

However, many Palestinians believed that the tactic of suicide bombing was counterproductive and was damaging their cause. In June 2003, after nearly three years of al-Aqsa Intifada that had cost the Palestinians more dearly than ordinary Israelis, Hamas called for a ceasefire and even agreed to suspend suicide attacks inside Israel. Hamas founder Shaykh Yasin told Reuters: 'Hamas has studied all the developments and has reached a decision to call a truce, or a suspension of fighting activities.' He added that the ceasefire carried conditions and a time limit.[11] Apparently the ceasefire was agreed between Marwan Barghouti, a jailed Fatah leader, and the heads of Hamas and Islamic Jihad in Damascus, Khaled Masha'al and Dr Ramadan Shalah respectively. Throughout 2004, Hamas persisted in its support for the 'temporary truce', despite continuing Israeli army raids on Gaza, and in 2005 it declared a 'unilateral ceasefire'.

This pragmatic approach to armed struggle contributed to Hamas's electoral victory in January 2006. Its spectacular triumph in the parliamentary elections was partly a protest at Fatah ineffectualness in negotiations and internal corruption. The victory was a result of a number of factors. First, the Islamic movement's anti-corruption and reformist agenda; supporters of Hamas regarded the Fatah leadership with disdain; believing they were strutting around the world in a lavish style, while many people lived in poverty and in appalling conditions in refugee camps (Prior 1999c: 36–8). Second, the failure of Fatah to liberate Palestine; Hamas considered the Oslo process to be an acquiescence to Israeli and American diktats, never an adequate solution; for Hamas, the Fatah leadership 'has sold the struggle, sold the blood and sold the rights of the Palestinian people' (interview with Jamil Hamameh, in Ahmad 1994: 110). Third, the vote for Hamas was also about 'the Power to Say No' to the orchestrator of the Oslo process, the USA – a staunch ally of the occupying power – and its political process which had led to Palestinian imprisonment; it was an expression of non-cooperation and non-violent resistance to American-led schemes in the Middle East.[12] The free and fair democratic elections in Palestine also created a major problem for American imperial calculations, exploding its propagandistic claims to be pushing for democracy across the region.

Yet Hamas in power is likely to be different from Hamas in opposition. After its election it chose to tone down its militant rhetoric. Its ascent to political power led its leaders to modify some positions. It was not entirely clear whether Hamas's rejection of suicide bombing inside Israel was tactical. But, as Khaled Hroub, director of the Cambridge Arab Media Project and a leading Palestinian expert on Hamas, argues, Hamas has always had a moderate wing; it has always had the potential to make the transition to a purely political organisation, and among members of Hamas suicide bombing was always controversial.

> If one looks at the conduct of Hamas in 1996 there was huge controversy even in the ranks of Hamas over its bombing campaign.... The concept of the two-state solution is now the cornerstone of their thinking. I doubt we will see the old Hamas again.[13]

This shift in Hamas's strategy was evident in the run-up to the Palestinian election of January 2006, when the movement, although still committed to armed struggle, dropped its call for the destruction of Israel from its election manifesto, a move that brought the Islamist movement closer to the mainstream Palestinian position of building a state within the boundaries of the occupied territories.[14]

Hamas, which was now leading the Palestinian Authority, was under pressure to seek approval from the international community. In April 2006 Yahya Musa, a Hamas member of the Palestinian Legislative Council, stated that Hamas had moved into a 'new era' which did not require suicide attacks. 'The suicide bombings happened in an exceptional period and they have now stopped', he said. 'They came to an end as a change of belief.' Ghazi Hamed, the spokesman for the government, said in future any military action would be restricted to the Palestinian territories occupied by Israel.[15] Nevertheless in early April 2006 the European Union announced it was stopping direct funding of the PA, while the United States halted aid projects. Hamas needs outside funding of $150 million each month to pay Palestinian Authority wages, and the Palestinian economy was on the verge of collapse.

Evolving Attitudes: From Historic Palestine as an Islamic *Waqf* to the Two-State Solution

Hamas's ultimate gaol is to establish a sovereign 'Islamic state' in historic Palestine with Jerusalem as its capital. For decades Palestinian nationalism was predominantly secular. The anti-colonial PLO National Covenant (*al-Mithaq al-Qawmi al-Filastini*) advocated secular territorial nationalism which would accommodate pre-1948 Jews in a secular democratic Palestine.[16] Hamas's Charter of August 1988, which expressed its objectives in thirty-six articles (English translation in Hroub 2000: 267–291; Ahmad 1994: 129–59) was the embodiment of the new Palestinian religious nationalism. In the Charter we find that Hamas's aim is an 'Islamic state', allowing the followers of other religions to exist, but only under the shadow of Islam (Article 6). Hamas's programme was not only to establish a Palestinian state and remove the Israeli settlers from the occupied territories, but also to establish an Islamic state in all of historic Palestine: 'Let every hand be cut off that signs a relinquishment of a grain of the soil of Palestine to the enemies of Allah who have usurped the blessed soil.'[17] On the introductory page of the Charter we find, 'Israel will be established and will stay established until Islam nullifies it as it nullified what was before it.' Later we are told 'There is no solution to the Palestinian question except by Jihad' (Article 13), and 'When an enemy occupies some of the Muslim lands, Jihad becomes obligatory for every Muslim. In the struggle against the Jewish occupation of Palestine, the banner of Jihad must be raised' (Article 15).

Hamas was strongly opposed to the PLO Algiers Declaration of 1988 and its central concept of a two-state solution, regarding it as a betrayal of its principles and covenant. Hamas's criticism of the PLO and its vision of a secular Palestinian state in the West Bank and Gaza intensified after 1988. Furthermore, by 1992 slogans in Gaza promoted Hamas as 'the sole legitimate representative of the Palestinian people', and in July of that year armed clashes occurred in Gaza, leaving three dead (Ahmad 1994: 65). Since the mid-1990s, however, major developments in the thinking of Hamas have taken place, with the Islamist movement placing greater emphasis on UN resolutions on Palestine and on international legitimacy, as well as on the idea of a long-term historic truce between Palestine and Israel (Hroub 1994: 24-37, 2000, 2004, 21-38). In late March 2005 Hamas, and its junior partner Islamic Jihad, decided in principle to join the PLO. Hamas felt it was strong enough and confident enough to join the PLO not as a spoiler or an 'onerous newcomer', as the movement was once portrayed by PLO factions, but as a welcome and full partner, even a potential saviour.[18] Hamas's vanguard role in the Palestinian Intifada against Israeli occupation and its electoral gains in Gaza and the West Bank more than qualified the movement to join the PLO, an organisation that has been dominated since the late 1960s by Fatah.[19]

Hamas's current attitudes, therefore, should not only be measured against the rhetoric of its 1988 Charter, but also be understood to have undergone significant and radical changes. While the Charter insisted on Muslim rights to, and sovereignty over, all historic Palestine, by early 2006 Hamas had become deeply wedded to the concept of the two-state solution it had fiercely denounced in the late 1980s. Indeed the idea of a Palestinian state in the West Bank and Gaza has become the cornerstone of Hamas's political thinking.[20]

Hamas's Charter views Islamic Palestine in fairly traditional Islamic terms: Jerusalem has the first of the two *qiblahs* (direction to which

Muslims turn when praying), is the third of the holy Islamic sanctuar-
ies, was the point of departure for the Prophet Muhammad's midnight
journey to the seventh heaven (Hamas Charter: Article 14). However, the
main innovative idea introduced by Hamas centred on the notion that
the land of Palestine as a whole was consecrated and endowed as *waqf*
in perpetuity for all generations of Muslims, and that therefore no part
of it should be relinquished. This idea is enshrined in Hamas's Charter.
Article 11 reads:

> The Islamic Resistance Movement believes that the land of Palestine is an
> Islamic *waqf* entrusted to the Muslim generations until Judgement Day.
> No one may renounce all or even part of it. Neither Arab state nor all Arab
> states combined, neither king or president nor all the kings and presidents,
> and neither organisation nor all organisations, be they Palestinian or Arab,
> have the right to do that because Palestine is an Islamic *waqf* [land] that has
> been entrusted to generations of Muslims until the Day of Judgement. Who,
> after all, has the right to act on behalf of Muslim generations until the Day
> of Judgement?
>
> This is its status in Islamic sharia [law] and the same goes for all the land
> were conquered by Muslims, where Muslims made the conquered lands a
> trust [*waqf* land] to all generations of Muslims until the Day of Judgement.
>
> And it was so when the commanders of the Islamic armies, after conquer-
> ing Iraq and al-Sham [Syria], sent to the Muslim Caliph, 'Umar ibn al-Khatab,
> asking for his advice concerning the conquered land: whether they should
> divide it among the army, or leave the land to the owners? After discussions
> and consultations between the Caliph of the Muslims, 'Umar ibn al-Khatab
> and companions of the Prophet (peace be upon him) they decided that the
> land should remain in the hands of the owners to benefit from its fruit. As
> for the real ownership of the land and the land itself, it should be endowed as
> a *waqf* for all Muslim generations until the Day of Resurrection. Those who
> are on the land have the right to land's benefit only. This *waqf* remains as
> long as earth and heaven last. Any action taken in contradiction to Islamic
> sharia with respect to Palestine is unacceptable action to be rescinded by
> its claimants.

On the face of it the rhetoric of Hamas's Charter, which insists on
Muslim rights to, and sovereignty over, all historic Palestine, leaves no
room for a political settlement with Israel (Ahmad 1994: 52). There is no
point in pursuing peace with Israel, since Hamas works towards 'raising
the banner of Allah on every inch of Palestine' (Article 6). 'As far as
the ideology of the Islamic Resistance Movement is concerned, giving

up any part of Palestine is like giving up part of its religion' (Article 13). However, Hamas's theological innovations, namely the insistence on all historic Palestine as an Islamic *waqf*, can be understood not in the historical or traditional terms of the Islamic institution of religious endowment but rather against the background of the modern Palestine-Israel conflict, and especially against the background of the 1948 Palestinian Nakba, including the expulsion of the Palestinians and the destruction of much of Palestinian society in 1948, in order to make way for Israel. Palestinians of all shades of opinion consider the Nakba as a heinous Zionist crime. In the post-Nakba period the Israeli state, under the Law of Absentee Property, seized Palestinian property, including virtually all the property of the Muslim *waqf*, a major property owner in historic Palestine (McDowall 1990: 126).[21] Historically the *waqf* land in Palestine was substantial, with one estimate suggesting that *waqf* property amounted to one-tenth of all land in Mandatory Palestine, as well as 70 per cent of all shops in some Arab cities (Lustick 1980: 59, 189-90).[22] It is no wonder, therefore, that the Islamic movement in Israel has led in recent years a widely publicised civil rights campaign of direct action to recover confiscated Muslim *waqf* property in Israel. This has included mass rallies and regular marches to the lands of Palestinian villages destroyed in 1948 as well the recovery of mosques and cemeteries in these villages. The activities of the Islamic Movement in Israel are carried out through the 'al-Aqsa Association', an NGO which campaigns for the release by the Israeli authorities of mosques and cemeteries existing in abandoned (almost completely destroyed) villages and the preservation and restoration of these *waqf* properties (Masalha 2005a: 44; Benvenisti 2002: 284).

Hamas has emphasised the universality and unity of the Islamic nation, and in its Covenant requests open borders for the mujahideen of the Arab and Islamic countries 'so that they can take their role and join their efforts with their Muslim brothers of Palestine' (Article 28). However, it insists on not interfering with the affairs of any Arab state, and points to the bad experience of such PLO interference. For their part, Arab countries are strongly supportive of Hamas. Sudan provides training for activists. Algeria's Islamists are the role model for Hamas, and Saudi Arabian funds, previously channelled to the PLO, now go to Hamas. Hamas needs the support of the Arab states to advance its goals, and the Arab states need Hamas to assist in the weakening of the PLO.

The religio-political discourse of Hamas contains the biblical paradigm and its legends. Historically Islam regarded Judaism as containing some of the most important components of the religious tradition to which it itself belonged; Islam and Judaism were perceived as belonging to the same tradition of prophecy and of divine revelation. Although critical of the human 'tampering' with the biblical text, the Quran affirms that the Torah is revelation from God and that the prophets of Judaism (Abraham and his two sons, Jacob, Moses and others) are prophets of God (Al-Faruqi 1986: 57–9). Furthermore in Arabic, Palestine (*Filastin*) had preserved the (religious) name of the Holy Land (*al-Ard al-Muqaddasah*), and the annual celebration of the Nabi Musa festival (pilgrimage to the prophet Moses' 'tomb' near Jericho) by Palestinian Muslims even contributed to the strengthening of the bond between the various parts of Palestine (Weinstock: 1979: 77). But Hamas also speaks of Palestine as the 'promised land': in Arabic *al-Watan al-Maw'ud or Ard al-Mi'ad* – a biblical expression that has little basis in the Muslim tradition and is evidently derives from the religio-political vocabulary of (religious and secular) Zionism (Sivan 1992: 71–81). Although a Muslim version of the biblical narrative is found in the Quran, which depicts the sacrifice enjoined by God on Ibrahim (Abraham) as involving Ishma'il (biblical Ishmael), the forefather of the Arabs, and not Isaac (Quran 37: 97-113), but that sacrifice tradition links Ibrahim to holy sites in Hijaz and is enshrined in the Haj (pilgrimage) tradition to Mecca. The traditional Islamic narrative has also been outlined by medieval Muslim commentators such as al-Tabari, al-Kisai and al-Tha'alabi. On the face of it Hamas's 'promised land' rhetoric appears to be aiming at expropriating and subverting the Zionist rhetoric (Sivan 1992: 71–81).

The discourse of Hamas, to use Foucauldian terms, is part of a world of (biblical) discourse divided between dominant and accepted (Zionist) discourse and excluded and dominated (Palestinian) discourse.[23] In essence, however, the biblicist rhetoric Hamas fails to counter is Zionist biblical mythology. In fact it can only reinforce biblically based 'fundamentalist' ideologies of Jews and (mainly American) Protestant evangelicals who, in their various shades, are fixated on the paradigm of 'promised land–chosen people' and advocate exclusive Israeli sovereignty over the 'whole Land of Israel' couched in ideologically absolute and uncompromising (rather than historically grounded and pragmatic) perspectives. Of course the relations between the dominant (Israeli–Jewish) religious power and the marginalised and occupied (both Palestinian Muslim and Christian) religious communities is a significant factor, and there is a basic difference between mainstream Israeli–Jewish and 'fundamentalist' attitudes and Muslim attitudes towards the question of the shrines in Jerusalem. Palestinian Muslims in occupied East Jerusalem are on the defensive, struggling against creeping Judaisation of the Old City and seeking to preserve the religious and prayer status quo on al-Haram al-Sharif, while Jewish and Christian 'fundamentalists' are on the offensive, running joint and well-funded campaigns in both Israel and the USA in favour of changing the status quo of the Muslim holy sites and of the building of the Jewish temple on the al-Haram al-Sharif.

As an Islamist movement, Hamas takes the Quran as its constitution. It bases its ideology firmly on the Quran and on the belief that Muslim lands should not come under the sovereignty of non-Muslims (Riddell 2001). According to Hamas, Islam must exercise political and religious sovereignty where it is dominant. For centuries Islam claimed dominance in social, political and religious arrangements in Palestine (and in the Middle East as a whole) through the Ottoman *millet* system. This system was closely linked to the famously tolerant Islamic rules on the treatment of non-Muslim minorities, including Jews and Christians, who were considered *dhimmi*, or members of protected minorities. These religious communities were autonomous, allowed to rule themselves with little interference from the Ottoman government. The *millet* had a great deal of power: communities set their own laws and collected and distributed their own taxes. All that was required was loyalty to the Ottoman sultan.

At the time, the *millet* system was far more liberal than any contemporary European arrangement for dealing with religious minority groups. However, by the democratic standards of the twenty-first century a political system based on the *millet*, with its *dhimmi* status, would be rightly viewed by Christian Arabs, the minority community in every Middle Eastern country, as a system of political exclusion and social degradation. Palestinian Christians, who are fully integrated within the Palestinian people as a whole, are particularly sensitive to issues of discrimination and their possible second-class status (Wagner 2003: 30). The late Shaykh Yasin, a religiously tolerant man, stated in an interview on 27 May 2000 that: 'Christians will have complete freedom in our state, even more than they have now' (Wagner 2003: 30). While Muslims rightly point to the record of greater tolerance towards Christians and Jews when Islam ruled Palestine, many (deeply secular) Palestinian Christians nonetheless wonder about their future status in a potentially revived *dhimmi* arrangement under Hamas (Wagner 2003: 30).

Hamas's leaders have always argued that Zionism and the Jewish state are based on discrimination against and ethnic cleansing of an entire ethnic group – non-Jewish Palestinians. Yet Hamas's aim is to establish ultimately a Muslim Palestine, in which Jews and Christians would be 'tolerated' (not equal) minorities. Thus Hamas needs to give a morally consistent and politically coherent answer to the fundamental question facing Palestinians, an answer that can also gain the respect of world public opinion: that there should be full equality under the law for all those who live in historic Palestine (Palestine–Israel) regardless of ethnicity or religious persuasion.[24] The Hamas Charter speaks of

> The Islamic Resistance Movement [as] a humanistic movement. It takes care of human rights and is guided by Islamic tolerance when dealing with the followers of other religions. ... Under the wing of Islam, it is possible for the followers of the three religions – Islam, Christianity and Judaism – to coexist in peace and quiet with each other. Peace and quiet would not be possible except under the wing of Islam. Past and present history are the best witness to that. (Article 31)

Hamas's current political tactics flow from the strategy of achieving Islamic sovereignty in Palestine. But Hamas's strategy is unlikely to lead to the abolition of an exclusionist Jewish state because, in order to achieve that goal, Hamas would have to embrace the concept of a state for all its citizens in Palestine–Israel, with full equality for all citizens not provided for by the sovereignty of Islam. Ultimately Hamas might end up embracing a Zionist-framed definition of its goal: a 'Muslim state' in the West Bank and Gaza; in other words a Bantustan Palestinian statelet in 22 per cent of Palestine, next to, broken into disconnected pieces by, and under the dominance of a Jewish state from which 80 per cent of the non-Jews had been driven out, dispossessed of all their property, never allowed to return and never compensated for their property, and in which the remainder of non-Jews are denied the rights of first-class citizenship.[25] However, Hamas cannot uphold the principle of full and genuine equality when another key part of its Charter says that

> It is the duty of the followers of other religions to stop disputing the sovereignty of Islam in this region, because the day these followers should take over there will be nothing but carnage, displacement and terror. (Article 31)

Hamas leaders are averse to embracing the secular democratic principle of complete equality in Palestine-Israel in the same way that the Zionist leaders of Israel are averse to upholding full equality for non-Jews.[26] In failing to uphold the principle of equality, Hamas would ultimately also fail to challenge the discriminatory nature of the Zionist enterprise on moral and political grounds.[27] In power Hamas would be under pressure to pursue more realistic goals, especially towards the right of Palestinian refugees to return to their home and land. But any realistic approach should not deflect from the realities of Israeli apartheid and the need for a strategy of challenging and exposing Israeli apartheid policies. In order to win the struggle against apartheid regimes like the Israeli Jewish state, there is a need to embrace the ideas of equality of citizenship, equality regardless of ethnicity or religious persuasion, and solidarity across the national divide.[28]

A new Palestinian regime dominated by Hamas will attempt to take over the key politically secular and socially liberal institutions of Palestinian Authority and set the political, social, cultural and educational agenda of the Palestinians living under Israeli military occupation. Clearly a more socially conservative agenda is on the cards in Palestine. Among Palestinians, Hamas is widely recognised as a pragmatic organisation; shortly after the elections a senior lecturer at Birziet University sent me the following email:

> Aside from pondering the national ramifications of this victory, every Palestinian now is thinking of his/her sphere and how that will be affected. So obviously we think of Birzeit, and whatever other organisations we are involved in. I think they [Hamas] will not have the bulldozer approach of 'Islamisation'. Rather, it will be a slow process, and we have to be vigilant. The old complacency regarding this threat is over, yet we should not be alarmists.[29]

The questions now are: first, whether Hamas will adopt a more radical approach to 'Islamisation'; and, second, the extent to which a Hamas-dominated regime will use the PA machinery to 're-Islamise' Palestinian society 'from above' (Jensen 2006). Shortly after news of its its election victory, jokes began to circulate in Palestine in Arabic on mobile phones as SMS messages, mocking Hamas's socially conservative agenda but also reflecting some anxiety about its real or imagined 'Islamisation' programme.[30]

Hamas in power is clearly wedded to the concept of the two-state solution. Its national religious rhetoric has little to offer beyond 'grandiloquence and the anaesthetising rhetoric' of a religious solution for a national secular situation (Prior 1999c: 261). Those outside Palestine, particularly in the refugee camps, have a strong sense of having been abandoned by the Palestinian leadership (Prior 1999c: 261). For an agreed future, religion in Palestine-Israel has to be separated from the state, and the national goals of both peoples, Palestinians and Israelis, must become inclusive. While the biblical discourse of 'promised land' and of the displacement by one people of the indigenous population is particularly objectionable (Prior 1999c: 261), the only obvious alternative is to envisage the creation of a democratic framework which respects the right of equal citizenship of all inhabitants of Palestine-Israel (including the return of those ethnically cleaned by Zionism), irrespective of religious affiliation.

Is the Hebrew Bible Historical? The Invention
of Tradition and the Challenge of Archaeology for
Biblical Scholarship and Nationalist Historiography

Biblical archaeology, with its biblical paradigm of 'promised land–chosen
people', has always had a tendency to privilege the narrative associated
with Israelis, Zionist settlers or Jewish nationalists over those of the
indigenous (predominantly Muslim) inhabitants of Palestine. Virtually all
biblical archaeologists were Western Christians (many of them churchmen)
or Jews with a strong commitment to the truth of the Bible, interpreting
their finds in light of the scriptures. No wonder, then, that archaeological
findings confirmed the Bible when researchers used the Old Testament
to identify, date, and interpret the significance of the towns, buildings,
pottery, and other artefacts they unearthed. This complete disregard
for the historical, demographic and political realities of (predominantly
Muslim) historic Palestine was at the heart of a colonial tradition: the
Western discipline of biblical archaeology – a tradition which from its
beginning in the nineteenth century was established to validate Western
roots in the Holy Land and authenticate the historicity of the Hebrew
Bible (see Chapter 1).

Driven by an invented tradition and the need to establish the 'veracity' of the Old Testament, the Hebrew archaeology of the Yishuv in
Palestine, which was sponsored by the British colonial power (1920–48),

was passionately Jewish nationalist. But while the attitudes of British archaeologists towards the Middle East began to change in the post-colonial period, Zionists and Israelis, by contrast, chose to maintain the colonial tradition of the West (Benvenisti 2002: 304). The ideologically driven character of this discipline became even more pronounced after the establishment of the State of Israel in 1948, when biblical archaeology became an obsession, firmly institutionalised as a cornerstone of Israel's civic religion, testifying to exclusive Zionist claims to the land of Palestine (Rose 2004: 7-25). The discipline of biblical archaeology has since been employed by Israeli academic institutions and the state to create a socially meaningful understanding of the past; its findings have been deployed by the state politically and educationally and have been presented to the Israeli public to foster Jewish nationalism and state-building and to legitimise the dispossession of the indigenous inhabitants of Palestine.

Fundamentalist readings of the Hebrew Bible are widely held among conservative evangelicals (Barr 1977: 120-59). The same evangelicals often disguise themselves as mainstream scholars (Lemche 2003). For them the Hebrew Scriptures are divine revelation and accurate history, conveyed directly from God to a wide variety of Israelite sages, prophets and priests. However, the historicity of the biblical patriarchs is also important for most mainstream churchmen, who feel that that unless these figures actually existed, their own religious faith would be somehow erroneous. Scholarly findings in archaeology, textual analysis, history, and newly translated ancient documents all point to a historical reality in ancient Palestine which is difficult for many traditional and fundamental-ist believers (Christian, Jews and Muslims) to reconcile with a faith that depends on holy scriptures, divine promises, prophecies, and revelations perceived as historical facts.[1] Many Christian and Jews, in particular, are still wedded to the notion that the five books of Moses were set down by Moses himself just before his death on Mount Nebo; that the books of Joshua, Judges and Samuel are regarded as sacred and recorded by Prophet Samuel; that King David was the author of the Psalms, and King Solomon the source of Proverbs and the Song of Solomon.

As we have seen in Chapter 1, for secular political Zionism the biblical narrative and ideology essentially functioned as the objective histori-cal account of the Jewish 'title to the land' – a claim not borne out by archaeological findings. However, this confidence that the Bible is a reliable witness to the historicity of the events it describes has collapsed over the last quarter of a century. The 'new' archaeology of the Holy Land raises the following questions: What if the Old Testament is largely fictional? What if Moses did not lead the Israelite tribes from Egypt to Canaan? What if the fabled walls of Jericho never fell before Joshua's armies? For Christian biblicists there are deep concerns about any questioning of the veracity of these claims and about the findings of the 'new' archaeology which challenges both biblical literalist and fundamentalist readings of the Hebrew Bible.[2] In Israel, furthermore, any attempt to question the historicity and reliability of the biblical descriptions is perceived as an attempt to undermine Jewish nationalism, the construction of Israeli identity in primordialist terms and, more crucially, the 'Jewish historic right to the land', and as shattering the myth of the State of Israel as continuing and renewing the ancient Kingdom of Israel (Herzog 1999: 6-8).

The new critical biblical scholarship and archaeology of ancient Palestine that has emerged in both Israel and the West presents a major challenge to the historicity of the Hebrew Bible and to both biblical scholarship and Israeli nationalist historiography. This critical archaeology, which suggests a reconstruction of the ancient past very different from that implied in the biblical narratives, did not emerge in a vacuum. Already in the late 1960s and early 1970s attempts began to separate history from legend, and the archaeology of ancient Palestine from biblical and theological studies (Thompson 1999: xi-xii; Dever 1995). Concentrating on Palestine's ancient history itself, rather than solely on its biblical associations, a critical trend of archaeologists and biblical scholars began to treat historical evidence and archaeological discoveries in the Holy Land as they would those anywhere else. They used settlement patterns, anthropological models, artefacts, architecture, animal bones, seeds, soil samples and other modern methods to produce a description based on scientific evidence (Finkelstein and Silberman 2001).

For Israelis the archaeological revolution raises fundamental emotive and ideological issues, partly because this critical scholarship is now being espoused by some leading archaeologists who are themselves living in Israel and teaching at Israeli universities (including Israel Finkelstein, Zeev Herzog and David Ussishkin) and by Israeli-Jewish biblical scholars who feel free from Zionist biases and the previous legendary conceptions of Western and Israeli biblical archaeology. They were able to look at the reality of ancient Palestine in a completely different way, thus contributing to the demolition of the Eurocentric concentration on the evidence of the Bible and making this new scholarship one of the most important developments of recent years.

Paradoxically the Israeli conquest of the West Bank in the 1967 war and its aftermath contributed to the rise of two contradictory currents in Israel: on the one hand, the messianic fundamentalist current of Greater Israel (discussed in Chapters 3–5) and, on the other, the 'new' archaeology. In the aftermath of the 1967 territorial conquests, Israeli archaeologists began to explore and analyse the hill country of the southern part of the West Bank ('biblical Judah'), looking for settlement patterns, evidence of lifestyles, and changes in demography and the environment. These surveys revolutionised the study of ancient Palestine (Finkelstein and Silberman 2001: 107). Indeed, since the late 1960s archaeological discoveries 'have revolutionized the study of early Israel and have cast serious doubt on the historical basis of such famous biblical stories as the wanderings of the Patriarchs, the Exodus from Egypt and conquest of Canaan, and the glorious empire of David and Solomon' (Finkelstein and Silberman 2001: 3).

For centuries Jews, Christians and Muslims believed (and continue to believe) in the historicity of Abraham (Ibrahim for Muslims) and the other biblical patriarchs. In 1974, however, Thomas L. Thompson, now Professor of the Old Testament at the University of Copenhagen, was among the first to question the historicity of the patriarchal narrative (1974). A year later Canadian scholar John Van Seters, in *Abraham in History and Tradition* (1975), not only questioned the historical validity of the patriarchal narrative but also showed that these biblical stories could only have been written in the sixth century BC or even later. Before and since the mid-1970s, the situation created by the mountains of findings excavated from 'biblical sites' paradoxically began to undermine the historical credibility of the Bible descriptions instead of reinforcing them; also, importantly, no evidence has been unearthed that can sustain the patriarchal period (or the legends of Abraham, Isaac and Jacob), dated between 2200 and 1900 BC or its chronology (Herzog 1999: 6–8). But, broadly speaking, the collapse of the historicity of the events described in the Hebrew Bible, Iron Age I,

over the last three decades, has been the result of three interrelated factors: archaeological evidence; textual and literary criticism; and, broadly
speaking, a post-colonial critique of biblical studies.

In *The Bible Came from Arabia* (1985), Kamal Salibi (then Professor of
History at the American University in Beirut) presents a highly ingenious
scholarly thesis that challenges Western biblical scholarship by putting
forward the theory that the actual 'lands of the Bible' were in south-western
Arabia and that the legend of the Jordan river crossing by Joshua was in
fact more to do with a *wadi* in the escarpment of Hijaz. Salibi's 'startling
discoveries' rest mainly on a linguistic analysis of biblical place names,
which, according to him, have been consistently mistranslated by biblical
scholars (Salibi 1985). Salibi's work is an exhaustive study of biblical place
names, which he located in an area bordering the Red Sea north of Yemen
– in Asir. The destruction of Judah by the Babylonian king Nebuchad-
nezzar in 586 BC finally put an end to the Israelites as a political entity in
south-west Arabia. In the subsequent migration of the Israelites in large
numbers to ancient Palestine, they took with them about thirty cherished
place names – not the hundreds that biblical archaeologists and scholars
claim to have identified in modern Palestine–Israel (Salibi 1985). There is
no archaeological evidence to support Salibi's thesis, which places Moses
and the Old Testament prophets on the map of Arabia; and no excavations
are likely to be allowed by the Wahhabi Saudi regime in the near future.
Whatever the merits of Salibi's place-names thesis, it is beyond the scope
of this chapter, which focuses on the post-1960s archaeology of the Holy
Land. The latter, however, shares at least one central argument with
Salibi's thesis: modern archaeology in Egypt and Palestine has failed to
produce evidence to support the biblical stories of the Israelites' captivity
in Egypt or to trace their Exodus through Sinai.

'It Ain't Necessarily So': The Challenge of New Archaeology, Literary Criticism and Post-colonial Studies

In 1986 the journalist and broadcaster John McCarthy was taken hostage,
together with several other Westerners, by Islamic fundamentalists in
Beirut. Apparently the Bible was the only book his Islamist prison guards
would allow them. During his long and painful ordeal, which lasted until

August 1991, McCarthy read the Bible twice (Rose 2004: 21). He became fascinated by the biblical epics. Following his release he stumbled across the works of a group of Israeli archaeologists from Tel Aviv University. The outcome was a British television documentary series entitled: *It Ain't Necessarily So* (November 2001, ITV), presented by McCarthy. The series shows McCarthy going to the Holy Land to examine the validity of stories from the Old Testament, with the help of leading archaeologists in the field. Apparently the ITV producers panicked about its radical content; consequently, McCarthy's six half-hour transmissions were given a midnight slot; and with minimum publicity audience figures were low (Rose 2004: 22).[3] The documentary series took in archaeology, new historiography and critical biblical research as the context for McCarthy's journey to the Holy Land and his attempt to explore the truth behind the stories: Joshua's conquest of Canaan – the Promised Land; Jericho's 'tumbling' walls. Who was Solomon? When did the Jews become monotheists? What was Zion? And when was the text of the Old Testament actually written?

Zeev Herzog, Professor of Archaeology at Tel Aviv University, and the director of its Institute of Archaeology, was one of the key advocates of this critical archaeology. Appearing on an Australian television programme in April 2000 – also entitled 'It Ain't Necessarily So' – Herzog debated the issue with Professor William Dever, a leading American archaeologist and former head of the University of Arizona's Near Eastern Studies Department. Already in October 1999, in a now-famous article in the Hebrew daily *Haaretz*, entitled 'The Old Testament: There Are No Findings on the Ground', Herzog argued:

> Following 70 years of intensive excavations in the Land of Israel, archaeologists have found out: The patriarchs' acts are legendary, the Israelites did not sojourn in Egypt or make an exodus, they did not conquer the land. Neither is there any mention of the empire of David and Solomon, nor of the source of belief in the God of Israel. These facts have been known for years, but Israel is a stubborn people and nobody wants to hear about it. (Herzog 1999: 6–8)

Herzog goes on to explain that Holy Land archaeology has shown that the Exodus and Joshua's conquest of Canaan could not have happened:

> This is what archaeologists have learned from their excavations in the Land of Israel: the Israelites were never in Egypt, did not wander in the desert, did not conquer the land in a military campaign and did not pass it on to the

12 tribes of Israel. Perhaps even harder to swallow is the fact that the united monarchy of David and Solomon, which is described by the Bible as a regional power, was at most a small tribal kingdom. And it will come as an unpleasant shock to many that the God of Israel, Jehovah [Yahweh], had a female consort [see below] and that the early Israelite religion adopted monotheism only in the waning period of the monarchy and not at Mount Sinai. Most of those who are engaged in scientific work in the interlocking spheres of the Bible, archaeology and the history of the Jewish people – and who once went into the field looking for proof to corroborate the Bible story – now agree that the historic events relating to the stages of the Jewish people's emergence are radically different from what that story tells. (Herzog 1999: 6-8; see also Harcourt 1997: 282-96)

The Bible is not history but literature and theology, Herzog argues; the 'new' archaeology of the Holy Land has completed a process that amounts to a scientific revolution in its field; archaeology – which has become an independent professional discipline with its own conclusions and its own observations – presents us with a picture of a reality of ancient Palestine completely different from the one described in the Old Testament; Holy Land archaeology is no longer using the Hebrew Bible as a reference point or a historical source; the old biblical archaeology is no longer the ruling paradigm in Holy Land archaeology; for the critical archaeologists the Bible is read like other ancient texts – as literature which may or may not contain some historical information (Herzog 2001: 72-93, 1999: 6-8).

Professor Dever, on the other hand, drew different conclusions. Although he does deny the historicity of Genesis–Joshua, gives the impression that his past certainties are under strain and concedes that no serious scholar today doubted the late date of the final redaction of the biblical tradition, he asserts that the biblical narrative may contain genuinely historical material, some of it possibly contemporary with the events the narrative purports to describe. He agrees that there is need for a fresh approach to 'ancient Israel', one that is critical, comparative, marked by dialogue between biblical scholars and archaeologists (Dever 2001: 25; Davies 2003).[4]

The critical archaeologists do not ignore the richness of the biblical narrative. Their argument is complex: that there is a need to distinguish between two distinct historical periods. The first is 'Iron Age I', which covers the earlier phases of the Hebrew Bible and the origins of the

Israelites, which describes a proto-history of the Israelites: the sojourn in Egypt; the wandering in Sinai; the very story of the patriarchs; the military conquest of Canaan. The main archaeological debate is about the historicity of the Bible during this period. Virtually all the events that are described in detail in the biblical stories appear to be contradictory. The current debate is not about the absence of archaeological evidence. Over the last seventy years, the 'new' archaeologists argue, the crucial evidence at digs in Israel–Palestine, Egypt, Jordan, and Lebanon suggest that most of the famous stories in the Hebrew Bible – the wanderings of the patriarchs; the Exodus from Egypt, which provides the foundation of the notion of 'liberation' within traditional Judaism; Joshua's conquest of Canaan; David's and Solomon's 'empire' – are without foundation.

The Myth of the United Kingdom of David and Solomon with its Capital Jerusalem

As we have seen in Chapter 1, Israeli claims for exclusive control over Jerusalem benefited greatly from the 'findings' of Israeli court archaeologists and Western orthodox biblical historiography, both of which relied on the historicity of the Hebrew Bible. The latter tells of the golden age of the united kingdom of the Israelites ruled over by a Judean monarch, first David and then his son Solomon. It describes a vast empire spreading from the Red Sea to the border of Syria, the splendour of Jerusalem and the first Temple built by Solomon, as well as other magnificent building projects. This 'united kingdom' subsequently split into Israel in the north and Judah in the south. But the archaeological discoveries contradict this picture. Although there is some archaeological evidence for the biblical monarchies of Judah and Israel from the ninth century to the sixth century BC, including in documents from neighbouring countries, mainly Assyria, there is also serious debate about the actual history of the two small tribal kingdoms. The archaeological evidence presents a picture completely at odds with the scale of the kingdoms of David and Solomon described in the Bible. The 'united monarchy' of David and Solomon, which the Bible describes as the zenith of the political, military and economic power of the Israelites, emerges from the recent archaeology not as a major regional power but as two modest tribal communities. Israel and Judea were from the outset two separate, tribal chiefdoms, and at times were in an adversarial relationship (Herzog 1999: 6–8).

A secularised Zionist version of Israeli mythologies that upheld Jerusalem as the 'national and religious capital' of the Israelites under David and Solomon is currently being promoted by left-wing Zionists and moderate Israelis, some of whom even utilise the findings of the critical archaeology to refute the biblical foundational myths of Israel. Daniel Gavron, a British Zionist journalist who emigrated to Israel in 1961 and became the head of English News at Israel Radio (he was also a co-founder of the *Palestine–Israel Journal*, which supports the two-state solution) wrote an article which was posted on the Israeli Foreign Ministry website in September 2003, entitled 'King David and Jerusalem: Myth and Reality'. The extraordinary thing about this public relations exercise is the fact that it endorses many of the findings of critical Israeli archaeologists (including Finkelstein and Nadav Naaman), but, at the same time, desperately clings on to old Zionist myths, and even articulates new ones centred on Jerusalem.[5] Gavron begins by commenting on the evidence produced by the new archaeology:

> To most Israelis it is axiomatic that the celebrations for the 3,000th anniversary of the conquest of Jerusalem by King David mark a real and tangible event; but this is far from certain. The biblical account of the capture of the city is the only one we have, and in the opinion of most modern scholars, the Bible is not an entirely reliable historical document. Corroborating evidence is required, and some indeed exists; but it is not conclusive. When all the available information has been assembled, the most that can be said is that there was probably an Israelite ruler called David, who made Jerusalem his capital sometime in the tenth century BCE. However, the precise date cannot be determined, and consequently there is no way of knowing exactly when the anniversary falls. ... The Bible is not – and was never intended to be – a historical document. A work of theology, law, ethics and literature, it does contain historical information; but if we want to evaluate this information we should consider when, how and why the Bible was compiled ... The historical evidence to back up these events is sparse, and, in some cases, contradictory. In particular, the account of Joshua's conquest of Canaan is inconsistent with the archaeological evidence. Cities supposedly conquered by Joshua in the 14th century BCE were destroyed long before he came on the scene. Some, such as Ai and Arad, had been ruins for a 1000 years. ... The conclusion is somewhat startling to Bible readers who know the Canaanites portrayed in the Bible as immoral idolaters: most of the Israelites were in fact formerly Canaanites.

The story of Abraham's journey from Ur of the Chaldees, the Patriarchs, the Exodus, Sinai, and the conquest of Canaan, all these were apparently based on legends that the various elements brought with them from their countries of origin. The consolidation of the Israelites into a nation was not the result of wanderings in the desert and divine revelation, but came from the need to defend themselves against the Philistines, who settled in the Canaanite coastal plain more or less at the same time the Israelites were establishing themselves in the hills.

Gavron goes on to reimagine Jerusalem as the 'national and religious capital' of the Israelites under David, implying that David did not expel the 'Jebusites' from his 'capital' city, and that therefore Israel today should also allow the Palestinians to live in Jerusalem:

> [The] founders of Israel were not Abraham and Moses; but Saul and David. It was apparently Saul who consolidated the hill farmers under his rule and created fighting units capable of confronting the Philistines. It was David who defeated the Philistines and united the hill farmers with the people of the Canaanite plains, thus establishing the Kingdom of Israel and its capital city. It is generally accepted among scholars today that there is genuine historical material in the Books of Samuel, which describe the careers of Saul and David; but even these books must be critically examined to distinguish between legend and fact, in as much as it can ever be known. Some of the materials in Samuel I and II, notably the lists of officers, officials, and districts, are believed to be very early, possibly even dating to the time of David or Solomon. These documents were probably in the hands of the Deuteronomists when they started to compile the material three centuries later.... The 3,000th anniversary celebration of David's capture of Jerusalem is perceived by some people, both in Israel and abroad, as an indication of an exclusive Jewish claim to the city. Although, as we have argued here, it is probable that David did take the city some three millennia ago, and make it his personal, national and religious capital, the biblical evidence points to the fact that the great Israelite monarch found a way to share his capital with his former adversaries. The Jebusites continued to live there; their property rights were respected and they were given a role in the administration of the city.[6]

These secularised nationalist claims that Jerusalem was always the 'capital city' of the 'united monarchy' under David and Solomon have no foundation in the history of ancient Palestine: they are fabricated modern myths (von Waldow 2004: 222-53) – myths which are crucial to the secular Zionist camp in Israel, but not to the religious orthodox or messianic ones. In fact the archaeological discoveries show Jerusalem was not even the spiritual centre of the biblically described, but in fact legendary united monarchy. Professor Herzog writes:

> The picture becomes even more complicated in the light of the excavations conducted in Jerusalem, the capital of the united monarchy. Large sections of the city have been excavated over the past 150 years. The digs have turned up impressive remnants of the cities from the Middle Bronze Age and from Iron Age II. ... No remains of buildings have been found from the period of the united monarchy (even according to the agreed chronology), only a few pottery shards. Given the preservation of the remains from earlier and later periods, it is clear that Jerusalem in the time of David and Solomon was a small city, perhaps with a small citadel for the king, but in any event it was not the capital of an empire as described in the Bible. This small chiefdom is the source of the 'Beth David' title mentioned in later Aramean and Moabite inscriptions. The authors of the biblical account knew Jerusalem in the 8th century BCE, with its wall and the rich culture of which remains have been found in various parts of the city, and projected this picture back to the age of the united monarchy. Presumably Jerusalem acquired its central status after the destruction of Samaria, its northern rival, in 722 BCE. (Herzog 1999: 6–8)

The actual ancient history of Palestine, in contrast with the biblical narrative, is not a history that is dominated by Jerusalem (Thompson 2003a: 7), although Finkelstein and Silberman believe that David and Solomon did exist, but only as minor highland chieftains ruling a population of perhaps 5,000 people. There is no archaeological evidence around 1005–970 BC for David's empire or conquests, nor for Solomon's (legendary) empire (970–931 BC). More crucially, there is no evidence even of monumental architecture in Jerusalem, which was no more than a village:

> As far as we can see on the basis of the archaeological surveys, Judah remained relatively empty of permanent population, quite isolated, and very marginal right up to and past the presumed time of David and Solomon, with no major urban centers and with no pronounced hierarchy of hamlets, villages, and towns. (Finkelstein and Silberman 2001: 132)

Current evidence refutes the existence of a unified kingdom:

> The glorious epic of the united monarchy was – like the stories of the patriarchs and the sagas of the Exodus and conquest – a brilliant composition that wove together ancient heroic tales and legends into a coherent and persuasive prophecy for the people of Israel in the seventh century BCE. (Finkelstein and Silberman 2001: 144)

Furthermore, there is no evidence of written documents or inscriptions for the palace of Solomon or the Jewish Temple; buildings once identified by Western archaeologists with Solomon have been shown by recent archaeology to date from other periods (Finkelstein and Silberman 2001: 144).

Israelites versus Canaanites and Philistines? An Invented Tradition and Mythological Ethnic and Religious Boundaries

These biblical stories and texts were written by multiple authors and put in their final form many centuries after the events they describe. They reflect the world of the later authors of the Hebrew Bible rather than actual historical facts. They also, then, express the ideology of a 'new' religious movement that arose among the ancient Israelites at a relatively late period. These accounts reflect a time when Babylon influenced exilic Judaism – after 587 BC and in the succeeding Persian period when both Babylon and ancient Palestine were under Persian rule (Davies 2002; Lemche 1991). In 529 BC the Persian emperor Cyrus the Great, who had conquered the Babylonians, allowed Jewish exiles wishing to return to Palestine to do so. The Hebrew Bible was, for the most part, written after the Babylonian exile and therefore was largely the product of exilic imagination: in the process of constructing a new tradition, Lemche argues, much of the previous Israelite history – including the exodus from Egypt, the conquest of Canaan and even the existence of the Canaanites – was an invented tradition, created to reflect the experiences of those returning from the Babylonian exile (Lemche 1991; Bowman 1999: 58-62).

The Hebrew Bible tells us that the Canaanites were the first people in Palestine. Yet nationalism is a modern European ideology; so, contrary to the mythologised biblical narrative, the Israelites, Canaanites and Philistines were not ethnic groups or distinct nationalities in ancient Palestine. However, the fact that the biblical narrative states that the Canaanites were the original inhabitants of Palestine, and that the names of Palestine and the Palestinians are derived from the ancient 'Philistines', have led many secular Palestinian nationalists to adopt the biblical paradigm to construct a Palestinian national identity based on mythologised ancient historical roots. The distinguished Palestinian lawyer and prolific author

Henry Cattan, for example, argues, in *Palestine, the Arabs and Israel: The Search for Justice* (1969) that the indigenous Arab inhabitants of modern Palestine, whether Muslim or Christian, were simply Arabised Canaanites:

> It is necessary at the outset to correct a current misconception. The Israelis were not the earliest inhabitants of Palestine. They were invaders. When the Israeli tribes, after their exodus from Egypt, invaded the land of Canaan in the 12th century B.C., they found a settled population and an established culture. The population of the country then included the settled Canaanites, the Gibeonites and the Philistines. The Philistines were never completely subdued by the invaders and retained control of their coastal plain along the Mediterranean. The rest of the country was occupied and settled by the Israelites, who established the Kingdom of Israel. This Kingdom lasted for two centuries and then split into the Kingdom of Israel in the north and the Kingdom of Judah in the south ... the Israelites who were themselves invaders ... were subsequently killed or deported [by the Romans]. ... The Palestine Arabs are the original inhabitants of Palestine ... [they] were Arabized [*sic*] as a result of the [Muslim] Arab conquest in the 7th century. The Palestinians of today are the descendants of the Philistines, the Canaanites and other early tribes. ... The Jews did not integrate into the ethnic stock formed by the original people of Palestine. (1969: 3-6)

Cattan, a Palestinian Christian born in Jerusalem in 1906, operates, in Foucauldian terms, in a world of discourse divided between accepted (Zionist-Jewish) discourse and excluded (Palestinian) discourse, between the dominant Israeli discourse and the dominated Palestinian one.[7] He found it necessary to have recourse to a mythologised ancient history of Palestine in order to create an anti-Zionist Palestinian counter-narrative. This appeal of ancient mythologies is found in his otherwise excellent book *Palestine and International Law: The Legal Aspects of the Arab–Israeli Conflict* (1976). His brilliant legal work aside, Cattan's historiography took to rehashing and appropriating the biblical narrative to construct a secular Palestinian narrative by emphasising the equal contribution of pagans, Muslims, Christians, Arabs and Jews to the material and cultural heritage of Palestine. However, in seeking to undermine the Zionist narrative, Cattan was in fact mirroring a mythological historiography in favour of a secular (although ethnically Arab) Palestinian nationalism.[8]

More recently, Palestinian scientist Mazin Qumsiyeh has suggested, in his *Sharing the Land of Canaan* (2004), a more realistic and less dichotomous approach to the debate on Canaanites and Israelites. He argues for coexistence in Palestine-Israel based on close historical, cultural and genetic affinities between the 'Canaanitic people': Mizrahi Jews and Palestinian Christians and Muslims (Qumsiyeh 2004: 28-30). Indeed it would not be unreasonable to argue that the modern Palestinians are more likely to be the descendants of the ancient Israelites (and Canaanites) than Ashkenazi Jews, many of whom were European converts to Judaism. Certainly historically – in contrast to the myth of 'exile and return' – many of the original Jewish inhabitants of ancient Palestine had remained in the country but had accepted Christianity and Islam many generations later. Today, however – in contrast to the mythologised Ashkenazi Zionist and Arab nationalist historiographies – more and more archaeologists and biblical scholars are convinced that the ancestors of the Israelites had never been in Egypt and that the biblical paradigm of a military conquest of Canaan is completely fictional. Indeed, the archaeological evidence undermines, in particular, the book of Joshua. If the Exodus from Egypt and the forty-year desert journey around Sinai could not have happened and the military conquest of the 'fortified cities' of Canaan (according to Deuteronomy 9:1: 'great cities with walls sky-high') were totally refuted by archaeology, who, then, were these Israelites, Philistines or Canaanites?

The term 'Israel' has many different meanings in the Bible (Davies 1992). The Israelites were, most likely, Canaanites who took a distinct developmental path. Israel Finkelstein, professor of archaeology at Tel Aviv University, proposed that they were the pastoral shepherds who wandered in this hill area throughout the Late Bronze Age. The archaeological evidence shows (a) that the population which later developed into the kingdoms of Judah and Israel originated from within the country – within Canaan or ancient Palestine; it did not come from Egypt or from any other place; (b) that in biblical times (as in modern times) the concept of ethnicity was fluid; (c) that Palestine was plagued by social fragmentation throughout antiquity (Thompson 2003a: 23; Lemche 1995: 13); (d) that the Iron Age I settlements on the central hills of ancient Palestine, from which the later kingdom of Israel developed, reflect continuity with Canaanite culture. The emergence of early Israelites, Finkelstein and Silberman write, was an outcome of the collapse of the Canaanite culture, not its cause. The early Israelites were themselves originally Canaanites (Finkelstein and Silberman 2001: 118).

The new critical biblical scholarship has taught us that the Israelites were no different from other Canaanites (Lemche 1991). Contrary to the vitriolic anti-Canaanite and anti-Philistine sentiment of the Old Testament authors, the new scholarship has shown that the biblical portrayal of the Israelites' origins in terms of a conflict between them and the Canaanites or the Philistines is not justification for assuming that such a conflict ever took place in history, either in the twelfth century or in any other period. Canaanites and Israelites never existed as opposing peoples fighting over Palestine (Thompson 2003a: 23; Lemche 1991). Lemche comments on the invention of the ethnic and racial divide between the Hebrews and Canaanites by the Bible writers during the post-exilic period:

> The 'Canaanites' embraced that part of the Palestinian population which did not convert to the Jewish religion of the exiles, the reason being that it had no part in the experience of exile and living in a foreign world which had been the fate of the Judaeans who were carried off to Babylonia in 587 BCE. The Palestinian – or rather old Israelite – population was not considered to be Jews because they were not ready to acknowledge the religious innovations of the exilic community that Yahweh was the only god to be worshipped. Thus the real difference between the Canaanites and the Israelites would be a religious one and not the difference between two distinct nationals. (1991: 162 n12)

The history of ancient Palestine and its peoples – often suppressed in favour of the biblical ideology (Whitelam 1996, 2002: 194-223) – is very different from the biblical narratives (Thompson, 2003a: 7) and the history of 'biblical Israel', which often involves literary and ideological problems (Thompson 2003a: 7-10). In the biblical narrative of the stories of Samson, Saul and David, the 'Philistines' are the 'people' of the southern and central coastal plain, where they play the role of Israel's enemy, parallel to the role of the Canaanites of the holy war stories of Joshua and Judges, as the evil which attempted to resist the (imaginary) construction of the Hebrews. But the Canaanites, Hebrews and Philistines were not ethnic designations of the Bronze or early Iron Age (Thompson 2003a: 5-6; Ahlström 1993: 334-70; Thompson 1992: 260-77).

The early term 'Canaan' (*Kinahhi*) does not refer to any historical people. It is a geographical term. It is used in reference to a people only in the sense of the various peoples who lived in the region or land of Kinahhi (Thompson 2003a: 5-6; Lemche 1991). It is used in reference to a people only in the sense of the various peoples who lived in the region of Kinahhi. It also overlaps with other geographical terms, such as *Churru, Retenu, Amurru* or *Hatti* (Rainey 1963: 43-45). One of the most important works produced by recent Israeli archaeology, *The Bible Unearthed: Archeology's New Vision of Ancient Israel and the Origin of Its Sacred Texts*, written by Israel Finkelstein and Neil Asher Silberman (2001), discusses the link between the archaeological finds and ethnicity. Finkelstein and Silberman note that even in modern times there is no agreed definition of ethnicity; that the concept is fluid, making its identification in terms of material culture a very difficult task. The identification of ethnic and racial boundaries between Canaanites and Israelites, or between Philistines and Israelites, in ancient cultures is highly problematic and completely fictional in the critical period of 'Israelite origins' (Iron I Age).

Furthermore, there are also mountains of archival evidence to suggest that monotheism came much later than the Bible suggests. Already in the late 1960s archaeologist William Dever discovered at excavations at Khirbet al-Kom near Hebron (al-Khalil) that Jehovah, the God of the Israelites, had a female consort called Asherah (Dever 2005). Asherah was also identified as a Canaanite deity, a fertility goddess. The inscription Dever discovered was written in ancient Hebrew, dating from the mid- to late eighth century BC; it ran: 'Blessed ... by Yahweh ... and his Asherah' (cited in Rose 2004: 23). Dever later recalled:

> When I first discovered it, I didn't really want to publish it, as a young scholar. It was too controversial. But then in the 1970s a second site was found by Israeli archaeologists – also in the eighth century in Sinai. And you have the same expression: 'may X be blessed by Yahweh and his Asherah.' (cited in Sturgis 2001: 173)

Since then several archaeological discoveries have been made connecting Jehovah to Asherah. The discovery of these inscriptions shows that in the minds of many Israelites, Jehovah – like other gods of the ancient Near East-had a consort and that the pagan polytheistic deities of the Israelites and Canaanites were widely shared, with radical implications for the theory of monotheism and when exactly monotheism was adopted. Herzog explains:

Jehovah and his consort: How many gods, exactly, did Israel have? Together with the historical and political aspects, there are also doubts as to the credibility of the information about belief and worship. The question about the date at which monotheism was adopted by the kingdoms of Israel and Judea arose with the discovery of inscriptions in ancient Hebrew that mention a pair of gods: Jehovah and his Asherah. At two sites, Kuntiliet Ajrud in the southwestern part of the Negev hill region, and at Khirbet el-Kom in the Judea piedmont, Hebrew inscriptions have been found that mention 'Jehovah and his Asherah', 'Jehovah Shomron and his Asherah', 'Jehovah Teman and his Asherah'. The authors were familiar with a pair of gods, Jehovah and his consort Asherah, and send blessings in the couple's name. These inscriptions, from the 8th century BCE, raise the possibility that monotheism, as a state religion, is actually an innovation of the period of the Kingdom of Judea, following the destruction of the Kingdom of Israel. (Herzog 1999: 6-8)

The Case for 'Minimalism' in Biblical Studies

The archaeological findings dovetailed with the conclusions of the critical school of Old Testament scholarship, which suggested that biblical conquest stories be viewed as etiological legends. In the 1980s and 1990s a group of critical biblical scholars emerged in Britain, Denmark, the USA, Italy and Israel, including Philip Davies (1992, 1994), Keith Whitelam (1996, 2002: 194-223), Thomas Thompson, Niels Lemche (1991, 1995). In the UK many of their books are published by Sheffield Academic Press.[9] Davies, Thompson, Lemche and Whitelam became closely associated with the 'minimalist' phenomenon; they were called the 'gang of four' by their detractors, as part of the smear campaign against them.[10] But there were scores of other biblical scholars and archaeologists highlighting different aspects, and reflecting different degrees, of minimalism.[11] The term 'minimalism' was coined by their detractors in the mid-1990s; it is not supposed to be flattering. However, while critics have reacted by attacking them as an isolated and extreme group, the minimalists are not a fringe group and their discourse is internationally debated as part of critical biblical scholarship.

Thompson argues for the necessity of distinguishing between interpretation of the Bible, which is the task of those engaged in biblical studies, and attempts to write a history of the region in the pre-biblical period, which is the domain of historians and particularly archaeologists.

Minimalism in biblical studies refers to a trend that, in the estimation of its opponents, plays down the historical character of the biblical narratives. Biblical minimalism is based on direct evidence from archaeology and historical geography supported by analogies that are primarily drawn from anthropology, sociology and linguistics. Secondary literature, such as we find in the Bible or other collected summaries of traditions such as Manetho, Berossus and Josephus in the Hellenistic period, gives us information about the use of past traditions.

According to Thompson there are three guiding principles of biblical minimalism. The first and most central principle is understanding the relationship between biblical interpretation and the writing of a history of pre-Hellenistic Palestine (Thompson 2003a). Second, the Bible is not a historical account of Palestine's past; nor did its authors try to write history. It is a secondary collection of tradition that is theologically motivated. The earliest surviving manuscripts of biblical books come from the Dead Sea scrolls. Nevertheless, the secondary and collective nature of biblical works allows us to speculate on earlier forms of these literary productions. Recognisably stereotypical themes and motifs provide a major key to understanding and interpreting the function and ideologically important motivations of the texts. Third is the hotly debated question about the historicity of the Bible as a tool used by historians to assess the value of a source for reconstructing events of the past. It is rare that historicity can be attributed to a literary or theologically oriented production. Since the Bible is filled with literary and theological motifs and themes, it is necessary to understand the authors' literary strategies before there is any attempt to use it in a historical synthesis.

Thompson also argues that (a) the biblical tradition is largely irrelevant to a history of 'ancient Israel' (Thompson 1987: 11–40); (b) a history of Israel's origins is not a history of ancient Palestine; (c) it is necessary to write a history of Israel's origins – on the basis of evidence rather than of ideology or theology – independent of the perspectives of biblical historiography; (d) the current understanding of Israel, whose origins we seek in the biblical tradition, comes from ideological and theological questions. The evidence from extra-biblical sources for Israel is wholly inadequate to the task of understanding origins, if we are searching for the origins of the Israel of the Bible.

Clearly the historicity of the Hebrew Bible is important for several groups, including conservative evangelical Christians, Israeli Zionists and not a few biblical archaeologists. The politics of these groups depend in some way upon the belief that the Old Testament relates real history. Once these interests are exposed, one can easily understand the rage and public outcry in the Israeli press and the orchestrated assault against biblical scholars who have questioned the historicity of the Old Testament (Herzog 2001: 72-93). But the linking of minimalism with 'anti-Semitism' – the deployment of the standard Zionist charge of anti-Semitism to intimidate academics – is completely spurious. While conservative evangelicals and Zionist nationalists reacted to the new scholarship by reiterating the dogma that the Bible equals history, the minimalists responded by saying that by separating the Bible from history, they were merely sheding bad history (Davies 2002, 2003). The critical archaeologists and biblical scholars were attacked by mainstream Zionists as 'anti-Bible', 'anti-Israel' and even 'anti-Semitic' (Lemche 2003).[12] Thompson illustrates the hostility towards critical scholarship exhibited by some biblical scholars and Israeli writers by citing one of the most vicious attacks on his work by Magen Broshi, former director of the Israel Department of Antiquities. This is found in a review of *The Bible in History: How Writers Create a Past* (1999), in *Jerusalem Post* (24 December 1999). The review ends with a slanderous note that informs the reader that Thompson's favoured readings are *The Protocols of the Elders of Zion*:

> Is it possible he does not believe in anything? Apparently there is a certain book that he does take seriously. A mutual acquaintance told me that Thompson confided in him that he is a staunch believer in The Protocols of the Elders of Zion.   •

Apparently this open accusation of 'anti-Semitism', which was repeated by several pro-Zionist propagandists, effectively put an end to the sales of Thompson's book on the American market (Lemche 2003).

A Minimalist School of Thought?

The minimalists have questioned the historicity of the Old Testament and the relationship between its historical narrative and the archaeological evidence. By separating the Hebrew scriptures from history and releasing them from any claims of historicity, they were not rejecting the Bible but rather providing new ways of reading the scriptures as literature, wonderful folk tales and beautiful poetry. Epics and legends like the story of Abraham or the binding of Isaac should be treated as moral tales (Thompson 1999); they were to do with the myths of origin which we find among the Assyrians, Babylonians; Arabs; even the Irish have a myth of origin: originating from one single person. But the minimalists were not a monolithic group; they all published separately and independently; there are also important differences among them (Davies 2002). Also crucially the minimalists do not deny there was an ancient Israel or that early Judaism was a religious factor in Palestine's history. *In Search of Ancient Israel*, by Davies (1992), who does not like the term minimalism (2003), has an entire chapter devoted to the historical Israel; but for him the Old Testament represents a narrow slice of the ancient world – maybe a few hundred years before Christ, rather than the 1,500 years that biblical theologians consider it to be. Thompson's work (1992) deals extensively with the states of Judah and Israel as historical entities. Lemche's detailed analysis of the historical and scholarly evidence for ancient Israel (1998) is the closest to denying that there was an ancient Israel, though he likewise is speaking of an Israel defined by biblical categories. The point at issue is not whether an ancient Israel ever existed, but whether the historical ancient Israel was like the portrait in the Bible.

Minimalism remains no more monolithic than any mainstream movement and there exist major differences among critical biblical scholars; not all minimalists like or use the term. Not all the 'minimalists' agree that they are part of a school, or a group; there is no such common agenda (Davies 2002; 2003). The scholarly approach of Thompson, Lemche, Whitelam and Davies is not identical and the four are following slightly different paths: some are influenced by new historical criticism and post-colonial studies, others by the recent archaeology of the Holy Land or by the sociology of ethnicity; some rely on anthropological modelling (Davies 2002). That Thompson, Whitelam, Lemche and Davies worked at some stage either in Copenhagen or in Sheffield may indeed suggest to superficial observers a 'school'. However, Thompson moved to Copenhagen only after his book *Early History of the Israelite People* was published (1992); he wrote it in Milwaukee. Whitelam's *The Invention of Ancient*

Israel was written in Stirling, Scotland, before its author was appointed to a chair in Sheffield in 1999. The four scholars have come to talk to each other through geographical proximity and through their shared notoriety; but not one of them developed his ideas in close contact with the others (Davies 2002).

There remains widespread disagreement among critical archaeologists and biblical scholars with regard to the question as to when the biblical narrative began to be written (Amit 1999: 20-33). Finkelstein and Silberman argue that Genesis was a 'national epic' created in the seventh century BC: although 'no archaeologist can deny that the Bible contains legends, characters, and story fragments that reach far back in time ... archaeology can show that the Torah and the Deuteronomistic History bear unmistakable hallmarks of their initial compilation in the seventh century BCE' (2001: 23). By contrast, both Thompson and Davies argue that the bulk of Old Testament literature was an invented tradition, and created during, and within the context, of the Persian empire by urban intellectuals (Thompson 1991, 2003a: 7, 24; Davies 1992, 2002; Lemche 1991: 7). Davies, in particular, asks what were the motives of the writers who compiled in stages an epic history that went back to creation, inventing a twelve-tribe nation that escaped from Egypt and annihilated the 'Canaanites,' generated several portraits of an ideal society set in a mythical wilderness scenario, and developed a monotheistic religion and assigned it to antiquity (Davies 2001: 239-52.). Davies's argument that the writings are not to be approached as history does not imply that there are no historical elements whatsoever: only that the picture as a whole is ideal, not real; that there never was a society as described by Joshua or Judges. This conflicts with the more radical views of Lemche that the account is Hellenistic (Lemche 1993: 163-93) – written 1,000 years after the events described. Whitelam, for his part, has not engaged in this question of dating at all but focuses rather on the ideology of representation of 'Israel' and 'Palestine' in ancient and modern sources. Only Lemche has written that the Tel Dan stela may be a forgery (Davies 2002). The inscription was 'discovered' at Tel Dan, previously known as Tell al-Qadi, in the Galilee, in 1993. Supposedly dating to the ninth or eighth centuries BC and containing the 'earliest reference' to 'David', its authenticity has been questioned not only by Lemche but also by several scholars. Whitelam and

Davies do not hold this opinion. These examples show that the widespread view that minimalists agree in their main opinions is not entirely true in all respects (Davies 2002).

The minimalists generally agree that the Bible is actually a record of what later generations mythologised about their history; that the representation of ancient Israel in the Hebrew Bible is largely idealised and fictionalised; that the story of David and Solomon is a literary text produced by biblical authors writing hundreds of years after the purported events. But while their critics, many of whom are neo-conservative authors, continue to insist on the historicity of the Old Testament (Davies 2002), the vast majority of biblical scholars lie in a spectrum between biblicist Albrightean scholars who adopt a fundamentalist approach to Holy Land archaeology (see Chapter 2) and the mimimalists. Davies, a leading scholar of the ancient world who has been carrying out textual analysis of the Bible for over thirty years, argues that the minimalists pursue the main lines of critical biblical scholarship over the last century (Davies 2002, 2003); that the mainstream view of critical biblical scholarship accepts that Genesis to Joshua (perhaps Judges) is devoid of reliable history; and that that it was in the Persian period that the bulk of the Hebrew Bible literature was either composed or achieved its canonical shape; that the later dating of much biblical literature is increasingly finding support among mainstream academics; although there were degrees of 'minimalism' over David, the historicity of David was generally being questioned by many scholars in the mainstream (Davies 2002, 2003).

Davies explains how and why the Jewish scriptures came into existence. What motivated the writers to create them? Who were the writers? Davies relies partly on archaeology and partly on anthropological modelling. He is not satisfied merely with concluding that the stories from Genesis to Joshua are unhistorical. Davies's theory is that the canonised writings represent a monumental project, partly conscious and partly unconscious, of defining the origins and nature of a society re-established in a small province of the Persian empire, a society composed of a group of Aramaic-speaking immigrants and a large number of indigenous, Hebrew-speaking 'people of the land'. The process of creating a religion, a society, took centuries but began essentially after the period of independent statehood had disappeared. Davies believes that the Hebrew Bible should not play a role in modern politics. The State of Israel was the result of modern forces rather than divine promises and ancient occupations. The Bible, he argues, is irrelevant – except in the indirect but very serious sense in which it has promoted the persecution of Jews in Europe, the main justification in his opinion for the establishment of a secure Jewish homeland in Palestine. What is important is not to politicise biblical studies but to depoliticise the discipline and distance it from any political stance towards the present Israel–Palestine crisis and thus permit that crisis to be seen in its modern and contemporary terms (2002).

Yet, as has already been argued in Chapters 1 and 2, the debate about 'ancient Israel' and modern colonial archaeology is also a debate about the modern State of Israel, most crucially because in the eyes of many people in the West the legitimacy of Zionism depends on the credibility of the biblical portrait. One facet of that debate is the argument in the public domain over the use of the term 'Israel' to denote the land west of the Jordan, both in ancient and in modern times. The inevitable outcome of the obsession with the Hebrew Bible in Western scholarship – by calling the land 'biblical' and by its exclusive interest in a small section of the history of the land – has resulted in a focus on the Israelite identity of a land that has actually been non-Jewish in terms of its indigenous population for the larger part of its recorded history. This state of affairs would not happen in any other area of the planet. It is due to the Hebrew Bible and its influence in the West, where an inherited Christian culture has supported the notion that Palestine has always been somehow essentially 'the land of Israel'. Traditional biblical scholarship has been essentially 'Zionist' and has participated in the elimination of the Palestinian identity, as if over 1,400 years of Muslim occupation of this land has meant nothing. This focus on a short period of history a long time ago participates in a kind of retrospective colonising of the past. It tends to regard modern Palestinians as trespassers or 'resident aliens' in someone else's territory.

The Bible, Post-colonialism and the Moral Critique: Michael Prior, Palestinian Liberation Theology and the Biblical Academy

The Public Intellectual as Moral Transformer of Society

Professor Michael Prior (1942–2004) was an outstanding biblical scholar, a Corkman,[1] a Vincentian priest,[2] a peace activist, a radical liberation theologian, an activist for the human rights of gypsies in London and an activist for Palestinian rights. During his two years study and teaching in the Holy Land in the 1980s and 1990s Professor Prior became an enthusiastic supporter of the Palestinian people.[3] He was also co-founder and chair of Living Stones for the Holy Land, an ecumenical trust dedicated to promoting links between the Palestinian Christians and Christians in Britain. Prior's scholarly work on the 'Bible and theology' and his moral critique of the Zionist project were outstanding and prophetic. His faith placed an emphasis on the humanity and equality of all people. The sudden and unexpected death of Prior on 22 July 2004 was devastating. His passing also saddened scores of his friends around the globe.

Prior's scholarship was influenced by a wide range of modern ideas and sources, including the liberation theology perspectives that emerged primarily out of Latin America in the 1960s and 1970s (and in Palestine in the 1980s and 1990s); secular humanist ideas, especially enlightenment human rights principles, originating outside the Scriptures. He was also

influenced by the emergence of a new Holy Land archaeology and a critical
biblical scholarship, also known as biblical 'minimalism', in the last two
decades (described in Chapter 7); by the emergence of new and critical
historiography of Israel–Palestine since the mid-1980s; and by Edward W.
Said's works on 'orientalism', post-colonial and cultural studies, Islam
and Palestine (see Chapter 9). Prior met Said a number of times – in
Jerusalem, at Bethlehem University and in London – and edited some of
his conference speeches.

Prior, like Said, passionately believed in the intellectual as a moral
transformer of society and, also like Said, his discourse engaged with
some of the great themes of religion and post-colonialism: truth and
reconciliation, critiques of structures of domination, the anti-Apartheid
struggle, liberation theology and social justice. Shortly before he died in
July 2004, Prior wrote:

> University people seldom distinguish themselves by their commitment to
> transform the world morally. Usually whatever idealism they once may have
> had has been well drained out, not infrequently by the imperative of the
> improvement of their career prospects. They can seldom afford to speak their
> truth. They have to keep their job, pay the mortgage and other expenses ...
> Their doctoral studies invariably focused on some specialist and esoteric
> aspect of a sub-discipline, which can, with a bit of luck, be prepared for
> publication, a *sine qua non* for securing even a part-time lecturing post.
> Having eventually gained a university position by 'playing the academic
> game', then, they in turn get down to the business of producing their own
> academic clones. In such manner the conventional university system goes
> along its very own emotionally-detached, intellectually-dispassionate and
> rationally value-neutral way. That, after all, is considered by the university
> academy and its powers to be the appropriate comportment of scholars, and
> is the surest way to climb the academic ladder. (Prior 2006: 278-9)

For Prior academics and intellectuals had a moral mission: to speak truth,
however uncomfortable, to people in power, to fight against racism and
oppression, and to work for a moral transformation of society (Prior
2006: 278-80).

Michael Prior and Palestinian Liberation Theology

Prior the Vincentian priest believed that the imperatives of the Gospel
faith require *moral* engagement as an article of faith and a starting point

of critical scholarship and post-colonial historiography. His regular visits to and experience in the Holy Land, his witnessing a kind of apartheid system, and his intellectual integrity drove him to examine critically the use of the Bible in Western colonialism in general and the role of the biblical paradigm of 'chosen people–promised land' in the Zionist enterprise in particular (Prior 1999a: 129–55, 1999b: 129–55, 1999b: 69–88, 2003a: 16–48).[4] By the mid-1990s Prior had emerged as a formidable critic of the impact of Israel's settler colonial policies on the Palestinians. His early works, including *Paul the Letter Writer and the Second Letter of Timothy* (1989), already illustrate his probing critique and the intellectual courage with which he began challenging conservative biblical scholarship and its failure to address, full square, the moral questions inherent in the biblical texts.

On the question of truth-speaking concerning Palestine-Israel, Prior became well known for his support for the dispossessed, the occupied and the disenfranchised Palestinians, and was convinced that they are the victims of a scandalous injustice. Prior early on realised that the liberation theology perspectives developed in Latin America in the 1960s and 1970s had an obvious relevance to the Israel-Palestine question; during his regular visits to the Holy Land he befriended many Palestinian Church leaders[5] and liberation theologians, including Dr Naim Ateek, Director of Sabeel, an ecumenical Centre for Palestinian Liberation Theology in Jerusalem. Sabeel embodies a grassroots liberation movement among Palestinian Christians and seeks to make the Gospel contextually relevant to Palestine-Israel. In Arabic, *sabeel* means 'the way' and a 'spring of water'. The organisation strives to develop a Palestinian theology based on justice, peace, nonviolence, liberation and reconciliation for the different ethnic and faith communities in the Holy Land. It is also highly critical of Christian Zionism, which has been 'successful in providing not only theological justification for Palestinian displacement, forced exile and continued oppression, but also is directly responsible for marshalling material resources' in support of Israeli settler colonialism.[6] In 1999 Prior co-edited with Canon Ateek the collection *Holy Land – Hollow Jubilee: God, Justice and the Palestinians* (Ateek and Prior: 1999), based on a major international conference organised by Sabeel in 1998, at which the keynote speaker was Edward Said.

The fundamental tenets of 'liberation theology' have been extensively discussed elsewhere.[7] The term describes the attempt by Latin American theologians to make the Gospel of Jesus Christ relevant to the social, economic and political conditions of Latin America. In a direct challenge to the established churches and their support for oppressive regimes, these theologians embarked upon an interpretation of the scriptures which found the words and deeds of Christ politically relevant and socially liberating. 'Liberation theology' requires both solidarity with the poor, the exploited, the oppressed and disenfranchised; and bridging the gap between abstract religious theories and their practical implementation. In *Jesus in Latin America* (1987), liberation theologian Jon Sobrino writes: 'Jesus, like the prophets, concentrates on those areas where the life of individuals is most precarious, most threatened, or even non-existent. For this reason, the program of his mission is one of partiality and announces a God of partisan life to those who lack it at the most elementary levels' (Sobrino 1987: 107–8). Clodovis Boff further explains: 'Existing liberation theology is a theology directed upon praxis – precisely a praxis of social transformation ... at once critical and utopian' (Boff 1993: 65). Liberation theology approaches involve giving priority to social justice and peace and developing a moral theology which emphasises solidarity with the struggle of the oppressed and marginalised.

In his first major work, *Jesus the Liberator: Nazareth Liberation Theology (Luke 4.16–30)* (1995), Prior attempted to combine a radical version of Latin American liberation theology with human rights approaches to the question of Palestine. He wrote:

> Only when 'the blind receive their sight, the lame walk, lepers are cleansed, and the deaf hear, the dead are raised up, poor people are evangelised' (Luke 7: 22) can the Church be at peace with its founder, the Nazareth preacher, and its Lord. (Prior 1995, 2001: 201)

Politically and theologically, Prior's subsequent works were noticeably more radical in challenging biblical literalists who defend a Zionist reading of the Bible. Inspired by Canon Ateek's work on Palestinian liberation theology (Ateek 1989), Prior discerned three major issues in Palestinian liberation theology perspectives: political freedom, justice and the Bible. Whereas mainstream theologians in the West look to the Bible for strength and liberation, it is being used by many Christians in the USA and by Zionist Jews in a way that offers Palestinians dispossession and slavery rather than freedom; exile and injustice rather than justice; and the destruction of their religious sites and national and political life.

The Redeeming Idea of Colonialism

In the early 1980s Prior, the biblical scholar, discovered that the biblical narrative is meaningless outside its worldly context. The question of Israel–Palestine also forced Prior the liberation theologian to recognise and reconfigure the key role of the biblical text within the project of European settler colonialism and empire. Already by 1918 some 85 per cent of the earth was in the hands of European colonising powers, with devastating effects on the indigenous populations of Africa, Asia and Latin America. Invariably the colonisers sought out some ideological principle to justify their deeds, and the Bible has often been, and still is for some (especially the Zionists), a text that redeems territorial conquests (Prior 1999a: 130–33). Prior's striking reflections on the Bible and the redeeming idea of colonialism are found in his important book: *The Bible and Colonialism: A Moral Critique* (1997a).[8] Benefiting from recent scholarship in post-colonial studies, Prior's major work was to show the extent to which colonial interests have been successful in utilising and manipulating the oral and written theological and political traditions contained in the Bible for their own benefit. Examples of such ideological manipulation become clear particularly in those chapters where Prior describes the conquest of the 'New World', the Zionist enterprise in Palestine and settler colonialism in Southern Africa. The book represents a deep analysis and a moral critique of the ways in which imperial colonialist discourse attempts to manipulate arguments and texts in order to legitimise its own agenda of domination, exploitation and the extermination of indigenous peoples and societies.

The publication of the Spanish edition of *The Bible and Colonialism* provided Prior with the opportunity to reflect (shortly before his death in 2004)[9] on the evolution of his thought, to point out the various influences on this book, and to bring his work up to date. More crucially, while the economic and political conditions in both Latin America and South Africa had remained difficult, the situation in Palestine had continued to deteriorate and the plight of the Palestinians under occupation had worsened. It is hardly surprising, therefore, that Prior begins the Introduction to this edition by pointing out that the main stimulus for writing this work

> came from having undertaken significant portions of my postgraduate Biblical Studies in the Land of the Bible. Studying in Jerusalem, 1983-84 and since, has been one of the catalysts for significant change, not only in my own perspectives, but in how I understand the task of a biblical scholar. Things might have been different had I confined myself to study in biblical institutes and libraries in Dublin, Rome, or London, which in fact provided my first academic base.

Remarkably groundbreaking, *The Bible and Colonialism* is Prior's most important work. In it he analyses the ways in which the Bible was deployed to justify Western settler colonialism and oppression in three different settings: in Latin America, South Africa and Palestine. Moreover, while the Bible, its 'mega narratives' and use in Christian ideology have played a huge part in imperialist expansion, the Western biblical academy has rarely bothered to subject the Bible to scholarly moral investigation. Prior (as well as other scholars[10]) has shown that the depiction of the land in biblical scholarship is of an 'empty space' waiting to be populated by Israel. In this book, Prior also devotes attention to the Palestinian catastrophe and to a critique of both Zionism and the biblical academy – the latter being complicit in perpetuating the foundation myths of Zionism and the State of Israel.

Prior subjected the 'Western' disciplines of Theology and Biblical Studies to a devastating critique. He was convinced that much of the two disciplines was either indifferent to or implicitly supportive of the dispossession of the Palestinians (Prior 2003c: 192-218):

> What is striking from a moral perspective is the widespread support which the Zionist enterprise enjoys in the West. Whereas elsewhere the perpetrators of ethnic cleansing would be charged with war crimes and crimes against humanity, the Zionist conquest is judged widely to be a just and appropriate political accomplishment, and, in some quarters, is accorded unique religious significance. Much of the rationale for such benevolent appraisal derives from a literalist interpretation of the land traditions, and some of the messianic texts of the Bible. In most Western theological and religious circles, Christian and Jewish, the Zionist prize is viewed as being no more than what the Jewish

people deserves in virtue of the promises of God outlined in the Bible. The claim that the Bible legitimises exclusively Jewish rights to *Eretz Yisrael* – in conformity with the exclusively Israelite rights to 'the land of Canaan' – is so pervasive, not only within the Jewish and Christian Zionist circles, but even within mainstream Christian Theology, and much of university biblical studies, that the very attempt to raise the issue is sure to elicit opposition. (Prior 1998: 41-81; see also 2001: 9-35, 2002: 44-45)

For Prior the biblical academy should not only study the original context of biblical texts but also explain how these texts have been deployed (used, misused and abused) in dubious colonial enterprises.

Reading the Bible with the Eyes of the Canaanites

'Reading the Bible with the Eyes of the Canaanites: In Homage to Professor Edward Said', was the title of a paper presented by Prior to a three-day conference (1-3 April 2004) organised by the Centre for Contemporary Approaches to the Bible, University of Wales at Lampeter, and the Catholic Biblical Association of Great Britain (Prior 2006: 273-96; see also 2003a: 65-82). Greatly influenced by Said's writings and the idea that our under-standing of a text should always be underpinned by our own *worldliness* (Prior 2006: 274-6), Prior's critique of Western biblical scholarship echoes Said's devastating attack on orientalism. Prior first came across the idea of reading the Bible 'with the eyes of the Canaanites' in an article written by Said in 1986 (Prior 2006: 277; Said 1986b: 289-303) – although Prior was critical of Said for not pursuing his 'Canaanite Reading' of the biblical narrative (Prior 2006: 277).

Yet the first person to develop this new perspective was the North American native scholar Robert Allen Warrior, who speaks of how strongly he was compelled by Martin Luther King's Exodus imagery of going to the mountaintop, seeing the Promised Land, and crossing the River Jordan. He writes of being stunned at the realisation that native Americans were in fact the Canaanites of the American colonial experience. He writes:

> The obvious characters in the story for Native Americans to identify with are the Canaanites, the people who already lived in the promised land. As a member of the Osage Nation of American Indians who stands in solidarity with other tribal people around the world, I read the Exodus story with Canaanite eyes. And, it is the Canaanite side of the story that has been

overlooked by those seeking to articulate theories of liberation. Especially ignored are those parts of the story that describe Yahweh's command to mercilessly annihilate the indigenous population. (Warrior 1991: 289; Prior 2006: 277)

Warrior observes that the land traditions of the Bible, conveniently ignored by most theologies of liberation, provide a model of conquest, oppression and genocide for native Americans, Palestinians and other indigenous peoples. Yahweh the conqueror, who delivers the Israelites from their oppression in Egypt, leads them in their conquest of the land of the Canaanites, the Hittites, the Amorites, the Perizzites, the Hivites and the Jebusites:

> With what voice will we, the Canaanites of the world, say, 'Let my people go and leave my people alone?' And, with what ears will followers of alien gods who have wooed us (Christians, Jews, Marxists, capitalists), listen to us? The indigenous people of this hemisphere have endured a subjugation now a hundred years longer than the sojourn of Israel in Egypt. Is there a god, a spirit, who will hear us and stand with us in the Amazon, Osage County, and Wounded Knee? Is there a god, a spirit, able to move among the pain and anger of the Nablus, Gaza, and Soweto of 1989? Perhaps. But we, the wretched of the earth, may be well advised this time not to listen to outsiders with their promises of liberation and deliverance. We will perhaps do better to look elsewhere for our vision of justice, peace and political sanity – a vision through which we escape not only our oppressors, but our oppression as well. Maybe, for once, we will just have to listen to ourselves, leaving the gods of this continent's real strangers to do battle among themselves. (Warrior 1991: 287-95)

Inspired by Warrior's radical critique of mainstream liberation theology and Said's critique of orientalism, Prior sought to radicalise liberation theology in general and Palestinian liberation theology in particular. He also benefited from the emergence of a post-colonial critical biblical scholarship in the two last decades. Biblical 'minimalism' (discussed in Chapter 7), whose key contributors include Philip Davies (1992), Thomas L. Thompson (1999, 2003a: 1-15, 2004), Niels Peter Lemche (1998, 2000: 165-93) and Keith W. Whitelam (1996), has emerged as an identifiable method of scholarship within biblical studies, and argues that the Bible's language is not a historical language. Minimalism has presented serious challenges to biblical scholars, Prior included. It was Prior's personal experiences and study of the Bible in the 'land of the Bible' which helped him to see 'with the eyes of the Canaanites'.[11] Prior continued to wrestle with the idea that biblical 'mega narratives' and key biblical traditions were politically oppressive and morally reprehensible. Was Yahweh (Jehovah) the great 'ethnic cleanser'? Did Yahweh not instruct the biblical Israelites to rid their 'promised land' of its indigenous inhabitants, the Canaanites? Few biblical scholars are prepared to confront these questions.

Prior argued that the land traditions of the Bible, which inspired modern political Zionism, appeared to mandate the genocide of the indigenes of Canaan. While it was possible to develop a Jewish theology of liberation with strong dependence on the Hebrew prophets, it would be no more difficult to construct a theology of oppression on the basis of other Old Testament traditions, especially those dealing with (the mythologised) Israelite origins that demanded the destruction of other peoples. According to the Hebrew Bible, the ancient Israelite shared the belief that Yahweh was a warrior directly involved in earthly battles; at least some ancient Israelites believed that Yahweh demanded the complete extermination of the enemy people. Prior concluded that the metanarratives of the Hebrew Bible present 'ethnic cleansing' as not only legitimate, but as required by the deity; that, according to modern standards of international law and human rights, what these biblical narratives mandate are 'war crimes' and 'crimes against humanity'. Prior believed that mainstream liberation theology was not radical enough in eliminating oppression for indigenous peoples, especially the Palestinians. To illustrate his thesis Prior cited the following metanarratives:[12]

(a) Although the reading of Exodus 3, both in the Christian liturgy and in the classical texts of liberation theologies, halts abruptly in the middle of verse 8 at the description of the land as one 'flowing with milk and honey', the biblical text itself continues, 'to the country of the Canaanites, the Hittites, the Amorites, the Perizzites, the Hivites, and the Jebusites'. Manifestly, the promised land, flowing with milk and honey, had no lack of indigenous peoples, and, according to the narrative, would soon flow with blood. As the Israelites were fleeing Egypt, Yahweh promises Moses and the people: 'When my angel goes in front of you, and brings you to the Amorites, the Hittites, the Perizzites, the Canaanites, the Hivites, and the Jebusites, and I blot them out, you shall not bow down to their gods, or worship them, or follow their practices, but you shall utterly demolish them and break their pillars in pieces' (Exodus 23.23-24).

(b) Matters got worse in the narrative of the Book of Deuteronomy which is canonised as Sacred Scripture. In fact it contains menacing ideologies and racist, xenophobic and militaristic tendencies: after the King of Heshbon refused passage to the Israelites, Yahweh gave him over to the Israelites who captured and utterly destroyed all the cities, killing all the men, women, and children (Deuteronomy 2.33-34). The fate of the King of Bashan was no better (3.3).

(c) Yahweh's role was central to the destruction of other peoples: 'When Yahweh your God brings you into the land that you are about to enter and occupy, and he clears away many nations before you – the Hittites, the Girgashites, the Amorites, the Canaanites, the Perizzites, the Hivites ... and when Yahweh your God gives them over to you ... you must utterly destroy them ... Show them no mercy ... For you are a people holy to Yahweh your God; Yahweh your God has chosen you out of all the peoples on earth to be his people, his treasured possession' (Deuteronomy 7.1-11; see also 9.1-5; 11.8-9, 23, 31-32).

(d) The Book of Deuteronomy tells the Israelites that when they approach towns along the way, they are to offer terms of peace to the inhabitants. If the people accept the peace terms, they are to be reduced to serving Israelites as forced labour; if they refuse, all the adult males are to be killed and the women, children, and animals are to be taken as spoils of war (Deuteronomy 20.10-15). When, however, the Israelites reach the lands where they are to dwell, they are to annihilate the inhabitants entirely so that they cannot tempt the Israelites to worship their gods (Deuteronomy 20.16-18). 'But as for the towns of these peoples that Yahweh your God is giving you as an inheritance, you must not let anything that breathes remain alive. You shall annihilate them – the Hittites and the Amorites, the Canaanites and the Perizzites, the Hivites and the Jebusites – just as Yahweh your God has commanded, so that they may not teach you to do all the abhorrent things that they do for their gods, and you thus sin against Yahweh your God' (Deuteronomy 20.16-18).

(e) The first part of the Book of Joshua (chapters 2-12) describes the conquest of key cities, and their fate in accordance with the laws of the Holy War. Even when the Gibeonites were to be spared, the Israelite elders complained at the lapse in fidelity to the mandate to destroy all the inhabitants of the land (9.21-27). Joshua took Makkedah, utterly destroying every person in it (10.28). A similar fate befell other cities (10.29-39): everything that breathed was destroyed, as Yahweh commanded (10.40-43). Joshua utterly destroyed the inhabitants of the cities of the north as well (11.1-23). Yahweh gave to Israel all the land that he swore to their ancestors he would give them (21.43-45). The legendary achievements of Yahweh through the agencies of

Moses, Aaron, and Joshua are kept before the Israelites even in their prayers: 'You brought a vine out of Egypt; you drove out the nations and planted it (Psalm 80.8; see also Psalms 78.54-55; 105.44).

(f) This is sometimes justified because the other peoples worship alien gods and thus do not deserve to live. There are similar commands in the Book of Numbers (chapter 31). Later in the biblical narrative, when the Israelites reach Jericho, Joshua orders that the entire city be devoted to the Lord for destruction, except for Rahab the prostitute and those in her house. All other inhabitants, as well as the oxen, sheep and donkeys are to be killed in the name of God (Joshua 6:21). In the First Book of Samuel, Samuel prophesies in the name of the Lord to Saul: 'Thus says the Lord of hosts, "I will punish the Amalekites for what they did in opposing the Israelites when they came up out of Egypt. Now go and attack Amalek and utterly destroy all that they have, do not spare them, but kill both man and woman, child and infant, ox and sheep, camel and donkey"' (1 Samuel 15: 2-3).

In the Spanish-language edition of *The Bible and Colonialism* (2005) Prior revisits the old ground,[13] in his original and deliberately combative style. First, the biblical narrative, with its 'divine promise' was inherently linked with the mandate to ethnically cleanse or exterminate the indigenous peoples; these 'war crimes' are legitimised by the divinity (Prior 2000b: 49-50, 2001: 9-35, 2002: 44-5). Second, the Exodus narrative portrays Yahweh as a tribal, ethnocentric God, with compassion only for the misery of his 'own people' (Exodus 3.7-8). Third, in the narrative of the Book of Deuteronomy the divine command to commit 'genocide' is explicit. Fourth, genocide and mass slaughter follow in the Book of Joshua. These highly dubious traditions of the Bible have been kept before subsequent generations of Jews and Christians in their prayers. Christians still pray, in Psalm 80 on Thursday mornings, 'You brought a vine out of Egypt; you drove out the nations and planted it.'

The historical evidence, however, strongly suggests that such genocidal massacres never actually took place, although these racist, xenophobic and militaristic narratives remained for later generations as powerful examples of divine aid in battle and of a divine command for widespread slaughter of an enemy. Regarding the divine demand in the Hebrew Bible to kill entire tribes, the later rabbinical tradition of post-biblical Judaism would view the wars of conquest of Canaan as a unique situation that offered no precedent for later wars. Some later Jewish commentators would interpret the struggle against the Amalekites as a symbolic metaphor for fighting genocidal evil.[14]

Despite Prior's extraordinary effort to sustain his main argument, especially with regard to the genocidal themes in the Book of Joshua and other 'mega narratives' of the Bible, his thesis has come under criticism from various scholars of ancient Palestine, including Professor Bernardo Gandulla, of the University of Buenos Aires. Gandulla, while sharing Prior's critique of the perverse use that Zionism and the State of Israel have made of the Bible to support their 'ethnic cleansing' policies in Palestine, points out that Prior's interpretation of biblical narrative as the epitome of war crimes and crimes against humanity perpetrated against the Canaanite population of ancient Palestine, suggesting that we should 'read the Bible with the eyes of the Canaanites', is a wrong interpretation, or at least a lyrical metaphor drawn from his appreciation of the text (Gandulla 2005b: 103-4).

The portrayal of the Israelites' origins in terms of a conflict between the ancient Hebrews and Canaanites is not justification for assuming that such a conflict ever took place in history, in either the twelfth century BC or any other period. As Lemche has pointed out, Canaanites and Israelites/Hebrews never existed as opposing peoples fighting over ancient Palestine (Lemche 1991). Although the Canaanites and Hebrews (as well the Philistines and Amorites) may all play the role of 'peoples' in the Bible's narrative, they were not ethnic designations of the Bronze or early Iron Age (see also Chapter 7). 'Canaanites' – the name is a variation on other biblical names such as the Amorites or Jebusites – were hardly distinguishable, and all three groups appear in different stories as the original population of Jerusalem. Furthermore, in the biblical stories of Samson, Saul and David, the 'Philistines' are the people of the southern and central coastal plain of Palestine, where they play the role of the Hebrews' enemy, parallel to the role of the Canaanites of the holy war stories of Joshua and Judges. In Genesis, however, the Canaanites live in the Negev, together with the Philistines, Hittites and Amorites, and, in the role of indigenous peoples of Palestine, are friendly to the patriarchs.

'Reading the Bible with the eyes of the Canaanites', Gandulla concluded, would only be possible if: (a) the actors of the Hebrew Bible narratives actually existed and were not mere ideological constructions, and (b) the bloody events described therein, especially in the Book of Joshua, had actually taken place. Biblical traditions have little or no historical worth because, as Neils Lemche has pointed out, they were not conceived as history even though they contain historical elements, since they are a reservoir of collective memory. The biblical narratives represent a set of epic cycles which have all the trimmings of violent conquests written long after the events by a population dominated by Greeks and Romans and driven by the need to legitimise and differentiate themselves from the Greco-Roman elite. Evidence supporting this interpretation can be found in the almost contemporary work of Flavius Josephus (*The Wars of the Jews*) (Gandulla 2005b: 103–4; also 2005a).

Gandulla argues that only if we consider that the Palestine of today and the Canaan of the past are one and the same indivisible cultural entity will it become possible not only to read the Bible but also to understand the ideology of domination from an independent Canaanite viewpoint, in which all who truly defend justice will find a common ground irrespective of the faith they practice. Perhaps this is the message to be discovered in Prior's metaphor (Gandulla 2005a: 103–4).

Zionism and the State of Israel: A Post-colonial Moral Critique

In his later writings Prior concentrated on the Bible's provision of alleged moral and theological legitimisation for the ethnic cleansing and oppression of the indigenous inhabitants of Palestine. This was the main focus of his major work, *Zionism and the State of Israel: A Moral Inquiry* (1999c). The dominant perspective of this study is the 'moral' question of the impact which the Zionist conquest and settlement have had on the indigenous population of Palestine. The book explores the sharp ethical issues arising from the use and abuse of the Bible by Christians, as much as by Jews, to justify the occupation and settlement of Palestine, with its catastrophic consequences in the forced expulsion and subjugation of the indigenous Palestinian people. The book includes a discussion of the Bible and modern biblical hermeneutics, post-biblical Jewish and Christian cultures, the history and development of Zionism, the international law of war and of occupation, and human rights in Palestine. The heart of the book deals with the biblical and mythical justification for Zionism. Prior

takes a liberal approach to biblical scholarship, arguing that the claim to
the divine promise of land is integrally linked with the claim of divine
approval for the extermination of the indigenous people (Prior 1999c).

The book also exposes the foundational myths of modern Zionism,
showing that its roots were in secular East European nationalism of the
late nineteenth century, and that support for Zionism by religious Jews
is a relatively recent phenomenon. Moreover, utilising the 'new' historiography of Palestine and Israel, he convincingly demonstrates that the
1948 Palestinian Nakba and expulsion of the Palestinians had been planned
by the founding fathers of Zionism and the State of Israel from the outset
(Masalha 1992, 1997, 2003).

Of course the various religious faiths at their best advocate non-violence,
peace, justice and compassion. Prior, however, found incitement to war and
violence in the very foundation documents of Judaism, Christianity and
Islam. In the Hebrew Bible, for instance, there is a dominant strand that
sees God as ethnocentric and militaristic (Prior 1999c: 181). Furthermore,
in their conquest of Canaan, the Israelites are commanded by Yahweh to
destroy the indigenous inhabitants of Palestine. Later in the days of the
Israelite kingdoms, they are urged to show no pity, but to massacre their
enemies. These Hebrew Scriptures were eventually adopted by Christians
as the first part of their Bible, described as the Old Testament, and were
used to justify atrocities that would not be condoned in the second part
of their Bible, the New Testament.[15] Today, both Christian Zionists in the
West and Israeli messianics continue to refer to the Hebrew Scriptures for
archetypal conflicts, which guide their attitudes towards the indigenous
inhabitants of Palestine: the Palestinian Muslims and Christians.

Prior was, inevitably, also critical of the classical works of Latin American liberation theology. Prior argues that even if you pursue the literature
of liberationist theological writers, you will have to search long and hard to
find any mention of the Israel–Palestine issue. He argues that this literature,
which emphasises the Exodus motif as the key for Christian theology, has
nothing to say about the fate of the indigenous peoples of ancient Palestine
that the biblical Israelites were instructed to dispossess and slaughter.

Still less do the liberation theologians have anything to say about the
settler colonial nature of modern Zionism or the plight of its Palestinian
victims. For liberation theologians in Latin America and the West, Prior

argues, it is apparently much easier to critique American imperialism in Latin America or monopoly capitalism than to speak the truth about Zionist settler colonialism and ethnic cleansing in the Holy Land.

Some mainstream Christian theologians in Britain and the USA have criticised Prior's methodology, arguing that he does not regard the Scriptures as the main source of his theology and that he takes ethical ideas from secular humanist sources outside the Bible and then uses them to critique the biblical texts. They further argue that Prior's radical and subversive approach is difficult to reconcile with the way many religious Jews and Christians (as well as the official teaching of the Roman Catholic Church) try to interpret the 'Word of God'. Some also argue that for Prior's critique of the biblical narrative to be accepted by a wider audience in the West it would have needed to show how principles taken from the Hebrew Bible must themselves guide the interpretation of certain other passages of the Scriptures (such as the conquest narratives) so as to resist a literalist 'ethnic cleansing'/'genocidal' moral mandate.

Prior, of course, would concede that he was also influenced by Enlightenment and secular humanist ideas originating outside the Scriptures, especially universal principles of human rights and international law: although he was a theologian by training, his methodological approach was multidisciplinary, grounded in the social sciences and benefiting from a range of secular and religious ideas and sources. When challenged at public meetings, Prior typically would respond to his critics by saying that the search for a hermeneutics of the Bible that is sound theologically will be found in the person of *Jesus the Liberator* (Prior 1995). Also, crucially, he would argue that the question of Palestine was not just a theological issue; it was essentially a moral and ethical one.

Prior was particularly brilliant at debunking the mythical notion of 'redemption' that was deployed in justification for the Zionist colonisation of Palestine during the last century. Prior's dedication to truth-telling, his moral courage and pioneer scholarship are manifested in his last edited book, *Speaking the Truth about Zionism and Israel* (2004), which included contributions from distinguished authors Naseer Aruri, Rosemary Radford Ruether, Ilan Pappé, and Archbishop Desmond Tutu. The last, one of the most influential theologians and critics of the apartheid regime of South Africa, won the Nobel Peace Prize in 1984. He also chaired South

Africa's Truth and Reconciliation Commission in 1995–98. He writes in the foreword to the Spanish edition of *The Bible and Colonialism:*

> The affairs of the Holy Land have long been a concern for Christians world-wide, and we in South Africa take a particular interest in them. The two countries have so much in common, and the forms of oppression in each demonstrate remarkable similarities. Over the last several years during which problems in South Africa have diminished, matters in the Holy Land have got increasingly worse, and the human tragedy has been multiplied. ... The transformation in South Africa culminating in the liberation of the 1990s should encourage all those who strive for justice and peace in the Holy Land. (Tutu 2004: 9)

Prior's experience convinced him that the Jewish–Christian dialogue was hijacked by a Zionist agenda; he carried out extensive research on groups such as Dabru Emet ('speaking the truth'), whose 'Jewish–Christian dialogue' was in fact a 'monologue in two voices' (Prior 2004b).[16] In his last article, 'A Disaster for Dialogue', published posthumously in the Catholic weekly *The Tablet* (London), 31 July 2004, Prior challenged the claim that opponents of Zionism are necessarily anti-Semitic. He also comments that the eighteenth International Catholic–Jewish Liaison Committee, which met in Buenos Aires in July 2004,

> released a joint statement repeating many of the constant emphases of the Jewish–Christian dialogue of recent years. There were wider global concerns too: economic disparity and its challenges, ecological devastation, the negative aspects of globalisation, and the urgent need for international peacemaking. One searches in vain, however, for an interfaith comment on the ever-deteriorating conditions in the Holy Land, and the challenge to justice and charity, or simply to justice and international legality, caused by the situation in Israel. There was not one mention of the Separation Wall dividing Jews and Palestinians.

In the same article – and throughout much of his later works – Prior argued powerfully that when liberal Catholics and Protestants in the West variously apply the biblical message of liberation to current situations of political and racial oppression abroad, or to issues of social oppression relating to gender or sexuality at home, their careful avoidance of any reference to apartheid Israel, to its 'apartheid wall' at the heart of Palestine, and to its current ethnic cleansing policies in Jerusalem and in Palestine as a whole, is all the more remarkable.

9

Cultural Resistance and the Secular Humanist Challenge: Edward W. Said, Zionism and Rethinking the Question of Palestine

With the passing of Edward W. Said on 25 September 2003 humanity and human culture lost a great champion. Said was the epitome of the scholar/critic/human rights activist. He often said that he wanted to help bring a Palestinian state into existence so that then he could play his proper role as critic, and criticise it (Mitchell 2003). Said was often described both as 'the conscience of Palestine' and as a citizen of the world. He was also described by the *New York Times* as 'one of the most influential literary and cultural critics in the world' (Aruri 2004: 141). His passionate engagement as a fearless intellectual in real-life issues was a constant inspiration for many Palestinians. His seminal work *Orientalism* (1978) had established him as a major international commentator, and by the 1990s he had achieved virtually cult status. Said was one of the greatest scholar/activist/critics of his generation, responsible for opening up entire new fields of thought and research for thousands of people within and outside the academic world (Mitchell 2003). He was a unique individual who has left an indelible legacy across many disciplines: internationally renowned critic of literature and culture, philosopher of history, music critic, Middle East specialist, political theorist, activist, and deeply humane voice of conscience. No one can easily fill his place on the many platforms on which he so powerfully represented the cause of Palestine.

Said's secular humanist discourse engaged with some of the great themes of religion: truth; critique of power and oppression; liberation and social justice. While by his own testimony his inspiration derived from secular humanistic values, people of religious sensitivities, such as Michael Prior, saw in Said also something of a priest, or, perhaps more accurately, a prophet – one who speaks on behalf of God. Prior wrote:

> I could never quite understand Said's apparent assumption that a project such as his could emanate only from a secular, humanistic perspective. I take the view that such engagement should flow naturally from religious idealism, in my case from Christianity, the religion in which Edward was brought up and from which he lapsed, a fact which … he seemed to feel obliged to advertise. (Prior: 2006: 276–7)

Said's works have been translated into twenty-six languages. His greatest achievements are, by common acclaim, *Orientalism* and *Culture and Imperialism* – twin works that have shaped and nourished the invigorating fields of post-colonial studies and cultural studies. It is Said the cultural theorist who has received the most attention from commentators and critics. Nevertheless, taken as a whole, Said's work on Palestine (and Islam) constituted the largest proportion of his political writings (Ashcroft and Ahluwalia 2001: 117), although it has received the least attention. Said's work on Palestine embodies the personal and political, and informs the theoretical position of Said the cultural theorist; the question of Palestine was central to Said's thinking and writings and to the way he constructed his own complex and post-colonial identity in exile. Born in pre-1948 West Jerusalem of wealthy Palestinian Protestant parents, Said spent his early life in Egypt being educated at a famous English public school. Said had a B.A. from Princeton University and an M.A. and Ph.D. from Harvard. After taking his doctorate in English literature he joined the faculty of Columbia University in 1963, and New York remained his home until his death. In *Reflections on Exile* (2000) Said makes it clear that the fact of his own exile and the fate of the Palestinians informed his social theories and gave both form and intimacy to the theoretical questions he pursued.

Said bridged the gap between the underprivileged and the ivory tower. He took up the cause of Palestine in venues that were likely to be closed to the underprivileged – lecture theatres, the concert stage, highbrow journals, television shows in the West, the numerous occasions honouring him and celebrating his work worldwide (Aruri 2004: 141). Said, of course, articulated the aspirations of many indigenous and oppressed peoples, and of the disenfranchised and marginalised. But the plight of the Palestinian people, the 1948 Nakba, the dispossession and dislocation of the Palestinians, the exile and refugeedom, overwhelming sense of loss and cultural resistance became a main feature of his political writings. However, although this deep sense of injustice, physical and legal dislocation, and exile is unremitting in Said's writings, it is nevertheless from these dehumanising experiences that the empowerment and resistance of the Palestinians emerges. Over the past three decades, Said the public intellectual played a key role in trying both to empower and to transform the international discourse on Palestine. Issues such as the dispossession of the Palestinians, memory and identity in exile, Palestinian oral history, the 'right of return' of the Palestine refugees, Zionist responsibility for the ongoing Palestinian catastrophe, the authoritarianism and corruption of the Palestinian Authority (PA) and, most recently, the one-state solution, have constituted much of Said's concerns.

Said, the Exodus Paradigm and the Question of Palestine

Prior to 1948 Palestine was overwhelmingly inhabited by Palestinian Arabs, who owned much of the land. The creation of the State of Israel entailed expulsion of the Palestinians and the turning of the majority into refugees.[1] In 1967 Israel occupied the West Bank and Gaza, the last two fragments of historic Palestine.[2] One of Said's favourite themes, which he explores in *Orientalism* and *The Question of Palestine*, is the relationship between power and knowledge. In terms of Palestine, the Zionist idea of a 'Jewish homeland', which saw, eventually, the destruction of Palestine and the establishment of Israel in 1948, was prepared for in advance by the knowledge accumulated by British biblical scholars and theologians, biblical archaeologists, colonial administrators, and experts who had been surveying the area and exploring the 'Bible lands' since the mid-nineteenth century. It was this knowledge that enabled the Zionists to maintain arguments similar to those of the British imperial project.

While historically the Palestine question favoured the victor (Israel) and marginalised the victim, Said injected into the historiographical debate his original thoughts about issues such as representation, power relations and the production of knowledge – issues very relevant to the writing of history.

The historical importance of biblical stories like Exodus for settler-colonial histories of Europeans, Americans and Israeli Zionists was the subject of an extraordinary debate between Edward Said and Michael Walzer, an American Jewish author (Said 1986b, 1988; Walzer 1986). The publication of Walzer's *Exodus and Revolution* in 1985 ignited a controversy which centred on how a religious narrative should be represented. Walzer presented an argument for the Exodus narrative as a paradigm for radical, progressive and even revolutionary politics (1985). Walzer developed Moses as a leader of a progressive national liberation movement on its way to the Promised Land, and by implication on a mission to establish the ethical relationship of man to God. In a compelling critique of Walzer's book, entitled 'Michael Walzer's *Exodus and Revolution*: A Canaanite Reading', Said took upon himself the task of reading the biblical narrative with the eyes of the Canaanites (Said 1986b). Said was impressed by Walzer's skills as a writer but not by his intellectual integrity or proficiency as a historian, and even less as a fair interpreter of the Israel–Palestine conflict. For Said, Walzer's Exodus politics – a contemporary reading of the Old Testament story – was a sophisticated obfuscation of reality, a thinly veiled apology for the settler-colonial policies of the Israeli state and a historical repetition of the narrative of the conquest of the land of Canaan (Hart 2000: 1–6; Said 1986b).

Like Said, the North American native author Robert Allen Warrior, a member of the Osage Nation, also found the Exodus paradigm, with its concept of 'Yahweh the conqueror', oppressive rather than liberating. He argues that the obvious characters for the Native American people and other indigenous people to identify with in this story are the Canaanites – the indigenous people who already lived in the Promised Land (1995: 289) – hence the biblical injunction to exterminate the indigenous inhabitants of Canaan by the Israelites while performing their mission inspired by God. Warrior observes: 'It is the Canaanite side of the story that has been overlooked by those seeking to articulate theologies of liberation';

'Especially ignored are those parts of the story that describe Yahweh's command to mercilessly annihilate the indigenous population' (Warrior 1991: 279). Both Warrior and Said are aware of the fact that the biblical stories are not necessarily rooted in reality; they thus make a clear distinction between the Exodus paradigm and the actual historical events in ancient Palestine. Like Warrior, Said argues that the Exodus paradigm demonstrates that there was no biblical Israel without the 'conquest of Canaan' and the expulsion or inferior status of Canaanites. Said, in his resistance 'Canaanite reading' of the Bible, observes:

> Walzer uses the rhetoric of contemporary liberation movements to highlight certain aspects of the Old Testament history and to mute or minimize others. The most troubling of these is of course the injunction laid on the Jews by God to exterminate their opponents, an injunction that somewhat takes away the aura of progressive national liberation which Walzer is bent upon giving the Exodus. (1988: 165-6)

It was Said, more than any other scholar, who gave theoretical under-pinnings to the influence of one's own worldliness on understanding a text in its worldliness (Prior 2006: 274). Yet Said, the radical secular humanist, never pursued his 1986 exhortation to read the biblical narrative with the eyes of the Canaanites (Prior 2006: 277) and for many years he paid less attention to the discourse of biblical studies – although from the mid-1980s onwards he began to highlight the peculiar features of the 'Redemptive' Zionist project, with its notions of 'land redemption–redemptive occupation' as the fulfilment of biblically ordained, divine promises. The Zionist restorative project, Said observed, vouchsafes the 'chosen people' with the extremely problematic gift of Redemption, elevating them into the status of divine agents, while reducing the unredeemed, displaced indigenous inhabitants of the land, the Palestinians, and putting them outside any moral concern (Said 1986b). But Said was criticised by biblical scholar Keith Whitelam, in his work *The Invention of Ancient Israel* (1996), for neglecting the field of biblical studies. In 1999 Said responded:

> [Keith] Whitelam is quite right to criticize my own work on the modern struggle for Palestine for not paying any attention to the discourse of biblical studies. This discourse he says was really part of Orientalism, by which Europeans imagined and represented the timeless Orient as they wished to see it, not as it was, or as its natives believed. Thus biblical studies, which created

an Israel that was set apart from its environment, and supposedly brought civilization and progress to the region, was reinforced by Zionist ideology and by Europe's interest in the roots of its own past. Yet, he concludes, 'this discourse has excluded the vast majority of the population of the region'. It is a discourse of power 'which has dispossessed Palestinians of a land and a past'. Whitlam's subject is ancient history and how a purposeful political movement could invent a serviceable past which became a crucial aspect of Israel's modern collective memory. When the mayor of Jerusalem a few years ago proclaimed that the city represented 3,000 years of unbroken Jewish dominance, he was mobilizing an invented story for the political purposes of a modern state still trying to dispossess native Palestinians who are now seen only as barely tolerated aliens. (Said 1999b: 15)

For Said, Zionism and its modern and recently invented mobilising myths have to be studied not in abstract, but mainly from the standpoint of its victims. He was a historian neither by profession nor by inclination. Yet the impact of his historical perspective – which we find not only in *The Question of Palestine* but also in many articles – on the rewriting of the history of Zionism from the perspective of its victims cannot be overestimated. Said's historical perspective on the Palestinian Nakba – combined with the new historiographical picture that has emerged from the archival material of recent years and Palestinian oral history – introduced us to the catastrophe inflicted upon the Palestinians in the 1948 war. Furthermore, Said was never uncritical when it came to the Palestinian leadership and its share in the disaster. It was the failure of the leadership to respond to the effectiveness of Zionism that became one of the main causes of the Palestinian refugee exodus of 1948.

In 1992 I published a book entitled *Expulsion of the Palestinians: The Concept of 'Transfer' in Zionist Political Thought, 1882–1992*, which is largely based on Hebrew archival material. This was followed by *A Land without a People* (1997) and *The Politics of Denial: Israel and the Palestinian Refugee Problem* (2003). The last two decades have seen major contributions by other Palestinian authors, some of whose accounts have been based on the oral history of the Palestinian refugees themselves. However, I think Said was the first to locate the Nakba in a wider perspective. His critical strength was in juxtaposing the Palestinian catastrophe, and all its horrors, with its *denial*, not only in Israel but also in the West. In many of his works Said exposed the Western media's attempts to sideline, if not altogether eliminate from the public domain, the tragedy of Palestine.

While most people opposed the exclusion and injustices of the apartheid regime in South Africa, Said pointed out, there has been a deep reluctance among both liberals and radicals in the West to condemn Zionist 'ethnic cleansing' and the exclusion of the Palestinians under Israeli apartheid policies. This unwillingness Said traced to the views of very influential European thinkers (many of whom were Christian Zionists), including George Eliot (in her novel *Daniel Deronda*), who considered Palestine to be essentially empty of inhabitants and the exclusive, rightful homeland of the Jews, completely ignoring the fact the land was already inhabited by other people who also considered it to be their homeland (see Chapter 2). Three main ideas were shared by European precursors of Zionism, including Eliot, Moses Hess (1812–1875)[3] and 'later almost every Zionist thinker and ideologue':

> (a) the nonexistent Arab inhabitants, (b) the complementary Western-Jewish attitude to an 'empty' territory, and (c) the restorative Zionist project, which would repeat by rebuilding a vanished Jewish state and combine it with modern elements like disciplined, separate colonies, a special agency for land acquisition etc. Of course, none of these ideas would have any force were it not for the additional fact of their being addressed to, shaped for, and out of an international (i.e., non-Oriental and hence European) context. (Said 1980: 68)

In *The Question of Palestine* Said also documents the manner in which Zionism began as a European conquering ideology and a settler colonial movement seeking to colonise Palestine, not unlike that of European colonial expansion in the nineteenth century: 'Zionism has appeared to be an uncompromisingly exclusionary, discriminatory, colonialist praxis' (Said 1980: 69). But the colonisation of Palestine also differed from other European settler colonial projects. Said thought that a peculiar feature of Zionist colonisation was the notion of a 'redemptive' occupation and the fulfilment of God's promise. For Said, Zionism (in both its secular and its religious versions) has reduced the inhabitants of Palestine to an aberration that had challenged the supremacist and xenophobic notions of God-given biblical status of the 'Promised Land' (Said 1980: 56–114). Said, the secular humanist, reflected: 'That Messianic, redemptive quality ... [is]

so foreign to me, so outside me, so unlike anything I have experienced'
(cited in Ashcroft 1996: 13).

Reading Said's thoughts about these topics, one can immediately connect his critique with the role of historiography in the Palestine conflict.
It was Said who undermined the hegemonic Zionist narrative in both
public and academic spheres. This narrative, which has dominated the
academic discourse in the West, insists that 'a people without land arrived
in a country without people', modernised it, and 'made its deserts bloom',
while it had to fight for its life against inexplicable barbaric attacks by
its Islamic and Arab neighbours. For Said, to write differently and more
truthfully about what happened was not merely to practise professional
historiography, but was also a political act of redemption and justice. Under
the influence of his work, the balance was redressed. The Palestinian
narrative – once regarded as sheer propaganda in the West, while the
Israeli version was respected as academic and serious – was legitimised,
while the founding myths of Israel were demolished and the hegemonic
Zionist narrative was itself exposed for its falsity and pretence.

No less important was the way Said related directly to the historian's
method in discussing the meaning and significance of the 'historical
document'. During a two-day conference of Israeli and Palestinian historians (including Ilan Pappé, Benny Morris, Itamar Rabinowitch, Zeev
Sternhell, Elias Sanbar and myself) in Paris in 1998, Said explained, in
a few sentences, to the attentive public, and to the less attentive Israeli
historians in particular, what a 'historical document' was (Pappé 2004b:
137). The Israeli historians taking part in the conference (especially
Morris and Rabinowitch) expressed their almost religious belief that
they were both ideologically and empirically impartial, and declared
that the only reliable sources for the reconstruction of the 1948 war were
documents in the IDF archives. Said made clear that a report by a soldier
from 1948 is as much an interpretation, and quite often manipulation,
of the reality as any other human recollection of the same event; it was
never the reality itself. By doing so, he pointed us to the vitality and
significance of oral history in the reconstruction of the past. The most
horrific aspects of the Nakba – the dozens of massacres that accompanied the ethnic cleansing – as well as a detailed description of what
'ethnic cleansing' had been from the point of view of those 'ethnically

cleansed' – can only be built when this historiographical approach is adopted (Pappé 2004a: 137).

Said subsequently wrote an article on the Paris event in *al-Ahram Weekly* online, entitled 'New History, Old Ideas' (1998),[4] referring to the so-called 'new' Israeli historians taking part in the conference. At that conference, as Ilan Pappé later commented, Said was at his best, partly because he was able to articulate what others felt but were unable to express in a meaningful manner. He wondered aloud how Israeli historians like Morris could relate to the Nakba's real essence – as the most traumatic catastrophe that befell the Palestinian people – without showing even a modicum of solidarity or sympathy with its victims. As he noted, Israeli historians such as Morris and Rabinowitch would never have tolerated such a treatment of the Jewish holocaust history (Pappé 2004b: 137).

As early as 1977, when few Palestinians were prepared to concede that Israeli Jews had claims to Palestine, Said said: 'I don't deny their claims, but their claim always entails Palestinian dispossession' (Ruthven 2003). More than any other Palestinian writer, Said qualified his anti-colonial critique of Israel, explaining its complex entanglements and the problematic character of its origins in the persecution of European Jews, and the overwhelming impact of the Zionist idea on the European conscience (Ruthven 2003). 'The question to be asked', Said wrote in *The Politics of Dispossession*,

> is how long can the history of anti-semitism and the Holocaust in particular be used as a fence to exempt Israel from arguments and sanctions against it for its behavior towards the Palestinians, arguments and sanctions that were used against other repressive governments, such as that of South Africa? How long are we going to deny that the cries of the people of Gaza … are directly connected to the policies of the Israeli government and not to the cries of the victims of Nazism? (Said 1995b: 171-2)

Identity Construction and Cultural Resistance: Israeli Apartheid and Palestinian Intifadas

Said began to write about the plight of the indigenous inhabitants of Palestine after 1967. His transformation from a university professor of English into a political activist can be traced to the shock of the 1967 war and its aftermath, especially the conquest of the entire area of historic Palestine by

Israel. Of course, there is more to the idea of Palestine than the Occupied Territories. In the 1970s Said – like many Palestinians – did not like the term 'Palestinian diaspora'. But by the 1990s I found Said was using the term *shatat falastini* (Palestinian diasporas) quite often. However, for him, there was always a 'larger Palestine' that existed outside historic Palestine, in the Palestinian communities in exile, dispossessed from their homeland; that larger Palestine has been completely marginalised.

The post-1967 reality appeared to transform Said's own sense of identity and position within American society (Ashcroft and Ahluwalia 2001: 118). After 1967 the Professor of English also discovers that the text is meaningless outside its worldly context. In the post-1967 period, the question of Palestine also forced the cultural theorist to recognise and reconfigure the key role of the Western text within the project of empire – the same empire that created the conditions for his dispossessed people (Ashcroft and Ahluwalia 2001: 118).

In many ways, Said's extraordinary life reflected the plight and suffering that have been at the core of the Palestinian experience, and many of his writings beyond literary and cultural criticism were inspired by his Palestinian experience. These include his books *The Question of Palestine* (1980); *After the Last Sky* (1986a); *Blaming the Victims: Spurious Scholarship and the Question of Palestine* (with Christopher Hitchens, 1988); *The Politics of Dispossession* (1995b); *Peace and Its Discontents* (1995a); and the memoir of his youth, *Out of Place* (1999a).[5] All remain seminal works, which both personalise and humanise the turbulence of the Palestinians and place them in the wider political context. All seek to document the anguish of the Palestinian predicament. Two points are worth noting here: Said's unique ability to articulate, in the public sphere, the essence of the Palestine question; and the freshness and relevance of his ideas to the present day.

On the question of truth-speaking concerning Palestine-Israel, the Zionist/orientalist hegemonic narrative of half-truths and downright lies had to be challenged by Said. His first sustained work on Palestine (and his first work to be published in Hebrew), *The Question of Palestine*, was first published in 1979 (Said 1980). A year earlier (1978), in *Orientalism*, Said had subjected Western 'Oriental Studies' to a devastating critique, exposing the underlying presumptions of the discipline. He concluded that Western biblical studies were part of and an extension of the 'Orientalist discourse', which has been written without any 'Oriental'/Arab/Muslim reader in view.

Said lived most of his life in the United States. For him, the total incapacity of the Palestinians to represent themselves is most pronounced in the United States, where the pro-Israeli (Zionist Christian and Jewish) lobby is most effective, where the question of Palestine was vigorously suppressed throughout the 1970s, and where the Arab and Muslim are still often portrayed as terrorists. The Israeli Likud prime ministers, Menahem Begin, Yitzhak Shamir, Benyamin Netanyahu and Ariel Sharon, are represented in the American press as statesmen, while the atrocities they have committed against the Palestinians (and against the British before 1948) are completely ignored. To oppose Zionist claims, especially after the Holocaust, Said argued in the 1970s, was to be viewed as aligning oneself with anti-Semitism. With the sharp rise of Islamophobia in the West in the wake of 9/11, these observations are even more relevant. In *Orientalism* Said argues that, in the post-Holocaust era and especially after the 1973 war and oil crisis, deeply embedded European anti-Semitism began to transfer itself to the racially menacing figure of the Arab:

> Cartoons depicting an Arab sheik standing behind a gasoline pump turned up consistently. These Arabs, however, were clearly 'Semitic': their sharply hooked noses, the evil mustachioed leer on their faces, were obviously reminders (to a largely non-Semitic population) that 'Semites' were at the bottom of all our 'troubles', which in this case was principally a gasoline shortage. The transference of a popular anti-Semitic animus from a Jewish to an Arab target was made smoothly, since the figure was essentially the same. (Said 1978: 285-6)

In a book edited with Christopher Hitchens, *Blaming the Victims* (1988), Said demonstrates that in the United States there is an ongoing campaign to suppress the Palestinian question. The suppression is made possible because of the extensive support the United States gives Israel in international forums and in direct aid:

> Israel is the recipient of more US aid than any foreign state in history. It is estimated that every Israeli citizen today is subsidized by the US at roughly $1.400 per annum; each member of the Israeli military is underwritten by the US at about $9,750 per year. Along with these munificent sums (which incidentally far exceed US federal subvention to many of its own disadvantaged citizens) has gone the equally significant political support, whose

symptoms are unswerving solidarity with Israel in any international forum of significance. (Said and Hitchens 1988: 2)

Blaming the Victims (which includes contributions from distinguished authors, including Noam Chomsky, Ibrahim Abu-Lughod, Rashid Kha-lidi, Elia Zureik and Norman Finkelstein) shows how the historical fate of the Palestinians has been justified in spurious academic scholarship by dismissal of their historical rights and claims to a home within the boundaries of historic Palestine, and even denial of their very existence (Said and Hitchens 1988).

Said's writings on Palestine, from his early work on Palestinian dispos-session, and throughout the 1970s and 1980s, were intended to address the expatriate (and exiled) Arab/Palestinian and Western audience. For nearly three decades Said was consumed with the task of documenting a Palestinian presence in the Western consciousness. In *The Politics of Dispossession*, he writes,

> My most specific task was ... to make the case for Palestinian presence, to say that there was a Palestinian people and that, like all others, it had a history, a society, and, most important, a right to self-determination. In other words, to try to change the public consciousness in the West in which Palestine had no presence at all. (Said 1995b: xvi)

Said's long engagement with Palestine's history and historiography had a very clear agenda. He saw the mutual recognition of Palestinian and Jewish suffering as a precondition for reconciliation. He wished Palestin-ians and Arabs to desist from denying or dwarfing the Jewish Holocaust and hoped that this would encourage Israeli Jews to cease their Nakba denial. As we shall see below, this secular humanist and progressive approach would lead Said to embrace a new political vision that can only derive from a long-term Palestinian–Jewish movement for equality, expressed within a single, secular democratic framework in Palestine-Israel.

Out of these conditions of Nakba, dispossession and dislocation, Israeli apartheid and 'ethnocratic' policies, a culture of resistance has arisen among the indigenous inhabitants of Palestine – both within the Occupied Territories and in exile – a will to defend their legal rights and cultural identity (Said 1980: 111). Said called the first Palestinian Intifada, which began in December 1987, 'surely one of the great anticolonial insurrections of the modern period' (Said 1995b: xxvii). For Said, the Palestinian first and second Intifadas (1987-93 and 2000-2007) essentially embodied not terrorism or violence (as the Western media like us to believe), but the right to resist an illegal, brutal occupation.

Said was highly effective in promoting the idea that the cause of Palestine (like the liberation of apartheid South Africa) should serve as a model for Arabs and fair-minded, idealistic people everywhere. For Said, there was some resonance with South Africa and the relegation of the indigenous inhabitants of South Africa to Bantustans but still within the boundaries of the country. The Palestinians, on the other hand, have been subjected to 'ethnic cleansing' and banishment both in the Occupied Territories and in the neighbouring Arab countries to which they were driven. This has caused additional pressure from the host countries, which have not been particularly accommodating to the Palestinians. The periodic expulsion of the Palestinians from one or another Arab state has meant insecurity of habitat for the refugees and an ambivalent relationship with the Arab states. This is, Said pointed out in the late 1970s, why the

> Palestinian does not construct his life outside Palestine; he cannot free himself from the scandal of his total exile; all his institutions repeat the fact of his exile. This is manifestly true also for the Palestinian Arabs now subject on the West Bank and in Gaza to Israeli domination and to those who reside in Israel. Every Palestinian achievement is flawed by this paradoxical truth, that any survival outside Palestine is ruined in a sense by its impermanence, its groundlessness, its lack of a specifically Palestinian sovereign will over the future of the Palestinian, despite the extraordinary symbolic successes of the PLO. (Said 1980: 154-5)

Said recognised the complexities of Palestinian identity within and outside Palestine and he took a particular interest in the contested Palestinian identity within Israel (the so-called 'Israeli-Arab' identity). He was also hugely influenced by ideas centred on the construction of Palestinian identity in exile by secular humanist Palestinian intellectuals such as Ibrahim Abu-Lughod and the Palestinian national poet Mahmoud Darwish. Abu-Lughod, a former professor of political science at Northwestern University in the USA, later returned to Palestine after forty years of exile and became vice-president of Birzeit University on the West Bank.[6] It was Abu-Lughod who after 1967 introduced Said to the world of national liberation struggles and post-colonial politics. Reflecting on fifty years of friendship with Abu-Lughod, Said wrote an article entitled 'My Guru', explaining that *Orientalism* had originated in an essay he had written shortly after 1967, for a special issue of a monthly journal guest-edited by Abu-Lughod, intended to look at the 1967 war from an Arab perspective: 'I used the occasion to look at the image of the Arabs in the media, popular literature, and cultural representations going back to the Middle Ages. This was the origin of my book *Orientalism*.'[7]

While Said and Abu-Lughod were 'external' refugees, constructing their secular and diasporic identity in the West, Darwish was an internally displaced Palestinian, brought up in Galilee as a Palestinian citizen in Israel, before leaving Israel and joining the PLO in exile in Beirut in the 1970s. The Palestinian identity and conditions of exile, Said pointed out, were best captured by Darwish in his short poem '*bitaqit hawiyya*' ('Identity Card'), which evokes the peculiar Palestinian predicament of a diasporic and contested identity being created outside Palestine. The short poem, which full of irony, defiance and even resistance, is governed by the imperative *Sajjil*, 'Record':

> 'sajjil ana 'arabi wa raqm hawiyyati khamsim alf
> Record!
> I am an Arab
> And my Identity Card is number fifty thousand
> I have eight children
> And the ninth
> is coming in midsummer
> Will you be angry?

Two stanzas later, Darwish says:

> Record!
> I am an Arab
> Without a name – without title
> Patient in a country
> With people enraged.
> (Said 1980: 154-6)[8]

In a number of his books, Said returns time and again to the issues that have become part of his own 'Palestinianness': displacement, landlessness, exile and identity. A key theme explored by Said in *The Politics of Dispossession* is that the history of Palestine has turned the insider (the Palestinian Arab) into the outsider. This point is illustrated by a photograph of Nazareth taken from a position in what is called Upper Nazareth – an area which did not exist in the time of Arab Palestine. Thus Arab Palestine is seen from the point of view of a new, invented Palestine, and the inside experience of the old Palestine has become the external experience in the photograph. And yet the Palestinians have remained. (Said 1995b: 109-10)

The Politics of Dispossession offers a glimpse of the issues that have dominated the construction of Said's own identity: 'You try to get used to living alongside outsiders and endless attempting to define what is yours on the inside' (Said 1995b: 53). Said argues that the Palestinians cannot reach the interior (*al-dakhil*), which refers to both historical Palestine, controlled by Israel and privacy, a kind of wall created by the solidarity forged by members of the group. Said is trying to explain that the quest for this inner state is part of the Palestinian experience. It is in this was that 'After the last sky there is no sky. After the last border there is no land' (Said 1995b: 108).

After the Last Sky, Said's collaborative book with the great Swiss photographer Jean Mohr, is probably Said's most profound reflection on the oppression of the Palestinian people. The book is a passionate and very moving meditation on displacement, landlessness, exile and identity. It is also an impassioned plea for international recognition of the justice of Palestinian claims and a critique of the brutal occupation and dispossession they have suffered for half a century. Moreover, the book is a mirror for the Palestinians, a critical reflection on their political mistakes, their cultural shortcomings. In this book, Said also recognises that the exclusion of others is central to the formation of identity (Said 1986b: 40). The heart of the Palestinian question is the problem of working out this fraught and disturbing issue of identity. How does one create the defining boundaries of one's identity without demonising the other?

In the 1970s Said, although backing the 'two-state solution', recognised that the future of the Palestinians is linked inexorably with that of the Israelis. In fact, he was one of the first Palestinians to argue the need for both communities, with their unique historical circumstances and engagements, to come to terms with their realities and recognise that this was the only way to achieve a lasting peace in the region. Said repeatedly called for a radical reassessment of the injustices on both sides of the national divide between Israelis and Palestinians. Said sought to dig deep beneath the assumptions and prejudices that have characterised the representation of Palestine in the West and the erasure of the Palestinians from history. The way forward for the Palestinians is to ensure that their reality, national existence, land and human rights are fully recognised.

From Liberation to Capitulation:
The PLO and the Oslo Process

Said was an early advocate of the 'two-state solution', implicitly recognising Israel's right to exist. This policy was adopted at the historic meeting of the Palestinian National Council (PNC) in Algiers in 1988. In fact, Said helped to draft the Palestinian Declaration of Independence at that famous meeting.

Said was also a speechwriter for Yasser Arafat (1929–2004) when he gave his famous 'Gun and Olive Branch' speech to the UN General Assembly in 1974. Indeed, in the 1970s and 1980s Said saw considerable hope and promise in the PLO and, in particular, in the leadership of Mr Palestine, Yasser Arafat. For Said, the PLO under Arafat came to symbolise freedom, as had the ANC under Nelson Mandela. The PLO, an organisation that operated in the difficult circumstances of exile, became the place where all Palestinians could be accommodated – a key achievement of the organisation in the 1970s:

> I myself am greatly impressed with the generous presence in the PLO of values, ideas, open debate, revolutionary initiative ... despite the shortcomings of its policies or its leadership, [the PLO] keep[s] the Palestinian cause alive, something greater than provisional organizations or policies. (Said 1980: 165)

The prominence of the PLO was attributed to the leadership of Arafat, which, Said asserted, approached the problems affecting Palestine with a great deal of clarity and focus on detail.

Yet early it became clear that Said was no apologist for Palestinian nationalism, secular or religious. In recent years he consistently criticised suicide bombings as greatly harming the Palestinian cause. In December 2002 he wrote: 'I do not hesitate now to say again that these efforts are morally repugnant and politically disastrous on all sorts of grounds'

(2002). Said was an internationalist, not an ardent nationalist. On the contrary, he was a particularly strident critic of much of the ethnic and religious nationalism that seems to pervade the Arab and Muslim worlds. Said sought to deploy universal principles that pointed to the injustices inflicted on his people. It is this commitment to internationalism that made Said an important figure among marginalised and oppressed people the world over.

To occupy such a position required sometimes taking a stand against the leadership of the cause that he supported so passionately, including Arafat and the PLO, and the Arab states. In 1989, four years before Oslo, Said was highly critical of the PLO, claiming that its representatives were corrupt and incompetent. The critique is one that Said repeated often, claiming that the PLO was wrong in its strategy of working through middlemen rather than focusing on American civil society and on civil rights groups in the West. By the early 1990s Said had become very disenchanted with the PLO leadership and spoke of the despair with which he witnessed them take decisions such as 'support' (real or imagined) for Saddam Hussein during the Kuwaiti crisis of 1990–91 and saw the manner in which 'we had already ceased being a people of liberation; we had accepted the lesser goal of a small degree of independence' (Said 1995b: xxiii).

Said was elected to the Palestinian National Council (PNC), the Palestinian parliament in exile, in 1977 and remained a highly active member until 1991. But he was an independent intellectual and he avoided taking part in the factional struggles within the PLO, while using his authority to make strategic interventions. It is important to note, however, that Said was not a member of the PLO. The turning point came in 1991 for Said. In the aftermath of the first Gulf War, an American-sponsored Middle East 'peace process' began with a much-diminished role for the PLO in the actual negotiations. It was at this stage that Said lost faith in the Palestinian leadership and resigned from the PNC.

Said argued for a tougher stand, with stronger guarantees, but found that the PLO was willing to 'rush to discard principles and strategic goals with equal abandon' (Said 1995b: xxxii). Subsequently Said became one of the fiercest critics of the September 1993 Declaration of Principles, which culminated in a degree of Palestinian autonomy in parts of the West Bank and Gaza. In an article in the *London Review of Books*, Said wrote:

What of this vaunted peace process? What has it achieved and why, if indeed it was a peace process, has the miserable condition of the Palestinians and the loss of life become so much worse than before the Oslo Accords were signed in September 1993? And what does it mean to speak of peace if Israeli troops and settlements are still present in such large numbers? Again, according to the Report on Israeli Settlement in the Occupied Territories, 110,000 Jews lived in illegal settlements in Gaza and the West Bank before Oslo; the number has since increased to 195,000, a figure that doesn't include those Jews who have taken up residence in Arab East Jerusalem. Has the world been deluded or has the rhetoric of 'peace' been in essence a gigantic fraud? (Said 2000a)

When Arafat was perceived to be abandoning the Palestinian consensus, Said's sharp criticism was directed at him and his close associates (in particular, the current PLO chairman Mahmoud 'Abbas, better known as Abu Mazen [Said 2003]), whom he publicly named as complicit in endorsing a Bantustan solution: a truncated, fragmented Palestinian entity that was not what the Palestinian people had struggled for. An independent, viable Palestinian state was not likely to emerge within the framework of Oslo. Said was not only critical of the PLO negotiators, he was also censorious about a certain disposition of passivity among the Palestinians, at home as well as in the diaspora – a disposition which allowed the Palestinian leadership to get away with mafia-like practices.

It is important to question why Said had become fiercely critical of the Oslo process, given that he was one of the first advocates of mutual recognition and the two-state solution. Fundamentally, for Said, the Oslo agreement was a capitulation on the part of the PLO, which had become a policing mechanism for the Israeli state; while Israeli settlements continued to expand, the conditions of the Palestinians in the occupied territories continued to deteriorate. Apartheid Israel had in effect consolidated its hold on the West Bank and Gaza, restricting further control of movements of the Palestinians and legitimising an oppressive occupation under the illusion of a peace process:

> It would therefore seem that the PLO has ended an Intifada, which embodies not terrorism or violence but the right to resist, even though Israel remains in occupation of the West Bank and Gaza and has yet to admit that it is, in fact, an occupying power. The primary consideration in the [Oslo] document is Israel's security, with none for the Palestinians from Israel's incursions. (Said 1995b: xxxv)

For Said, there was also no atonement for past injustices, no remorse for Palestinian losses and dispossession, but an indefinite subjugation of Palestinians in the Occupied Territories. More crucially, there was no hope for the millions of Palestinian refugees in exile.

Said's anger and frustration were reflected in his writings from that time onwards, which continued to highlight the Palestinian predicament, to raise questions about all the parties, but above all to adhere to the secular humanist principles and values that had driven him from the beginning. Critical of the PLO and its pro-Western sponsors in the region, such as Mubarak's Egypt, Said occupied an ambivalent place in Palestinian politics after his resignation from the PNC.

In *Peace and its Discontents: Gaza-Jericho 1993–1996* (1995a) Said abandons his traditional Western audience and speaks directly to the Palestinians and the Arabs. A version of this book was originally published in Cairo in November 1994, under the title *Gaza–Jericho: An American Peace*. The essays were originally written on a bi-weekly basis for *Al-Hayat*, the leading Arabic-language daily, edited in London but printed in every Arab capital, and they were also published in Cairo's *Al-Ahram Weekly*. It was no longer the case that Said just needed to highlight the Palestinian cause in the West; rather, it was important to engage with the Palestinian people themselves. In the book's Introduction Said explains that this 'is the first of my books to have been written from start to finish with an Arab audience in mind' (Said 1995a: xix). The book documents his sense of outrage and betrayal at the signing of the Oslo agreement.

During the Oslo process, under American pressure, Arafat and the Palestinian leadership eventually amended the PLO Charter so as to accept the reality of a 'Jewish state' on 77 per cent of historic Palestine, leaving room for a Palestinian state on the remainder. However, Said quickly realized that in endorsing an 'ethnocratic' Jewish state – based on Israeli demographic racism – the Palestinian leadership was actually moving away from basic universal values of non-discrimination based on religion, ethnicity or race. Said now also saw that many Western liberals, who had campaigned for the dissolution of the white supremacist regime of South Africa, were becoming slavishly devoted to the 'two-state solution' in order to preserve 'Jewish ethnocracy' in Israel (and Palestine).

It is not that Said was opposed to peace and reconciliation between

Palestinians and Israelis – peace was, after all, a cause that he passionately pursued for three decades. Rather, he was concerned about a continuing infringement upon Palestinian rights, now sanctioned by the peace process. True reconciliation cannot be imposed; it must be achieved by genuine negotiation, something that did not occur in the case of the Oslo process. For Said, there had been a Palestinian capitulation that meant that Israel gained recognition and legitimacy without any concessions, 'without in effect conceding sovereignty over the Arab land, including annexed East Jerusalem, captured illegally by war' (Said 1995a: xxi).

For Said the Oslo process meant the world no longer saw the inherent problems that continued to plague Palestine. The daily haemorrhage of Palestinian lives and property accelerated without respite, while Western media reported horrifically sensational suicide bombings, complete with pictures and names of the victims as well as gut-wrenching details:

> As for the continued practice of extra-legal assassinations, Israel is allowed to get away with phrases from journalists who use words like 'alleged' or 'officials say' to cover their own irresponsibility as reporters. The *New York Times* in particular is now so clotted with such phrases in reporting on the Middle East (Iraq included) that it might as well be re-named 'Officials Said'. the fact that illegal Israeli practices continue to deliberately bleed the Palestinian civilian population is obscured, hidden from view, though it continues steadily all the time: 65 per cent unemployment, 50 per cent poverty (people living on less than $2 a day), schools, hospitals, universities, businesses under constant military pressure, these are only the outward manifestation of Israeli crimes against humanity. Over 40 per cent of the Palestinian population is malnourished and famine is now a genuine threat. Non-stop curfews, the endless expropriation of land and the building of settlements (now numbering almost 200), the destruction of crops, trees, houses have made life for ordinary Palestinians intolerable. Many are leaving, or as is the case with the inhabitants of Yanun village, must leave because settlers' terror against them, the burning of their houses, and threats against their lives make it impossible to stay. Ethnic cleansing is what this is all about, although Sharon's demonic plan is to do it in tiny daily increments that won't properly be reported and are never seen cumulatively as part of a general pattern. (Said 2002)

The Palestinian Authority and Palestinian Rights in Jerusalem

Said was highly critical of the Arabs, the Muslims and, especially, the Palestinians for failing to mobilise their considerable resources to counteract

Israel's behaviour in Jerusalem. In the mid-1990s the Arab League summit, scheduled as a response to Israel's announced expropriations, had been summarily cancelled. Moreover, despite mountains of evidence proving Israel's bad faith, the Palestinian Authority (PA) spinelessly proceeded with its negotiations, while doing absolutely nothing either locally or internationally to mobilise international public opinion against Israel's continued assault on Jerusalem. In the 1993 Declaration of Principles (Oslo Accords) Jerusalem was split off from the West Bank and Gaza, in effect conceded to Israel from the outset of negotiations. Powerful Israel, with full US backing, could do what it wished with Jerusalem, and the Palestinian leadership was convinced that there was no alternative but to make numerous concessions. Said accused the Palestinian leadership of 'prior moral capitulation', piling up one concession on another. The Palestinian 'architect' of the Oslo Accords, Abu Mazen, had assured Hanan Ashrawi not to worry about her reservations about the Declaration of Principles. 'We shall sign now', he assured her, adding chivalrously, 'you can bargain with them to try to get back the things we have conceded' (cited in Prior 2006: 281).

The incompetent PA, Said reminded his audience at an International Conference on Jerusalem in London in 1995, usually negotiated without consulting Palestinian or international lawyers, with no experience in settling international disputes, and with no real conviction in winning anything. He observed:

> The problem of Jerusalem in the peace process today is therefore largely a problem of the incompetence, the insouciance, the unacceptable negligence of the Palestinian leadership, which has in the first instance actually agreed to let Israel do what it wishes in Jerusalem, and in the second instance evinces not the slightest sign that it is capable of comprehending, let alone executing the truly Herculean task that is required before the battle for Jerusalem can really be joined. (cited in Prior 2006: 281-2)

What could be done? Said argued that Palestinians needed a new strategy of negotiating and winning the peace that Palestinians desire. This general negotiating strategy should be based on a new vision and a clear statement of purpose to guide their struggle. In the first instance, Israel should not be allowed to subvert the Palestinian-Muslim-Christian multicultural reality in Jerusalem. Palestinians should also insist that it was not Israel's right to dispose of Jerusalem to the exclusion of Palestinians and others. Diaspora Palestinians, who constitute the majority of Palestinians in the world should take the initiative on Jerusalem and on the other Occupied Territories, and do so in a coordinated fashion. Moreover, speaking of East Jerusalem was not enough: the whole city should be a place of co-existence and sharing between the Palestinians and the Israelis, with joint sovereignty and a cooperative vision (cited in Prior 2006: 281-2).

Democratic Change Must Come from Below: The Role of Civil Society

Said was always wary of the kind of rule that Arafat instituted (Ashcroft and Ahluwalia 2001: 135). To the end, he remained a thorn in the side of the PA. The most distinguished Palestinian intellectual became the subject of censorship by the representatives of the PA; Said remained one of the standard-bearers of the liberal conscience in the increasingly illiberal climate of intolerance and corruption surrounding Arafat and his authoritarian regime. The Palestinian leadership, Said argued, had made a terrible mistake by paying little attention to Palestinian civil society, to the needs of oppressed people living under brutal Israeli occupation. Assessing Arafat's undemocratic legacy, Said wrote in December 2002:

> It is a lamentable reality that during his 10 years of misrule Arafat actively prevented the creation of a constitution despite all his ridiculous gibberish about 'Palestinian democracy'. His legacy is neither a constitution nor even a basic law, but only a decrepit mafia. (Said 2002)

Despite the appalling conduct of the PA and 'despite Sharon's frantic wish to bring an end to Palestinian national life' (Said 2002), Said remained fundamentally an optimist. He was not just a strong believer in Palestinian civil society, but also positive about how incredibly resourceful the Palestinians, as a people, were:

> our popular and civil institutions still function under extreme hardship and duress. Somehow teachers teach, nurses nurse, doctors doctor, and so on. These everyday activities have never stopped if only because necessity dictates unstinting effort. Now those institutions and those people who have truly served their society must bring themselves forward and provide a moral and intellectual framework for liberation and democracy, by peaceful means

and with genuine national intent. In this effort Palestinians under occupation and those in the *shatat* or diaspora have an equal obligation to make the effort. Perhaps this national initiative [*al-Mubadara al-Wataniyya*, below] may provide a democratic example for other Arabs as well. (Said 2002)

For Said, real reforms and democracy must come from below. People in the Middle East must change; 'democracy cannot be imported or imposed on the Middle East; it was also the prerogative of citizens who can make it and desire to live under it' (Said 2002). Writing in December 2002, on the eve of the American-led invasion of Iraq, Said complained bitterly about the sorry state of Palestinian and Arab politics. The following quotation is from an article entitled: 'Real Change Means *People* Must Change: Immediate Imperative', written by Said for *CounterPunch* (2002) is worth quoting at length:

> [Regarding] the sorry state of Palestinian and Arab politics, ... its leaders and elites [were] never more corrupt, rarely more injurious to their people as now. Neither collectively nor individually have these people put up any systematic strategy, much less even a systematic protest against Washington's announced plans to re-draw the map of the Middle East after the invasion of Iraq. All these regimes can do now seems to be either to market themselves as indispensable to the U.S. or to suppress any sign of dissent in their midst...
>
> Representatives who represent only themselves ... the absence of any semblance of democracy within, and without, such regimes – these are not reassuring prospects for the future. What is especially noticeable about the general situation is the powerlessness and silence of the overwhelming major-ity of the people, who suffer their humiliation within an envelope of overall indifference and repression. Everything in the Arab world is done either from above by basically unelected rulers or behind a curtain by undesignated ... middlemen. Resources are bartered or sold without accountability; political futures are designed for the convenience of the powerful and their local sub-contractors; human compassion and care for the citizens' well being have few institutions to nurture them.
>
> The Palestinian situation embodies all this with startling drama. As the culmination of its 35-year-old military occupation the Israeli army has spent the last nine months destroying the rudimentary infrastructure of civilian life on the West Bank and in Gaza: people there, in effect, live in cages, with electrical and concrete fences or Israeli troops to guard and interdict their free movement. Yasser Arafat and his men, who are at least as responsible for the current paralysis and devastation because of what they signed away in Oslo, and for having given legitimacy to the Israeli occupation, seem to be hanging on anyway, even as extraordinary stories of their corruption

and illegally acquired wealth dribble out all over the Israeli, Arab and international media.

It is deeply troubling that many of these men have recently been involved in secret negotiations with the EU, with the CIA, with the Scandinavian countries on the basis of their former credibility as surrogates and servants of Arafat. In the meantime Mr Palestine himself continues to issue orders and ludicrous denunciations, all of them either futile or years out of date ... he and his henchmen like the sinister Mohamed Rashid (aka Khalid Salam) continue to employ large sums of money to bribe, to corrupt, and to prolong their rule past all decency. No one seems to be paying attention as the infamous Quartet announces a peace conference and reform with one voice on one day, withdrawing the plan the next, while encouraging Israel in its repression on the third day.

What could be more preposterous than the call for Palestinian elections, which Mr Arafat of all people, imprisoned in an Israeli vice, announces, retracts, postpones, and re-announces. Everyone speaks of reform except the very people whose future depends on it, i.e. the citizens of Palestine, who have endured and sacrificed so much even as their impoverishment and misery increases. Isn't it ironic, not to say grotesque, that in the name of that long-suffering people schemes of rule are being hatched everywhere, except by that people itself? Surely the Swedes, the Spanish, the British, the Americans and even the Israelis know that the symbolic key to the future of the Middle East is Palestine, and that is why they do everything within their power to make sure that the Palestinian people are kept as far away from decisions about the future as possible. And this during a heated campaign for war against Iraq, during which numerous Americans, Europeans and Israelis have openly stated that this is the time to re-draw the map of the Middle East and bring in 'democracy' ...

Democracy cannot be imported or imposed: it is the prerogative of citizens who can make it and desire to live under it. Ever since the end of World War Two, the Arab countries have been living in various states of 'emergency', which has been a license for their rulers to do what they want in the name of security. Even the Palestinians under Oslo had a regime imposed on them that existed first of all to serve Israel's security, and second, to serve (and help) itself. ... [I]t is today imperative that Palestinians take steps to restore the fashioning of their destiny to their own hands.

The political stage in Palestine is now divided between two unattractive and unviable alternatives. On one side there is what is left of the Authority and Arafat, on the other the Islamic parties. Neither one nor the other can possibly secure a decent future for the citizens of Palestine. The Authority is so discredited, its failure to build institutions so basic, its corrupt and cynical history so compromised in every way as to render it incapable of being entrusted with the future. Only rogues will pretend otherwise, as some of its security chiefs and prominent negotiators are now pretending. As for the

Islamic parties, they lead desperate individuals into a negative space of endless religious strife and anti-modern decline. If we speak of Zionism as having failed politically and socially, how can it be acceptable to turn passively to another religion and look there for worldly salvation? Impossible. Human beings make their own history, not gods or magic or miracles. Purifying the land of 'aliens', whether it is spoken of by Muslims, Christians or Jews, is a defilement of human life as it is lived by billions of people who are mixed by race, history, ethnic identity, religion or nationality.

But a large majority of Palestinians and, I think, Israelis, know these things.... [I]n its weakened state Palestinian society is being targeted for 'reform' by parties whose real interest is to liquidate Palestine as a political and moral force for years to come.... What Sharon and the Quartet now propose is an extension of the same unacceptable regime.

Idle talk of elections by Arafat and his lieutenants is meant to reassure outsiders that democracy is on the way. Far from it – these people simply want to continue their corrupt and bankrupt ways by any means possible, including outright fraud. The 1996 elections, it should be remembered, were conducted on the basis of the Oslo process, the main aim of which was to continue Israeli occupation under a different title. The Legislative Assembly (*al-majlis al-tashri'i*) was in reality powerless before both Arafat's edict and the Israeli veto...

As a people under occupation we need a leadership whose main goal is to rid us of Israeli depredations and occupations, and to provide us with an order that can fulfil our needs for honesty, national scope, transparency and direct speech. Arafat has a history of double talk. (Said 2002)

Said was not a mindless militant intellectual. Fiercely independent, he will always be remembered more for his monumental writings and for his uncompromising approach to the PA than for his ability to organise Palestinian opposition or to establish civil society institutions that would have allowed disaffected Palestinian individuals, within and outside Palestine, to play a more effective role in generating democratic change from below.

Abu Mazen and the 'Road Map to Nowhere'

For Said, the Oslo process, and the Palestinian leadership's conduct during the process, made the overall situation of the Palestinians a good deal worse. Furthermore, for Said, Mahmoud 'Abbas – the self-styled 'architect' of the Oslo process,[9] who later in January 2005 was elected president of the PA – inspired no confidence. Shortly before his death in September 2003,

Said wrote an article in the *London Review of Books* sharply critical of both Arafat and Abu Mazen.[10] The latter had just been installed as a new PA prime minister and had just met US Secretary of State Colin Powell in Ramallah for the purpose of implementing the 'Road Map', sponsored by the Quartet: the USA, the UN, the EU and Russia. Said has this to say about Abu Mazen:

> I first met him in March 1977 at my first National Council meeting in Cairo. He gave by far the longest speech, in the didactic manner he must have perfected as a secondary school teacher in Qatar, and explained to the as-sembled Palestinian parliamentarians the differences between Zionism and Zionist dissidents. It was a noteworthy intervention, since most Palestinians in those days had no real notion that Israel was made up not only of funda-mentalist Zionists who were anathema to every Arab, but of various kinds of peacenik and activist as well. In retrospect, Abu Mazen's speech launched the PLO's campaign of meetings, most of them secret, between Palestinians and Israelis: these long dialogues in Europe about peace had considerable effect in their respective societies on shaping the constituencies that made Oslo possible.[11]

During the PLO's Beirut years, between 1971 and 1982, Abu Mazen was stationed in Damascus, but then joined the exiled Arafat and his staff in Tunis for the next decade or so. Said writes:

> I saw him there several times and was struck by his well-organised office, his quiet bureaucratic manner and his evident interest in Europe and the United States as arenas where Palestinians could do useful work promoting peace. After the Madrid conference in 1991, he was said to have brought together PLO employees and independent intellectuals in Europe and formed them into teams, to prepare negotiating files on subjects such as water, refugees, demography and boundaries in advance of what were to become the secret Oslo meetings, although to the best of my knowledge, none of the files was used, none of the Palestinian experts was directly involved in the talks, and none of the results of this research influenced the final documents that emerged.

Throughout 2003 the Quartet were calling for the implementation of the Road Map, a 'peace plan' which gave the PA leaders, and Abu Mazen in particular, another lease of political life. Phase one of the plan was supposed to be realised by the restructuring of the PA, the elimination of all 'violence and incitement' against Israelis, and the installation of a Palestinian government that met the requirements of Israel. Israel for its part undertook to improve the 'humanitarian situation' in the Occupied Territories by easing restrictions and lifting curfews. The plan had nothing to say about removing the over 400,000 illegal Jewish settlers in the West Bank, Gaza and East Jerusalem. Phase two, described as a transition, was focused on the option of creating an independent Palestinian state with 'provisional borders' and 'attributes of sovereignty'. Phase three was to end the conflict completely, also by way of an international conference whose job would be to settle the thorny issues: refugees, settlements, Jerusalem, borders. The real onus, Said wrote, was placed on the Palestinians, who must stop 'violence' while the military occupation remained in place. The misleading symmetry of the plan's structure left Israel in charge of the whole process, while Palestinian human rights remained suppressed.[12]

Said pointed out one key serious omission from the Road Map: the gigantic Apartheid Wall (or 'Separation Wall'), being built in the West Bank by Israel: 347 kilometres of concrete running north to south, of which 120 kilometres had already been erected. It is 8 metres high and 2 metres thick; its cost was put at $1.6 million per kilometre. The wall does not simply divide Israel from a hypothetical Palestinian state on the basis of the 1967 borders: it actually takes in new tracts of Palestinian land, sometimes 5 or 6 kilometres at a stretch. It is surrounded by trenches, electrified wire and moats; there are watchtowers at regular intervals. Almost a decade after the end of South African apartheid, this racist wall is going up with scarcely a protest from most Israelis, or from their American allies who will pay for it. It is estimated that when the wall is completed, almost 300,000 Palestinians will be separated from their land. In effect the Road Map would reduce the envisaged Palestinian state to roughly 40 per cent of the West Bank.

The Road Map, Said powerfully argued, was in essence a plan for pacification: it was about putting an end to Palestine as a problem. The way Palestinians were expected to behave – no violence, no protest, more democracy, better leaders and institutions – all this was based on the notion that the underlying problem has been the ferocity of Palestinian Intifada and resistance, rather than the occupation and settlement activities that had given rise to it. Of course not a word was said about what Palestinians had endured at the hands of Israel since 1948. Not a single word was said in the Road Map about the Israeli policy of targeted assassinations, the closures since 1993, the wholesale destruction of Palestinian infrastructure and property, and the large number of deaths and maimings.[13]

Beyond Zionist 'Ethnocracy' and Palestinian Religious Nationalism: The Secular Democratic Vision

The search for an alternative to the deeply flawed Oslo process (and subsequently to the Road Map), anchored in universal human rights and international law, which would also uphold the Palestinian 'right of return' and self-determination, led Said to the one-state solution: a secular democratic state based on post-apartheid South Africa, and on equality for every single human being in Palestine–Israel and justice. One democratic state based on non-discrimination with equal rights for Palestinians, Israelis, Jews, Muslims, Christians and atheists is closer to the values of the liberal democracies than a state created specifically for one 'ethnicity', namely the Jewish one, whose laws uphold the superior rights of one ethnicity/race/religion over that of another, including the Palestinian citizens of Israel, who constitute one-fifth of the total population of Israel. The 'one-state solution' became the motto of Said's struggle in his final years: a joint Palestinian–Israeli struggle. Said's rethinking of the Palestine question was an indictment of the narrow brand of ethnic (both Israeli Jewish and Palestinian Arab) nationalism that seemed either unwilling or incapable of re-examining the foundational myths and mistakes of the past.

For Said, Zionist settler colonialism in the West Bank, Israel's 'ethnocractic' regime, and, more recently, Israel's 'Apartheid Wall' at the heart of Palestine have all brought about the death of the two-state solution. This also means that the architects of the Oslo Accord had inadvertently set the stage for a single non-sectarian state in historic Palestine. Such a vision was based on Said's unique concept of identity, which reflected his universalist, non-ethnic, non-sectarian perspective. Call it a 'bi-national solution' or a 'federal system', the common denominators are still equal rights, equal citizenship, religious plurality, and coexistence between Israeli Jews and Palestinians. Said was not politically naive; such a vision can only derive from a long-term, joint Arab–Jewish struggle for equality, expressed within a single, secular democratic framework (Aruri 2004: 142). For Said, secular and liberal bi-nationalism was not only desirable but also the only realistic way for Palestine–Israel. In his last decade Said was the principal voice for a pluralist coexistence in historic Palestine. His rethinking of the Palestine question in secular humanist and universalist terms – extending far beyond the Palestine issue, to touch wide and diverse audiences – is the key to understanding his extraordinary and enduring legacy.

Said passionately believed that only by a fundamental critique of the Zionist project in historic Palestine, and only when the Palestinians themselves managed to rediscover, rethink, reform and reconstruct their democratic secular polity and transform it from an empty slogan into a viable programme for the present realities in Palestine–Israel, could the hope for real peace be rekindled.

Also crucially, for Said, the clear shift in Palestinian politics from secular to religious nationalism, as reflected in the rise in the Occupied Territories of the Islamic movement Hamas, was not the way forward. For him, there was a political alternative to the religious nationalism of Hamas and the authoritarianism of Fatah and the PA. He enthusiastically endorsed (and even 'attached' himself to) the new Palestinian National Initiative (PNI, *al-Mubadara al-Wataniyya*), which was announced in the Occupied Territories in June 2002, whose leading figure is Mustafa Barghouti. Barghouti is a Moscow-trained doctor whose main work has been as director of the impressive Village Medical Relief Committees, which have brought health care to more than 100,000 rural Palestinians. Other leaders of the *al-Mubadara* were independent-minded figures such as Haidar 'Abdel-Shafi and Rawia al-Shawwa. The latter ran in the Palestinian presidential election in January 2004. The *al-Mubadara* advocates the idea of a national unified authority, elected to serve the people and its need for liberation, for democratic freedoms, and for public debate and accountability. *Al-Mubadara*, however, unlike Said, continues to advocate a two-state solution.

To summarise what Said wrote about his new vision for Palestine:

• This vision has to be based on liberation from, rather than cooperation with, the Israeli occupation. Throughout the post-Oslo period Said argued for liberation and not a readjustment of the occupation to suit ruling elites, Palestinian VIPs and the Israeli occupation.

- The society created must be representative of a broad base in civil society and therefore include no military or security people and no hangers-on in Ramallah.
- The values of responsible, modern citizenship are central to any new vision of Palestine; 'The old ways are over and should be buried as expeditiously as possible.' Said thought that it was crucial that 'the Palestinian people be led now by modern, well-educated people for whom the values of citizenship are central to their vision'.
- Above all, Said believed that real change can only come about from below, when people actively will that change, make it possible themselves.
- That change among the Palestinians must be brought about by peaceful means and non-violent resistance.
- In Palestine it should be possible to have elections now, not to reinstall the henchmen of the PA but to choose delegates for a constitutional and truly representative assembly.

Said remained committed to demanding the right to narrate the story of Palestine (Ashcroft and Ahluwalia 2001: 135), to articulate the story of loss, dispossession, exile and homelessness. The loss entailed by this condition, however, resulted in a very strident empowerment: Said, who became one of the most celebrated exiles, gave his people and their predicament a voice, against all odds. Any retrospective review of Said's personal and intellectual impact should continue along the two paths he opened up – the Palestinian and the wider international – and that nourished each other in his life and work. Said's involvement in the Palestine issue and his presence in the more general debates around culture and power were invaluable. His secular humanism and his insights into Palestine reality will live on. His work on Palestine embodied the personal and political and informed his theoretical position, one where the secular, humanist intellectual is rooted firmly within worldliness – albeit a constantly shifting world where rigid borders had little meaning for one who remained an exile.

Said's role as 'spokesperson' for Palestine involved many shifts, turns and complexities. Always avoiding the politics of factionalism and refusing to follow any party line, he was determined to speak truth to power, no matter who held it. Of course, Said was not a 'spokesperson' for Palestine in the usual sense: he was not a mouthpiece for those in power. While by his own account his commmitment was rooted in the values of humanism, for some commentators his status was seemingly closer to that of prophet – conference audiences tended to view his performances with a reverence usually only observed in liturgical settings. W.J.T. Mitchell, editor of *Critical Inquiry* and for many years a personal friend of Said, argued that Said was indeed a 'spokesperson' in the way the Hebrew Bible prophets spoke for and to Israelites:

> a chiding, challenging voice, sometimes in the wilderness, sometimes in the opera house or symphony hall, sometimes at the movies or in the preface to a book of poems or a graphic documentary, and sometimes in the academic lecture theater, always speaking the unwelcome truth to power. (Mitchell 2003)

Said, true to his public commitment as a fearless public intellectual, continued to stir debate, strive for open discussion, ask awkward questions. It was this commitment that drove him and allowed him to envision a different future for Palestine-Israel, one based on mutual recognition and the end of the subjugation of the Palestinian people. His views on Zionism and the Palestinians remained remarkably consistent. Although acutely aware in his last decade that he had a terminal illness, Said remained an optimist, against all odds. He never gave up the struggle to relocate the Palestinian refugee issue at the heart of the public and global agenda. He consistently stressed the need to work tirelessly to change American public opinion on Palestine; meanwhile he was encouraged by what he recognised as a significant change in European public opinion. In his memoir, Said tells us that he felt 'out of place' for much of his life in exile; he remained unfulfilled and unsettled. Nevertheless, he created (in the words of his friend and Columbia University colleague Joseph Massad (2003) an intellectual world not just for himself but also for us, one to which we can all belong.

Epilogue

The extraordinary influence of the Hebrew Bible in the largely secular West, where an inherited Christian tradition supports the notion that Palestine has always been somehow 'the land of Israel', has led to the Bible's deployment in favour of Zionism and settler colonialism in Palestine. Therefore the debate about 'ancient Israel' and modern archaeology is also a debate about Zionism and the State of Israel, most crucially because in the eyes of many people in the West the legitimacy of Zionism depends on the credibility of the biblical portrait.

The inevitable outcome of the obsession with the Hebrew Bible in the West – an obsession illustrated by description of the land as 'biblical' and by an exclusive interest in a small section of the history of the land – has resulted in a focus on the Israelite identity of a land that has actually been non-Jewish in terms of its indigenous population for the larger part of its recorded history. No wonder, therefore, that biblical scholarship has, by and large, been essentially 'Zionist' and has participated in the deletion of Palestinian identity and culture, as if over 1,400 years of Muslim occupation of this land has meant nothing. The biblical academia in Israel and the West has been deeply complicit in Israeli occupation and its apartheid policies on several counts, including its view of indigenous Palestinians

as trespassers or 'resident aliens' in someone else's territory and its obsession with a short period of ancient history. Thus it participates in a kind
of retrospective Western colonising of the past and provides a moral
justification for what amounts to ethnic cleansing and apartheid policies
in Palestine. In his seminal work *The Invention of Ancient Israel: The
Silencing of Palestinian History* (1996), Whitelam links the problems of
the modern biblical discipline to the Palestine–Israel conflict and examines
the political implications of the terminology of biblical scholarship chosen
to represent this area. He has shown how the naming of the land implied
control and possession; how the religious term 'the land of Israel' and
Palestine have been invested with, or divested of, meaning in both Western
and Israeli scholarship. Despite the fact that Western biblical scholarship
has continually employed the term the 'Land of Israel', Whitelam argues,
the term has been emptied of any real meaning. Palestine has no intrinsic
meaning of its own, no history of its own; but provides a background for
the history of Israel.

Commensurate with this lack of history is the absence of the inhabitants
of the land. The history of Palestine and its inhabitants in general is subsumed and silenced by the concern with, and the search for, ancient Israel
(Whitelam 1996: 40–45). Whitelam also subjects the biblical paradigm of
'promised land–chosen people', and the biblical academy as a whole, to
a devastating critique and exposes the underlying presumptions of the
discipline. Inspired by the work of Edward W. Said, Whitelam concludes
that biblical studies have been part of and an extension of the orientalist
discourse in the West, which has been written without any 'oriental'
subject in view. For Said, in this orientalist discourse the indigenous
cultures of Palestine were presented as incapable of unified action and
national consciousness. Whitelam further develops Said's arguments,
showing that the history of ancient Palestine has been ignored and silenced
by the discourse of biblical studies, which has its own agenda: 'Western
scholarship has invented ancient Israel and silenced Palestinian history'
(Whitelam 1996: 1, 3) Ancient Palestine, Whitelam insists, has a history
of its own, and needs to be freed from the grasp of biblical studies:

> The problem of Palestinian history has remained unspoken within bibli-
> cal studies, silenced by the invention of ancient Israel in the image of the
> European nation state. Only after we have exposed the implications of this

invention will Palestinian history be freed from the constraints of biblical studies and the discourse that has shaped it (Whitelam 1996: 36).

Whitelam, whose argument confirms the conclusions of other critical biblical scholars (Davies, Thompson and Lemche) that 'ancient Israel' is an ideological construct based upon a misreading of the biblical traditions and divorced from historical reality. He observes that the practice of representative biblical works on the ancient history of Palestine the refer to

> the geographical region as Palestine but never refer to its inhabitants as Palestinians is a denial and silencing of Palestinian history. We are continually presented with images of a land in which its inhabitants are anonymous or non-existent. The history of Palestine effectively only begins with the history of Israel and becomes coterminous with it ... Biblical studies is, therefore, implicated in an act of dispossession which has its modern political counterpart in the Zionist possession of the land and dispossession of its Palestinian inhabitants. (Whitelam 1996: 46)

The silencing of indigenous Palestinians in biblical historiography is matched by the attitudes within mainstream biblical archaeology,[1] which views Palestine only in its capacity to illustrate biblical history (Whitelam 1996: 52), thus providing justification for modern Zionist myths and chauvinist claims to the land of Palestine. Whitelam further explains:

> What we have in biblical scholarship from its inception to the present day is the presentation of a land, 'Palestine', without inhabitants, or at the most simply temporary, ephemeral inhabitants, awaiting a people without a land. This has been reinforced by a reading of the biblical traditions and archaeological findings, interpreted on the basis of a prior understanding of a reading of the Bible, which helps to confirm this understanding. The foundation of the modern state has dominated scholarship to such an extent that the retrojection of the nation state into antiquity has provided the vital continuity which helps to justify and legitimize both. The effect has been to deny any continuity or legitimacy to Palestinian history ... Europe has retrojected the nation state into antiquity in order to discover its own roots while at the same time giving birth to the Zionist movement which established a 'civilized' state in the alien Orient thereby helping to confirm this continuity in culture and civilization. The irony of this situation is that for the past there is a Palestine but no Palestinians, yet for the present there are Palestinians but no Palestine.... In the scholarship of the past and in the reality of the present, Palestine has become 'the land of Israel' and the

history of Israel is the only legitimate subject of study. All else is subsumed in providing background and understanding for the history of ancient Israel which has continuity with the present state and provides the roots and impulse of European civilization. (Whitelam 1996: 58)

Israel continues to impose, with the support of the US administration, its South African-style apartheid system on the Palestinians, thus pre-empting any possibility of a viable Palestinian state in the future. The conviction by Zionist Israelis (both secular and religious) and their American Christian allies that God and the Bible have given the 'Jews' the 'promised land' exclusively and in perpetuity is one of the underpinnings of the Israeli apartheid system in Palestine. Trading on biblical myths, the same ethnocentric ideology led to the 1948 Palestinian catastrophe and the exile today of millions of Palestinian refugees. The outcome of the 1948 ethnic cleansing of Palestine left Israel in control of over 5 million acres of Palestinian land. After 1948, the Israeli state took over the land of the Palestinian refugees, who were barred from returning, while the remaining Palestinian minority was subjected to apartheid-style laws and regulations that effectively deprived it too of most of its land. The entire drive to take over Palestinian land was conducted according to strict legality. Between 1948 and the early 1990s, the Israeli Knesset (parliament) enacted some thirty statutes that transferred land from private Arab to state (Jewish) ownership. Israel has denied the right of the Palestinian refugees to return to their ancestral towns and villages, in violation of international law and all UN resolutions on this issue. Subsequent policies adopted by the State of Israel – demographic, legal and political – have aimed at consolidating a Jewish ethnocracy – an apartheid regime whose land and settlement policies derive from mythologised biblical claims and modern invented traditions.

With the Zionist construction of Israel as a 'racial state', Israel has positioned itself above the morality of international law, while continuing to evoke international and biblical morality in its defence.[2] All the evidence shows that the State of Israel was founded upon the ethnic cleansing of the indigenous Palestinians. Yet since 1948 Israel has practised the politics of denial (Masalha 2003). The Israeli establishment has done everything in its power to quash the early buds of Israeli self-awareness and recognition of Israel's role in the Palestinian catastrophe. Official Israeli spokespersons and Israeli academia have continued to erase the Palestinian Nakba as a historical event. Holocaust denial is abhorrent; in some European countries it is a crime. Israel's denial of responsibility for the Palestinian Nakba is also abhorrent. The question of moral responsibility for the 1948 Palestinian catastrophe has, of course, major ramifications for the refugee question, giving rise to issues of compensation, restitution of property and the 'right of return'. The Palestinian refugee problem has remained at the centre of the Arab–Israeli conflict since 1948. It was mainly the refugees themselves who opposed schemes to resettle them in Arab countries. In general, Palestinians and Arabs refused to discuss an overall solution to the Arab–Israeli conflict before Israel declared that it accepted the repatriation of refugees, in accordance with UN General Assembly Resolution 194 (III) of December 1948. The resolution states that 'the refugees wishing to return to their homes and live at peace with their neighbours should be permitted to do so at the earliest practicable date'. A comprehensive and durable settlement of the conflict will depend on addressing the refugee problem seriously. For over five decades, the right of return has been central to the Palestinians' struggle against dispossession and expulsion from their ancestral homeland and to their struggle for national reconstitution. Only by understanding the centrality of the Nakba that befell the Palestinian people in 1948 is it possible to understand their sense of the right of return. The wrong done to the Palestinians can only be righted through an acknowledgement of their right to return to their homeland and, should they choose, their right to restitution of property.

The conviction held by Zionists that God and the Bible have given the 'Jews' Palestine in perpetuity also underpins the definition of the state as a state of the 'entire Jewish nation' and not merely of its citizens, granting automatic citizenship to any Jew wishing to immigrate by dint of the racially discriminating 'Law of Return', while opposing the right of return for Palestinians made refugees by the establishment of Israel in 1948 and by subsequent expulsions following the 1967 war and the occupation of Palestinian territories. Furthermore, the State of Israel, through the offices of the Jewish National Fund, has designated 95 per cent of the state territory as 'state lands' held in perpetuity for the Jewish people, and has enacted laws that differentiate between Jew and non-Jew, making it illegal for non-Jews (read Palestinians) to lease state lands; between 1948 and 1973, the Jewish Agency established 594 Jewish settlements and not one Arab settlement.[3] State demographic racism towards the one million Palestinian Israeli citizens is discussed extensively in my *A Land without a People* (1997). Citing demographic anxiety, according to which Jews might become a minority by 2020, the Israeli state continues to enact racial laws based on Jewish belonging – Judaism here conceptualised not merely as religion, but also as nationality and ethnicity – to preserve Jewish demographic superiority. Recent examples are the 'Citizenship and Entry Act' (2003), which prohibits non-Jewish (read: Palestinian) spouses of Israeli–Palestinian citizens – who constitute one-fifth of the total population of Israel – to enter the state, and the proposal to deport hundreds of Israel-born children of migrant workers.[4]

Israel continues to speak of 'Judea' and 'Samaria' as parts of 'biblical Israel', referring to an expanded nation with biblically sanctioned borders, and continues to consolidate Jewish-only settlement blocs and construct its annexation wall in the West Bank. With complete disregard for the land's actual inhabitants, successive Israeli governments have insisted on calling the Occupied Territories of the West Bank by their biblical names, claiming biblical rights to lands confiscated from Palestinians. The claim that the occupation of the West Bank derives from biblical rights continues to provide 'moral legitimacy' for Israeli colonisation policies and the oppression of the Palestinians. Furthermore, the deployment of the Old Testament with the aim of driving Palestinians out of Jerusalem and the continuing threats to the Muslim shrines in the city is another disturbing feature of current Israeli policies. Prime minister Ehud Olmert was obsessed during his mayorship of Jerusalem between 1993 and 2003 with Judaisation policies in Arab East Jerusalem. While announcing his new government on 5 May 2006, he pledged to redraw the country's borders and make the main Jewish colonies in the West Bank part of expanded Israel permanently. Typically affirming a belief among Israelis that they have a legitimate claim to biblical territory beyond the River Jordan, he said: 'I believe with all my heart in the people of Israel's eternal historic right to the entire land of Israel.'[5] While millions of Palestinians outside the Occupied Territories, particularly in the refugee camps, have a sense of having been abandoned by the Palestinian leadership, the continuing Palestinian catastrophe is illustrated by Israel's ongoing racist demographic battle with the Palestinians, a battle for 'maximum land and minimum Arabs'.

As Jeff Halper, coordinator of the Israeli Committee Against House Demolitions, shows, the Israeli 'realignment plan' unveiled by Olmert at his speech to a joint session of the US Congress on 26 May 2006 was based on the creation of massive 'facts on the ground'. The Israeli 'Separation Wall' (*Gader haHafrada*), like the South African apartheid system, is based on concepts of racial segregation (separate and unequal). The 'Apartheid Wall', with its tortuous route deep into West Bank territory, will be declared Israel's 'demographic border' with the Palestinians, taking 10 per cent of the West Bank, adding a hundred more stories of Palestinian land loss to the occupation's brutal history. The Israeli plans sandwich the Palestinians between the Separation Wall and yet another 'security' border, the Jordan Valley, giving Israel two eastern borders. In addition Israel plans to incorporate the major settlement blocs (plus half a million Israeli settlers), thus carving the West Bank into a number of small, disconnected, impoverished 'cantons' – which are not the basis for a viable Palestinian state. More crucially, Israeli colonisation plans remove from the Palestinians their richest agricultural land and all their water.[6] The Israeli plans also create a 'greater' Israeli Jerusalem over the entire central portion of the West Bank, thus cutting the economic, cultural, religious and historic heart out of any future Palestinian state. Israel plans also to retain control of Palestinian airspace, the electromagnetic sphere and even the right of a Palestinian state to conduct its own foreign policy.

In the summer of 2006 the American-Israeli (biblical) 'axis of imperialism', backed by the British government of Tony Blair, launched Israel's devastating assault on Gaza and Lebanon, leading to the death of hundreds of Palestinian and Lebanese civilians. While the rest of the world looked on, and much of the Western media was preoccupied with the dismantling of the 'infrastructure of terrorism' of Hizbullah and Hamas, Israel, which has in fact killed four times more civilians than the Palestinians,[7] has used its untrammelled force to break Arab and Muslim will and drag the whole region back to the days of direct western colonialism. Contrary to claims made by the Israeli *hasbara* (propaganda) machine, claims often uncritically rehashed by the BBC and other Western media outlets, virtually no element of the four-decade Israeli occupation – the expropriation of most West Bank land, the establishment of some 300 settlements, the demolition of 12,000 Palestinian homes, the uprooting of a million olive and fruit trees, the construction of a massive system of highways to link the settlements into Israel proper – can be explained by security. As Jeff Halper writes:

> every single element of Israel's Occupation is patently illegal: settlements and the construction of a massive system of Israel-only highways that link the West Bank settlements to Israel proper; the extension of Israel's legal and planning system into occupied Palestinian areas; the plunder of Palestinian water and other resources for Israeli use; house demolitions and the expropriation of Palestinian lands; the intentional impoverishment of the local population; military attacks on civilian populations – to name but a few. Even when Israel's construction of the 'Separation Barrier' was ruled illegal by the International Court of Justice in the Hague and its ruling ratified by the General Assembly, nothing was done to stop it.[8]

Nonetheless there are promising developments. With the rise of new historiography in Israel–Palestine in the last three decades, two exciting scholarly developments have also emerged: biblical minimalism and the new archaeology of the Holy Land. Both developments have combined to produce an academic revolution in biblical studies. Minimalism has emerged as an identifiable method of scholarship within biblical studies, showing that the Bible's language is not a historical language. The minimalist approach, which arose out of the need for scholars to account for the huge discrepancies between the biblical texts and the discoveries of archaeologists, effectively exposed the problems of confusing biblical stories and legends with historical evidence, the difficulties resulting from the ways in which the authors of the Hebrew Bible talk about the past, and the use of myths of origin and the dangers of confusing them with notions of history. Using archaeology for the purpose of reconstructing the ancient history of Palestine, the minimalists propose treating the biblical literature purely as a story rather than as historiographical literature which can shed real light on the actual history of ancient Palestine.

The findings of the new archaeology of Israel–Palestine and of the postcolonial biblical scholarship contribute to the debate about the historicity of the Hebrew Bible and reveal the mythological origins of the biblical paradigm. They also expose the underlying premises of a discourse which mobilises Old Testament mythologies for a settler colonial enterprise and an apartheid system in Palestine. Of course the shaping and construction of the modern identities of Israelis and Palestinians should not be couched in primordialist or mythological terms, rooted either in mythological Old Testament history, in the case of Zionist Israelis, or in mythologised Canaanite roots, in the discourse of some secular Palestinian nationalists (e.g. Cattan 1969: 3-4). As Edward Said shows, the discourse on contemporary identities in Palestine-Israel should be shaped not by historical legends and mythologised nationalist historiographies but by humanist and progressive approaches derived from a joint Palestinian–Jewish struggle against the discredited colonial legacy of Zionism and for equality and democracy in Palestine-Israel.

Both Edward Said and Michael Prior were formidable critics of Zionism. They passionately believed that only by a fundamental critique of the Zionist project in historic Palestine and only when the Palestinians themselves managed to rediscover, rethink, reform and reconstruct their democratic secular polity and transform it from an empty slogan into a viable programme for the present realities in Palestine-Israel, could the hope for real peace be rekindled. Prior, like his hero Said, was the epitome of the scholar-activist and a fearless intellectual. His extraordinary knowledge and his unique style are evident throughout his extensive writings. As a co-founder and co-editor (with Prior) of *Holy Land Studies: A Multidisciplinary Journal*[9] I learned a great deal from Prior's editorial skills. Yet I will always treasure most his passionate commitment to the dispossessed, oppressed and disenfranchised; and his moral courage in challenging both the Zionist misuse of ancient history and the deployment of the biblical narrative in support of settler colonialism. Prior's work reflected his desire for a just resolution of the Israeli-Palestinian dispute. His dedication to truth-telling was a major challenge to the field of biblical scholarship; his tenacious message will continue to reverberate until justice for the Palestinians is done and peace and reconciliation in Palestine-Israel are achieved.

Prior has shown that the religio-political discourse of the Islamic movement Hamas is wedded to the biblical paradigm and its legends. Hamas, currently in government, has clearly accepted the concept of the two-state solution. However, its national religious rhetoric has little to offer beyond 'grandiloquence and the anaesthetising rhetoric' of a religious solution for a national secular situation (Prior 1999a: 261). In a similar vein, for Said the clear shift in Palestinian politics from secular to religious nationalism, as reflected in the rise in the Occupied Territories of Hamas, was not the way forward. For him, as we have seen, there was a political alternative to the religious nationalism of Hamas and the authoritarianism of Fatah and the PA: a new secular democratic vision for Palestine-Israel based on liberation from, rather than cooperation with, the Israeli occupation.

Said and Prior were right to argue that religion in Palestine-Israel has to be separated from the state and the national goals of both peoples. Palestinians and Israelis must become inclusive. While the biblical discourse of 'promised land' and of the displacement by one people of the indigenous population is particularly objectionable (Prior 1999a: 261), the only obvious alternative is to envisage the creation of a democratic framework which respects the right of equal citizenship of all inhabitants of Palestine-Israel (including the return of those ethnically cleansed by Zionism), irrespective of religious affiliation.

The obstacle to such a programme, of course, is the Zionist principle of racial and ethnic separation (*hafrada*). To achieve a unified state, with equality of rights for all citizens, the basic intentions of Zionism would have to be re-evaluated, and its essentially discriminatory, complex base and structure would have to be dismantled. A federation of two states, with permeable borders, and a wide range of collaboration is the preferred option, and could serve as an intermediate stage to a unified state. Perhaps the dismantling of apartheid South Africa and the movement towards an agreed settlement in Northern Ireland encourage one to believe that such a future might be possible. In any case, some anti-apartheid solution must be devised which will accommodate both Israeli Jews and Palestinian Arabs. The challenge for all national and religious communities in the Holy Land – as well as for religious politics in Jerusalem – is to develop a pluralistic, secular democratic and humanist mode of existence based on equality for all the citizens of Israel-Palestine and the recognition of shared principles, values and interests amid acknowledged religious and political differences.

The project of the decolonisation of Palestine formed the grounding premiss of Said's work. For him, almost every category of Jewish experience – homelessness, dispossession and displacement – applied to the Palestinian case. Ilan Pappé – who argues that Said's works have had a great deal of impact on the evolution of post-Zionism in Israel in the 1990s (Pappé 2004a;[10] Nimni 2003) – has this to say in his tribute to Edward Said:

> In more concrete terms we needed a clear articulation of an agenda that was based on principals of universal human rights, and that rejected the set of ideals that accompanied us from the cradle, ideas that were deeply rooted in colonialism and nationalist fanaticism. This is where Edward Said appeared in our life, like a lighthouse navigating us away from the rocks of murkiness and confusion arising from growing up in a Zionist state, on to a safe harbour of reason, morality and consciousness. (Pappé 2004b: 135)

Said argued that the Palestinians need a clear statement of purpose and principle to guide their way, and this demanded the rethinking of their general strategy of negotiation with Israel. In the first place, they must insist that it was not Israel's right to dispose of Jerusalem to the exclusion of Palestinians and others and that the massive Palestinian–Muslim–Christian multicultural reality in Jerusalem should not be subverted by Israel. The whole city should be a place of coexistence and sharing between the Palestinians and the Israelis, with joint sovereignty and a cooperative vision. Moreover, it would not be sufficient for the Palestinians merely to lament their Nakba and facts of dispossession. For Said, facts never speak for themselves, but must be articulated, disseminated, reiterated and recirculated. Diaspora Palestinians, who constitute the majority of Palestinians in the world, must therefore take the initiative on Jerusalem and on all the other Occupied Territories, and do so in a coordinated fashion. Not that Said was arguing against peace. But real peace was possible only between equals, who together decide consciously and deliberately to share the land among each other decently and humanely. Israel, in his opinion, had used the peace process as a subterfuge; only to go on holding the land as if it were its sole proprietor, with concessions to Bantustan-like 'separation' and cantonisation for the lesser race of human beings. Palestinians, on their part, had accepted Israel as a sovereign state entitled to peace and security. Was it the Palestinian destiny merely to capitulate and accept the dictates of the strong? Surely not. Rather, the Palestinians must redefine their goals, recognise that they are realisable, and work for them. And since the Palestinian Authority was incapable of doing so, the challenge should be taken up by the Palestinian diaspora, strategically organised, and working in collaboration with other constituencies – the gigantic Islamic and Arab constituency, the Western and Christian constituencies, and others scarcely considered hitherto.

Said's engagement with Palestine's history was guided by a clear and constructive agenda. He wanted Palestinians and Arabs to stop denying or downplaying the Jewish Holocaust, and hoped that this would encourage Israeli Jews in turn to cease their Nakba denial and lead them to acknowledge the evils they had inflicted on the Palestinians. Said remained to the end a great believer in history, not as a force that enslaves the present, but as one that liberates it, for the sake of a better future. Said's secular democratic vision is the only alternative to Redemptionist Zionism, both secular and religious. Such a vision, which is based on a joint Palestinian-Jewish struggle for equality and universal human rights, is the only realistic way forward for Palestine-Israel.

Notes

Introduction

1. The word 'Bible' is derived from the Greek word *biblia*, meaning 'books'. The collection of Jewish and Christian sacred texts came to be increasingly regarded as a single entity. With the exception of a few passages in Aramaic, the Old Testament was written in Hebrew. As Aramaic became the common language among Jews following the Babylonian Exile (6th century BC), however, translations for the use of the faithful were made into Aramaic. Greek was the next language to predominate in much of the ancient world. The earliest translation into Greek of the Pentateuch, or the first five books (Genesis, Exodus, Leviticus, Numbers and Deuteronomy, which in Hebrew are called the Torah or Law) was the Septuagint. The spread of Christianity inspired additional Greek and Latin translations of the Bible. St Augustine complained of the 'infinite variety of Latin translations'. To remedy the problem, in the year 382 AD Pope Damasus I commissioned the leading biblical scholar St Jerome to prepare a standard Bible in Latin. Jerome translated the Old Testament directly from the Hebrew and used Aramaic manuscripts rather than the Greek Septuagint. For the New Testament Jerome used existing Latin and Greek manuscripts. His work, completed in 405 AD, gradually gained widespread acceptance among Latin-speaking Christians – it was referred to as the Vulgate Bible. Written in an everyday Latin, it was consciously designed to be both more accurate and easier to understand than its predecessors and took its name from the phrase *versio vulgata*, 'the common [i.e., popular] version' (Herzog 2001: 72–93).

Chapter 1

1. The term 'biblicism' is not used widely in the English language. Some writers use it to describe literalist and fundamentalist positions centred on the Bible. But the word is used here for a position of softer than religious fundamentalism. Following

James Barr, the term is used here for a position that maintains that the Bible is the sole source for Christian theology (Barr: 1977: 6).

2. The earliest human habitation at Jericho dates from about 8000 BC.

3. Kohn 1958, in Khalidi 2005: 812–13.

4. Kohn 1958, in Khalidi 2005: 813.

5. For the Lithuanian Eliezer Ben-Yehuda (1857-1922), a pioneer in reviving Hebrew, the colonisation of Palestine and the replacement of Yiddish and other European languages by Hebrew as the language of instruction in Zionist colonies in Palestine went hand in hand. Ben-Yehuda settled in Palestine in 1881, and in 1889, with several collaborators, established Va'ad Lashon Ha-'Ivrit (the Hebrew Language Committee), whose tasks included coining new Hebrew words.

6. Avishai Margalit, 'The Myth of Jerusalem', *New York Review of Books* 38, no. 21, 19 December 1991.

7. Michael Gillespie, 'Bill Moyers, Modernity, and Islam', Media Monitors Network, 20 July 2002, www.mediamonitors.net/gillespie6.html (accessed 18 February 2004).

8. Zvi Zameret, 'Ben-Gurion's Bible', at www.matan.org.il/Data/UploadedFiles/Free/massekhet_zvizammeret_abs_125.doc (accessed 15 March 2006).

9. Ibid.

10. Ibid.

11. Cited by Daniel Lazare, 'False Testament: Archaeology Refutes the Bible's Claim to History', *Harper's Magazine*, March 2002, www.worldagesarchive.com/Reference_Links/False_Testament_(Harpers).htm (accessed 20 April 2006).

12. Gillespie, 'Bill Moyers, Modernity, and Islam'.

13. Oz 1988: 21.

14. Kohn 1958, in Khalidi 2005: 818–19. See also Masalha 2000; Shlaim 2000.

15. Vladimir Jabotinsky, 'The Iron Wall: We and the Arabs', first published in Russian under the title 'O Zheleznoi Stene', *Rasswyet*, 4 November 1923; published in English in *Jewish Herald* (South Africa), 26 November 1937; quoted in Brenner 1984: 74-5; and in Masalha 1992: 28-9, 2000: 56) the article is available at www.marxists.de/middleast/ironwall/ironwall.htm (accessed 2 June 2006).

16. In 1854 he joined the Society for the Promotion of Christianity Among the Jews.

17. Herzl recorded one meeting in Vienna with Hechler in detail:

> Yesterday, Sunday afternoon, I visited the Rev Hechler. ... He lives on the fourth floor; his windows overlook the Schillerplatz. ... The room which I entered was lined up with books on every side, floor to ceiling. Nothing but Bibles. A window of the very bright room was open ... and Mr Hechler showed me his biblical treasures. Then he spread out before me his chart of comparative history, and finally a map of Palestine. It is a large military staff map in four sheets which, when laid out, covered the entire floor ... He shows me where, according to his calculations, our new Temple must be located: in Bethel! Because that is the centre of the country. He also showed me models of the ancient temple: 'We have prepared the ground for you.' (quoted in Merkley 1998: 16-17)

18. For a collection of Israeli-Zionist views, see Doron 1988.

19. See Margalit, 'The Myth of Jerusalem', www.nybooks.com/articles/3055.

20. Oz 1988: 22. Oz's article was originally published in *Davar* in 1967.

21. Cited from the back cover of 'Jerusalem of Gold', Fontana Records, SRF, 67572, MGF 27572.

22. See *Ma'ariv*, 11 June 1967.

23. Uri Avnery 'Death of a Myth, ZNet, 13 May 2005, www.zmag.org/content/show-article.cfm?ItemID=7850.

24. Ibid.

25. Ibid.

26. The *shofar* is a horn used in Jewish high holidays to commemorate events of major significance.

27. Translated from Hebrew, in Davis and Mezvinsky 1975: 220.

28. Oz 1988: 22, originally published in *Davar* in 1967.

29. Piterberg explains that his critical discussion of the foundational myths of Zionism was informed by Evron 1995; Myers 1995; Raz-Krakotzkin 1993-94.

30. Har-Tzion owned a large cattle ranch situated on the lands of the destroyed Arab village of Kawkab al-Hawa in the Beisan valley, the inhabitants of which were driven out in 1948.

31. *Ma'ariv*, supplement, 22 January 1979, p. 6; cited also in Kahane 1980: 230.

32. *Davar*, 9 February 1979, p. 17.

33. In his book *Heros of Israel*, Haim Hertzog (president of Israel from 1983 to 1993) quotes Ariel Sharon's description of Har-Tzion as 'The fighting symbol not only of the paratroopers, but of the entire Israel Defence Forces' (Herzog 1989: 271) See also Dayan (1978: 96-101). In March 1955 Har-Tzion and his colleagues were involved in a little-known massacre of Bedouin in the Negev (see Hanokh Bartov in *Ma'ariv*, 26 January 1979, p. 14.) In the wake of those atrocities the then Prime Minister Moshe Sharett entered in his personal diary: 'I am dumbfounded about the essence and fate of this people, which is capable of having a noble soul ... but in addition produces from the ranks of its best youth young men who are capable of murdering human beings in clear mind and cold bloodedness by thrusting knives in the bodies of defenceless young Bedouins' (Sharett 1978: 823).

34. His real name was Simon ben Kosiba, although he was usually called Bar Kochba (son of the star), a reference to his claim to be a Jewish Messiah. After the end of the disastrous rebellion, the rabbis called him 'Bar Koziba', which means 'son of the lie'.

35. For excerpts of Shamir's address, see *Journal of Palestine Studies* 21, no. 2 (Winter 1992): 128-31.

36. Ibid. See also Netanyahu 1993: 39-40.

37. See also Benny Morris in the *Guardian*, G2, 3 October 2002.

38. As reported in the *New Judea* 13, nos 111-12 (August-September 1937): 220.

39. Protocol of the Jewish Agency Executive meeting of 7 June 1938, *Jerusalem Confidential* 28, no. 51, Central Zionist Archives, Jerusalem.

40. David Ben-Gurion, 'Lines for Zionist Policy', 15 October 1941, in Masalha 1992: 128-9.

41. *Doar Hayom* (Jerusalem), 28 April 1930. See also *Sefer Ussishkin* [*The Book of Ussishkin*], Jerusalem, 1934 [Hebrew]: 233-7.

42. *'Al Darchei Mediniyutenu: Mo'atzah 'Olamit Shel Ihud Po'alei Tzion* (1938).

43. Protocol of the Jewish Agency Executive meeting of 12 June 1938, vol. 28, no. 53, Central Zionist Archives, Jerusalem.

44. One of the first to label it *Nakba* was Constantine Zurayk, a distinguished philosopher of Arab history and liberal intellectual, in his booklet *The Meaning of the Disaster* (1956), a self-critical analysis of the socio-economic causes of the Arab defeat in the 1948 war, written and published while the war was still going on. An English edition was published in 1956. The term also became the title of the monumental work of Palestinian historian 'Arif Al-'Arif (1958-60).

45. Kohn 1958, in Khalidi 2005: 836.
46. Avi Shlaim, 'The New History of 1948 and the Palestinian Nakba', 18 March 2004, www.miftah.org/PrinterF.cfm?DocId=3336.
47. Ibid.
48. Ibid.
49. The term 'politicide' was used by Kimmerling in connection with Ariel Sharon's war against the Palestinians (2003).
50. Quoted in William Martin, 'Who Is Pushing Whom into the Sea?', 11 March 2005, www.counterpunch.org/martin03112005.html (accessed 14 March 2005).
51. Ibid.
52. Ibid.
53. Guy Erlich in *Ha'ir*, 6 May 1992 [Hebrew].
54. Begin sent a congratulatory note to the Irgun fighters who had carried out the Deir Yasin massacre: 'Accept congratulations on this splendid act of conquest. Tell the soldiers you have made history in Israel' (quoted by *Corner Stone* 11, Easter 1998, at www.sabeel.org/old/news/t11/index.htm).
55. Don C. Benjamin, 'Stories and Stones: Archaeology and the Bible, an introduction with CD Rom', 2006, www.doncbenjamin.com/Archaeology_&_the_Bible.pdf, p. 254 n78.
56. Yadin Roman, at www.eretz.com/archive/jan3000.htm.
57. Approximate one-quarter of all geographical names were derived from the Arabic names on the basis of the similarity of sounds. Abu El-Haj 2001: 95.
58. Michelson et al. 1996.
59. See, for instance, David Ben-Gurion, 'Al Gvulot Historiim Ve-Gvulot Hamdina' [On Historical Borders and the Borders of the State], *Mabat Hadash*, 19 April 1967.
60. Zameret, 'Ben-Gurion's Bible'.
61. On Albright and the politics of biblical archaeology, see Long 1997. See also Chapter 2.
62. Y. Ariel, 'The Antiquity Robbery and Dayan's Collection' [Hebrew], *Haaretz*, 13 April 1986, p. 9; Y. Ariel 'A Complaint about a Digging Made by M. Dayan in a Historical Site' [Hebrew], *Haaretz*, 17 November 1968 [Hebrew]). See also Dayan 1976: 258.
63. Cited by Daniel Lazare, 'False Testament: Archaeology Refutes the Bible's Claim to History', *Harper's Magazine*, March 2002, www.worldagesarchive.com/Reference_Links/False_Testament_(Harpers).htm (accessed 20 April 2006)
64. In December 1971 a list of accusations against Dayan was published by Dan Ben-Amotz in the anti-establishment Hebrew magazine *Ha'olam Hazeh*.
65. R. Miberg, 'The Man Who Came To Take', *Hadashot*, Supplement, 17 September 1991 [Hebrew].
66. These figures were mentioned in a letter by the inhabitants' committee, cited in *Reconstruct Emmaus*, Association for the Reconstruction of Emmaus, Saint-Sulpice, Switzerland, December 1987, p. 3.
67. Quoted in David Sharrock (reporting from Jerusalem), *Guardian*, 1 January 1998, p. 9. Sharrock's report is based on *Haaretz*, 31 December 1997. See also *Haaretz*, 2 January 1998.
68. Cited by Sharrock, *Guardian*, 1 January 1998.
69. See the *Jerusalem Diary of Sister Marie-Therese*, in *Cahiers du Temoignage Chretien*, Paris, 27 July 1967; Hirst 1984: 225.
70. For further details see, Khalidi 1992: 139-40; Dumper 1994: 116.

71. *Jerusalem Diary of Sister Marie-Therese*, in *Cahiers du Temoignage Chretien*.
72. See Aronson 1990: 19. For further discussion of Israel's settlement policies in occupied East Jerusalem, see Dumper 1992: 32-53, 1994: 117-20; Michal Sela', in *Davar*, 30 December 1991, pp. 9-10; Friedman 1992: 96-100, 113-21. According to Benziman, Shlomo Lahat and his assistant Ya'acov Salman played a key role in the eviction of Arab residents from the Jewish quarter of the Old City of Jerusalem after June 1967 (Benziman 1973: 45).

Chapter 2

1. Regina Sharif states that the first printed literature dealing with Christian Zionist and millenarian speculations appeared in Europe in the 1590s (Sharif 1983: 17).
2. Cited by Ami Isseroff, 'British Support for Jewish Restoration', www.mideastweb. org/britzion.htm (accessed 11 February 2006).
3. As early as 1821 the Anglican Church, through its Church Missionary Society and the London Jews Society (more properly 'The Society for Promoting Christianity among the Jews', founded in 1808 to convert the Jews to Christianity), was considering the establishment of a post. The London Jews Society established the first permanent Anglican mission station in Jerusalem in 1833, two years after the crisis caused by the capture of the city by Muhammad 'Ali. In 1841, a Protestant bishopric in Jerusalem was established under joint British and Prussian auspices.
4. Russian interest in the Holy Land increased particularly after the Crimean War, as Russia availed itself of the opportunity of furthering Russian political concerns through protection of Orthodox interests in the Ottoman Empire. This was witnessed as early as 1860 with the commencement of the building of a Russian cathedral and of a vast complex of hostels, offices and hospitals for the care for Russian pilgrims to Jerusalem.
5. German influence was reflected in the German Evangelical Church's administration of the hospital of the German deaconesses, the Syrian Protestant Orphanage, the Leper Hospital in the German colony, and the Lutheran Church of the Redeemer.
6. Not to be outdone, the Church of Scotland mission was established, which, in addition to St Andrew's in Jerusalem, provided medical and educational services in several centres in Palestine.
7. www.pef.org.uk/Pages/Warren.htm.
8. 'The White Man's Burden' is a famous poem written by Kipling in 1899.
9. Shaftesbury was the nephew-in-law of Lord Melbourne (prime minister through most of the period 1834-41), and the step son-in-law of Lord Palmerston (foreign minister for most of the 1840s and early 1850s, and then prime minister for most of the period 1855-65). Merkley 1998: 13.
10. See also Masalha 1992, 1997, 2003.
11. Cited by Isseroff, 'British Support for Jewish Restoration'; Masalha 1992, 1997, 2003.
12. Darby n.d.
13. Cited by Isseroff, 'British Support for Jewish Restoration'.
14. Numbers 32:1; Genesis 31:25; Genesis 37:25.
15. Cited by Isseroff, 'British Support for Jewish Restoration'.
16. For further discussion of the founding myths of Zionism, see Masalha 1992, 1997; Piterberg 2001; Sternhell 1998.

17. Cited by Isseroff, 'British Support for Jewish Restoration'.
18. Here Said uses Karl Marx's adage 'they cannot represent themselves; they must be represented' in an epigraph to *Orientalism.*
19. FOSH, Hebrew abbreviation for Plugot Sadeh. The FOSH was disbanded in 1939 to create a larger mobile force known as the HISH (Heyl Sadeh or Field Force). During the Second World War FOSH veterans were trained by the British for commando raids.
20. Ron Grossman, 'Remembering One of Israel's Founding Fathers – A Protestant Scotsman', *Chicago Tribune*, 29 April 1998: 5.1, quoted Wagner 2003: 117.
21. Grossman, quoted in Wagner 2003: 117.
22. For conservative evangelical attitudes to Wellhausen, see Barr 1977: 121-2.
23. William Foxwell Albright, 'Archaeological Discovery in the Holy Land', *Bibliotheca Sacra* 79 (1922): 402, 412, 416, cited in Long 2003: 143, 229.
24. *Bulletin of the American Schools of Oriental Research* 6 (May 1922): 9, cited in Long 2003: 139, 228.
25. Viewing the Bible as a reliable history, Frederic Kenyon wrote: 'The Christian can take the whole Bible in his hand and say without fear or hesitation that he holds in it the true Word of God, handed down without essential loss from generation to generation throughout the centuries (Kenyon 1958: 55).
26. Dr Barry Morgan, Archbishop of Wales and Bishop of Llandaff Welsh Centre for International Affairs, Anniversary Lecture on 20 November 2003, www.wcia.org. uk/dsp_whatsnew_detail.cfm?Page=whatsnew&WhatsNewId=16&lang=we.
27. Quoted by Michael Gillespie, 'Bill Moyers, Modernity, and Islam', www.media-monitors.net/gillespie6.html (accessed 4 March 2006).
28. W.R. Price and J.J.H. Price Goodman, *Jerry Falwell, An Unauthorized Profile*, cited in Halsell 1986: 72.
29. L. Nelson Bell, 'Editorial', *Christianity Today*, 12 July 1967, quoted in Wagner 1992): 4, 13.
30. See Armstrong 1996. For further discussion on early manifestations of sacred geography, see see Eliade 1958: 368, 1959: 373.
31. The building of Anastasis probably took ten years (326-335 AD). It was a complex of monumental structures, including a rotunda built over the tomb, a great basilica, and columned courtyards (Wasserstein 2002: 7).
32. Norman K. Gottwald, 'Biblical Scholarship in Public Discourse', The Bible and Interpretation, December 2002, www.bibleinterp.com/articles/Biblical_Scholarship. htm.
33. In May 1984 Risenhoover and Krieger organised a White House briefing for evangelical and American Zionist organizations on Middle East issues. The meeting was attended by Hall Lindsay and Jimmy Swaggart (Wagner 1992). See also Lisa Pevtzov, 'Apocalypse Now, Operation Conquest – The Temple Mount Yeshiva', *Jerusalem Post* Magazine, 18 February 1994, p. 6.
34. www.sorisrael.com/tours.htm (accessed 25 February 2006).
35. John Mearsheimer and Stephen Walt, 'The Israel Lobby', *London Review of Books* 28, no. 6 (23 March 2006).
36. Mearsheimer and Walt, 'The Israel Lobby'.
37. Romesh Ratanar, 'The Right's New Crusade: Lobbying for Israel', *Time*, 6 May 2002, p. 26.
38. Middle East Council of Churches 1988: 9.
39. Servan-Schreider 1988: 13. For how Christian Zionists justify occupation through the use of biblical terminology ('Judaea and Samaria'), see Evans 1980: 129-48.

40. Wagner, 'Beyond Armageddon'; also Haija 2006: 75-95.
41. Speech by President Jimmy Carter on 1 May 1978, *Department of State Bulletin* 78, no. 2015, p. 4, cited in Sharif 1983: 136.
42. *Jerusalem Post*, March 1979, cited in Sharif 1983: 135.
43. Ronnie Dugger, 'Does Reagan Expect a Nuclear Armageddon?', *Washington Post*, 18 April 1984.
44. In the 1990s pro-Zionist Senator Bob Dole introduced legislation in the American Senate which required the US embassy to be rebuilt in Jerusalem by 31 May 1999, and authorising $100 million for 'preliminary' spending for the next threee years. Earlier, on 24 October 1995, Dole had stated: 'Israel's capital is not on the table in the peace process, and moving the United States embassy to Jerusalem does nothing to prejudice the outcome of any future negotiations'. Middle East Realities, 'Lie of the Week'.
45. 'International Christian Zionist Congress Proclamation, Affirmation of Christian Zionism', International Christian Embassy, Jerusalem. 25-29 February 1996; 'Why Should Christians be Friends of Israel?' Christian Friends of Israel leaflet, n.d.
46. Eusebius of Caesarea, *Church History*, Book II, Chapter 6, at: www.preteristarchive.com/StudyArchive/e/eusebius_historian.html.
47. Tuvia Sagiv, 'The Temples of Mount Moriah', www.templemount.org/mtmoriah.html#1.
48. Karen Armstrong, 'Islam's Stake: Why Jerusalem Was Central to Muhammad', /www.time.com/time/2001/jerusalem/islam.html (accessed 3 March 2006).
49. Sagiv, 'The Temples of Mount Moriah'.
50. Interview with Dr Ilan Pappé, of Haifa University, 7 May 2003.
51. Interview with 'Adnan al-Husseini, director of the Muslim Waqf in Jerusalem, 29 April 2003. Interview with Jamal Abu-Tu'ameh, solicitor based in East Jerusalem, who is in charge of the legal side of the Muslim Waqf; he also represented the Muslim Waqf in legal cases involving the Israeli High Court.
52. From Michael Prior's interviews with representatives of the 'International Christian Embassy, Jerusalem' (19 March 2003), and with Dr Clarence H. Wagner, Chairman and President (CEO) of Bridges for Peace, and Editor in Chief-Publications (24 March 2003).
53. Bill Durland, 'Christian Zionism: Will Fear or Freedom Triumph?', http://western-quaker.net/Christian%20Zionism_Sept%2004.htm (accessed 3 March 2006).
54. Jeff Halper, 'A New Apartheid Regime or Peace? Israel-Palestine after the January-March Elections', speech at St Mary's College, Twickenham, 17 February 2006.
55. Halper, 'A New Apartheid Regime or Peace?' See also Sizer 2004: 197.
56. Andy Goldberg, 'Israel Plans a Hell of a Party at Armageddon', *Sunday Times*, 17 November 1996, p. 18.
57. Wagner, 'Beyond Armageddon'.
58. Lindsey 1995: front cover.
59. Wagner, 'Beyond Armageddon'.
60. Andrew Walker, cited in an interview with Geoffrey Levy, *Daily Mail*, 2 September 1994, p. 18.
61. Wagner, 'Beyond Armageddon'.
62. Patrick Cockburn, *Independent*, 30 September 1996, p. 9.
63. Haim Shapiro, 'Sharon to Christians: This Land Was Promised Only to the Jews, Pope Told Me', *Jerusalem Post*, 22 September 2002.

Chapter 3

1. Kimmerling 1999: 339-63; see also Cook 2006: 174-5.
2. The term 'Jewish fundamentalists' is used to describe those individuals, parties or movements with a religious fundamentalist approach to religion and state, invariably wanting Israel to become a *halachic* state – that is, one governed by Jewish religious law.
3. Avishai Margalit, 'The Myth of Jerusalem', *New York Review of Books* 38, no. 21 (19 December 1991).
4. Michael Neumann, 'What's So Bad About Israel?, *Counter Punch*, 6 July 2002, www.counterpunch.org/neumann0706.html (accessed 5 February 2006)
5. Interview with Dr Ilan Pappé, a leading Israeli 'new historian', 6 May 2003.
6. The NRP has been a member of all Israeli governments since 1948, with the exception of short periods in 1958-59 and in June 1992-June 1996.
7. Michael Neumann, 'What's So Bad About Israel?'
8. Over 200 illegal Israeli settlements and 400,000 settlers are now in situ. The core of Gush Emunim is the illegal settlements established in the Arab territories since 1967 (Sprinzak 1991: 130; Newman 1985: 533; Lustick 1988: 10).
9. Quoted in David Shaham, *Yedi'ot Aharonot* supplement, 13 April 1979.
10. *Hatzofeh*, 23 June 1967.
11. *Yedi'ot Aharonot*, 20 December 1974.
12. See for instance *Torah Ve'avodah [Torah and Work]*, no. 6 (Jerusalem, 1984 [Hebrew]).
13. Yisrael Rosen in *Nekudah*, November 1987.
14. Quoted in *Jerusalem Post International*, 30 January 1988.
15. Gush Emunim's main organ, *Nekudah*, has been assiduously popularising the 'transfer' idea since its first appearance in December 1979. By 1986, its circulation reached 10,000. Copies were sent to subscribers in the Occupied Territories and in Israel, including public institutions and public and academic libraries. *Nekudah* also appears in the form of pamphlets with a circulation of 50,000 (Benvenisti 1986: 160; Yisrael Rosen in *Nekudah*, November 1987).
16. See also *Journal of Palestine Studies* 10, no. 1 (Autumn 1980), p. 150; Rubinstein 1982: 91. The settlers statements were also published in the Gush Emunim journal *Nekudah*. See Yehuda Litani in *Haaretz*, 15 May 1984, p. 15. Another settler of 'Ofra, echoing the widely publicized aphorism of the late Prime Minister Golda Meir, said in June 1980: 'after all there are no Palestinian people. We invented them, but they don't exist.' See *Jerusalem Post International*, 8-14 June 1980.
17. *Ma'ariv*, 18 March 1983.

Chapter 4

1. Jonathan Silverman, 'Whose Jerusalem ? Whose Land? On the Holiness of Jerusalem in Judaism and Islam', 8 January 2002, www.cdn-friends-icej.ca/holiness.html (accessed 10 January 2003).
2. Interview with Dr Ilan Pappé, of Haifa University, 7 May 2003.
3. Silverman, note 14 above.
4. Interview with Shaykh 'Ikrima Sabri, the Mufti of Palestine, 14 March 2003.
5. Daniel Pipes, 'The Muslim Claim to Jerusalem', *Middle East Quarterly,* September 2001, www. danielpipes.org/article/84 (accessed 10 November 2003).

6. Daniel Pipes, 'Jerusalem Means More to Jews than to Muslims', *Los Angeles Times*, 21 July 2000.
7. Pipes, 'The Muslim Claim to Jerusalem'.
8. Silverman, note 14 above.
9. Interview with 'Adnan al-Husseini, Director of the Muslim Waqf in Jerusalem, 29 April 2003; Interview with Jamal Abu-Tu'ameh, solicitor based in East Jerusalem, who is in charge of the legal side of the Muslim Waqf; he also represented the Muslim Waqf in legal cases involving the Israeli High Court.
10. The obsession with Islam is exemplified in the publications of Paul Eidelberg, Professor of Politics at Bar-Ilan University, a stronghold of Zionist messianism and of Jewish fundamentalism. His published work is typical of the fundamentalist current within Israeli academia, which is particularly obsessive about Islam and Muslims. In his *Jerusalem vs. Athens* he writes:

> Judaism is the acme of freedom and creativity – the Jew represents the very heart of human potentiality ... the difference between Ishmael and Isaac. Ishmael was born of Hagar, an Egyptian slave, and before Abraham's circumcision. Concerning Ishmael: His hand will be against everyone, and everyone's hand will be against him (Gen. 16:12). This is exactly descriptive of Ishmael's highly sensual descendants, the bellicose Moslem world whose Koran is a gospel of war. In contrast, Isaac, born of Sarah, was a man of peace, as have ever been his descendants. (Eidelberg 1983: 216 and 366 n14)

Five years later Eidelberg, while still teaching at Bar Ilan University, proposed the removal of all Muslims from Jerusalem and the entire area of historic Palestine (in an article in *Haumah* journal, Spring 1988; see Eidelberg 1988: 238-48).
11. See also Amnon Rubinstein's in *Haaretz*, 9 May 1976.
12. 'Amos Ben-Vered in *Haaretz,* 23 October 1979, p. 8.
13. *Ma'ariv*, 14 June 1985.
14. *Ma'ariv,* 5 July 1985, p. 19.
15. Since the eruption of the 'al-Aqsa Intifada' in September 2000, scores of Palestinians civilians have been killed and wounded by armed Jewish settlers in the West Bank and Gaza.
16. In Elfi Pallis, *Middle East International*, 24 April 1981, p. 12.
17. Husam Suwaylim in *al-Hayat* (London), 29 December 1999, p. 14.
18. *Frontline*, 5 April 2005, www.pbs.org/wgbh/pages/frontline/press/2311.html (accessed 15 January 2005).
19. See *Haaretz*, 25 September 1984, p. 9, and 30 May 1985.
20. See Yehoshafat Harkabi's letter in *Haaretz*, 11 May 1984, p. 22.
21. Uri Avnery, 'Profile of Ehud Olmert', 16 April 2006, at www.redress.btinternet.co.uk/uavnery154.htm (accessed 20 April 2006).
22. Natour's letter Gershon Baskin, IPCRI, Jerusalem, posted on 4 March 2006, www.place4peace.com/article.php?sid=1120
23. See also letter to the editor by Knesset member Meir Purush, of the orthodox Yahdut Ha'Torah party, in *Haaretz*, 16 April 2006.

Chapter 5

1. Gush Emunim was formally established in February 1974. See Chapters 3 and 4.
2. See *American Zionist*, May/June 1976.
3. The Mishnah, consisting of five chapters, treats the following subjects of *'avoda zara*: (1) prohibitions concerning dealings with Gentiles (who are presumed to be

idolaters) on their festival periods; objects which may or may not be sold or hired to Gentiles as they may be required for idol worship; prohibitions of sale or lease of real estate in the 'land of Israel' to Gentiles; (2) prohibitions arising from Gentiles being suspected of incest and murder; laws concerning articles belonging to Gentiles; (4) the prohibition of actual idolatrous objects (images, shrines) and the way in which these are to be abolished or destroyed; (5) laws about wine produced or handled by non-Jews, which is presumed to have been used, or intended for use, as a libation before an idol. The two Talmuds also convey much information on idolatory, including 'oriental religions, Christianity and Gnosticism', although in medieval times copies were rare, probably due to Christian censors. This led many Jewish scholars to issue declarations to the effect that statements in the tractate *'avoda zara* were directed only against the nations of antiquity, not against Christianity, and to adopt a lenient attitude to some of its prohibitions.

4. A. Ben-Vered in *Haaretz*, 23 October 1979, p. 8.

Chapter 6

1. Article 7 of the Hamas Charter reads: 'The Islamic Resistance Movement is a link in the chain of Jihad against the Zionist occupation. It is tied to the initiation of Jihad by the martyr 'Izzedin al-Qassam and his *mujahid* brothers in 1936. And it is connected to the other episode in the Jihad of the Palestinian people, the Jihad of the Muslim Brotherhood in the 1948 War and the Jihad operations of the Muslim Brotherhood in 1967 and thereafter'.
2. For instance Ahmad 1994; and Hroub 2000.
3. Danny Rubinstein in *Davar*, 19 February 1988, p. 16.
4. Cited in Avishai Margalit, 'The Terror Master', *New York Review of Books*, 5 October 1995, pp. 18-19.
5. It was only in May 1988 that Hamas identified itself as the military wing of the Brotherhood (Ahmad 1994: 19-20).
6. Danny Rubinstein in *New Outlook*, January–February 1993, p. 14.
7. *Middle East Economic Digest*, 8 January, 1993, p. 6.
8. Haim Baram in *Middle East International*, 23 June 1995, p. 4.
9. 'How Israel Misjudges Hamas and Its Terrorism', *Washington Post*, 19 October 1997, quoted in Hroub 2000: 246.
10. Conal Urquhart, 'Hamas in Call to End Suicide Bombings', *Observer*, 9 April 2006.
11. *Guardian,* 27 June 2003, www.guardian.co.uk/israel/Story/0,2763,986666,00. html; see also Tracy McVeigh in the *Observer*, 29 June 2003.
12. Jeff Halper, 'The Power of Saying No', Media Monitor Network, 21 March 2006, http://world.mediamonitors.net/content/view/full/28435.
13. Cited in Urquhart, 'Hamas in Call to End Suicide Bombings'.
14. Chris McGreal, 'Hamas Drops Call for Destruction of Israel from Manifesto', *Guardian*, 12 January 2006, p. 17.
15. Urquhart, 'Hamas in Call to End Suicide Bombings'.
16. Article 7: 'Jews of Palestinian origin are considered Palestinians if they are willing to live peacefully and loyally in Palestine.'
17. Leaflet of March 1988, quoted in Shaul Mishal, 'Paper War – Words Behind Stones: The Intifada in Leaflets', *Jerusalem Quarterly* 51 (1989), in Ahmad 1994: 52.
18. Khaled, Amayreh, 'Joining Forces', *Al-Ahram Weekly*, 1 April 2005.
19. Ibid.

20. Khaled Hroub, quoted in Urquhart, 'Hamas in Call to End Suicide Bombings'.
21. Under this law, some mosques and other specifically religious buildings were exempted.
22. In comparison, lower estimates were given by Jiryis, who states that, according to the British Commission of Enquiry on Palestine 1936, one-sixteenth of the total area of Palestine was *waqf* property (Jiryis 1968: 63).
23. This world of discourses is described in an excellent article entitled 'The Politics of Tour Guiding', in Bowman 1991: 121-34.
24. John Spritzler, 'Why Won't Hamas Tell the World Why There Should Not Be a Jewish State in Palestine?', 26 February 2006, http://newdemocracyworld. org/War/Why%20wont%20Hamas.htm.
25. Ibid.
26. Ibid.
27. Ibid.
28. Ibid.
29. Personal communication.
30. The below were translated by colleagues in Ramallah:
    • From now on the traffic police will stop people and ask for drivers' licenses, insurance papers and *wadu* (ablution, purification ritual before prayer) pitchers for inspection – slightly modified version: A policeman stops a motorist in Gaza and instead of inquiring about his seat belt, asks if he has had *wadu*;
    • From now on, the Palestinian police will be wearing *dishdashes* for uniform;
    • From now on the colour of the Palestinian *knafeh* will be green;
    • The traffic lights will only display a green colour, but this should not confuse the motorists much. For movement, instructions will appear as follows: *Sir, 'ala barakat Allah* (go, with the blessing of God);
    • A special offer from the Call of Heaven restaurant (previously known as Vache's café/bar): special morning prayer meal for half price, with a mug of draft *kharroub* (carob). Note: the *miswak* (plant material that the prophet used in lieu of toothpicks) will be offered free of charge;
    • After forming the government, Khaled Mish'al and Mahmoud Zahhar (Hamas leaders) decide to call Hamas *hamam* (doves);
    • New labour laws with the new Hamas government: office hours shall begin immediately following morning prayer (at sunrise exactly); prayer is to be completed collectively behind the *mudir* (the boss); fasting is enforced on Mondays and Thursdays in governmental offices;
    • Declare your Islam by the end of the month and get a 50 per cent reduction in your *jizyah* (tax) fees;
    • New penalty law under the Hamas government: watching Rotana Clip (singing and dancing): 30 whips; watching a Nancy (famous Arabic singer) clip: 80 whips; not growing a beard: 50 whips; ownership of a satellite dish: stoning to death.

Chapter 7

1. However to judge by recent cover stories in *Time* magazine and *National Geographic* the biblical patriarchs have remained established historical figures. Sarah Belle Dougherty, 'Fiat Lux: Archeology and the Old Testament [Review Article]', *Sunrise* magazine, February/March 2003, www.theosophical.org.uk/Biblunsbd. htm.

2. Not all Christian fundamentalists are literalist, i.e. 'take the Bible literally'. For many of them the debate is not about the *literality* of the Bible, but about its inerrancy; for them the Bible does not contain error; 'In order to avoid imputing error to the Bible [Christian] fundamentalists twist and turn back and forth between literal and non-literal (symbolic, metaphoric, transferred) exegesis' (Barr 1973: 168).
3. *It Ain't Necessarily So: Investigating the Truth of the Biblical Past* is the title of a 2001 book written by Matthew Sturgis, John McCarthy foreword (London: Headline).
4. At a conference in October 1999 at Northwestern University Dever attacked minimalist Biblical scholars as 'anti-Israel', 'anti-Bible' and 'nihilistic' (Davies 2002).
5. Daniel Gavron, 'King David and Jerusalem: Myth and Reality', 6 Sep 2003, www.mfa.gov.il/MFA/MFAArchive/2000_2009/2003/9/King%20David%20and%20Jerusalem-%20Myth%20and%20Reality (accessed 20 May 2006).
6. Ibid.
7. This world of discourses is described in an excellent article entitled 'The Politics of Tour Guiding', Bowman 1991: 121-34.
8. The same mythologised biblical historiography is found, with minor modifications, in Cattan 1981: 19-23, 1988: 3-5.
9. Sheffield Academic Press also published Amit (1999). Some works were published with Routledge.
10. Thomas L. Thompson 'A View from Copenhagen: Israel and the History of Palestine', *The Bible and Interpretation*, www.bibleinterp.com/articles/copenhagen.htm (accessed 20 April 2006).
11. Many scholars are associated with the recent critical biblical scholarship, although not all of them are called minimalists. These include Israel Finkelstein, David Ussishkin, Zeev Herzog, Neil Asher Silberman, Yairah Amit, Gösta Ahlström, John Van Seters, Rainer Albertz, Axel Knauf, Robert Carroll, David Gunn, Etienne Nodet, Herbert Niehr, Graham Auld, Giovanni Garbini, Carlo Zaccagnini, Mario Liverani, Pietro Fronzaroli, Fred Cryer, Tilde Binger, Allan Rosengren, Hans Jørgen Lundager Jensen, Margreet Steiner, Terje Oestigaard, Margit Sjeggestad, Diana Edelman, Flemming Nielsen, Thomas Bolin, Ingrid Hjelm, Greg Doudna, Bernd Diebner and Henk Franken.
12. Thompson 'A View from Copenhagen'. In November 1999 the Internet journal *Miqra* published a piece by Hershel Shanks, the editor of the magazine *The Biblical Archaeology Review*, with accusations of anti-Semitism against Professors Zeev Herzog, Niels Peter Lemche and Philip Davies.

Chapter 8

1. Born in Cork, Ireland.
2. The Vincentian priests, inspired by their patron, St. Vincent de Paul, work with poor and disadvantaged people. Michael also taught for St Mary's College, University of Surrey, for many years – in fact he was the last Vincentian to teach at the College.
3. In recent years Prior was a regular visitor to Jerusalem, partly in connection with a research project on the religious politics of Jerusalem, funded by the Arts and Humanities Research Council (formerly AHRB), UK.

4. On the use of the Bible by one key Zionist leader see, Ben-Gurion 1954; 1972.
5. Prominent Palestinian Christians included the Latin Patriarch of Jerusalem, Michel Sabbah, the Greek Orthodox Archbishop Timotheos, the Anglican Bishop Samir Kafity, and the then Vice-President of Birzeit University, Dr Gabi Baramki.
6. For further discussion of Sabeel's liberation theology, see www.sabeel.nu/media/docs/palestinian_liberation_theology_intro.pdf (accessed 3 February 2005).
7. For works on liberation theology in Latin America, including its origins, historical context and development over the years, see Ellacuria and Sobrino (1993); Sobrino (1987, 1990, 1993); Ellacuria (1976); Boff (1993).
8. The book was also translated into Arabic and published by Cadmus books (Damascus, 2003).
9. The Spanish-language edition of *The Bible and Colonialism*, *La Biblia y el Colonialismo*, came out in 2005 (Buenos Aires: Editorial Canaan).
10. See for instance, Whitelam 1996: 44; Masalha 2000.
11. On the experiences of other 'Western' Christians in the Holy Land, see Prior 2000a.
12. See Michael Prior in the December 2000 issue of *The Link* (published by Americans for Middle East Understanding, New York), reproduced online at www.bintjbeil.com/E/occupation/ameu_bible.html (accessed 25 January 2005).
13. Prior has published many articles on the use of the Bible in journals such as *Scripture Bulletin*, *New Blackfriars*, *Studies in World Christianity*, *The Link*, *Epworth Review*, *Holy Land Studies: A Multidisciplinary Journal*, *Living Stones Bulletin*.
14. Father Leo Lefebure, 'Sacred Violence and Interreligious Conflict: The Background of a Tragedy', *Chicago Studies* 41, no. 1 (Spring 2002), www.everydayzen.org/teachings/essay_sacredviolence.asp.
15. See also Dr Barry Morgan, Archbishop of Wales and Bishop of Llandaff, 'Anniversary Lecture' to the Welsh Centre for International Affairs, 20 November 2003, www.wcia.org.uk/dsp_whatsnew_detail.cfm?Page=whatsnew&WhatsNewId=16&lang=we (accessed 12 February 2005).
16. For a somewhat critical discussion of *Dabru Emet*'s agenda, see also Ellis 2002: pp. 88–9.

Chapter 9

1. For further discussion, see Masalha 1992; 1997.
2. On the post-1967 period, see Masalha 2000.
3. Hess was a secular German Jew and a socialist. See Chapter 1.
4. *Al-Ahram Weekly* online, no. 378 (21–27 May 1998).
5. Said wrote and edited twenty-five books; many are listed in the bibliography.
6. He died on 23 May 2001 at the age of 72 in his Ramallah home after a long illness.
7. Edward Said, 'My Guru', *London Review of Books* 23, no. 24 (13 December 2001), www.lrb.co.uk/v23/n24/said01_.html (accessed 28 September 2005).
8. For a full text of the poem see www.barghouti.com/poets/darwish/bitaqa.asp (accessed 12 October 2004).
9. See Mahmoud Abbas's memoir, *Through Secret Channels: The Road to Oslo* (1995).
10. Edward Said, 'A Road Map to Where?' *London Review of Books* 25, no. 12 (19 June 2003).

11. Ibid.
12. Ibid.
13. Ibid.

Epilogue

1. For further discussion on the biblical archaeology and nation-building in Israel, see Abu El-Haj 2001; Ben-Yehuda 2002.
2. Ronit Lentin, '"No Woman's Law Will Rot This State": the Israeli Racial State and Feminist Resistance', *Sociological Research Online* 9, no. 3 (2004), www.socresonline.org.uk/9/3/lentin.html.
3. Ibid.
4. Shulamit Aloni, 'Perhaps Not the End', *Haaretz*, 26 September 2003, cited in Lentin, '"No Woman's Law Will Rot This State": The Israeli Racial State and Feminist Resistance'.
5. Chris McGreal, 'Prime Minister Pins His Colours to "New Look" Israel', *Guardian*, 5 May 2006.
6. Jeff Halper ' Countdown to Apartheid', www.icahduk.org/art/Countdown%20to%20Apartheid-Halper-0506.htm.
7. Ibid.
8. Jeff Halper, 'The Power of Saying No', Media Monitor Network, 21 March 2006, http://world.mediamonitors.net/content/view/full/28435.
9. Currently published by Edinburgh University Press.
10. Paper by Ilan Pappé presented to Edward Said: Contexts and Consequences conference, Sussex University, 14 May 2004.

Bibliography

Abbas, Mahmoud (Abu Mazen) (1995) *Through Secret Channels: The Road to Oslo* (Reading: Garnet Publishing).

Abu Amr, Ziad (1993) 'Hamas: A Historical and Political Background', *Journal of Palestine Studies* 12, no. 4 (Summer): 5–19.

——— (1994) *Islamic Fundamentalism in the West Bank and Gaza* (Indiana: Indiana University Press).

Abu El-Haj, Nadia (2001) *Facts on the Ground: Archaeological Practice and Territorial Self-fashioning in Israeli Society* (Chicago: University of Chicago Press).

Abu-Lughod, Ibrahim, Roger Heacock and Khaled Nashef (eds) (1991) *The Landscape of Palestine: Equivocal Poetry* (Birzeit, Palestine: Birzeit University Publications).

Abu-Shakrah, Jan Demarest (1985) *Israeli Settler Violence in the Occupied Territories: 1980–1984* (Chicago: Palestine Human Rights Campaign).

Aharoni, Yohanan (1967) *The Land of the Bible* (London: Burns & Oates).

Ahlström, Gösta W. (1993) *The History of Ancient Palestine from the Palaeolithic Period to Alexander's Conquest* (Sheffield: Sheffield Academic Press).

Ahmad, Hisham H. (1994) *From Religious Salvation to Political Transformation: The Rise of Hamas in Palestinian Society* (Jerusalem: Passia).

Akenson, Donald Harman (1992) *God's Peoples: Covenant and Land in South Africa, Israel, and Ulster* (McGill: Queen's Studies in the History of Religion). www.mqup. mcgill.ca/images/site/pix.gif.

Albright, William F. (1946) *From the Stone Age to Christianity* (New York: Doubleday).

——— (1949a) *The Archaeology of Palestine* (Baltimore: Penguin).

——— (1949b) *The Biblical Period from Abraham to Ezra* (New York: Harper & Row).

Al-Faruqi, Isma'il (1986) 'Judaism, Zionism and Islam', in *Judaism or Zionism: What Difference for the Middle East?* (London: Zed Books): 52–65.

Al-Raheb, Hani (1985) *The Zionist Character in the English Novel* (London: Zed Books).

Amit, Yairah (1999) *History and Ideology: An Introduction to Historiography in the Hebrew Bible* (Sheffield: Sheffield Academic Press).

Anderson, Benedict (1991) *Imagined Communities: Reflections on the Origin and Spread of Nationalism* (London and New York: Verso).

Anderson, Irvin H. (2005) *Biblical Interpretation and Middle East Policy: The Promised Land, America, and Israel* (Gainesville, FL: University Press of Florida).

Appleby, R. Scott (ed.) (1997) *Spokesmen for the Despised: Fundamentalist Leaders of the Middle East* (Chicago and London: University Press of Chicago).

Aran, Gideon (1997) 'The Father, the Son and the Holy Land: The Spiritual Authorities of Jewish-Zionist Fundamentalism in Israel', in R. Scott Appleby (ed.), *Spokesmen for the Despised* (Chicago and London: University Press of Chicago): 294-327.

Ariel, Yisrael (1980) 'Devarim Kehavayatam' [Things as They Are], *Tzippiyah I: Anthology of Contemporary Problems, Israel, the Land, and the Temple* (Jerusalem: Hamateh 'Lema'an Ahai ve Rea'ai Publication [Hebrew]).

Al-'Arif, 'Arif (1958-60) *Al-Nakba: Nakbat Bayt al-Maqdis Wal-Firdaws al-Mafqud, 1947-1952* [The Disaster: The Disaster of Jerusalem and the Lost Paradise, 1947-55], 3 vols (Sidon and Beirut: Al-Maktaba al-'Asriyya).

'Al Darchei Mediniyutenu: Mo'atzah 'Olamit Shel Ihud Po'alei Tzion (c.s.)-Din Veheshbon Male (1938) [A Full Report about the World Convention of Ihud Po'alei Tzion, C.S., 21 July-7 August] (Tel Aviv: Central Office of Hitahdut Po'alei Tzion Press [Hebrew]).

Armstrong, Karen (1988) *Holy War: The Crusades and Their Impact on Today's World* (London: Macmillan).

——— (1996) *Jerusalem: One City, Three Faiths* (New York: Ballantine Books).

Aronoff, Myron J. (1985) 'The Institutionalization and Cooptation of a Charismatic, Messianic, Religious-Political Revitalization Movement', in David Newman (ed.), *The Impact of Gush Emunim* (London: Croom Helm): 46-69.

Aronson, Geoffrey (1990) *Israel, Palestinians and the Intifada* (London: Kegan Paul).

Aruri, Naseer H. (ed.) (2001) *Palestinian Refugees and their Right of Return* (London and Sterling, VA: Pluto Press).

——— (2004) 'Professor Edward W. Said, Scholar-Activist', *Holy Land Studies: A Multidisciplinary Journal* 2, no. 2 (March): 140-43.

Ashcroft, Bill (1996) 'Conversation with Edward Said', *New Literature Review* 32 (1996): 3-22.

Ashcroft, Bill, and Pal Ahluwalia (2001) *Edward Said: Routledge Critical Thinkers* (London and New York: Routledge).

Ateek, Naim S. (1989) *Justice and Only Justice: A Palestinian Theology of Liberation* (Maryknoll, NY: Orbis Books).

Ateek, Naim S., and Michael Prior (eds) (1999) *Holy Land – Hollow Jubilee: God, Justice and the Palestinians* (London: Melisende).

Aviner, Shlomo (1982) 'Haumah Veartzah' [The People and its Land], *Artzi*, vol. 1 (Jerusalem [Hebrew]).

——— (1983) 'Yerushat Haaretz Vehabe'ayah Hamusarit' [The Inheritance of the Land and the Moral Problem], *Artzi*, vol. 2 (Jerusalem [Hebrew]).

——— (2000) *Lemikdashkha Tashuv: Yerushalayim Ve-Hamikdash* [You Will Return to Your Temple: Jerusalem and the Temple] (Bet El settlement, West Bank: Sifriyat Hava [Hebrew]).

Barr, James (1973) *The Bible in the Modern World* (London: SCM Press).
———— (1977) *Fundamentalism* (London: SCM Press).
Bar-Yosef, Eitan (2003) 'Christian Zionism and Victorian Culture', *Israel Studies* 8, no. 2 (Summer): 18–44.
Bar-Zohar, Michael (1977) *Ben-Gurion*, vol. 2 (Tel Aviv: 'Am 'Oved [Hebrew]).
Baumgarten, Helga (2005) 'The Three Faces/Phases of Palestinian Nationalism, 1948–2005' *Journal of Palestine Studies* 34, no. 4 (Summer): 25–48.
Beit-Hallahmi, Benjamin (1992) *Original Sins: Reflections on the History of Zionism and Israel* (London: Pluto Press).
Ben-'Ami, Aharon (ed.) (1977) *Sefer Eretz Yisrael Hashlemah* [The Book of the Whole Land of Israel] (Tel Aviv: Friedman Press [Hebrew]).
Ben-Amotz, Dan (1974) *Kriah Tamah* [Reflections in Time] (Tel Aviv: Bitan [Hebrew]).
———— (1982 *Seporei Abu-Nimr* [The Stories of Abu-Nimr] (Tel Aviv: Zmora-Bitan [Hebrew]).
Ben-Dov, M., M. Naor and Z. Aner (1983) *The Western Wall* (Jerusalem: Ministry of Defence Publishing House).
Ben-Ezer, E. (1997) *Courage: The Story of Moshe Dayan* (Tel Aviv: Ministry of Defence).
Ben-Gurion, David (1954) *The Rebirth and Destiny of Israel* (New York: Philosophical Library).
———— (1970) *Recollections* (ed. Thomas R. Bransten) (London: MacDonald).
———— (1972) *Ben-Gurion Looks at the Bible* (London and New York: W.H. Allen).
———— (1971–72) *Zichronot* [Memoirs], vols 3 and 4 (Tel Aviv: 'Am 'Oved [Hebrew]).
———— (1982) *Yoman Hamilhamah* [War Diary], vols 1–3 (Tel Aviv: Misrad Habitahon Publications [Hebrew]).
Ben-Maimon, Moshe (1985) *Misheh Torah, Hu Hayad Hahazakah, Sefer 'Avoda* 9 (Jerusalem: Mosad Harav Kook [Hebrew]).
Benvenisti, Meron (1986) *Conflicts and Contradictions* (New York: Willard Books).
———— (2002) *Sacred Landscape: The Buried History of the Holy Land since 1948* (Berkeley: University of California Press).
Benvenisti, Meron (with Ziad Abu-Zayed and Danny Rubinstein) (1986) *The West Bank Handbook* (Jerusalem: Jerusalem Post).
Ben-Yehuda, Nachman (2002) *Sacrificing Truth: Archaeology and the Myth of Massada* (Amherst, NY: Prometheus Books).
Benziman, 'Uzi (1973) *Yerushalayim: 'Ir Lelo Homah* [Jerusalem: A City without a Wall] (Tel Aviv: Schocken [Hebrew]).
Boff, Clodovis (1993) 'Epistemology and Methodology of the Theology of Liberation', in Ignacio Ellacuria and Jon Sobrino (eds), *Mysterium Liberationis* (Maryknoll, NY: Orbis Books): 57–84.
Bowman, Glenn (1991) 'The Politics of Tour Guiding: Israeli and Palestinian Guides in Israel and the Occupied Territories', in David Harrison (ed.), *Tourism and the Less Developed Countries* (London: Belhaven Press): 121–34.
———— (1999) 'The Exilic Imagination: The Construction of the Landscape of Palestine From Its Outside', in Ibrahim Abu-Lughod, Roger Heacock and Khaled Nashef (eds), *The Landscape of Palestine: Equivocal Poetry* (Birzeit, Palestine: Birzeit University Publications): 53–77.
Brenner, Lenni (1984) *The Iron Wall: Zionist Revisionism from Jabotinski to Shamir* (London and New York: Zed Books).
Bresheet, Haim (1989) 'Self and Other in Zionism: Palestine and Israel in Recent Hebrew Literature', in *Palestine: Profile of an Occupation* (London: Zed Books): 120–52.

Bright, John (1980) *A History of Israel*, 3rd edn (London: SCM).

Broshi, Magen (1987) Religion, Ideology and Politics and their Impact on Palestinian Archaeology', *Israel Museum Journal* 6: 17-32.

Brown, Robert McAfee (1990) *Gustavo Gutierrez: An Introduction to Liberation Theology* (Maryknoll, NY: Orbis Books).

Budeiri, Musa (1995) 'The Nationalist Dimension of Islamic Movements in Palestinian Politics', *Journal of Palestine Studies* 24, no. 3 (Spring 1995): 89-95.

Burgat, François (2003) *Face to Face with Political Islam* (London: I.B. Tauris).

Burge, Gary M. (2003) *Whose Land? Whose Promise?* (Cleveland: Pilgrim Press).

Burke, Kevin F. (2000) *The Ground Beneath the Cross: The Theology of Ignacio Ellacuria* (Washington DC: Georgetown University Press).

Carter, Jimmy (1985) *The Blood of Abraham* (London: Sidgwick & Jackson).

Cattan, Henry (1969) *Palestine, the Arabs and Israel: The Search for Justice* (London: Longman).

—— (1976) *Palestine and International Law: The Legal Aspects of the Arab–Israeli Conflict*, 2nd edn (London: Longman).

—— (1981) *Jerusalem* (London: Croom Helm).

—— (1988) *The Palestine Question* (London and New York: Croom Helm).

Chapman, Colin (2002) *Whose Promised Land?* (Oxford: Lion Publishing).

Chomsky, Noam (1975) *Peace in the Middle East? Reflections of Justice and Nationhood* (Glasgow: Fontana/Collins).

—— (1983) *The Fateful Triangle: The United States, Israel and the Palestinians* (London: Pluto Press).

Cohen, Aharon (1948) 'Our Arab Policy During the War', memorandum dated 10 May 1948, in Giv'at Haviva (Israel), Hashomer Hatza'ir Archives, 10.10.95 (4).

Cohn-Sherbok, Dan (2006) *The Politics of Apocalypse: The History and Influence of Christian Zionism* (Oxford: Oneworld Publications).

Cook, Jonathan (2006) *Blood and Religion: The Unmasking of the Jewish and Democratic State* (London and Ann Arbor, MI: Pluto Press).

Coote, R.B., and Keith W. Whitelam (1987) *The Emergence of Early Israel in Historical Perspective* (Sheffield: Sheffield Academic Press).

Cragg, Kenneth (1992) *The Arab Christian: A History in the Middle East* (London: Mowbray).

Crawford, A.W.C (Lord Lindsay) (1847) *Letters on Egypt, Edom and the Holy Land*, vol. 2 (London: H. Colburn).

Culver, Douglas J. (1995) *Albion and Ariel: British Puritanism and the Birth of Political Zionism* (New York: Peter Lang).

Cygielman, Victor (1977) 'The Clericalization of Israel', *New Outlook* 20, no. 7 (October–November): 28-37.

Darby, J.N. (1962) *Letters of J.N. Darby*, vol. 2 (London: Morish).

Davies, Philip R. (1992) *In Search of Ancient Israel* (Sheffield: Sheffield Academic Press).

—— (1994) 'A House Built on Sand', *Biblical Archaeology Review* 20: 54-5.

—— (2001) 'The Intellectual, the Archaeologist and the Bible', in J. Andrew Dearman and M. Patrick Graham (eds), *The Land That I Will Show You: Essays on the History and Archaeology of the Ancient Near East in Honor of J. Maxwell Miller* (Sheffield: Sheffield Academic Press): 239-52.

—— (2002) 'Minimalism, "Ancient Israel", and Anti-Semitism', *The Bible and Interpretation*, www.bibleinterp.com/articles/Minimalism.htm (accessed 30 March 2006).

——— (2003) 'Final Comments on Minimalism', *The Bible and Interpretation*, June, www.bibleinterp.com/articles/Davies_Final_Comments.htm (accessed 25 April 2006).

Davis, Uri, and Norman Mezvinsky (eds) (1975) *Documents from Israel 1967–1973* (London: Ithaca Press).

Dayan, Moshe (1969) *Mapah Hadashah, Yehasim Aherim* [A New Map, Other Relationships] (Tel Aviv: Maʿariv [Hebrew]).

——— (1976a) *Story of My Life* (London: Weidenfeld & Nicolson).

——— (1976b) 'The Cave of Machpela – The Cave beneath the Mosque', *Qadmoniyot* 36: 129-31 [Hebrew]).

——— (1978) *Lehyot ʿIm HaTamakh*' (Jerusalem: ʿEdanim [Hebrew]). *Living with the Bible* (London: Weidenfeld & Nicolson, 1978).

——— (1981) *Shall the Sword Devour Forever?*' (Jerusalem: ʿEdanim [Hebrew]); in English, *Breakthrough: A Personal Account of the Egypt–Israel Peace Negotiations* (New York: Knopf).

Dayan, Yael (1986) *My Father, His Daughter* (Jerusalem: ʿEdanim [Hebrew]).

Dever, William G. (1995) 'The Death of a Discipline', *Biblical Archaeology Review* (September): 54-8.

——— (2001) *What Did the Biblical Writers Know and When Did They Know It? What Archaeology Can Tell Us about the Reality of Ancient Israel* (Grand Rapids, MI: Wm. B. Eerdmans).

——— (2005) *Did God Have a Wife? Archaeology and Folk Religion in Ancient Israel* (Grand Rapids, MI: Wm. B. Eerdmans).

Doron, Adam (ed.) (1988) *The State of Israel and the Land of Israel* (Tel Aviv: Beit Berl College [Hebrew]).

Dugdale, Blanche E.C. (1936) *Arthur James Balfour: First Earl of Balfour* (London: Hutchinson).

Dumper, Michael (1992) 'Israeli Settlement in the Old City of Jerusalem', *Journal of Palestine Studies* 21, no. 4 (Summer): 32-53.

——— (1994) *Islam and Israel: Muslim Religious Endowments and the Jewish State* (Washington DC: Institute for Palestine Studies).

Dyer, Charles (1991) *The Rise of Babylon: Signs of the End Times* (Wheaton, IL: Tyndale House).

——— (1993) *World News and Biblical Prophecy* (Wheaton, IL: Tyndale House).

Eidelberg, Paul (1983) *Jerusalem vs. Athens: In Quest of a General Theory of Existence* (Lanham, MD: University Press of America).

——— (1988) 'Netrul Ptzatzat Hazman Ha'arvit: Habe'ayah Hademografit' [Neutralisation of the Arab Time-bomb: The Demographic Problem], *Haumah* 90 (Spring): 238-48 [Hebrew].

Eilat, Yisrael (1983) 'The Cancer of the State', in *Davar*, 10 November [Hebrew].

El-Asmar, Fouzi (1986) 'The Portrayal of Arabs in Hebrew Children's Literature', *Journal of Palestine Studies* 16, no. 1 (Autumn): 81-94.

Eliade, Mircea (1958) *Patterns in Comparative Religion* (London and New York: Sheed & Ward).

——— (1959) *The Sacred and the Profane: The Nature of Religion* (New York: Harcourt Brace Jovanovich).

Eliot, George (1876, 1899) *Daniel Deronda* (London).

Elitzur, Yehuda (1978) 'The Borders of Eretz Israel in the Jewish Tradition', in Avner Tomaschoff (ed.), *Whose Homeland* (Jerusalem: The World Zionist Organization): 42-53.

Ellacuria, Ignacio (1976) *Freedom Made Flesh: The Mission of Christ and His Church* (Maryknoll, NY: Orbis Books).

Ellacuria, Ignacio, and Jon Sobrino (eds) (1993) *Mysterium Liberationis: Fundamental Concepts of Liberation Theology* (Maryknoll, NY: Orbis Books).

Ellis, Marc E. (1991) *Oh Jerusalem! The Contested Future of the Jewish Covenant* (Minneapolis: Fortress).

——— (2002) *Israel and Palestine Out of the Ashes: The Search for Jewish Identity in the Twenty-First Century* (London and Sterling, VA: Pluto Press).

Elon, Amos (1971) *The Israelis: Founders and Sons* (London: Weidenfeld & Nicolson).

——— (1996) *Jerusalem: City of Mirrors* (London: Flamingo).

——— (1997a) *A Blood-Dimmed Tide: Dispatches from the Middle East* (New York: Columbia University Press).

——— (1997b) 'Politics and Archaeology', in Neil Asher Silberman and David B. Small, *The Archaeology of Israel* (Sheffield: Sheffield Academic Press): 35-47.

Epstein, Isidore (1990) *Judaism: A Historical Presentation* (London: Penguin).

Evans, Mike (1980) *Israel, America's Key to Survival* (Plainfield, NJ: Haven Books).

Evron, Boaz (1995) *Jewish State or Israeli Nation?* (Bloomington: Indiana University Press). Hebrew version: *Hahisbon Haleumi* [The National Reckoning] (1986).

Finkelstein, Israel, and Neil Asher Silberman (2001) *The Bible Unearthed: Archaeology's New Vision of Ancient Israel and the Origin of its Sacred Texts* (Free Press: New York).

Finkelstein, Norman G. (1995) *Image and Reality of the Israel–Palestine Conflict* (London and New York: Verso).

Flapan, Simha (1987) *The Birth of Israel: Myths and Realities* (New York: Pantheon Books).

Fox, Marvin (1971) 'Trinity', *Encyclopaedia Judaica* VII (Jerusalem: Keter): 671-2.

Friedman, Robert I. (1992) *Zealots for Zion: Inside Israel's West Bank Settlement Movement* (New York: Random House).

Gandulla, Bernardo (2005a) *Los Hebreos en el Gran Canaán: del Bronce Antiguo al Bronce Tardío* (Buenos Aries: Editorial Canaán).

——— (2005b) 'The Bible and Colonialist Discourse', review of Michael Prior's *La Biblia y el Colonialismo: una crítica moral*, *Holy land Studies: A Multidisciplinary Journal* 4, no. 1 (November): 103-4.

Gellner, Ernest (1983) *Nations and Nationalism* (London: Blackwell).

Gerstner, John (1991) *Wrongly Dividing the Word of Truth* (Brentwood, TN: Wolgemuth & Hyatt).

Gertz, Nurith (2000) *Myths in Israeli Culture: Captives of a Dream* (London: Vallentine Mitchell).

Glock, Albert E. (1999) 'Cultural Bias in Archaeology', in Tomis Kapitan (ed.), *Archaeology, History and Culture in Palestine and the Near East* (Atlanta, GA: Scholars Press and American Schools of Oriental Research): 324-42.

Goitein, S.D. (1974) *Jews and Arabs: Their Contacts through the Ages*, 3rd edn (New York: Schocken).

Golani, Moti (1998) *Israel in Search of a War: The Sinai Campaign 1955–1956* (Guildford: Sussex Academic Press).

Goldberg, Louis (1982) *Turbulence over the Middle East* (Neptune, NJ: Loizeaux Brothers).

Gorenberg, Gershom (2000) *The End of Days: Fundamentalism and the Struggle for the Temple Mount* (Oxford and New York: Oxford University Press).

Gorny, Yosef (1994) *The State of Israel in Jewish Public Thought* (London: Macmillan).

———— (1987) *Zionism and the Arabs, 1882–1948* (Oxford: Clarendon Press).

Graham, Billy (1983) *Approaching Hoofbeats: The Four Horsemen of the Apocalypse* (Waco: Word).

———— (1992) *Storm Warning* (Milton Keynes: Word).

Grossman, David (1988) *The Yellow Wind* (London: Jonathan Cape).

Guedalla, Philip (1925) *Napoleon and Palestine* (London: George Allen & Unwin).

Gunner, Göran (2003) '9/11 and Armageddon: The Christian Right and George W. Bush', *Holy Land Studies: A Multidisciplinary Journal* 2, no. 1: 35-50.

Gurvitz, Yehuda, and Shmuel Navon (eds) (1953) *What Story Will I Tell My Children?* (Tel Aviv: Amihah).

Haddad, Hassan, and Donald Wagner (eds) (1986) *All in the Name of the Bible* (Brattleboro, VT: Amana Books).

Hagee, John C. (2001) *The Battle for Jerusalem* (Nashville: Thomas Nelson).

Haija, Rammy M. (2006) 'The Armageddon Lobby: Dispensationalist Christian Zionism and the Shaping of US Policy Towards Israel-Palestine', *Holy Land Studies, A Multidisciplinary Journal* 5, no. 1 (May): 75-95.

Halevi, Ilan (1987) *A History of the Jews* (London: Zed Books).

Hall, Martin (1984) 'The Burden of Tribalism: The Social Context of Southern African Iron Age Studies', *American Antiquities* 49, no. 3: 455-67.

Halsell, Grace (1986) *Prophecy and Politics: Militant Evangelists on the Road to Nuclear War* (Westport, CT: Lawrence Hill).

Hamas (1988) *Mithaq Harakat al-Muqawama al-Islamiyya* [The Charter of the Islamic Resistance Movement] (*Filastin*).

Harcourt, Hugh R. (1997) 'In Search of the Emperor's New Clothes: Reflections on Rights in the Palestine Conflict', in Tomis Kapitan (ed.), *Philosophical Perspectives on the Israeli–Palestinian Conflict* (New York: M.E. Sharpe): 282-96.

Harkabi, Yehoshafat (1986) *Hakhra'ot Goraliyot* [Fateful Decisions] (Tel Aviv: 'Am 'Oved [Hebrew]).

Hart, William D. (2000) *Edward Said and the Religious Effects of Culture* (Cambridge: Cambridge University Press).

Heller, Yosef (1984) *Bamavak Lemedinah: Hamediniyut Hatziyonit Bashanim 1936–48* [The Struggle for the State: The Zionist Policy 1936-48] (Jerusalem [Hebrew]).

Herzog, Chaim (1989) *Heroes of Israel: Profiles of Jewish Courage* (London: Weidenfeld & Nicolson).

Herzog, Zeev (1999) 'Hatanach: Ein Mimtzaim Bashetah' ['The Bible: There Are No Findings on the Ground', also often translated into English as 'Deconstructing the Walls of Jericho'], *Haaretz*, 29 October 1999: 6-8 [Hebrew].

———— (2001) 'Deconstructing the Walls of Jericho: Biblical Myth and Archaeological Reality', *Prometheus* 4: 72-93.

Hess, Yisrael (1980) 'Mitzvat Hagenocide Batorah' [The Genocide Commandment in the Torah], *Bat Kol* (26 February) [Hebrew].

Hillenbrand, Carole (1999) *The Crusades: Islamic Perspectives* (Edinburgh: Edinburgh University Press).

Hirst, David (1984) *The Gun and the Olive Branch* (London: Faber & Faber).

Hitti, Philip K. (1956) *History of the Arabs* (London and New York: Macmillan and St. Martin's Press).

Hobsbawm, Eric (1990) *Nations and Nationalism since 1780* (Cambridge: Cambridge University Press).

Hobsbawm, Eric and Terence Ranger (1996) *The Invention of Tradition* (Cambridge: Cambridge University Press).

Hroub, Khalid (1994) 'Harakat Hamas Bein al-Sulta al-Filastiniya wa-Israeel': Min Muthallath al-Quwa al-Mitraqa wa-sindan', *Majallat al-Dirasat al-Filastiniyah* 18 (Autumn): 24-37.

―――― (2000) *Hamas: Political Thought and Practice* (Washington DC: Institute for Palestine Studies).

―――― (2004) 'Hamas after Shaykh Yasin and Rantisi', *Journal of Palestine Studies* 33, no. 4 (Summer): 21-38.

Hunt, Dave (1983) *Peace, Prosperity and the Coming Holocaust: The New Age Movement in Prophecy* (Eugene, OR: Harvest House).

―――― (1990) *Global Peace and the Rise of Antichrist* (Eugene, OR: Harvest House).

Hunter, Alastair G., and Philip R. Davies (eds) (2002) *Sense and Sensitivity: Essays on Reading the Bible in Memory of Robert Carroll* (Sheffield: Sheffield Academic Press).

Hyamson, Albert M. (1950) *Palestine under the Mandate* (London: Methuen).

Idinopulos, A., and A. Thomas (1991) *Jerusalem Blessed, Jerusalem Cursed: Jews, Christians and Moslems in the Holy City from David's Time to Our Own* (Chicago: Ivan R. Dee).

Ihud Po'alei Tzion (1938) *'Al Darchei Mediniyutenu: Mo'atzah 'Olamit Shel Ihud Po'alei Tzion (c.s.)-Din Vehesbon Male, 21 July-7 August* [A Full Report about the World Convention of Ihud Po'alei Tzion, C.S.] (Tel Aviv: Central Office of Hitahdut Po'alei Tzion Press).

Inbari, Pinchas (1984) 'Underground: Political Background and Psychological Atmosphere', *New Outlook* (June-July): 10-11.

International Christian Embassy in Jerusalem (1996) 'International Christian Zionist Congress Proclamation, Affirmation of Christian Zionism', 25-29 February 1996; 'Why Should Christians Be Friends of Israel?', Christian Friends of Israel leaflet, www.netvision.net.il/php/tehilah.

James, Edgar C. (1991a) *Arabs, Oil and Armageddon* (Chicago: Moody Press).

―――― (1991b) *Armageddon and the New World Order* (Chicago: Moody Press).

Jensen, Michael Irving (2006) '"Re-Islamising" Palestinian Society "From Below": Hamas and Higher Education in Gaza', *Holy Land Studies: A Multidisciplinary Journal* 5, no. 1 (May): 57-74.

Jewish Agency Executive (1938) Protocol of the Jewish Agency Executive meeting of 12 June, vol. 28, no. 53 (Jerusalem: Central Zionist Archives [Hebrew]).

Jiryis, Sabri (1968) *The Arabs in Israel* (Beirut: Institute for Palestine Studies).

Joffe, Lawrence (1996) *Keesing's Guide to the Mid-East Peace Process* (London: Cartermill).

Johnson, Paul (1993) *A History of the Jews* (London: Phoenix).

Jones, Clive (1999) 'Ideo-Theology and the Jewish State: From Conflict to Conciliation?', *British Journal of Middle Eastern Studies* 26, no. 1: 9-26.

Juergensmeyer, Mark (ed.) (1992) *Violence and the Sacred in the Modern World* (London: Frank Cass).

Kahane, Meir (1980) *Lesikim Be'enekhem* [They Shall Be Strings in Your Eyes] (Jerusalem: Hamakhon Lara'ayon Hayehudi [Hebrew]).

Kanaana, Sharif (1992) *Still on Vacation! The Eviction of the Palestinians in 1948* (Ramallah and Jerusalem: Shaml-Palestinian Diaspora and Refugee Centre).

Kapitan, Tomis (ed.) (1999) *Archaeology, History and Culture in Palestine and the Near East: Essays in Memory of Albert E. Glock* (Atlanta, GA: Scholars Press and American Schools of Oriental Research).

Kaplan, Robert (1993) *The Arabists: The Romance of an American Elite* (New York: Free Press).

Katz, Jacob (1961) *Exclusiveness and Tolerance: Studies in Jewish–Gentile Relations in Medieval and Modern Times* (Oxford: Oxford University Press).

Katznelson, Berl (1949) *Ketavim* [Writings], vol. 12 (Tel Aviv: Mapai Publication [Hebrew]).

Kellner, Menachem (1991) *Maimonides on Judaism and the Jewish People* (New York: State University of New York Press).

Kenyon, Frederic G. (1958) *Our Bible and the Ancient Manuscripts* (New York: Harper).

Kenyon, Kathleen (1960, 1970) *Archeology in the Holy Land* (New York: Praeger).

Khalidi, Rashid (1992) 'The Future of Arab Jerusalem', *British Journal of Middle Eastern Studies* 19, no. 2: 139-40.

——(1997) *Palestinian Identity: The Construction of Modern National Consciousness* (New York: Colombia University Press).

Khalidi, Walid (ed.) (1992) *All That Remains: The Palestinian Villages Occupied and Depopulated by Israel in 1948* (Washington DC: Institute for Palestine Studies).

——(1999) *Deir Yassin: Friday, 9 April 1948* (Beirut: Institute for Palestine Studies [Arabic]).

——(ed.) (2005) *From Heaven to Conquest: Reading in Zionism and the Palestine Problem until 1948* (Washington DC: Institute for Palestine Studies).

Kim, Hanna (1984) 'To Annihilate Amalek', *'Al-Hamishmar*, 12 March [Hebrew].

Kimmerling, Baruch (1999) 'Religion, Nationalism and Democracy in Israel', *Constellations* 6, no. 3: 339-63. Hebrew version: *Zmanim* (Tel Aviv University School of History) 50 (December 1994).

——(2003) *Politicide: Ariel Sharon's War against the Palestinians* (London and New York: Verso).

Kletter, Raz (2003) 'A Very General Archaeologist: Moshe Dayan and Israeli Archaeology', *Journal of Hebrew Scriptures* 4, no. 5, www.arts.ualberta.ca/JHS/abstracts-articles.html#A27.

Kohn, Hans (1958) 'Zion and the Jewish National Idea', *Menorah Journal*, 46, nos 1 and 2; also in Walid Khalidi (ed.), *From Heaven to Conquest: Reading in Zionism and the Palestine Problem until 1948* (Washington DC: Institute for Palestine Studies): 807-39.

Kook, Tzvi Yehuda (1982) 'Bein 'Am Veartzo' [Between People and Its Land] *Artzi* 2 (Spring): 15-23 [Hebrew].

Kristiansen, Wendy (1999) 'Challenge and Counterchallenge: Hamas's Response to Oslo', *Journal of Palestine Studies* 28, no. 3 (Spring): 19-36.

Leaman, Oliver (1990) *Moses Maimonides* (London and New York: Routledge).

Leibowitz, Yeshayahu (1987) *The Faith of Maimonides* (New York: Adama Books).

Lemche, Niels Peter (1991) *The Canaanites and Their Land* (Sheffield: Sheffield Academic Press).

——(1993) 'The Old Testament – a Hellenistic Book?', *Scandinavian Journal of the Old Testament* 7: 163-93.

——(1995) *Ancient Israel: A New History of the Israelite Society* (Sheffield: Sheffield Academic Press).

——(1998) *The Israelites in History and Tradition* (Louisville: Westminster John Knox Press).

——(2000) 'Ideology and the History of Ancient Israel', *Scandinavian Journal of the Old Testament* 14, no. 2: 165-93.

—— (2003) 'Conservative Scholarship – Critical Scholarship: Or How Did We Get Caught by This Bogus Discussion', *The Bible and Interpretation* (September), www. bibleinterp.com/articles/Conservative_Scholarship.htm.

Leor, Dov (1986) 'The Arabs and Us', *Artzi* 4 (Spring) [Hebrew].

Lewis, Bernard (1973) *Islam in History: Ideas, Men and Events in the Middle East* (London: Alcove Press).

Lienesch, Michael (1993) *Redeeming America: Piety and Politics in the New Christian Right* (Chapel Hill, NC: North Carolina Press).

Lindsey, Hal (1970) *The Late Great Planet Earth* (London: Lakeland).

—— (1973) *Satan is Alive and Well on Planet Earth* (London: Lakeland).

—— (1981) *The 1980s: Countdown to Armageddon* (New York: Bantam).

—— (1983) *Israel and the Last Days* (Eugene, OR: Harvest House)

—— (1986) *Combat Faith* (New York: Bantam).

—— (1989) *The Road to Holocaust* (New York: Bantam).

—— (1995) *The Final Battle* (Palos Verdes, CA: Western Front).

—— (1997) *The Apocalypse Code* (Palos Verdes, CA: Western Front).

Litvinoff, Barnet (ed.) (1983) *The Letters and Papers of Chaim Weizmann*, vol. I, Series B (Jerusalem: Israel University Press).

Lockman, Zachary, and Joel Beinin (eds) (1999) *Intifada: The Palestinian Upspring against Israeli Occupation* (London: I.B. Tauris).

Long, Burke O. (1997) *Planting and Reaping Albright: Politics, Ideology, and Interpreting the Bible* (Pennsylvania: Penn State University Press).

—— (2003) *Imagining the Holy Land: Maps, Models and Fantasy Travels* (Bloomington and Indianapolis: Indiana University Press).

Lustick, Ian (1980) *Arabs in the Jewish State*: *Israel's Control of a National Minority* (Austin, TX: University of Texas Press).

—— (1987) 'Israel's Dangerous Fundamentalists', *Foreign Policy* 68: 118–39.

—— (1988) *For the Land and the Lord: Jewish Fundamentalism in Israel* (New York: Council on Foreign Relations).

McDonagh, John (2004) 'The Philistines as Scapegoats: Narratives and Myths in the Invention of Ancient Israel and in Modern Critical Theory', *Holy Land Studies: A Multidisciplinary Journal* 3, no. 1 (May): 93–111.

MacDonald, James (1951) *My Mission in Israel, 1948–1951* (London: Gollancz).

McDowall, David (1990) *Palestine and Israel: The Uprising and Beyond* (London: I.B. Tauris).

—— (1994) *The Palestinians: The Road to Nationhood* (London: Minority Rights Publications).

McGowan, A. Daniel, and Marc H. Ellis (eds) (1998) *Remembering Deir Yassin: The Future of Israel and Palestine* (New York: Olive Branch Press).

Mahoney, John F. (1992) 'About This Issue', *The Link* (Americans for Middle East Understanding) 25, no. 4 (October/November).

Mansfield, Stephen (2003) *The Faith of George W. Bush* (New York: Tarcher/Penguin).

Marsden, George (1991) *Understanding Fundamentalism and Evangelicalism* (Grand Rapids, MI: Eerdmans).

Masalha, Nur (1988) 'On Recent Hebrew and Israeli Sources for the Palestinian Exodus, 1947–49', *Journal of Palestine Studies* 18, no. 1 (Autumn): 121–37.

—— (1990) (with Franklin Vivekananda) 'Israeli Revisionist Historiography of the 1948 and its Palestinian Exodus', *Scandinavian Journal of Development Alternatives* 9, no. 1 (March): 71–9.

——— (1992) *Expulsion of the Palestinians: The Concept of 'Transfer' Zionist Political Thought, 1882–1948* (Washington DC: Institute for Palestine Studies).

——— (1997) *A Land without a People* (London: Faber & Faber).

——— (2000) *Imperial Israel and the Palestinians: The Politics of Expansion* (London and Sterling VA: Pluto Press).

——— (2002) 'Reinventing Maimonides: From Universalist Philosopher to Religious Fundamentalist (1967–2002)', *Holy Land Studies: A Multidisciplinary Journal* 1, no. 1 (September): 85-117.

——— (2003) *The Politics of Denial: Israel and the Palestinian Refugee Problem* (London and Sterling VA: Pluto Press).

——— (ed.) (2005) *Catastrophe Remembered: Palestine, Israel and the Internal Refugees: Essays in Memory of Edward W. Said* (London: Zed Books).

Massad, Joseph (2003) 'Edward Said's Journey to Ithaka', *Al-Ahram Weekly* online (5-9 October), http://weekly.ahram.org.eg/2003/659/op11.htm.

Matar, Nabil I. (1989) 'Protestantism, Palestine and Partisan Scholarship', *Journal of Palestine Studies* 18: 52-70.

——— (1999) 'Renaissance Cartography and the Question of Palestine', in Ibrahim Abu-Lughod, Roger Heacock and Khaled Nashef (eds), *The Landscape of Palestine: Equivocal Poetry* (Birzeit, Palestine: Birzeit University Publications): 139-51.

Merkley, Paul C. (1998) *The Politics of Christian Zionism, 1891–1948* (London: Frank Cass).

Meskell, L. (ed.) (1998) *Archaeology under Fire: Nationalism, Politics and Heritage in the Eastern Mediterranean and Middle East* (London and New York: Routledge).

Michelson, Menachem, et al. (1996) *Jewish Holy Places in the Land of Israel* (Tel Aviv: Ministry of Defence).

Middle East Council of Churches (1988) *What is Western Fundamentalist Christian Zionism?* (Limassol: Middle East Council of Churches).

Milton-Edwards, Beverley (1999) *Islamic Politics in Palestine* (London: I.B. Tauris).

Milton-Edwards, Beverley, and Alastair Crooke (2004) 'Elusive Ingredient: Hamas and the Peace Process', *Journal of Palestine Studies* 33, no. 4 (Summer): 39-52.

Mishal, Shaul, and Avraham Sela (2000) *The Palestinian Hamas: Vision, Violence and Coexistence* (New York: Columbia University Press).

Mitchell, J.T. (2003) 'A Critical Conscience: Remembering Edward Said' (1 October), http://chronicle.com/free/2003/10/2003100105n.htm.

Moody, William R. (1900) *The Life of Dwight L. Moody* (Murfreesboro, TN: Sword for the Lord).

Morris, Benny (1986a) 'Yosef Weitz and the Transfer Committees, 1948-49', *Middle Eastern Studies* 22, no. 4 (October): 522-561.

——— (1986b) 'Operation Dani and the Palestinian Exodus from Lydda and Ramle in 1948', *Middle East Journal* 40, no. 1 (Winter): 82-109.

——— (1986c) 'The Causes and Character of the Arab Exodus from Palestine: The Israel Defence Forces Intelligence Branch Analysis of June 1948', *Middle Eastern Studies* 22 (January): 5-19.

——— (1986d) 'Jewish Attacks Caused Most of Arab Exodus', *Jerusalem Post*, March 2: 1.

——— (1987) *The Birth of the Palestinian Refugee Problem, 1947–1949* (Cambridge: Cambridge University Press).

——— (1990) *1948 and After* (Oxford: Clarendon Press).

——— (1995) 'Falsifying the Record: A Fresh Look at Zionist Documentation of 1948', *Journal of Palestine Studies* 24, no. 3 (Spring): 44-62.

——— (1999) 'Operation Hiram Revisited: A Correction', *Journal of Palestine Studies* 28, no. 2 (Winter): 68-76.

——— (2000) *Righteous Victims: A History of the Zionist–Arab Conflict, 1881–1999* (London: John Murray).

Murray, Iain H. (1971) *The Puritan Hope: Revival and the Interpretation of Prophecy* (Edinburgh: Banner of Truth).

Myers, David N. (1995) *Reinventing the Jewish Past: European Jewish Intellectuals and the Zionist Return to History* (New York: Oxford University Press).

Netanyahu, Binyamin (1993) *A Place among the Nations* (London: Bantam).

Newman, David (1982) *Jewish Settlement in the West Bank: The Role of Gush Emunim*, Occasional Paper 16 (Durham: Centre for Middle Eastern and Islamic Studies, University of Durham).

——— (ed.) (1985) *The Impact of Gush Emunim* (London: Croom Helm).

——— (1994) 'Gush Emunim (Bloc of the Faithful)', in *New Encyclopedia of Zionism and Israel*, vol. 1 (London and Toronto: Associated University Presses).

Nimni, Ephraim (2003) *The Challenge of Post-Zionism: Alternatives to Israeli Fundamentalist Politics* (London and New York: Zed Books).

Nisan, Mordechai (1983) 'Judaism and Politics', *Jerusalem Post*, 13 January.

——— (1984) in *Kivunim* (official publication of the World Zionist Organization) 24 (August): 151-6.

——— (1987) *Hamedinah Hayehudit Vehabe'ayah Ha'arvit* [The Jewish State and the Arab Problem] (Tel Aviv: Hadar [Hebrew]).

——— (1991) 'Arab Hostages', *Modelet* 28-29 (February–March): 21.

——— (1990/91) 'The Persian Gulf Crisis and the New Order in the Middle East', *Haumah* 102 (Winter): 139-41 [Hebrew].

——— (1992) *Toward a New Israel: The Jewish State and the Arab Question* (New York: AMS Press [in Hebrew, 1986]).

Omran, Abdel-Rahim (1980) *Population in the Arab World: Problems and Prospects* (New York and London: Croom Helm).

Osband, Linda (1989) *Famous Travellers to the Holy Land* (London: Prion).

Oz, Amos (1988) 'The Meaning of Homeland', *New Outlook* 31, no. 1 (January); reproducing an article originally published in the daily *Davar* in 1967.

Pappé, Ilan (1992) *The Making of the Arab–Israeli Conflict, 1947–1951* (London: I.B. Tauris).

——— (2004a) *A History of Modern Palestine: One Land, Two Peoples* (Cambridge: Cambridge University Press).

——— (2004b) 'Palestine and Truth, Culture and Imperialism: The Legacy of Edward W. Said', *Holy Land Studies: A Multidisciplinary Journal* 2, no. 2 (March): 135-9.

Pearlman, Moshe (1965) *Ben-Gurion Looks Back* (London: Weidenfeld & Nicolson).

Peres, Shimon (1993) *The New Middle East* (Dorset: Element Books).

Peri, Yoram (1984) 'Expulsion is not the Final Stage', *Davar*, 3 August [Hebrew].

Peteet, Julie (2005) 'Words as Interventions: Naming in the Palestine-Israel Conflict', *Third World Quarterly* 26, no. 1 (March): 153-72.

Pichnik, Rabbi (ed.) (1968) *Shanah Beshanah, 5728* [Year by Year] (Jerusalem: Hekhal Shlomo Publication [Hebrew]).

Piterberg, Gabriel (2001) 'Erasures', *New Left Review* 10 (July–August): 31-46.

Prior, Michael (1989) *Paul the Letter Writer and the Second Letter of Timothy* (London: Continuum).

——— (1995) *Jesus the Liberator: Nazareth Liberation Theology* (Sheffield: Sheffield Academic Press).

——— (1997) *The Bible and Colonialism: A Moral Critique* (Sheffield: Sheffield Academic Press).

——— (1997a) 'Settling for God', *Middle East International* 565 (19 December): 20-21.

——— (1998) 'The Moral Problem of the Land Traditions of the Bible', in Michael Prior (ed.), *Western Scholarship and the History of Palestine* (London: Melisende): 41-81.

——— (1999a) 'The Bible and the Redeeming Idea of Colonialism', in *Studies in World Christianity* 5, no. 2: 129-55.

——— (1999b) 'Zionism and the Bible', in Naim Ateek and Michael Prior (eds), *Holy Land – Hollow Jubilee* (Maryknoll, NY: Orbis Books): 69-88.

——— (1999c) *Zionism and the State of Israel: A Moral Inquiry* (London: Routledge).

——— (ed.) (2000a) *They Came and They Saw: Western Christian Experiences of the Holy Land* (London: Melisende).

——— (2000b) 'Zionist Ethnic Cleansing: the Fulfilment of Biblical Prophecy?' *Epworth Review* 27: 49-60.

——— (2001) 'The Right to Expel: The Bible and Ethnic Cleansing', in H. Aruri (ed.), *Palestinian Refugees and their Right of Return* (London and Sterling, VA: Pluto Press): 9-35.

——— (2002) 'Ethnic Cleansing and the Bible: A Moral Critique', *Holy Land Studies: A Multidisciplinary Journal* 1, no. 1 (September): 44-5.

——— (2003a) 'A Moral Reading of the Bible in Jerusalem', in Thomas L. Thompson (ed.), *Jerusalem in Ancient History and Tradition* (London and New York: T. & T. Clark): 16-48.

——— (2003b) 'En paz, en el lugar descanso: Una appreciation de Edward W. Said', in Saad Chedid (ed.), *El Legado de Edward W. Said* (Buenos Aires: Editorial Canaan): 65-82.

——— (2003c) 'The State of the Art: Biblical Scholarship and the Holy Land', *Holy Land Studies: A Multidisciplinary Journal* 1, no. 1 (March): 192-218.

——— (2004a) *Speaking the Truth about Zionism and Israel* (London: Melisende).

——— (2004b) 'The State of Israel and Jerusalem in the Jewish-Christian Dialogue: A Monologue in Two Voices', *Holy Land Studies: A Multidisciplinary Journal* 3, no. 2 (May): 145-70.

——— (2005) *La Biblia y el Colonialismo: una crítica moral* (Buenos Aires: Editorial Canaan).

——— (2006) 'Reading the Bible with the Eyes of the Canaanites: In Homage to Edward Said', in *A Living Stone: Selected Essays & Addresses*, ed. Duncan Macpherson (London: Melisende): 273-96.

Prior, Michael, and William Taylor (eds) (1994) *Christians in the Holy Land* (London: World of Islam Festival Trust).

Qumsiyeh, Mazin B. (2004) *Sharing the Land of Canaan: Human Rights and Israel-Palestinian Struggle* (London: Pluto Press).

Rachlevsky, Seffe (1998) *Hamuro Shel Mashiah* [Messiah's Donkey] (Tel Aviv: Yedi'ot Aharonot).

Rainey, A. (1963) 'A Canaanite at Ugarit', *Israel Exploration Journal* 13: 43-5.

Rajwan, Nissim (1968) 'Aspects of Judeo-Arabic Culture', *New Outlook* 11, no. 1: 31-42.

Ram, Uri (1995) 'Zionist Historiography and the Invention of Modern Jewish Nationhood: The Case of Benzion Dinur', *History and Memory* 7, no. 1: 91-124.

Rash, Yehoshu'a (1986) 'Uriel Tal's Legacy', *Gesher* 32, no. 114: 71-83 [Hebrew].

Rausch, David A. (1979) *Zionism within Early American Fundamentalism, 1878-191: A Convergence of Two Traditions* (New York: Mellen Press).

———(1993) *Fundamentalist Evangelicals and Anti-Semitism* (Valley Forge: Trinity Press International).

Ravitzky, Aviezer (1996) *Messianisn, Zionism and Jewish Religious Radicalism* (Chicago and London: University of Chicago Press).

Raz-Krakotzkin, Amnon (1993–94) 'Exile within Sovereignty', *Teoriya ve-Bekorit* [Theory and Criticism], 2 parts, 4: 23–56 and 5: 113–32 [Hebrew].

Riddell, Peter (2001) 'From Qu'ran to Contemporary Politics: Hamas and the Role of the Sacred Scripture', in Christopher Partridge (ed.), *Fundamentalism* (Carlisle: Paternoster Press).

Roberts, Keith (1990) *Religion in Sociological Perspective* (Belmont, CA: Wadsworth).

Rogan, Eugene L., and Avi Shlaim (eds) (2001) *The War for Palestine: Rewriting the History of 1948* (Cambridge: Cambridge University Press).

Rolef, Susan Hattis (ed.) (1993) *Political Dictionary of the State of Israel* (New York: Macmillan).

Ronel, Eti (1984) 'Inside Israel: The Battle for Temple Mount', *New Outlook*, February 1984: 11–14.

Rose, John (2004) *The Myths of Zionism* (London: Pluto Press).

Rosen, Moishe (1991) *Beyond the Gulf War: Overture to Armageddon* (San Bernardino: Here's Life Publishers).

Rosenthal, Erwin I.J. (1961) *Judaism and Islam* (London and New York: Thomas Yoseloff).

Rosenthal, Franz (1975) *The Classical Heritage of Islam* (London: Routledge & Kegan Paul).

Rosenthal, Gilbert (ed.) (1990) *Maimonides: His Wisdom for Our Time* (New York: Walker).

Rubinstein, Amnon (1980) *Mehertzel 'Ad Gush Emunim Uvehazarah* [From Herzl to Gush Emunim and Back Again] (Tel Aviv: Schocken Press [Hebrew]).

Rubinstein, Danny (1982) *Mi La-H' Elai: Gush Emunim* [On the Lord's Side: Gush Emunim] (Tel Aviv: Hakibbutz Hameuhad [Hebrew]).

Ruether, Rosemary Radford (1998) 'Christianity and the Future of the Israeli–Palestinian Relations', in Daniel McGowan and Marc H. Ellis (eds), *Remembering Deir Yassin: The Future of Israel and Palestine* (Yew York: Olive Branch Press): 112–22.

Ruether, Rosemary Radford, and Herman J. Ruether (2002) *The Wrath of Jonah: The Crisis of Religious Nationalism in the Israeli–Palestinian Conflict*, 2nd edn (Minneapolis: Fortress Press).

Runciman, Steven (1954) *A History of the Crusades*, vol. 1 (Cambridge: Cambridge University Press).

Ruthven, Malise (2003) 'Edward Said: Controversial Literary Critic and Bold Advocate of the Palestinian Cause in America', *Guardian*, 26 September.

Sabbagh, Karl (2006) *Palestine: A Personal History* (London: Atlantic Books).

Sachar, Howard M (1976) *A History of Israel: From the Rise of Zionism to Our Time* (New York: Alfred A. Knopf).

Sahliyeh, Emile (1988) *In Search of Leadership: West Bank Politics since 1967* (Washington DC: Brookings Institution Press).

———(1995) 'A Comparative Analysis of the Islamic Movement in the West Bank, the Lebanese Shi'a, and the Radical Sikhs of India', in Martin E. Marty and Scott Appleby (eds), *Fundamentalisms Comprehended* (Chicago: University of Chicago Press).

Said, Edward W. (1978) *Orientalism* (London: Routledge & Kegan Paul).

———(1980) *The Question of Palestine* (London: Routledge & Kegan Paul).

—— (1981) *Covering Islam* (New York: Vintage).

—— (1986a) *After the Last Sky* (with Photographs by Jean Mohr) (London: Faber & Faber).

—— (1986b) 'Michael Walzer's *Exodus and Revolution*: A Canaanite Reading', *Arab Studies Quarterly* 8, no. 3 (Summer): 289–303.

—— (1988) 'Michael Walzer's *Exodus and Revolution*: A Canaanite Reading', in Edward Said and Christopher Hitchens (eds), *Blaming the Victims: Spurious Scholarship and the Palestinian Question* (London and New York: Verso): 161–78.

—— (1995a) *Peace and its Discontents: Gaza-Jericho 1993–1995* (New York: Vintage).

—— (1995b) *The Politics of Dispossession: The Struggle for Palestinian Self-Determination 1969–1994* (London: Vintage).

—— (1999a) *Out of Place: A Memoir* (London: Granta Books).

—— (1999b) 'Palestine: Memory, Invention and Space', in Ibrahim Abu-Lughod, Roger Heacock and Khaled Nashef (eds), *The Landscape of Palestine: Equivocal Poetry* (Birzeit, Palestine: Birzeit University Publications): 3–20.

—— (2000a) *Reflections on Exile and Other Literary and Cultural Essays* (London: Granta).

—— (2000b) 'Palestinians under Siege', *London Review of Books*, 14 December.

—— (2002) 'Real Change Means *People* Must Change: Immediate Imperative', *CounterPunch*, 21 December.

—— (2003) 'A Road Map to Where?' *London Review of Books*, 19 June.

Said, Edward W., and Christopher Hitchens (eds) (1988) *Blaming the Victims: Spurious Scholarship and the Palestinian Question* (London and New York: Verso).

Salaita, Steven (2006) *Anti-Arab Racism in the USA* (London: Pluto Press).

Salibi, Kamal (1985) *The Bible Came from Arabia* (London: Jonathan Cape).

Schiff, Zeev, and Eitan Haber (eds) (1976) *Leksikon Levitahon Yisrael* [Israel, Army and Defence: A Dictionary] (Tel Aviv: Zmora, Bitan, Modan [Hebrew]).

Schlink, Basliea M. (1991) *Israel at the Heart of World Events* (Darmstadt-Eberstadt: Evangelical Sisterhood of Mary).

Schnall, David J. (1984) *Beyond the Green Line: Israeli Settlements West of the Jordan* (New York: Praeger).

—— (1985) 'An Impact Assessment', in David Newman (ed.), *The Impact of Gush Emunim* (London: Croom Helm): 13–26.

Segev, Tom (1986a) 'Man and His Land', *Archaeology* (Bulletin of the Israel Association of Archaeologists) 1: 61–2 [Hebrew].

—— (1986b) *1949: The First Israelis* (New York: Free Press).

Servan-Schreider, Jean-Jacques (1988) *The Chosen and the Choice* (London: Futura).

Shahak, Israel (1988) 'Israeli Apartheid and the Intifada', *Race & Class* 30, no. 1 (July–September): 1–12.

—— (1994) *Jewish History, Jewish Religion* (London: Pluto Press).

Shahak, Israel, and Norton Mezvinsky (1999) *Jewish Fundamentalism in Israel* (London: Pluto Press).

Shaham, David (1979) *Yedi'ot Aharonot* supplement, 13 April; in Donald S. Will, 'Zionist Settlement Policy', *Journal of Palestine Studies* 11, no. 3 (Summer 1979): 40.

Shalev, Aryeh (1991) *The Intifada: Causes and Effects* (Tel Aviv and London: Westview Press).

Shamir, Moshe (1991) *Hamakom Hayarok* [The Green Place] (Tel Aviv: Dvir Publishing House [Hebrew]).

Shanks, Michael (1992) *Experiencing the Past: On the Character of Archaeology* (New York: Routledge).

Shapira, Anita (1984) *Berl: The Biography of a Socialist Zionist* (Cambridge: Cambridge University Press).

—— (1992) *Land and Power: The Zionist Resort to Force* (New York: Oxford University Press).

Sharett, Moshe (1978) *Yoman Ishi* [Personal Diary], vol. 3, entry for 8 March 1955 (Tel Aviv: Sifriyat Ma'ariv [Hebrew]).

Sharif, Regina (1983) *Non-Jewish Zionism: Its Roots in Western History* (London: Zed Books).

Shem-Ur, Ora (1989) *Te'ud Politi: Hamefarkim* [The Liquidators: A Political Documentation] (Tel Aviv: Nogah Press [Hebrew]).

Shepherd, Naomi (1987) *The Zealous Intruders: The Western Rediscovery of Palestine* (London: Collins).

Shiloah, Tzvi (1989) *Ashmat Yerushalayim* [The Guilt of Jerusalem] (Jerusalem: Karni Press [Hebrew]).

Shindler, Colin (2002a) *The Land Beyond Promise: Israel, Likud and the Zionist Dream* (London and New York: I.B. Tauris).

—— (2002b) 'Likud and the Search for Eretz Israel: From the Bible to the Twenty-First Century', in Efraim Karsh (ed.), *Israel, the First Hundred Years*, vol. III: *Israel Politics and Society since 1948: Problems of Collective Identity* (London: Frank Cass): 91–117.

Shlaim, Avi (1996a) *Collusion across the Jordan* (Oxford: Oxford University Press).

—— (1996b) 'The Last Testament of Yehoshafat Harkabi', *Middle East International*, 5 January.

—— (2000) *The Iron Wall: Israel and the Arab World* (London: Penguin).

Shragai, Nadav (1995) *Har Ha-Bayet: Ha-Maavak 'Al Har Ha-Bayet, Yehudim Ve-Muslimim, Dat Ve-Politika Meaz 1967* [The Temple Mount: The Struggle for the Temple Mount, Jews and Muslims, Religion and Politics since 1967] (Jerusalem: Keter [Hebrew]).

Silberman, Neil Asher (1982) *Digging for God and Country* (New York: Alfred A. Knopf).

—— (1989) *Between Past and Present*: *Archaeology, Ideology and Nationalism in the Modern Middle East* (New York: Holt).

—— (1993) *Prophet amongst You: The Life of Yigael Yadin* (Reading, MA: Addison-Wesley).

—— (1997) 'Structuring the Past: Israelis, Palestinians and the Symbolic Authority of the Archaeological Monuments', in Neil Asher Silberman and David Small (eds), *The Archaeology of Israel: Constructing the Past, Interpreting the Present* (Sheffield: Sheffield Academic Press): 62–81.

—— (1998) 'Whose Game Is It Anyway? The Political and Social Transformations of American Biblical Archaeology', in L. Meskell (ed.), *Archaeology under Fire* (New York, Routledge): 175–88.

Silberman, Neil Asher, and David B. Small (1997) *The Archaeology of Israel: Constructing the Past, Interpreting the Present* (Sheffield: Sheffield Academic Press).

Simon, Merrill (1984) *Jerry Falwell and the Jews* (Middle Village, NY: Jonathan David).

Sivan, Emmanuel (1992) 'The Mythologies of Religious Radicalism: Judaism and Islam', in Mark Juergensmeyer (ed.), *Violence and the Sacred in the Modern World* (London: Frank Cass, 1992): 71–81.

Sizer, Stephen (2004) *Christian Zionism: Road-map to Armageddon?* (Leicester: Inter-Varsity Press).

Skutel, H.J. (1983) 'Purifying Zion', *Journal of Palestine Studies* 12, no. 2: 83-5.

Slater, Robert (1991) *Warrior Statesman: The Life of Moshe Dayan* (New York: St Martin's Press).

Smith, Anthony D. (1971) *Theories of Nationalism* (London: Duckworth).

——— (1981) *The Ethnic Revival* (Cambridge: Cambridge University Press).

——— (1984) 'Ethnic Myths and Ethnic Revivals', *European Journal of Sociology* 22: 283-305.

——— (1986) *The Ethnic Origin of Nations* (London: Blackwell).

——— (1991) *National Identity* (London: Penguin).

Sobrino, Jon (1987) *Jesus in Latin America* (Maryknoll, NY: Orbis Books).

——— (1990) Companions of Jesus: The Jesuit Martyrs of El Salvador (Maryknoll, NY: Orbis Books).

——— (1993) *Witnesses to the Kingdom: The Martyrs of El Salvador and the Crucified Peoples* (Maryknoll, NY: Orbis Books).

Sprinzak, Ehud (1977) 'Extreme Politics in Israel', *Jerusalem Quarterly* 15 (Fall): 33-47.

——— (1991) *The Ascendance of Israel's Radical Right* (Oxford and New York: Oxford University Press).

Stein, Leonard (1961) *The Balfour Declaration* (Jerusalem: Magnes Press of the Hebrew University)

Sternhell, Zeev (1998) *The Founding Myths of Israel: Nationalism, Socialism and the Making of the Jewish State* (Princeton, NJ: Princeton University Press).

Sturgis, Matthew (2001) *It Ain't Necessarily So: Investigating the Truth of the Biblical Past* (London: Headline).

Sykes, Christopher (1973) *Crossroads to Israel, 1917–1948* (Bloomington and London: Indiana University Press).

Talhami, Ghada Hashem (2000) 'The Modern History of Islamic Jerusalem: Academic Myths and Propaganda', *Middle East Policy* 7, no. 2 (February): 113-29.

Talmon, Jacob L. (1965a) 'Who Is a Jew?' *Encounter* 24, no. 5 (May).

——— (1965b) *The Unique and the Universal* (London: Secker & Warburg).

Tamarin, Georges (1973), *The Israeli Dilemma: Essays on a Welfare State* (Rotterdam: Rotterdam University Press).

Taraki, Lisa (1990) 'The Islamic Resistance Movement in the Palestinian Uprising', in Zachary Lockman and Joel Beinin (eds), *Intifada: The Palestinian Upspring against Israeli Occupation* (London: I.B Tauris): 117-77; reproducing an article published in *Middle East Report* 156 (January-February 1989).

Teshuvot Harambam [Maimonides Response] (1937) *Mekitzi Nirdamim* (Jerusalem) 1.149: 284-5 [Hebrew together with original Arabic text].

——— (1940) *Mekitzi Nirdamim* (Jerusalem) 2.448: 725-8.

Tessler, Mark (1986) 'The Political Right in Israel: Its Origins, Growth and Prospects', *Journal of Palestine Studies* 15, no. 2 (Winter) 31: 12-55.

Teveth, Shabtai (1969) *The Cursed Blessing. The Story of Israel's Occupation of the West Bank* (London: Weidenfeld & Nicolson).

——— (1972) *Moshe Dayan* (London: Weidenfeld & Nicolson).

——— (1985) *Ben-Gurion and the Palestinian Arabs* (Oxford: Oxford University Press).

Thompson, Thomas L. (1974) *The Historicity of the Patriarchal Narratives: The Quest for the Historical Abraham* (Berlin: Walter de Gruyter)

——— (1987) 'The Origin Tradition of Ancient Israel I', *Journal for the Study of the Old Testament* Supplementary Series 55 (Sheffield: Sheffield Academic Press).

——(1991) 'Text, Context and Referent in Israelite Historiography', in David Edelman (ed.), *The Fabric of History* (Sheffield: Sheffield Academic Press): 65-92.

——(1992) *Early History of the Israelite People* (Brill: Leiden).

——(1999) *The Bible in History: How Writers Create a Past* (London: Jonathan Cape); American edition, *The Mythical Past* (New York: Basic Books).

——(2003a) 'Is the Bible Historical? The Challenge of "Minimalism" for Biblical Scholars and Historians', *Holy Land Studies: A Multidisciplinary Journal* 3, no. 1 (May): 1-27.

——(ed.) (2003b) *Jerusalem in Ancient History and Tradition* (London and New York: T. & T. Clark).

Tomaschoff, Avner (ed.) (1978) *Whose Homeland* (Jerusalem: World Zionist Organization).

Toon, Peter (ed.) (1970) *Puritans, the Millennium and the Future of Israel: Puritan Eschatology 1600–1660* (Cambridge: James Clarke).

——(1970) 'The Latter-Day Glory', in Peter Toon (ed.), *Puritans, the Millennium and the Future of Israel: Puritan Eschatology 1600–1660* (Cambridge: James Clarke).

Tuchman, Barbara W. (1982) *Bible and Sword: England and Palestine from the Bronze Age to Balfour* [1956] (London, Macmillan).

Tutu, Desmond Mpilo (2004) 'Foreword', in Michael Prior (ed.), *Speaking the Truth about Zionism and Israel* (London: Melisende).

Urbach, Ephraim (1974) 'Avoda Zara', in *Encyclopaedia Hebraica* XXVI (Jerusalem: Encyclopaedia Publishing Company [Hebrew]): 614-23.

Van Seters, John (1975) *Abraham in History and Tradition* (New Haven, CT: Yale University Press).

Verete, Mayir (1970) 'The Balfour Declaration and Its Makers', *Middle Eastern Studies* 6, no. 1: 48-76.

Vital, David (1988) *Zionism: The Formative Years* (Oxford: Clarendon Press).

Von Waldow, H. Eberhard (2004) 'Statehood and Jerusalem in Ancient Israel: Myths and Realities', *Holy Land Studies: A Multidisciplinary Journal* 2, no. 2 (March): 222-53.

Wagner, Donald (1992) 'Beyond Armageddon', *The Link* 25, no. 4 (October-November): 4, www.ameu.org/uploads/vol25_issue4_1992.pdf (accessed 20 April 2006).

——(1995) *Anxious for Armageddon* (Scottdale, PA and Waterloo, ON: Herald Press).

——(2003) *Dying in the Land of Promise* (London: Melisende).

Walker, P.W.L. (ed.) (1994) *Jerusalem, Past and Present in the Purposes of God*, 2nd edn (Carlisle: Paternoster Press).

Walvoord, John F. (1962) *Israel in Prophecy* (Grand Rapids, MI: Zondervan).

——(1974) *Armageddon, Oil and the Middle East Crisis* (Grand Rapids, MI: Zondervan).

Walzer, Michael (1985) *Exodus and Revolution* (New York: Basic Books).

——(1986) '*Exodus and Revolution*: A Canaanite Reading', *Arab Studies Quarterly* 8, no. 3 (Summer): 289-303.

Warrior, Robert Allen (1989) 'Canaanites, Cowboys and Indians: Deliverance, Conquest, and Liberation Theology Today', *Christianity and Crisis* 49: 261-5.

——(1991) 'A Native American Perspective: Canaanites, Cowboys, and Indians', in R.S. Sugirtharajah (ed.), *Voices from the Margin: Interpreting the Bible in the Third World* (London: SPCK): 287-95.

Wasserstein, Bernard (2002) *Divided Jerusalem: The Struggle for the Holy City* (London: Profile Books).

Weitz Yosef (1940) *Diary,* A246/7 (Jerusalem: Central Zionist Archives [Hebrew]).

———— (1941) *Diary,* A246/7, dated 17 July 1941 (Jerusalem: Central Zionist Archives [Hebrew]).

————(1948) *Diary,* A246/7, dated 18 April 1948 (Jerusalem: Central Zionist Archives [Hebrew]).

Weinstock, Nathan (1979) *Zionism: False Messiah* (London: Ink Links).

Werblowsky, R.J. Zwi (1971) 'Jewish Attitudes toward Christianity', *Encyclopaedia Judaica* V (Jerusalem: Keter): 513-14.

Wetherell, David Fielding (2005) 'The Use and Misuse of the Religious Language: Zionism and the Palestinians', *Holy Land Studies: A Multidisciplinary Journal* 4, no. 1 (May): 69-86.

Whitelam, Keith (1996) *The Invention of Ancient Israel: The Silencing of Palestinian History* (London and New York: Routledge).

———— (2002) 'Representing Minimalism', in Hunter and Davies (eds), *Sense and Sensitivity*: 194-223.

Wiemer, Reinhard, (1983) 'Zionism and the Arabs after the Establishment of the State of Israel', in Alexander Schölch (ed.), *Palestinians over the Green Line* (London: Ithaca Press): 26-63.

Wolpo, Shalom Dov (ed.) (1983) *Da'at Torah Be'inyanei Hamatzav Beertz Hakodesh* [The Opinion of the Torah Regarding the Situation in the Holy Land], 3rd edn (Israel: Kiryat Gat [Hebrew]).

Wrba, Marian (ed.) (1996) *Austrian Presence in the Holy Land in the 19th and Early 20th Century. Proceedings of the Symposium in the Austrian Hospice in Jerusalem on March 1-2, 1995* (Tel Aviv: Austrian Embassy).

Yehoshu'a, A.B. (1989) *Hakir Vehahar* [The Wall and the Mountain] (Tel Aviv: Zmora-Beitan [Hebrew]).

Zahhar, Mahmud (1995) 'Hamas: Waiting for Secular Nationalism to Self-Destruct', Interview, *Journal of Palestine Studies* 24, no. 3 (Spring): 81-8.

———— (1998) *Ishkaliyat: Al-Khitab al-Siyasi al-Mu'asir* (Al-Khalil, Palestine: Dar al-Mustaqbal).

Zangwill, Israel (1920) *The Voice of Jerusalem* (London: William Heinemann).

———— (1937) *Speeches, Articles and Letters* (London: Soncino Press).

Zerubavel, Yael (1995) *Recovered Roots: Collective Memory and the Making of Israeli National Tradition* (Chicago: University of Chicago Press).

Zucker, Dedi (1983) *Report on Human Rights in the Occupied Territories, 1979-83* (Tel Aviv: International Centre for Peace in the Middle East).

Zurayk, Constantine K. (1956) *Palestine: The Meaning of the Disaster* [*Ma'na al-Nakba*] (Beirut: Khayat).

Index

Arab League, 299
Arabic language, 189, 191, 209
Arabo-Islamic civilisation, Middle
    Ages, 188; cultural heritage, 211;
    –Jewish symbiosis, 9, 184, 186, 189
Arafat, Yasser, 226-8, 297, 302, 304;
    authoritarian rule, 300; critique of,
    296; UN General Assembly speech
    1974, 294
archaeology, *see* biblical archaeology
Arendt, Hannah, 20
Ariel, West Bank Jewish settlement,
    161
Ariel, Ya'acov, 160
Ariel, Yisrael, 157, 160, 199
Ariel, Yo'ezer, 179
Armageddon, 'Battle' of, 125, 127;
    'lobby', 112; 'theology', 8, 117, 126,
    129
Armstrong, Karen, 106
Aruri, Naseer, 277
Asherah, Jehova's consort, 255
Ashrawi, Hanan, 299
Ateek, Naim, 131, 265-6
'Ateret Cohanim, Jerusalem yeshiva,
    174-5, 177
atrocities, Israeli 'War of
    Independence', 61-2
Avi-Yonah, Michael, 81
Aviner, Shlomo, 143, 147-8, 162, 179
avoda zara, 201-2
'Ayn Karim village, 66
'Ayyash, Yahya, targeted assassination
    of, 227

Balfour, Arthur, Declaration, 45, 93,
    98, 100-101
Bantustan(s) model, 237, 291, 296, 320
Bar-Ilan religious university, 149
Bar-Kohkva, Simon, 42; revolt, 57
Barak, Ehud, 173
Baram, Haim, 228
Barghouti, Marwan, 229
Barghouti, Mustafa, 307
Barr, James, 87-8, 112
Batei Din, national rabbinical court,
    141
Bayt Nuba village, 79, 81
Begin, Menahem, 23, 60, 63, 116-17,
    144, 220, 289
Beirut, 244
Beit-Hallahmi, Benjamin, 21
Bell, L. Nelson, 109

Ben-Amotz, Dan, 40
Ben-Gurion (Green), David, 4-5, 8,
    16-17, 24-8, 30, 33-6, 46, 48-9,
    55-61, 63, 66-8, 71-2, 77-8, 81, 131,
    155
Ben-Moshe, Eytan, 80
Ben-Tzion Ishbezari, Moshe, 149
Ben-Tzvi (Shimshelevitz), Yitzhak, 27,
    36, 49, 67
Ben-Yair, Elaazar, 30
Ben-Yosef, Moshe, 153, 205
Benei 'Akiva, state funding, 142
Benvenisti, Meron, 22, 69
Benziman, 'Uzi, 80-83
Betar: biblical location, 4, 30; Zionist
    movement, 23, 29, 62
Bethlehem, 110; University, 264
Bible, the, *see* Hebrew Bible
Bible lands, British surveying of, 281
biblical archaeology: biblicised, 3-4,
    102-4, 240; critical, 242-3, 245-6,
    254, 264; distorted chronology, 70;
    fundamentalist, 261; ideology of,
    241
'biblical Israel', boundaries
    contestation, 75
biblical place names, study of, 244
biblical scholarship/studies, 269;
    critical, 256; depoliticisation need,
    262; discourse of, 283; post-
    colonial, 244, 270, 317
biblicism, Christian, 87
Birzeit University, West Bank, 62, 238,
    291
Blair, Tony, 316
Bleich, J. David, 161
Boff, Clodovis, 266
Bonaparte, Napoleon, 91
Boone, Pat, 113, 118
Borochov, Ber, 31
Bowman, Glenn, 114
Brightman, Thomas, 89-90
Brit Shalom movement, 51
British Mandate, *see* Palestine
British Palestine Exploration Fund, 92
British Royal (Peel) Commission,
    Palestine, 34, 54
Broshi, Magen, 258
Buber, Martin, 63
bulldozers, Israeli, 67, 81-2
Burgat, François, 215
Bush, George H., 113
Bush, George W., 120; biblicist

WHERE NOW FOR PALESTINE?

The Demise of the Two-State Solution

Edited by Jamil Hilal

'Thoroughly researched and thoroughly informative
on a burning issue of our time.' – Ghada Karmi

'Whatever position one holds on the question of a two-state solution or
of a bi-national state for Palestine/Israel, it is important to understand
the arguments put forward. This collection of essays engages the reader
directly and honestly, bringing many new and important angles to the
debate over bi-nationalism. The arguments and facts presented here
succeed in bringing the bi-nationalist position from the margins of the
debate to a more central position.' – Mick Dumper, Reader in Middle
East Politics

Where Now for Palestine? marks a turning point for the Middle East.
The attacks of 9/11, the death of Arafat and the elections of Hamas and
Kadima have meant that the Israel/Palestine 'two-state solution' now
seems illusory.

This collection critically revisits the concept of the 'two-state solution'
and maps the effects of local and global political changes on both
Palestinian people and politics. The authors discuss the changing face of
Fateh, Israeli perceptions of Palestine, and the influence of the Palestinian
diaspora. The book also analyses the environmental destruction of Gaza
and the West Bank, the economic viability of a Palestinian state and
the impact of US foreign policy in the region. This authoritative and
up-to-date guide to the impasse facing the region is required reading
for anyone wishing to understand a conflict entrenched at the heart of
global politics.

Hb ISBN 978 1 84277 839 5
Pb ISBN 978 1 84277 840 1

CATASTROPHE REMEMBERED

Palestine, Israel and the Internal Refugees:
Essays in Memory of Edward W. Said

Edited by Nur Masalha

'In this remarkable book, twelve writers brilliantly evoke the spirit of
Edward Said to tell the unvarnished truth about Palestine and Israel.'
– John Pilger

'This is a work of enormous significance by distinguished scholars of
singular courage and integrity. The spirit and legacy of Edward Said are
embodied in these papers that seek to rectify grave historical omissions
and distortions pertaining to the plight and rights of the Palestinians,
particularly in their displacement and exile. Such a narrative of
affirmation, authenticity and rectification is the essential antidote to
the mendacious accounts of exclusion and denial that have perpetuated,
and even justified, the continued victimization of the Palestinian
nation.' – Dr Hanan Ashrawi, former Dean of Faculty of Arts, Bir Zeit
University, Palestine; and recipient of the 2003 Sydney Peace Prize

The 1948 Palestine War is known to Israelis as 'the War of Independence'.
But for Palestinians, the war is forever the Nakba, the 'catastrophe'.
The war led to the creation of the State of Israel and the destruction of
much of Palestinian society by the Zionist forces. For all Palestinians,
the Nakba has become central to history, memory and identity. This book
focuses on Palestinian internal refugees in Israel and internally displaced
Palestinians across the Green Line. It uses oral history and interviews to
examine Palestinian identity and memory, indigenous rights, international
protection, the 'right of return', and a just solution in Palestine/Israel.

Contributors include several distinguished authors and scholars such
as William Dalrymple, Professor Naseer Aruri, Dr Ilan Pappé, Professor
Isma'il Abu Sa'ad and Dr Nur Masalha.

Hb ISBN 978 1 84277 622 3
Pb ISBN 978 1 84277 623 0

CHECKPOINT WATCH

Testimonies from Occupied Palestine

Yehudit Kirstein Keshet

'This important book offers an insightful perspective of the system
of Israeli military checkpoints and blockades in the West Bank, their
devastating impact on the Palestinian population, and the arbitrary use
of a control mechanism for reasons which often have little to do with
security considerations. The first-hand accounts and observations of
the Watchers – Israeli women from all walks of life – also provide an
interesting insight into how different sectors of Israeli society see – or
fail to see – the impact of such a system and its injustices.' – Donatella
Rovera, Researcher on Israel and the Occupied Territories, Amnesty
International

'It is impossible to guess when and how the harsher Israeli version of the
Apartheid Pass System will collapse. When it does, CheckpointWatch
will have had an important role in its collapse.' – Amira Hass

This is a critical exploration of Israel's curfew-closure policy in the
Occupied Palestinian Territories through the eyes of CheckpointWatch,
an organisation of Israeli women monitoring human rights abuses. It
combines observers' reports from checkpoints and along the Separation
Wall, with information and analysis of the bureaucracy supporting the
ongoing occupation and the wider project of ethnic-cleansing. It critically
reviews CheckpointWatch's transformation from a feminist, radical protest
movement and analyses Israeli media representation of the organisation
and of human rights activism in general. The author contends that the
dilemmas that women activists face, torn between opposition to the occupation and loyalty to the state, reflect political divisions within Israel
society as a whole.

Hb ISBN 978 1 84277 718 3
Pb ISBN 978 1 84277 719 0

THE CHALLENGE OF POST-ZIONISM

Alternatives to Israeli Fundamentalist Politics

Edited by Ephraim Nimni

'The emergence of "post-Zionist" scholarship and – as yet small – sector of opinion is one of the most welcome developments of recent years.'
– Perry Anderson, *New Left Review*

As an antidote to the growing Israeli fundamentalism, in recent years a lively debate has developed in the Israeli media, intellectual circles and academia about the defining characteristics of Israel and the future. The argument, known as post-Zionism, challenges some of the fundamental myths surrounding the early history and contemporary identity of the Israeli State. This argument is voiced by individuals and groups with different political agendas, but at the centre of the argument is the desire to downplay the influence of Judaism in the definition of the state, and to move towards the idea that Israel should become a secular state of all its citizens. This argument has profound and radical implications for the Israeli-Palestinian conflict and for Israeli politics, for it implies an improvement in the status of the Arab citizens of Israel and downgrades the status of Jews who are not citizens of Israel.

This volume presents this emerging debate. Its contributors include some of its main protagonists, Israeli citizens of Jewish and Palestinian background, including A'sad Ghanem, Uri Ram and Ilan Pappé. They explore post-Zionism's meanings, ambiguities and prospects. Other contributors place it in its political context as Israeli society seems to be reaching an ideological crossroads. They also put forward criticisms of post-Zionism, and explore its implications for 'out' groups, including Palestinians, Israeli women and Jewish people living outside Israel. The book concludes with a fascinating assessment by Edward Said of the implications of this debate for a reconciliation between Israelis and Palestinians. The significance of this volume goes beyond Israel's own emerging post-colonial identity and contains implications for theories of the post-colonial state generally.

Hb ISBN 978 1 85649 893 7
Pb ISBN 978 1 85649 894 4

REFUSENIK!

Israel's Soldiers of Conscience

Compiled and edited by Peretz Kidron

'Our greatest admiration must go to those brave Israeli soldiers who refuse to serve beyond the 1967 borders.... These soldiers, who are Jews, take seriously the principle put forward at the Nuremberg trials in 1945-46: namely, that a soldier is not obliged to obey unjust orders – indeed, one has an obligation to disobey them.' – Susan Sontag, novelist, essayist and playwright

'Resistance to crimes of state, and refusal to participate in them, has been and remains one of the most significant achievements of people of decency and courage throughout history. The Israelis who have undertaken this honorable course merit the greatest admiration and respect. Their testimonies are a memorable contribution to this noble cause.' – Noam Chomsky

'It was once said of people who lived near concentration camps but claimed no knowledge of what went on inside, that those who didn't know, didn't want to know. Jews who still try to defend retention of the West Bank are in a similar category.'
– David J. Goldberg in *The Jewish Chronicle*

Hundreds of Israeli soldiers, called up to take part in controversial campaigns like the 1982 invasion of Lebanon or policing duties in the Palestinian territories today, have refused orders. Many of these 'refuseniks' have faced prison sentences rather than take part in what they regard as an unjust occupation in defence of illegal Jewish settlements.

In this inspirational book, Peretz Kidron, himself a refusenik, gives us the stories, experiences, viewpoints, even poetry, of these courageous conscripts who believe in their country, but not in its actions beyond its borders.

Hb ISBN 978 1 84277 450 2
Pb ISBN 978 1 84277 451 9

APARTHEID ISRAEL

Possibilities for the Struggle Within

Uri Davis

'Uri Davis's new book is a devastating critique of Israel's internal apartheid system and by extension the entire ideology of political Zionism. It is difficult to do justice to such an impassioned and detailed work, but I would particularly draw attention to its dedication to universal moral principles, unassailable logic and attention to factual detail that I believe are the distinctive hallmarks of this brilliant book.'
– Hisham Sharabi

'Based on the struggle to end apartheid in South Africa, and borrowing from his long years in the peace movement, Uri Davis presents, what is for me, the only sensible way forward in the present deadlock: a roadmap based on civil rights, human dignity and international justice. It ... has the moral strength to convince victimizers and victims alike that there is a valid alternative to the present Israeli system of discrimination and occupation.' – Ilan Pappé, historian and author of *The Making of the Arab-Israeli Conflict, 1947–1951*

'*Apartheid Israel* represents the most thorough critique to date of Israel's legal and political structure from a human rights perspective. At the same time it points towards an alternative vision for conflict-ridden Israel/Palestine, building on the author's own exceptional experience as an Israeli academic and human rights activist for decades. Current developments make this book more urgent reading than ever before.'
– Nils Butenschøn, Director, Norwegian Centre for Human Rights, Faculty of Law, University of Oslo

Hb ISBN 978 1 84277 338 3
Pb ISBN 978 1 84277 339 0

A THREAT FROM WITHIN

A Century of Jewish Opposition to Zionism

Yakov M. Rabkin

'An extremely interesting and valuable book' – Noam Chomsky, Massachusetts Institute of Technology, Cambridge, MA

'Timely, well researched and thorough treatment of probably the most controversial issue in today's Jewish world. Fascinating contemporary material ... the author deserves our thanks for presenting our case so eloquently.' – *Jewish Telegraph*

'Yakov Rabkin argues that Jewish rejection of the Zionist state should be taken seriously.' – *Jewish Chronicle*

'This book sheds light on religious anti-Zionism, which, demographically and ideologically, represents the most serious threat to Israel as a State and as a collective identity. In fact, it is a more grievous and dangerous challenge than Arab and Palestinian hostility. The State, by increasing its achievements, leads the country straight into an abyss. To paraphrase Marx, one could say that Israel, by virtue of its spectacular development, is digging its own tomb.' – Dr Joseph Hodara, Professor of Sociology, Bar-Ilan University, Israel

'I can only welcome the publication of this unconventional book based on often ignored historical facts. It is up to us to draw lessons from it.' – Rabbi Moshe Gérard Ackermann, Director of the Nerlitz Institute of Jewish Studies, Jerusalem

'Yakov Rabkin has produced an altogether remarkable book that tells the story and analyses the ideas of the Orthodox Jewish movement opposed to Zionism and the State of Israel. I am enormously impressed by the author's historical scholarship, by his brilliant analysis of a complex literature and by the lucidity of his prose. This is an extraordinary book.' – Dr Gregory Baum, Professor of Theology, McGill University

Hb ISBN 978 1 84277 698 8
Pb ISBN 978 1 84277 699 5

THE JEWS AND THEIR FUTURE

A Conversation on Judaism and Jewish Identities

Esther Benbassa and Jean-Christophe Attias

'This duo have a real penchant for provoking their readers. They love to shake old certainties and orthodoxies. And in this new book, they have transcended themselves by penning a magnificently iconoclastic dialogue.' – Pierre Vidal-Naquet, *Le Nouvel Observateur*

'Readers will be grateful to these authors for having opened up, and so richly, the "Jewish Question" today: highlighting the situation of Jewish people in the Diaspora.' – Sylvain Cypel, *Le Monde*

'This book positively invites debate. But on condition one first recognises the deep knowledge and open-minded spirit that inspires it.' – *L'Histoire*

'These authors share a common passion for the history of Judaism, and an equal repugnance for prejudices, taboos, even panic that characterizes Judaism when it thinks it is under attack. Taking the form of a dialogue in the manner of certain old rabbinical texts, even socratic, they whisper their disquiet (intellectual, even spiritual) at the self-indulgence contemporary Judaism tends to engage in more than it would like to admit.' – Jean-Luc Allouche, *Libération*

'What does it mean to be Jewish today? Is it to live in the cocoon of the Shoah and the fear of a resurgence of fascism? Is it to cover one's head, to support Sharon? Or is it to have a sense of belonging across boundaries? To answer these questions, the authors revisit the iconic images of the Diaspora, Zionism, anti-Semitism, and also of the "Jewish mother", the tensions between Ashkenazi and Sephardic Jews – and deconstruct them with a delicate hand.' – François Dufay, *Le Point*

Hb ISBN 978 1 84277 390 1
Pb ISBN 978 1 84277 391 8